D0792423

# CONTENTS

*Criminology as Peacemaking*

# Criminology as Peacemaking

EDITED BY

## Harold E. Pepinsky
AND
## Richard Quinney

INDIANA UNIVERSITY PRESS
*Bloomington and Indianapolis*

The paper used in this publication meets the minimum requirements of American
National Standard for Information Sciences—Permanence of Paper for Printed
Library Materials, ANSI Z39.48-1984.

∞™

Manufactured in the United States of America

Library of Congress Cataloging-in-Publication Data

Criminology as peacemaking / edited by Harold E. Pepinsky and Richard
Quinney.
p.    cm.
Includes index.
ISBN 0-253-34357-7 (cloth) ; ISBN 0-253-206596 (pbk.)
1. Criminology—Methodology.   I. Pepinsky, Harold E.
II. Quinney, Richard.
HV6018.C74   1991
364—dc20                                              90-42361
CIP

1   2   3   4   5   95   94   93   92   91

# PREFACE

The peacemaking perspective is steadily making its way into criminology. In recent years there have been proposals and programs that foster mediation, conflict resolution, reconciliation, and community. They are part of an emerging *criminology of peacemaking*, a criminology that seeks to alleviate suffering and thereby reduce crime. This is a criminology that is based necessarily on human transformation in the achievement of peace and justice. Human transformation takes place as we change our social, economic, and political structure. And the message is clear: Without peace within us and in our actions, there can be no peace in our results. Peace is the way.

There is a full awareness by now that the criminal justice system in this country is founded on violence. It is a system which assumes that violence can be overcome by violence, evil by evil. Criminal justice at home and warfare abroad are of the same principle of violence. This principle sadly dominates much of our criminology. Fortunately, more and more criminologists and practitioners in criminal justice are realizing that this principle is fundamentally incompatible with a faith that seeks to express itself in compassion, forgiveness, and love.

For several years in distinctive ways, the contributors to *Criminology as Peacemaking* have helped generate a network of professionals dedicated to such an expressive criminology. They have written essays for this book in an effort to present the criminology of peacemaking to an even larger audience of criminologists, social scientists, and practitioners in corrections and criminal justice. And it is the resolute conviction of the editors that peacemaking in criminology is part of the continuing movement for a world of peace and social justice. May we all be a way of peace.

# P A R T
# O N E

# Religious and Humanist
# Peacemaking Traditions

*Richard Quinney*

---

## O N E

# The Way of Peace

## *On Crime, Suffering, and Service*

Let us begin with a fundamental realization: No amount of thinking and no amount of public policy have brought us any closer to understanding and solving the problem of crime. The more we have reacted to crime, the` farther we have removed ourselves from any understanding and any reduction of the problem. In recent years, we have floundered desperately in reformulating the law, punishing the offender, and quantifying our knowledge. Yet this country remains one of the most crime-ridden nations. In spite of all its wealth, economic development, and scientific advances, this country has one of the worst crime records in the world.

With such realization, we return once again—as if starting anew—to the subject of crime, a subject that remains one of our most critical indicators of the state of our personal and collective being. If what is to be said seems outrageous and heretical, it is only because it is necessarily outside the conventional wisdom both of our understanding of the problem and of our attempt to solve it. Only by entering another world—yet one that is very simple and ultimately true—can we become aware of our own condition.

A few elementary observations serve as the basis for our understanding: (1) Thought of the Western rational mode is conditional, limiting knowledge to what is already known. (2) The truth of reality is emptiness; all that is real is beyond human conception. (3) Each life is a spiritual journey into

3

the unknown and the unknowable, beyond the egocentric self. (4) Human existence is characterized by suffering; crime is suffering; and the sources of suffering are within each of us. (5) Through love and compassion, beyond the egocentric self, we can end suffering and live in peace, personally and collectively. (6) The ending of suffering can be attained in a quieting of the mind and an opening of the heart, in being aware. (7) Crime can be ended only with the ending of suffering, only when there is peace— through the love and compassion found in awareness. (8) Understanding, service, justice: all these flow naturally from love and compassion, from mindful attention to the reality of all that is, here and now. (9) A *criminology of peacemaking*, the nonviolent criminology of compassion and service, seeks to end suffering and thereby eliminate crime. Let us elaborate on this understanding.

## Awareness of Human Suffering

Suffering is the condition of our existence. The forms of suffering are all around us. In our personal lives, there are tensions and anxieties. Each day we experience the physical pains in our bodies and the psychological hurts in our hearts and minds. Our interpersonal relations often are carried out in violence of one kind or another, if only in the withholding of what might be offered. We have created societies that are filled with the sufferings of poverty, hunger, homelessness, pollution, and destruction of the environment. Globally, nations are at war and threaten not only one another, but all of earthly life, with nuclear destruction. All these human problems, or forms of suffering, are a result of how we have lived our lives, moment by moment, day by day. The threat of nuclear war began as suffering on a very personal level and elevated gradually and systematically to the collective condition (see Walsh, 1984). The forms of suffering are symptoms of the sufferings within each of us.

If the social and global sufferings ever are to be ended, we must deal with the suffering of personal existence. What is involved, finally, is no less than the transformation of our human being. Political and economic solutions without this transformation inevitably fail. The solution is very near to us. There is no shortcut to the ending of suffering.

Our suffering, then, and our ending of this suffering, begins in the human mind. *The Dhammapada*, the ancient text of Buddhism, states: "All that we are is a result of what we have thought" (1936: 3). We act out of our thoughts, and we create social worlds out of these thoughts. Being human, we have constructed webs of meaning; and with these shared meanings we have constructed our interpersonal relations, our social structures, and our societies. All is a result of what we have thought.

The reconstruction of our existence—the ending of suffering—thus begins by giving attention to the mind. It is this mind, a modern mind that is busy and scattered, that creates its own suffering. To be able to observe the mind as it is, to be able to see clearly with the mind, we begin with what must seem at first a paradox: letting go. The author of *A Gradual Awakening* observes: "In letting go of who we imagine ourselves to be, letting go of our thinking, our attempt to control the world, we come upon our natural being which has been waiting patiently all these years for us to come home" (Levine, 1979: 39). This open state of mind is what one Zen master calls a "beginner's mind." He (Suzuki, 1970: 21) writes: "If your mind is empty, it is always ready for anything; it is open to everything. In the beginner's mind there are many possibilities; in the expert's mind there are few." We are ready to see things as they really are—beyond concepts and theories—when we have no thought of achievement, no thought of self. When our mind is open and thus compassionate toward all things, it is boundless in its understanding.

Without empty mind—without mindfulness—we are attached to our ideas, our thoughts, our mental constructions; and we take these productions to be reality itself. Many of our concepts are so deeply ingrained in our minds, in our education, and in our culture, that we forget that they completely condition our perceptions of reality (see Krishnamurti, 1975). In attachment to these mental productions, we are chained in the cave, observing merely the shadows of appearance on the wall before us. Awareness is a breaking of the chains of conditioned thought and a viewing of the reality beyond the shadows.

Without awareness, we humans are bound to the suffering caused by a grasping mind. Being attached to our thoughts, we take the thoughts to be our true selves. The mind that is attached to its own thoughts is the mind of a self-centered and possessive being. All conditioned and attached thought arises from the discursive mind of the egocentric self. That is why the sacred texts of the esoteric traditions, such as the wisdom literature of early Hinduism as found in the *Upanishads* and the *Bhagavad-Gita*, suggest that truth can be known only through union with Brahman, through that which is beyond the ego-self and its attempt at purely rational thought. In contemplation and meditation, we can see the essence of all things as they rise and pass away.

The higher wisdom, the awareness of reality, can be attained only with the loss of the conditioned ego and with the realization of the transcendental Self. In other words, the essence of our existence is the interpretation of ourselves with all things. In *Samadhi*, a treatise on self development in Zen Buddhism, Mike Sayama (1986: 12) writes: "The task before us is no longer to differentiate from nature and develop the ego, but transcend the ego and realize true Self that is one with the universe." Only then can one be at home. Peace and harmony come with the awareness of the oneness of all things and the transcendence of this small self to the wholeness of reality. All of this is to be found outside of the abstracting interpretations of the rational mind.

As we mature, we move beyond the rational and linear mode of thought to a more intuitive and transcendent mode. We lose the grasping and craving self of the individualized ego and find ourselves in the realm of the universal Self. It is not natural—it is unhealthy—for the academic and the intellectual (sociologist, criminologist) to continue strictly in the rational mode of speculative and dualistic thought as he or she matures, although this is the approved and rewarded form for the modern academic. To continue solely in the rational mode of thought is retrogressive for the maturing person, and for a discipline as well.

The author of *Samadhi* concludes: "At the most mature level of human being, a person realizes the true self which is one with the universe and experiences a meaning beyond question and articulation. Such a person transcends anxiety, is fearless and is moved by compassion" (Sayama, 1986: 98). Rather than a life primarily of acquisition and scholarly production, life now demands an inner awakening, a spiritual development. One no longer clings to rationality and the ego as the final realities; one is not trapped in the world of interpretive abstractions taking form according to attachments of an egocentric existence. Once we have mastered rationality and moved to the possibilities of perennial wisdom, we can begin to live in compassionate oneness with all that is; we can begin to understand the world by fully being aware of it.

The truth is that no amount of theorizing and rational thinking can tell us much about reality. To enter into the essential realm requires a mind that is unattached and compassionate. In a book on perennial wisdom, Aldous Huxley (1985: x) writes: "It is a fact, confirmed and re-confirmed during two or three thousand years of religious history, that the ultimate Reality is not clearly and immediately apprehended, except by those who have made themselves loving, pure in heart and poor in spirit." When we allow the higher Self to dwell in the depth of the particular self—when the egocentric, rational self is lost—we can attend to the unknown and unknowable mysteries of the world.

And the final expression of this realization may not be in more talk and more words, but in silence. Saint John of the Cross observed, "For whereas speaking distracts, silence and work collect thoughts and strengthen the spirit" (quoted in Huxley, 1970: 218). With the wisdom gained by awareness, there may be no further need to talk and to write discursively. One then practices what is realized—with attention and silence, in charity and humility, in the service of others.

## Right Understanding

The way to awareness, and thus the ending of suffering, begins with right understanding. An understanding of the true nature of reality involves the recognition that everything is impermanent, that nothing remains the same. Within the flux of reality is the fact that every action brings a certain result. For instance, whenever our actions are motivated by greed, hatred, or delusion, the inevitable result is suffering. All of this occurs within a reality that is beyond the abstractions of a grasping and craving mind.

The true reality, beyond human conception, is what Zen Buddhism refers to as *Sunyata:* nothingness, emptiness, the void. In a recognition of the fullness of the unnameable, of emptiness, we may begin to see clearly and compassionately the concrete reality of our existence. With this understanding, as Alan Watts (1957: 125) notes, we are "at the point where there is nothing further to seek, nothing to be gained." When we are empty—within the emptiness of all—we are in the realm of ultimate reality.

Beyond Western scientism, there is liberated action freed of the separation of ourselves from the world. Watts (1957: 131) quotes a Zen line: "Only when you have no thing in your mind and no mind in things are you vacant and spiritual, empty and marvelous." This takes us beyond the products of Western thought, beyond the malaise and destruction that have resulted from being separated from the ineffable reality of our existence. By a "dropping off of body-and mind," as Keiji Nishitani (1982) of the Kyoto School of Japanese Zen terms it, we allow ourselves to live in the wonder of absolute nothingness. We return to a home—we arrive at the "home-ground"—where all things are in harmony with what they actually are and ought to be. It is a "coming home with empty hands," and each being has found its place among all other things. But let us beware. Even this talk takes us into the place of mental abstractions, the place where we again lose touch with reality.

It is the presumed objectivity and rationality of modern science that we hope to avoid in a new criminology. We hope to avoid the personal and social consequences of positive science because, as one humanistic philosopher (Skolimowski, 1986: 306) has noted: The mind trained in objective science "over a number of years becomes cold, dry, uncaring, always atomized, cutting, analyzing. This kind of mind has lost the capacity for empathy, compassion, love." Our mode of thinking affects the way we live, and in the meantime we have not gotten any closer to understanding. We seek a mind that, instead of producing conflict and violence, heals—a compassionate mind rather than an objective mind. The compassionate mind is found beyond the boundaries of Western scientific rationality.

Being on the simple path of right understanding, we create thought, words, and deeds that will end our suffering. The forest monk, Achaan Chah, writes: "Only when our words and deeds come from kindness can we quiet the mind and open the heart" (1985: 50). Our work is not only to grow in wisdom and compassion but also to help others in their suffering. This takes place not necessarily in further theoretical work, but in moment-by-moment, day-by-day, step-by-step awareness of what actually is. We are on a wandering path to emptiness, to an awareness of the fullness and wholeness of all things.

That we criminologists are to be engaged in spiritual work in order to eliminate crime may require further reflection. To be fully human presupposes the development within oneself of a quality of being that transcends material existence. It is a quality that is not acquired automatically, but one that develops slowly and needs to be tended carefully. Through inner work, we forge a link between the profane and the sacred. Indeed, all of life becomes filled with the sacred. Such a quality within each of us assures a life of growing wisdom, compassion, and service.

Nothing any longer is profane, without the transcendent dimension. The simplest actions, from eating and walking to talking and working, have a sacramental character signifying something beyond themselves. Our lives are within a realm that demands a spiritual as well as material existence. This is why the great religious traditions continue to emphasize a constant discipline of recollection, meditation, study, prayer, contemplation, and at least some measure of solitude and retirement. The Trappist monk, Thomas Merton, thus writes: "If the salvation of society depends, in the long run, on the moral and spiritual health of individuals, the subject of contemplation becomes a vastly important one, since contemplation is one of the indications of spiritual maturity. It is closely allied to sanctity. You cannot save the world merely with a system. You cannot have peace without charity" (1979: 8). Seeing the truth, in contemplation and medita-tion, sets us on a path that promotes a humane and peaceful existence. Such an existence is a reality which we can attain only in a life lived in the depth of the sacred. A life devoted to criminology cannot avoid the impor-tance of this truth. Care has to be given to the inner life of each of us.

This life of giving attention to spiritual matters, of going beyond the self to all that is in the world, is a socially committed life. The contemplative life is not self-indulgent, for social issues cannot be faced appropriately without inner spiritual preparation (see Merton, 1962). Oppression in the world is caused by selves that are not spiritually aware, by those who live by greed, fear, egoism, and the craving for power over others. As Jacob Needleman (1980: 212–19) observes in *Lost Christianity*, the "outer" world is not out there, and the "inner" world is not solely one of personal emotions and thoughts. Both are of the same space, in interpenetration of everything. The objective is a compassionate living of each moment with all other beings—for the ending of suffering.

## Compassion and Service

We are all of us interrelated—and "not just people, but animals too, and stones, clouds, trees" (Aitken, 1984: 10). Those who are enlightened in the service of others, the *Bodhisattvas* of the world, realize fully the reality of the interpenetration of all things. By experiencing the ephemeral and trans-parent nature of reality, by being aware of the oneness of all things, we can know the potential of peace and harmony.

Were there complete perfection and unity, there would be no suffering. Suffering has arisen out of disunity and separation from the embracing totality, and it can be ended only with the return of all sentient beings to a condition of wholeness. We have fallen from the grace of wholeness into a separation from one another and from the ground of all being, a separation that is assured by craving and grasping selves, by selves that are really an illusion. If human beings were constantly and consciously in a proper relationship with the sacred and with the natural and social environment, there would be only as much suffering as creation makes inevitable (see Huxley, 1970: 233–34). But our own created reality is one of separation, and therefore one of suffering.

Thus the healing of separation is necessary if suffering is to be ended. To begin to end suffering, we must be aware of the causes of suffering within ourselves and search for the reasons that make us suffer. The Tibetan Buddhist master, Rinpoche Kalu, says that the suffering we experience in the world "is caused by the six afflictions—ignorance, desire, pride, anger, jealousy, and greed" (Kalu, 1987: 13). The most hopeful way to attain world peace, to end global suffering, he adds, is by developing within ourselves compassion and loving-kindness toward others.

In the practice of loving-kindness, what Buddhists call *metta*, there is developed the feeling of caring and connectedness. From within, thoughts of goodwill and benevolence are extended outward, embracing all others in an increasingly wider circle. In compassion, the suffering of others is recognized out of one's own suffering, and the suffering is shared. Jack Kornfield (1985: 63) writes: "Compassion is the tender readiness of the heart to respond to one's own or another's pain without grief or resentment or aversion. It is the wish to dissipate suffering. Compassion embraces those experiencing sorrow, and eliminates cruelty from the mind." Looking directly at suffering, both the suffering in the world and the suffering in one's own heart and mind, we love others (as ourselves) and act in compassion to end suffering—to heal separation.

We begin our practice, then, by being aware of the ways in which suffering is manifested in each of us. "The more conscious we are in dealing with our own suffering, the more sensitive we will be in treating the pain of others" (Dass and Gorman, 1985: 86). Our responsibility is to do what we can to alleviate the concrete conditions of human suffering. "We work to provide food for the hungry, shelter for the homeless, health care for the sick and feeble, protection for the threatened and vulnerable, schooling for the uneducated, freedom for the oppresed" (Dass and Gorman, 1985: 87). When we acknowledge *what is* and act as witnesses in this shared reality, without attachment and judgment, we open ourselves to all suffering. Acting out of compassion, without thinking of ourselves as doers, we are witnesses to what must be done.

The path to the ending of suffering is through compassion rather than through the theories of science and the calculations of conditioned thought. Our sufferings are, in fact, exacerbated by science and thought. The discoveries necessary for dealing with suffering are within our being.

The truth that relieves suffering lies in the concrete moment of our awareness, an awareness that frees us from conditioned judgments, creates loving-kindness within us, and allows us to realize the absolute emptiness of all phenomena.

As long as there is suffering in this world, each of us suffers. We cannot end our suffering without ending the suffering of all others. In being witnesses to the concrete reality, and in attempting to heal the separation between ourselves and true being (the ground of all existence), we necessarily suffer with all others. But now we are fully aware of the suffering and realize how it can be eliminated. With awareness and compassion, we are ready to act.

## The Way of Peace and Social Justice

From the inner understanding of our own suffering, we are prepared to act in a way of peace. As in Mahatma Gandhi's philosophy of *Satyagraha*, truth force, social action comes out of the informed heart, out of the clear and enlightened mind. The source of social action is within the human heart that has come to understand fully its own suffering and therefore the suffering of others. If human actions are not rooted in compassion, these actions will not contribute to a peaceful and compassionate world. "If we cannot move beyond inner discord, how can we help find a way to social harmony? If we ourselves cannot know peace, *be* peaceful, how will our acts disarm hatred and violence?" (Dass and Gorman, 1985: 165). The means cannot be different from the ends; peace can come only out of peace. "There is no way to peace," said A. J. Muste. "Peace is the way." .

In other words, without *inner* peace in each of us, without peace of mind and heart, there can be no *social* peace between people and no peace in societies, nations, and in the world. To be explicitly engaged in this process, of bringing about peace on all levels, of joining ends and means, is to be engaged in *peacemaking* (Musto, 1986: 8–9). In peacemaking, we attend to the ultimate purpose of our existence—to heal the separation between all things and to live harmoniously in a state of unconditional love.

The radical nature of peacemaking is clear: No less is involved than the transformation of our human being. We will indeed be engaged in action, but action will come out of our transformed being. Rather than attempting to create a good society first, and then trying to make ourselves better human beings, we have to work on the two simultaneously. The inner and the outer are the same. The human transformation in relation to action is described by Thich Nhat Hanh, the Vietnamese Buddhist peace activist, as a realization that begins in the human heart and mind:

> To realize does not only mean to act. First of all, realization connotes transforming oneself. This transformation creates a harmony between oneself and nature, between one's own joy and the joy of others. Once a person gets in

touch with the source of understanding and compassion, this transformation is accomplished. When this transformation is present, all one's actions will carry the same nature and effect—protecting and building life with understanding and compassion. If one wishes to share joy and happiness with others, one should have joy and happiness within oneself. If one wishes to transmit serenity, first one should realize it oneself. Without a sane and peaceful mind, one's actions could only create more trouble and destruction in the world. (Hanh, 1985: 2; also see Hanh, 1987)

The transformation of ourselves and the world becomes our constant practice, here and now.

The practice is, in the true sense, spiritual and religious. In Buddhist terms, we become enlightened in the practice; and in Christianity, the transformation involves an inner conversion—a new age coming in both cases only when we have made ourselves ready. As a commentator (Musto, 1986: 251) on the Catholic peace tradition writes, "Peace is not so much political revolution as personal conversion; it is not individual human ego and power at stake, but God's will to peace that only humans can accomplish on earth, as they are the recipients of God's gift and challenge to peace."

And there can be no peace without justice. This is the biblical command. A good social life—one based on equality, with the elimination of poverty, racism, sexism, and violence of all kinds—is a peaceful existence. The Old Testament Isaiah (32:17) states: "Justice will bring about peace, right will produce calm and security." Peace, the result of all the benefits of the covenant, is granted to those who fulfill the covenant by living in justice. "Peace and justice," Ronald Musto (1986: 13) observes, "are thus inextricably bound: cause and effect, journey and goal." By living the covenant—by creating justice—there is peace. The peacemakers are truly "the children of God."

All of this is to say, to us as criminologists, that crime is suffering and that the ending of crime is possible only with the ending of suffering. And the ending both of suffering and of crime, which is the establishing of justice, can come only out of peace, out of a peace that is spiritually grounded in our very being. To eliminate crime—to end the construction and perpetuation of an existence that makes crime possible—requires a transformation of our human being. We as human beings must *be* peace if we are to live in a world free of crime, in a world of peace.

In recent years, we have seen several attempts at peacemaking in criminology. There have been writings and some programs employing conflict resolution, mediation, reconciliation, abolition, and humanistic action (see, for example, Abel, 1982; Currie, 1985; Pepinsky, 1988; Tifft and Sullivan, 1980; Sullivan, 1980). They offer the concrete beginnings of a *criminology of peacemaking*, a criminology that seeks to end suffering and thereby eliminate crime. It is a criminology that is based necessarily on human transformation in the achievement of peace and justice. Human transformation takes place as we change our social, economic, and political structure. And the message is clear: Without peace within us and in our actions, there can be no peace in our results. Peace is the way.

We are fully aware by now that the criminal justice system in this country is founded on violence. It is a system that assumes that violence can be overcome by violence, evil by evil. Criminal justice at home and warfare abroad are of the same principle of violence. This principle sadly dominates much of our criminology. Fortunately, more and more criminologists are realizing that this principle is fundamentally incompatible with a faith that seeks to express itself in compassion, forgiveness, and love. When we recognize that the criminal justice system is the moral equivalent of the war machine, we realize that resistance to one goes hand-in-hand with resistance to the other.

The resistance must be in compassion and love, not in terms of the violence that is being resisted. A definition of "nonviolence" by a recent resister (Taylor, 1986: 1) is appropriate: "Nonviolence is a method of struggling for human liberation that resists and refuses to cooperate with evil or injustice, while trying to show goodwill to all opponents encountered in the struggle, and being willing to take suffering on oneself, rather than inflicting it on others." We are back again to the internal source of our actions: Action is the form the essence of our being takes. Thich Nhat Hanh, whose thoughts follow that same definition of nonviolence, writes:

> The chain reaction of love is the essential nature of the struggle. The usual way to generate force is to create anger, desire, and fear in people. Hatred, desire, and fear are sources of energy. But a nonviolent struggle cannot use these dangerous sources of energy, for they destroy both the people taking part in the struggle and the aim of the struggle itself. Nonviolent struggle must be nurtured by love and compassion. (Quoted in Taylor, 1986: 2)

When our hearts are filled with love and our minds with willingness to serve, we will know what has to be done and how it is to be done. Such is the basis of a *nonviolent criminology*.

We begin, then, by attending to the direction of our innermost being, the being that is the whole of reality. Out of this source, all action follows. In the words of Lao-tzu, "No action is taken, and yet nothing is left undone" (1963: 184). Everything is done out of compassion to help lessen the suffering of others.

Living in harmony with the truth, we do everything as an act of service. Criminology can be no less than this, a part of the reality of all that is—a way of peace.

An earlier version of this essay appeared in the 1988 winter edition of *The Quest*, pages 66 to 75.

## REFERENCES

Abel, Richard L. 1982. *The Politics of Informal Justice.* Vol. 1. New York: Academic Press.

Aitken, Robert. 1984. *The Mind of Clover: Essays in Zen Buddhist Ethics.* San Francisco: North Point Press.

*The Bhagavad-Gita.* 1962. Tr. Juan Mascaro. New York: Penguin Books.

Chah, Achaan. 1985. *A Still Forest Pool.* Ed. Jack Kornfield and Paul Breiter. Wheaton: Theosophical Publishing House.

Currie, Elliott. 1985. *Confronting Crime: An American Challenge.* New York: Pantheon Books.

Dass, Ram, and Paul Gorman. 1985. *How Can I Help? Stories and Reflections on Service.* New York: Alfred A. Knopf.

*The Dhammapada.* 1936. Tr. Irving Babbitt. New York: New Directions.

Goldstein, Joseph. 1983. *The Experience of Insight.* Boston: Shambhala.

Hanh, Thich Nhat. 1987. *Being Peace.* Berkeley: Parallax Press.

———. 1985. "Action and Compassion in the World." *Buddhist Peace Fellowship Newsletter* 7 (3): 2.

Huxley, Aldous. 1970 (1945). *The Perennial Philosophy.* New York: Harper and Row.

Kalu, H. E. Rinpoche. 1987. "The Value of Retreat." *Buddhist Peace Fellowship Newsletter* 9 (Winter): 13.

Kornfield, Jack. 1985. "The Buddhist Path and Social Responsibility." *ReVision* 8 (Summer-Fall): 63–67.

Krishnamurti, J. 1975. *Freedom from the Known.* New York: Harper and Row.

Lao-tzu. 1963. *The Way of Lao Tzu.* Tr. Wing-Tsit Chan. Indianapolis: Bobbs-Merrill.

Levine, Stephen. 1979. *A Gradual Awakening.* Garden City: Anchor Books.

Merton, Thomas. 1979. *The Ascent to Truth.* New York: Harcourt Brace Jovanovich.

———. 1962. *New Seeds of Contemplation.* New York: New Directions.

Musto, Ronald G. 1986. *The Catholic Peace Tradition.* Maryknoll, N.Y.: Orbis Books.

Needleman, Jacob. 1980. *Lost Christianity: A Journey of Rediscovery.* New York: Bantam Books.

Nishitani, Keiji. 1982. *Religion and Nothingness.* Tr. Jan Van Bragt. Berkeley: University of California Press.

Pepinsky, Harold E. 1988. "Violence as Unresponsiveness." *Justice Quarterly* 5 (December): 539–63.

Sayama, Mike. 1986. *Samadhi: Self Development in Zen, Swordsmanship, and Psychotherapy.* Albany: State University of New York Press.

Skolimowski, Henry. 1986. "Life, Entropy and Education." *American Theosophist* 74: 305–10.

Sullivan, Dennis. 1980. *The Mask of Love: Corrections in America, Toward a Mutual Aid Alternative.* Port Washington, N.Y.: Kennikat Press.

Suzuki, Shunryu. 1970. *Zen Mind, Beginner's Mind.* New York: Weatherhill.

Taylor, Richard. 1986. "What Are Nonviolent Tactics?" *Pledge of Resistance Newsletter* (Summer): 1–2, 8.

Tifft, Larry, and Dennis Sullivan. 1980. *The Struggle to Be Human: Crime, Criminology, and Anarchism.* Sanday, Orkney: Cienfuegos Press.

*The Upanishads.* 1965. Tr. Juan Mascaro. New York: Penguin Books.

Walsh, Roger. 1984. *Staying Alive: The Psychology of Human Survival.* Boston: Shambhala.

Watts, Alan W. 1957. *The Way of Zen.* New York: Pantheon Books.

*Kevin Anderson*

---

T W O

# Radical Criminology and the Overcoming of Alienation

*Perspectives from Marxian and*
*Gandhian Humanism*

Recently Joseph Weis, the outgoing editor of the mainstream journal *Criminology*, introduced a special issue which focused on theory by bemoaning what he termed the "exhaustion of paradigms" in criminological theory. (Weis, 1987: 83). In that same issue of *Criminology*, Jack Gibbs writes in a rather tendentious article:

> Criminologists should be sobered on recognition that Merton's theory and Sutherland's theory were formulated more than 40 years ago, while Hirschi's theory (1969) is now nearly 20 years old. Yet those theories are still treated at length in introductory texts. Perhaps a concern with old theories does not necessarily doom a field. . . . Yet critics of orthodox criminology have not really formulated alternatives to Merton, Sutherland, and Hirschi; rather they appear to have rejected etiological questions. (Gibbs 1987, 823–33).

Gibbs's sharpest criticism is directed at the critical criminologists, who are furthest from his own agenda of getting back to "etiological questions."

This essay will hardly satisfy Gibbs, but it does attempt to address the impasse of radical criminological theory in the 1980s, albeit not in Weis's scientist notion of an "exhaustion of paradigms." Instead, I attempt to formulate a new grounding for radical criminology in the humanism of Gandhi and Marx.

Radical criminological theory seems to offer at least four directions today: (1) holding fast to 1970s dogmatic Marxism (O'Malley, 1987); (2) moving from theory toward research in substantive areas (Greenberg, 1986); (3) abandoning radical thought for moderate liberalism (Hirst and Jones, 1987); or (4) moving toward a reformulation of radical criminology as a humanism (Hartjen, 1985).

Although the fourth perspective seems to me the most promising, my intent here is to first lay out a concept of radical humanism by an examination of Gandhian and Marxian thought. It is argued below that we need such a deeply grounded humanist vision if we are to reconstruct radical criminological theory in the coming period. This concept of humanism will then be used to assess aspects of radical criminology over the past two decades.

In the post–World War II world, various forms of radical humanism arose in response to the crises in politics and in theory produced by Nazism, Stalinism, Hiroshima, and the rise of Third World liberation movements. Such varied thinkers as the African revolutionary Frantz Fanon, the French existentialists Jean-Paul Sartre and Maurice Merleau-Ponty, the Catholic worker-priests, Mahatma Gandhi, and the Marxist humanists arose and debated how the alienation of both Western capitalism and established Communism could be overcome. Many of these debates centered on discussion of the young Marx's *1844 Essays,* which were just then gaining a wide circulation in Europe. I focus below on two quite different strands from this heterogeneous debate: Gandhian and Marxian humanism.

## Gandhian and Marxian Humanism

As is well known, Gandhi and Marx have two very different views of society and of social change. First, Marxian humanism arose mainly out of an examination of the crisis of industrial capitalism, while Gandhian humanism arose out of the problematic of an ancient agricultural civilization seeking to liberate itself from British imperialism. Second, Marxian humanism considers class struggle and revolution as part of the struggle for human self-emancipation, while Gandhian humanism adheres to reconciliation of classes and to nonviolence as a principle. Third, Marxian humanism is secular, rejecting religious categories, while Gandhian humanism derives itself explicitly from Hindu and Jain religious categories.

At the same time, there are less often noted similarities between these two forms of radical humanism. First, both of them are a radical rejection of Western capitalist civilization. Second, both posit for the future a vision of a society free of alienation. Third, both share a confidence that human liberation is on the immediate historical agenda.

I will deal with Gandhi first, for two reasons: One, even though Marx wrote earlier than Gandhi, the post-Marx Marxists did not see him as a humanist thinker. Such a view developed only after World War II with the discussions around the young Marx. Therefore, the discussion of Gandhian humanism, which began in the 1930s, is actually older than that of Marxian humanism. Two, as a Marxist humanist, I will be using Marxian categories to critique Gandhian ones; and in order to do so, it is first necessary to set out Gandhian categories.

## Gandhian Humanism

Gandhi's humanism did not involve either a religious rejection of the world or a religious fundamentalism intervening in the secular world, despite many misconceptions on this issue. As Margaret Chatterjee, a leading Indian philosopher, writes in her study of Gandhi's religious thought: Gandhi was "not fighting a battle against the inroads of secularism" but "was in fact throughout his life concerned with very secular goals"; and further, he "understood that the free Indian state needed to be secular if communal harmony was to be safeguarded" (Chatterjee, 1983: 4–5).[1] Chatterjee compares Gandhi's critical and radical Hinduism in this regard not to Islamic fundamentalism, but rather to Catholic liberation theology in Latin America today.

To be sure, Gandhi's radical Hinduism contained some contradictory elements. On the one hand, Gandhi was committed to uprooting untouchability, women's oppression in some forms, and other extremely oppressive features of Hindu society. He was also committed to harmonious relations with other religious groups, especially Muslims, a stance which led to his assassination at the hands of Hindu fundamentalists.

On the other hand, some features of Gandhian humanism would seem almost retrogressive. These include his promulgation of cow-protection as a major goal of the rural Gandhian movement, his advocacy of spinning on a handloom as an alternative to industrial capitalism, and his deeply traditional religious style. His style and dress was that of a traditional Hindu holy man, even though his aims and goals were essentially nontraditional.

Gandhi's Hindu-based concept of satyagraha, active but nonviolent noncooperation with oppression, was his major theoretical contribution. This concept was not only a political tactic, but also a philosophical-religious principle. It originated during Gandhi's stay in South Africa, where he led the Indian community in passive resistance to racist laws. Satyagraha also underlay his leadership of the struggle against British rule in India, 1919–47. It was a contradictory weapon and a contradictory philosophy.

Satyagraha's limits were seen after the Amritsar massacre of 1919, when hundreds of peaceful Indian demonstrators were machine-gunned to death by British soldiers. India seemed to many to be on the verge of revolution, in a period of world upheaval following the Russian Revolution. Far from deepening the movement into a confrontation with British imperialism after Amritsar, Gandhi used all of his considerable prestige to stop the movement in its tracks because it had strayed beyond his nonviolent tactics.

During the same period, on the other hand, Gandhi surprised many of his Marxist critics by aligning himself firmly against the native-Indian textile mill owners of Ahmedabad when their workers went on strike. The mill owners were financial supporters of his Congress Party. Yet at the same time, Gandhi limited the strike, forcing the workers to stop actively preventing scabs from working. When tension rose after two weeks on strike, Gandhi went on a fast, which quickly convinced the mill owners to negotiate with their workers (Gandhi, 1948).

The more radical character of Gandhian humanism was revealed as he compelled the nationalistic movement, until then based in the cities among the middle class, to penetrate the most oppressed part of the population—the indigo-growing peasantry of poverty-stricken Bihar. He led a protracted grass-roots struggle there against absentee British landlords, whose demands for rent payments in a year of crop failure were driving the peasants into famine.

In the famous Salt March of the 1930s, the disciplined nonviolent tactics of the Gandhian demonstrators exposed British imperialism to the world when it clubbed the nonviolent resisters mercilessly. This inaugurated four years of new independence agitation.

Still more radical was the Quit India Movement launched in 1942 in the midst of World War II. It should be recalled that pro-Soviet Marxists opposed anti-imperialist movements against the Western powers in this period because they might interfere with the struggle against Hitler's Germany, in which Stalin's Russia was allied with the Western nations: Britain, France and the United States. The Quit India Movement took on a near-insurrectionary character, especially in Bihar (Copley, 1987; Henningham, 1983). None of this, however, enabled the Indian movement to avoid the conflagration of 1942–47, which tragically dismembered the land on the eve of independence, leaving scars which fester today in interreligious pogroms.

At the same time, however, Gandhi's satyagraha had transcended India to become a universal for worldwide movements for peace, social justice, and national liberation. Especially in this regard, we should mention the independence struggle in African countries such as Zambia, where Kenneth Kaunda based the nationalist movement on Gandhian principles, as well as the peace and civil-rights movements in the Western capitalist lands. As the noted Gandhian scholar and former secretary to Gandhi, N. K. Bose, has suggested in an essay on Gandhi's socialist humanism:

> The supreme problem which faces mankind today is the problem of war. . . .
> [Gandhi] tried to find a substitute for war which would be equally effective,
> but which would not leave men debased, as they now are, after a conflict. It

was in pursuit of this that he invented the technique of satyagraha, by which conflicts could be conducted at a civilized level. (Bose, 1965: 89)

In an age of nuclear weapons, the attraction of satyagraha continues to grow and is found especially in the antinuclear movement.

On the critical and radical character of Gandhian humanism, one surprising testimonial is that of A. R. Desai, the Marxist sociologist and Gandhi critic, whose groundbreaking study of Indian nationalism first appeared in the 1940s. Desai writes:

> He was the first national leader who recognized the role of the masses and mass action in the struggle for national liberation. . . . Under his leadership, the Indian people became heroic, patriotic and intrepid fighters for national emancipation. . . . It was a stirring spectacle, that of tens of thousands of women, who for centuries were chained to the narrow domestic life and whom an authoritarian social system had assigned the position of helots at home, stepping out in the streets and marching with their male fellow-patriots in illegal political demonstrations. (Desai, 1976: 347)

Desai also notes Gandhi's commitment to the eradication of the age-old oppression of untouchability, not as an afterthought, but as a major part of his political program.

The radical Gandhian scholar N. K. Bose goes further, stressing Gandhi's paramount commitment to humanist goals: "It is clear that Gandhi was inspired by the highest ideals of democracy and equalitarianism. He was a humanist even before he was a nationalist" (Bose, 1965: 94). This does not mean that Gandhi's opposition to untouchability was without contradictions, however. His frequent paternalism toward untouchables, more accurately today called Dalits (oppressed), got Gandhi into much difficulty with their leading spokesperson, Dr. B. R. Ambedkar.

Gandhi's concept of a new India (Hind Swaraj) was closely related to satyagraha. He saw the self-sustaining Indian village community as the basis for a national regeneration: a village reformed of untouchability and landlord oppression, but equally rejecting modern industrial civilization.

As early as 1924 Gandhi had objected to what he termed the modern "craze" for machinery, which he held creates unemployment and alienation in Western capitalist civilization: "It is an alteration of the conditions of labor that I want. This mad rush for wealth must cease, and the laborer must be assured, not only a living wage, but a daily task that is not mere drudgery" (cited by Bose, 1965: 94). Gandhi's main concern was not the industrial worker, but rather the peasant. He hoped to avoid the exploitative character of capitalist development for India's majority, the peasants, in their 700,000 villages.

Gandhi's concept was that of a village which would be "self-contained, manufacturing mainly for use" (Gandhi, 1962: 291), as he wrote in 1936. Six years later, he outlined its self-governing structure: ". . . it will have pan-chayats (village councils) for settling disputes. . . . Since there will be no system of punishments in the accepted sense, this panchayat will be the legislature, judiciary and executive combined" (Gandhi, 1962: 295–96). When Gandhi outlined his concept of a republic based on each village having one vote in district and national administration, the American journalist Louis Fischer was quick to remark: "That is very much like the Soviet system." Gandhi replied: "I did not know that. I don't mind" (295).

Even as he opposed untouchability, Gandhi did not call for the abolition of caste within his self-governing village, but for its reform. In fact some have connected the concept of panchayat itself with that of caste. As Richard Lannoy notes in his discussion of early Indian culture: "When the occasion warranted it, a panchayat, or council of elders from the dominant caste, was convened either to·settle the differences between castes or internal disputes within castes" (Lannoy, 1971: 165). Gandhi's concept of panchayat in no way included such a traditional notion of upper-caste domination, but his ambiguity on the problem of caste itself left the door open for others to continue caste oppression in the new India. Gandhi's often expressed view that all would become Sudras (low-caste workers) in the new India did not solve this problem, although it did indicate the direction of his concept of panchayat.

Perhaps Gandhi's humanist vision of India's future, including his sharp critique of alienation, is best summed up in the following statement made in 1946, two years before his assassination:

> Independence must begin at the bottom. Thus, every village will be a republic or panchayat having full powers. . . . In this structure composed of innumerable villages, there will be everwidening, never ascending circles. Life will not be a pyramid with the apex sustained from the bottom. But it will be an oceanic circle whose center will be the individual always ready to perish for the village, the latter ready to perish for the circle of villages, till at last the whole becomes one life composed of individuals, never aggressive in their arrogance but ever humble, sharing the majesty of the oceanic circle of which they are integral units. (Cited by Borman, 1986: 260)

While we cannot know what Gandhi's view would have been of the prob-lems which postindependence India has faced since 1948, one thing should be noted, a fact which distinguished Gandhi from other Third World independence leaders of the period: Gandhi was remarkable for his refusal to take any formal leadership positions, either in the Congress Party or in the new Indian state. Some twenty-five years ago, a Marxist humanist writer singled out the uniqueness of this rejection by Gandhi of party and state positions (Dunayevskaya, 1962). This rejection of the centralized state and the single party is a major if implicit part of his vision of a panchayat republic based in the villages.

## Marxian Humanism

Marxist humanism needs to be differentiated from a variety of Marxist and neo-Marxist perspectives. Elsewhere (Anderson, 1986) I have shown some of its variety and distinguished it, not only from established Marxism but also from the neo-Marxist currents of either the Frankfurt School or the existential Marxists, by arguing that the latter neo-Marxists tended to assume the permanent character of human alienation, while the Marxist humanists did not. Not current until the 1950s, and based at that time most widely among East European dissident Marxists, Marxist humanism was a product both of increasing disillusionment with established Communism and of new discussions of the humanist writings of Marx, especially his *1844 Essays*. In its most radical and critical version, that of Raya Dunayevskaya (1982, 1985), Marxist humanism becomes a critique of all post-Marx Marxists. Below, however, I will discuss Marxian humanism strictly in terms of Marx's own writings.

Crucial to Marxian humanism is the Marxian concept of dialectic. While it is often stressed that materialism versus idealism separated Marx's dialectic from that of the founder of the modern concept of dialectic, Hegel, there are in fact strong idealist elements in Marx's dialectic as well, which is better expressed as a unity of idealism and materialism. Marx's break with Hegel's dialectic is not so much on the ground of materialism versus idealism, but rather on the basis of concrete versus abstract humanism. This is seen in Marx's profound 1844 "Critique of the Hegelian Dialectic" where he sets apart his own humanism from that of Hegel by referring to "real, corporeal man, with his feet firmly rooted on the solid ground, inhaling and exhaling all the powers of nature" (Marx, 1844: 181). Hegel's dialectic was both the point of origin for Marx's dialectic and a source to which he constantly returned.

Marx's concept of negativity as a "moving and creating principle" (Marx 1844: 176) is rooted firmly in Hegel's *Phenomenology of Mind*. In fact, Marx cites this idea as Hegel's greatest contribution to thought. This humanism of the young Marx, with the human being as the center of the universe and with negativity as a creative principle, clashes to some degree with Gandhian humanism's stress on the human being as rooted in nature and in reconciliation rather than negation.

Also beginning in 1844, Marx developed his concept of alienated labor. By the time he published *Capital* (1867) this concept had developed into his concepts of reification and fetishism of commodities. Here the objectivity of alienation under capitalism became more apparent, as did its opposite, freely associated labor. The latter was something the worker aimed for, according to Marx. Throughout, Marx included sharp critiques of modern industry and its machine technology. Already in the *Communist Manifesto*, the worker under capitalism was seen as reduced to "an appendage of the machine" where the labor process itself had robbed the worker of all individuality and humanity: "Owing to the extensive use of machinery and to division of labor, the work of the proletarians has lost all individual character, and, consequently, all charm for the workman" (Marx and Engels, 1848: 227).

This was hardly a view found only in the young Marx. It was worked out further and deepened in *Capital*, in the famous 150-page chapter on machinery:

> Factory work exhausts the nervous system to the uttermost; at the same time, it does away with the many-sided play of the muscles, and confiscates every atom of freedom, both in bodily and in intellectual activity. Even the lightening of the labor becomes an instrument of torture, since the machine does not free the worker from the work but rather deprives the work itself of all interest. (Marx, 1867: 548)[2]

In *Capital* the stress is also on the "negation of the negation," the positive overcoming of this reification in the negation of the system's own earlier negation of the freedom of the worker.

This is seen as well in Marx's concept of the possibility in the future of "a new economic foundation for a higher form of the family and of relations between the sexes":

> It is of course just as absurd to regard to the Christian–Germanic form of the family as absolute and final as it would have been in the case of the ancient Roman, the ancient Greek, or the Oriental forms, which, moreover, form a series in historical development. It is also obvious that the fact that the collective working group is composed of individuals of both sexes and all ages must under the appropriate conditions turn into a source of humane development, although in its spontaneously developed, brutal, capitalist form, the system works in the opposite direction, and becomes a pestiferous source of corruption and slavery, since here the worker exists for the process of production, and not the process of production for the worker. (Marx, 1867: 621)

Thus for the industrialized capitalist lands at least, the system of production needed to be transcended even in its form of the family, and no return to the past was possible.

Further, in the 1867 preface to the first edition of *Capital*, Marx had written that: "The country that is more developed industrially only shows, to the less developed, the image of its own future" (Marx, 1867: 91). This type of statement by Marx suggested to some the inevitability of the capitalist phase for all societies. If so, this is Marx's sharpest difference with Gandhi, who, as seen above, wanted to preserve aspects of the traditional self-sustaining Indian village.

But is Marx really the type of technological and historical determinist some have seen in the 1867 preface and in other isolated statements in his writings? The answer is a definite no in regard to his last writings, 1873–83. But first it should be mentioned that the context of the statement in the 1867 preface is a comparison of Britain with Germany, where Marx is stressing that Germany, already partially industrialized, will soon suffer the fate of Britain.

More important is how Marx alters this sentence in the French edition of *Capital*, the last one which he personally prepared for the printer. There the sentence from the preface reads quite differently: "The country that is more developed industrially only shows, *to those which follow it on the industrial path*, the image of their own future" (Marx, 1873–75: 549; my translation, emphasis added). Marx explicitly corrects his earlier text here, apparently to make sure that the reader would see that he is leaving open the future of noncapitalist lands. As I have argued elsewhere, there were many other changes from the 1867 edition to the French edition, some of them never included in the English or German editions of *Capital* by either Engels or subsequent editors (Anderson 1983).

This point about *Capital* does not rest solely on isolated passages from that or other works by Marx but on the whole corpus of his late writings, the most extensive of which were his *Ethnological Notebooks*, a study of anthropological data on India, Australia, Hawaii, and Native Americans. In addition, Marx researched and wrote in his last years about the traditional Russian *mir*, a self-governing village structure with a primitive communist form. Where some had interpreted his writings to argue that the *mir* and other such forms must inevitably disappear into capitalism, which only then could be transcended to create socialism, Marx wrote in 1877 to a Russian journal that "if Russia continues along the path it has followed since 1861, it will lose the finest chance ever offered by history to a people and undergo all the fateful vicissitudes of the capitalist regime" (Marx, in Shanin, 1983: 135). In 1881 he wrote Vera Zasulich that the village "commune is the fulcrum for a social regeneration in Russia. But in order that it might function as such, the harmful influences assailing it on all sides must first be eliminated, and it must then be assured the normal conditions for a spontaneous development" (Marx, in Shanin, 1983: 124). These discussions have generated intense interest in India in the 1980s, as I can attest from my trip there in 1986.

Here some parallels would seem to emerge with Gandhian humanism. But unlike Gandhi, Marx called for world revolution, including inside the village commune. In 1882, one year before his death, he wrote in the preface to a new Russian edition of the *Communist Manifesto:* "If the Russian Revolution becomes the signal for a proletarian revolution in the West, so that the two complement each other, then Russia's peasant communal land-ownership may serve as the point of departure for a communist development" (Marx, in Shanin, 1983: 139).

## Gandhi and Marx Compared

In addition to the concentration in his last writings on what is today termed the Third World, Marx also focused there on the problem of women's liberation. His own *Ethnological Notebooks*, which Engels read and attempted to popularize in his *Origin of the Family* (1884), reveal a far more profound, truly dialectical view of women's liberation then the schematic and deterministic view presented by Engels. Left unpublished until the 1970s, Marx's *Ethnological Notebooks* show a drawing together, albeit in unfinished form, of a lifetime of ideas on the man/woman relationship. Dunayevskaya (1982, 1985) argued forcefully that these *Notebooks* can become ground for a Marxian humanist concept of women's liberation.

While neither Marx nor Gandhi wanted to develop blueprints of a new society, Marx did sketch out (1) a theoretical concept of the new society, (2) a specific view in some of his writings on the Paris commune and other revolutionary attempts of that society, and (3) a view of what he was not for in some of his polemics against statist forms of socialism.

As early as the *Communist Manifesto*, Marx and Engels had written of a society of the future where "the free development of each is a condition of the free development of all" (Marx and Engels, 1848: 171). In *Capital* Marx had counterposed his concept of freely associated labor to the reification of the capitalist production process. But it was in *Grundrisse* that he developed his general concept of a humanist future most eloquently:

> In fact, however, when the limited bourgeois form is stripped away, what is wealth other than the universality of individual needs, capacities, pleasures, productive forces, etc., created through universal exchange? The full development of human mastery over the forces of nature, those of so-called nature as well as of humanity's own nature? The absolute working-out of his creative potentialities, with no presupposition other than the previous historic development, which makes this totality of development, i.e., the development of all human powers as such the end in itself, not as on a predetermined yardstick? Where he does not reproduce himself in one specificity, but produces his totality? Strives not to remain something he has become, but is in the absolute movement of becoming? (Marx, 1857–58: 488)

This type of humanism was thus not restricted to the *1844 Essays*, but rather permeates Marx's mature "economic" writings as well.

Where Gandhi talked of putting his satyagraha into practice in the villages of India, Marx's claim was different: that the workers and the other revolutionary groups were in the process of creating such a new society themselves. Gandhi's revolutionary ideas could deepen and clarify their struggle, give it a total vision; but his role was not so much that of initiator. It is not that Gandhi was elitist, but rather that he did not base his vision of the new society on a concrete analysis of the mass creativity of the movements of the oppressed. This made Gandhi's panchayat republic somewhat of an abstract universal, as against Marx's vision of a new society.

Marx's concreteness can be seen in his discussion of the Paris Commune of 1871. There Marx wrote of the new society which the Parisian workers created. As Dunayevskaya stresses:

> What was new was that the Commune, by releasing labor from the confines of value production, showed *how* people associated freely without the despotism of capital or the mediation of things. Contrast the *expansiveness* of that movement with the mutilation of labor under capitalism, which robs the workers of all individuality and reduces them merely to a component of labor in *general*. (Dunayevskaya, 1958: 101)

Marx, in his discussion of the Commune, gets very specific about its form of organization and sees it as an alternative to capitalist concepts of democracy.

In passing, Marx also noted the seemingly miraculous elimination of ordinary crime during the Commune:

> No longer was Paris the rendezvous of British landlords, Irish absentees, American ex-slaveholders, and shoddy men, Russian ex-serfowners, and Wallachian boyards. No more corpses at the morgue, no nocturnal burglaries, scarcely any robberies; in fact, for the first time since the days of February 1848, the streets of Paris were safe, and that without any police of any kind. "We," said a member of the commune, "hear no longer of assassination, theft, and personal assault; it seems indeed as if the police had dragged along with it to Versailles all its conservative friends." (Marx, 1871: 549)

Marx thus stressed the concrete overcoming of alienation, of the state, and of crime in the Commune. The Commune itself was ended by an immense crime of government: the slaughter by the Versailles military of 20,000 Parisians and the imprisonment or deportation of many more. At the same time, the Commune's brief existence opened up new theoretical vistas for the movement: it was only after the Commune that Marx was able to get a French publisher to serialize and translate *Capital* in a popular periodical that workers read. What the French readers got was also a more theoretically developed text, since Marx created a new French edition of *Capital* rather than permitting a mere translation.

Where Gandhi's critique of the nationalist party was implicit in his failure to assume any leadership post, Marx's critique of elitist forms of organization, including some socialist ones, is explicit. This is especially true of his *Critique of the Gotha Program* (1875) where Lassallean socialists in Germany are accused both of statism and of ties to the concept of the nation-state. Nor does Marx simply counterpose the type of organization in the Paris commune to statist socialism. He connects this question back to his overall theoretical framework of overcoming "the antithesis between mental and physical labor" toward a society based on the concept "from each according to his ability, to each according to his needs" (Marx, 1875: 10).

## Implications for Critical Criminology

The need to reformulate social theory, including criminological theory, on a radical humanist basis flows from the above discussion of socialist humanism in Gandhi and Marx. Gandhian humanism is also generating many discussions today, not only as a tactic, but increasingly as a social theory (Pantham, 1986; Chatterjee, 1983). More than two decades ago, at the height of the social movements of the 1960s, Erich Fromm (1965) brought together Marxian and Gandhian humanism in a single collection which included many writers on East European and Western Marxist humanism such as Mihailo Markovic, Karel Kosik, Raya Dunayevskaya, Herbert Marcuse, and Lucien Goldmann. This collection also included N. K. Bose's key essay on Gandhian socialist humanism. Thus, as early as 1965, a theoretical grounding had been developed for a socialist humanist criminology. Why then did one not fully develop at the time, and why may it be possible to develop one today?

In the late 1960s, as the New Left broke sharply with liberalism and moved toward varieties of revolutionary thought, all too many dropped the concept of humanism along with liberalism, some even considering it to be "bourgeois." At a theoretical level, this new "radical" antihumanism was epitomized by the structuralist Marxism of Louis Althusser, which concealed beneath its subtleties an authoritarian and dogmatic, even Stalinist, mode of thought.

Althusserian Marxist criminology was launched in 1972 by Paul Hirst, who from the outset rejected the revolutionary humanism of the young Marx: "Marx's later works (i.e. those works post-1844, that is, beginning with the German Ideology) contain a consistent and developed critique not only of bourgeois authors Hegel, Feuerbach, Proudhon, Smith, Ricardo, etc., but also of the 'young' Marx who shared their theoretical positions" (Hirst, 1972a: 30). This second-hand-Althusserian Hirst, whose arrogance was equaled only by ignorance, then proceeded to chop up Marx into "three different periods": (1) 1840–42, the Kantian critique of law; (2) 1842–44, the Feuerbachian period; and (3) 1845–82, the formation and development of historical materialism (Hirst, 1972a: 30).

Thus, where even the most anti-Hegelian Marxists have usually admitted that at least the young Marx was a Hegelian and a humanist, Hirst and Althusser had him as a "Kantian liberal" in the period 1840–42, a characterization few serious Marx scholars would accept. Hirst therefore considered both Marx's doctoral thesis on Epicurus and Democritus, with its critique of Hegel's concept of freedom, and his 1842 critique of the laws on the theft of wood to have been pre-Marxian and even based on liberalism.

Then, after distorting Marx beyond recognition, Hirst proceeded to argue that "mode of production" only—and not alienation, reification, or humanism—must become the starting point for a Marxist criminology.

Having by the 1980s abandoned much of his earlier Althusserian Marxism, Hirst is today arguably a Kantian liberal himself when he and a colleague write: "Marxism is a failure as a political theory because it stakes all on an impossible alternative, an advanced society with modern industry but without either a separate public power or a formal legal framework" (Hirst and Jones, 1987: 22). Perhaps against an earlier Hirst, he argues also that: "Few now support the crasser forms of the revolutionary Marxist approach to law" (22). But one consistency from the 1972 Hirst to the 1987 one is his firm belief in the need for a strong state: first Marxist, and today liberal. While some writers such as Elliott (1986) have chronicled Hirst's trajectory most critically, at least one radical criminological theorist, Pat O'Malley, shows that it is still possible today to see Hirst as the "first to face the problem directly" of how to found a Marxist criminology without any reference to the recent Hirst (O'Malley 1987: 70)!

In a recent survey of Marxist criminology, Greenberg (1986) discusses a wide variety of solid research on specific problems such as prisons, juvenile delinquency, police, law, etc.; but he rejects any attempt to directly ground Marxist criminology in classical theoretical texts: "It became clear that if a Marxist criminology were to be created, it had to be based more on Marx's general theoretical insights and methods than on the writings of Marx and Engels or their followers" (Greenberg, 1986: 171). The Marxist criminology of the 1970s, which Greenberg rightly criticizes, cannot, in my view, be overcome merely by shifting to what Merton once termed theories of the middle range. At some stage, broad theoretical grounding will need to be developed anew. To wait for more data to begin to do so is an empiricist answer to theoretical problematics and is definitely not in the tradition of Marxian and other forms of radical humanist theory.

Beirne (1987) has shown another possible direction by his critical probing into the origins of criminological theory in a detailed and incisive study of Tarde. But he does not tie his study directly to the problematics of a radical criminology today.

Over the years, some of the best radical criminological theory has attempted to move toward a socialist humanist concept. Taylor, Walton, and Young (1973) were certainly more inclined toward this direction than was Hirst. Unfortunately, Taylor and Walton's debate with Hirst (1972a, 1972b) reveals their own near-capitulation to Hirst's claim to speak in the name of Marxian theory as a major authority.

Taylor, Walton, and Young do in their major book call for:

> . . . building links between the insights of interactionist theory, and other approaches sensitive to men's subjective world, and the theories of social

structure implicit in orthodox Marxism. More crucially, such a linkage would enable us to escape from the straightjacket of an economic determinism and the relativism of some subjectivist approaches to a theory of contradiction in a social structure which recognizes in "deviance" the acts of men in the process of actively making, rather than passively taking, the external world. It might enable us to sustain what has until now been a polemical assertion made (in the main) by anarchists and deviates themselves, that much deviance is in itself a political act. (Taylor, Walton, and Young, 1973: 220–21)

The overly generalized concept of deviance as a political act seems today highly questionable; but at the time, it was part of the process of the creation of radical criminological theory, and perhaps a necessary step. Still left hanging, however, is the notion of subjectivity in the social theory of deviance. A concept of subjectivity can be found not only in the interactionist and phenomenological literature but also, as I have argued, in radical humanist theory, particularly in Marxist humanism.

While Taylor, Walton, and Young implicitly rejected Hirst's Althusserian bifurcation of the young and the mature Marx by making some use of Marx's category of alienation from his *1844 Essays*, they in no way developed this into a concept of Marxist humanism. Instead, they actually quoted Hirst approvingly on Marx's view of crime and deviance and accepted him as an authority on Marx. They did so despite Hirst's own (1972b) total dismissal of their mildly critical response to his view of Marx on crime and deviance.

Another major theoretical contribution during the 1970s was Richard Quinney's work, where radical humanism was initially grounded in phenomenology and existentialism. This was later connected to various forms of Marxism, with a revolutionary bent (Quinney, 1977). One difference between Quinney's work and that of most other Marxist criminologists in this period was that he continued to explore the theoretical and even philosophical bases of a radical and humanist criminology. His consistently humanist approach included the individual as well as the social in a dialectical interplay, occasionally making direct use of Marxist humanist writers such as Karel Kosik. More recently Quinney (1980, 1982) has moved toward a religious metaphysic as the grounding for a radical humanism, somewhat different from both the Gandhian and the Marxian humanism which I have discussed above.

A more recent discussion of humanism was that of Hartjen (1985: 461), who sees a need for "criminologists to get out of the crime control business and into the business of human understanding." Part of a special issue of the *Journal of Sociology and Social Welfare* on "Humanistic Perspectives in Criminology," edited by Ronald Kramer and Stuart Hills, this discussion, while not overly theoretical, shows the ongoing importance of the question of humanism in radical criminology. In addition, the Yugoslav Marxist humanist Mihailo Markovic's recent discussions of liberal and socialist concepts of human rights have made an important contribution to a radical humanist theory of law (Markovic, 1979, 1989).

In the above discussion, I have attempted to ground radical criminological theory in the writings of Marx and Gandhi on humanism. This led in turn to a critique of radical criminological theory up to now. It is my hope that others will take up this challenge as a way of moving beyond the current weaknesses of radical criminological theory.

## NOTES

1. In this context, the term "communal harmony" refers to overcoming the often murderous conflicts between religious, caste, and ethnic groups, which still plague modern India.

2. The translation here has been slightly altered, using the French edition of *Capital* (Marx, 1873–75), the last one which Marx personally prepared for the printer. For further details on this point, see Dunayevskaya (1982) and my own exploratory article (Anderson, 1983).

## REFERENCES

Anderson, Kevin. 1983. "The 'Unknown' Marx's *Capital*: The French Edition of 1872–75, 100 Years Later." *Review of Radical Political Economics* 16 (4): 71–80.
———. 1986. "Sources of Marxist Humanism: Fanon, Kosik, Dunayevskaya." *Quarterly Journal of Ideology* 10 (4): 15–31.
Beirne, Piers. 1987. "Between Classicism and Positivism: Crime and Penalty in the Writings of Gabriel Tarde." *Criminology* 25 (4): 785–819.
Borman, William. 1986. *Gandhi and Non-Violence*. Albany: SUNY Press.
Bose, Nirmal Kumar. 1965. "Gandhi: Humanist and Socialist." In Erich Fromm (ed.), *Socialist Humanism*. New York: Doubleday.
Chatterjee, Margaret. 1983. *Gandhi's Religious Thought*. Notre Dame: University of Notre Dame Press.
Copley, Antony. 1987. *Gandhi: Against the Tide*. New York: Basil Blackwell.
Desai, A. R. 1976. *The Social Background of Indian Nationalism*. Bombay: Popular Prakashan.
Dunayevskaya, Raya. 1962. "The China–India War in a Nuclear State–Capitalist Age." *The Raya Dunayevskaya Collection. Marxist-Humanism: A Half-Century of Its World Development*. Detroit: Wayne State University Archives (microfilm), 1986. 1958.
———. 1988. *Marxism and Freedom: From 1776 Until Today*. New York: Columbia University Press.
———. 1982. *Rosa Luxemburg, Women's Liberation and Marx's Philosophy of Revolution*. New Jersey: Humanities Press.
———. 1985. *Women's Liberation and the Dialectics of Revolution*. New Jersey: Humanities Press.

Elliott, Gregory. 1986. "The Odyssey of Paul Hirst." *New Left Review* 159 (October): 81–105.

Fromm, Erich (ed.). 1965. *Socialist Humanism.* New York: Doubleday.

Gandhi, Mahatma. 1948. *Autobiography: The Story of My Experiments with Truth.* New York: Dover.

———. 1962. *The Essential Gandhi.* Ed. Louis Fischer. New York: Vintage.

Gibbs, Jack. 1987. "The State of Criminological Theory." *Criminology* 25 (4): 821–40.

Greenberg, David. 1986. "Marxist Criminology." In Bertell Ollman and Edward Vernoff (eds.), *The Left Academy*, Vol. 3. New York: Praeger.

Hartjen, Clayton. 1985. "Humanist Criminology: Is It Possible?" *Journal of Sociology and Social Welfare* 13 (3): 444–68.

Henningham, Stephen. 1983. "Quit India in Bihar and the Eastern United Provinces: The Dual Revolt." In Ranajit Guha (ed.), *Subaltern Studies*, Vol. 2. Delhi: Oxford University Press.

Hirst, Paul Q. 1972a. "Marx and Engels on Law, Crime and Morality." *Economy and Society* 1 (1): 28–56.

———. 1972b. "A Reply to Taylor and Walton." *Economy and Society* 1 (3): 351–56.

Hirst, Paul Q., and Phil Jones. 1987. "The Critical Resources of Established Jurisprudence." In Peter Fitzpatrick and Alan Hunt (eds.), *Critical Legal Studies.* New York: Basil Blackwell.

Lannoy, Richard. 1971. *The Speaking Tree.* New York: Oxford University Press.

Markovic, Mihailo. 1979. "The Principle of Equal Self-Determination as a Basis for Jurisprudence." *Archiv für Rechts-und Sozialphilosophie* 13: 181–92.

———. 1989. "The Relation Between Political and Social Rights." *Quarterly Journal of Ideology* 13: 4.

Marx, Karl. 1844 (1961). "Economic and Philosophical Manuscripts." In Erich Fromm (ed.), *Marx's Concept of Man.* New York: Ungar.

———. 1976. *Capital.* Vol. 1. Tr. Ben Fowkes. London: Penguin. 1857–1858.

———. 1973. *Grundrisse.* Tr. Martin Nicolaus. New York: Vintage. 1871.

———. 1977. *The Civil War in France.* In David McLellan (ed.), *Karl Marx: Selected Writings.* New York: Oxford University Press, 1873–75.

———. 1963. *Le Capital.* In Karl Marx, *Oeuvres, Economie I*, Ed. Maximilien Rubel. Paris: Gallimard. 1875.

———. 1966. *Critique of the Gotha Program.* New York: International.

Marx, Karl and Friedrich Engels. 1848 (1977). *The Communist Manifesto.* In David McLellan (ed.), *Karl Marx: Selected Writings.* New York: Oxford University Press.

O'Malley, Pat. 1987. "Marxist Theory and Marxist Criminology." *Crime and Social Justice* 29: 70–87.

Pantham, Thomas. 1986. "Habermas' Practical Discourse and Gandhi's Satyagraha." *Praxis International* 6 (2): 190–204.

Quinney, Richard. 1977. *Class, State and Crime.* New York: David McKay.

———. 1980. *Class, State and Crime.* Second edition, New York and London: Longman.

———. 1982. *Social Existence: Metaphysics, Marxism and the Social Sciences.* Beverly Hills: Sage.

Shanin, Teodor. 1983. *Marx and the Russian Road.* New York: Monthly

Taylor, Ian, and Paul Walton. 1972. "Radical Deviancy Theory and Marxism: A Reply to Paul Q. Hirst." *Economy and Society* 1 (2): 229–33.

Taylor, Ian, Paul Walton, and Jock Young. 1973. *The New Criminology.* New York: Harper and Row.

Weis, Joseph G. 1987. "From the Editor: Special Issue on Theory." *Criminology* 25 (4): 783–84.

*J. Peter Cordella*

---

## T H R E E

# Reconciliation and the Mutualist Model of Community

As the societal eclipses the communal, as conflict is redefined as crime, and as reconciliation is replaced by retribution, the possibility of a return to the mutualist model of community becomes increasingly remote. The social contract model of community, with its assumption of the self-interested nature of man, has become so thoroughly accepted as *the* model of society that the establishment of a true and satisfying *community* in modern times is dismissed as regressive thinking.[1] It is argued that self-interested human nature precludes the return to communal organization. Existing examples of mutualist communities such as the Hutterites, Amish, and Mennonites are dismissed as aberrations, groups that have failed to overcome the limitations of religious traditionalism in the face of increasing formal rationalization of the dominant society. It is argued that these communitarian-based religious sects are of little importance to understanding the social problems of modern society because they have failed the all important test of rationality.[2]

Ironically, when conflict and its resolution are examined, it is the social contract model with its assumption of self-interest that appears to fail the most important test of rationality, an openness to reanalysis. Societies based on a system of absolute individual rights, which is the prerequisite for the contractarian approach, seem to be limited to repressive, punitive, violent responses to conflict. Because of the imperative to constantly reinforce *individual rights*, such a society can only respond in a rigidly procedural and absolute manner. To fail to do so would weaken its claims to legal legitimacy.

The legitimacy of the contractarian model is bound up with the absolute monopoly that officials of state have over ownership and response to conflict.[3] Officials refuse to view conflict within its larger communal context, defining it simply as an infringement on individuals' rights. Such a static definition precludes the possibility of more substantive responses to conflict such as reconciliation.[4]

Conversely, the communitarian religious societies of past and present employ a much less rigid definition of conflict and employ a more substantive response to it.[5] The communitarian system generally views conflict as a weakening of communion among its members, which implies a need for restoration to full communion. The solution, therefore, is inclusion rather than exclusion, readmittance rather than isolation, reinterpretation rather than adjudication—a system guided more by the altruistic than the adversarial.

These very simply are the elements of reconciliation. In order to understand fully the concept of reconciliation as an alternative to punishment, one must examine the mutualist model of community which makes reconciliation not only possible but necessary.

Throughout the history of Christianity there have been examples of mutualist-based religious communities that parallel the established religious movements of the time. Beginning with the Pentecost movement of the third century, the succession has included the Donatists, Paulicians, Cathari, Bogomils, and the Waldenses, as well as the medieval Franciscan tertiaries. While it would be historically incorrect to view these communities as an apostolic succession of the early Christian church, it is important to note that they shared a similar philosophy, both of religion and of social structure, which more clearly reflected the philosophy and structure of the early church than did the dominant church that overshadowed each of them.

## Reconciliation and the Mutualist Model of Community

At the heart of the mutualist model is the conviction that human freedom is ultimately meaningful and fulfilling only in community. Rather than making freedom of the individual an end in itself, as is the case in Western liberal democracies, the mutualist model turns its attention to the goal of such freedom. Community as envisioned in the mutualist model can be "judged by its effectiveness in fulfilling morally purposive functions. These functions, however, must be functions of some higher controlling intention."[6] It is *intention* that distinguishes the mutualist from both the contractarian and organic approach. For most of us today, our interaction with others is increasingly contractual in nature. Our union with others is predicated on the belief that it is the best way of advancing our own interests. The motive for our friendships and ultimately our community affiliation is the antithesis of mutuality. Even within an organic society that is designed to meet the needs of the general populace most equitably, our intentions are decidedly individualistic. We believe that what is best for us is ultimately best for everyone. Society becomes "nothing more than an aggregate of self-interested individuals . . . resulting in a social order that is designed on the presumption that people are self-interested."[7]

The presumption of self-interest, with its roots in Enlightenment philosophy, has become the dominant assumption of both the contractarian and organic models of society.[8] These two models differ as to how to structure society in light of human self-interest, but they are in agreement that self-interest is dominant in human nature. The mutualist philosophy provides a decidedly different view of human nature, a view that has been prominent throughout Judeo-Christian history but whose influence has steadily declined as a result of the ascendancy of the Enlightenment vision.

The mutualist vision of human nature is most clearly captured in the philosophy of John Macmurray. Macmurray argues that we possess a bipolar nature of love and fear. While fear can dominate our actions, it is inherently subordinate to love and presupposes love. This bipolar motivation dominates all personal relations, both on an individual and societal level. When fear is subordinate to *love*, the motivation for personal relations is heterocentric.[9] When fear for oneself becomes the dominant motivation, personal behavior becomes egocentric. The preoccupation with individual rights and the punitive reinforcement of these rights in today's liberal democratic society are clearly manifestations of the motivation of fear. Macmurray, in a discussion of conflict, provides us with an analysis of the role of fear in the transition from a mutualist-based community to a contractually-based society: "If we quarrel, each of us withdraws from the other into himself, and trust is replaced by fear. We can no longer be ourselves in relation to one another. We are in conflict, and each of us loses his freedom and must act under constraint."[10]

Macmurray goes on to suggest that there are two options available to us as a response to conflict. One option would require us to overcome the fear that led to our conflict. Macmurray defines this option as reconciliation: "There may be reconciliation which restores the original confidence: the negative motivation overcome and positive relation reestablished."[11]

Or we can accept fear as a permanent element of our relationship. The acceptance of such fear can occur on a societal as well as a personal level. The repercussions of the acceptance of fear can be seen on both levels in Macmurray's discussion of the second option:

> Or we may agree to cooperate on conditions which impose a restraint upon each of us and which prevent the outbreak of active hostility. The negative

> motivation, the fear of the other, will remain but will be suppressed. This will make possible cooperation for such ends as each of us has an interest in achieving. But we will remain isolated individuals, though it may appear to satisfy our need of one another, will not really satisfy us.[12]

Applied to a societal level, such an analysis illustrates the limits of individual rights. Even when individual rights are guaranteed to all by statute and state force, the fear of losing those rights, although suppressed, remains because we perceive the self-interest of others as a constant threat to our individual rights. In order to protect our individual rights, therefore, we surrender most of our conflicts to officials of state who in turn respond punitively to the perceived violations. Anything less than a punitive response, these officials argue, would threaten the legitimacy of the rights-based approach.

The punitive response, however, is rooted in fear, which drastically limits the possibility of the reunion of individual and community. Punitive responses by their very nature imply isolation from the community. Macmurray sees punitive responses to conflict as contributing further to the climate of fear. As people witness the isolation of those who are punished, they become increasingly fearful of their own vulnerability. As their fear increases, their demand for protection in the form of individual rights becomes greater, and their need for State intervention grows. These factors coalesce to make the individual more isolated. The distance between individuals becomes greater, their interactions become less mutual and more contractual, and their context becomes less communal and more societal. The reason for such a shift, according to Macmurray, is simply motivation: "For what we need is to care for one another, and we are only caring for ourselves. We have achieved society but not community. We have become associates not friends."[13]

In contractual society, unlike community, mutuality is limited to the most private of relations. The absence of trust in the public realm precludes the possibility of mutuality. The very reason for law, both civil and criminal, is a lack of trust among the members of a society. Any resolution of conflict that requires some level of trust is dismissed as ineffective. The law, with its mandate to punish, is perceived as the only effective means of addressing conflict.[14] Such a perception contributes to the increasing monopolization of conflict by officials of state. Conflict, like so many aspects of society, is defined in functional rather than personal terms.

A contractual society, like a community, is a group that works cooperatively but whose individual members do not share in a common life. It is made up of individual lives united by self interest:

> A society, like a community, is a group that acts together but the individuals within society are not united in a common life. Society is made up of individual lives united in common purpose: A society whose members act

together without forming a fellowship can only be constituted by a common
purpose which each one, in his own interest, desires to achieve and which
can only be achieved by cooperation. The relations of its members are
functional . . . the society has an organic form; it is an organization of
functions; each member is a function of the group.[15]

A contractual society can be viewed as a collection of special interest
groups with individuals migrating from group to group, depending upon
which group can best protect and expand their individual resources. Conversely, in a community it is the common life that binds individuals:

> Any community of persons as distinct from a mere society is a group of
> individuals united in a common life, the motivation of which is positive. Like
> a society, a community is a group which acts together but unlike a mere
> society, its members of which are in communion with one another. It cannot
> be defined in functional terms. It is not an organic structure and it cannot be
> maintained by organization but only by motives which sustain the personal
> relations of its members. It is constituted and maintained by a mutual
> affection.[16]

## Church vs. Sect: The Mutualist Question

Mutual affection, common life, and reconciliation are the common themes
found in each of the communitarian religious sects. Despite the perceived
differences that they inherited from each of their progenitors, their doctrine, social lives, and social structure are remarkably similar. These similarities are rooted in their interpretation of early Christianity as a mutualist
blueprint. Additionally, each of these communities either operated on the
margin of or separate from the religious denomination of their origin. The
Donatists, for example, began within the church as a movement which had
as its goal the establishment of mutualist communities within the larger
framework of the universal church. The Franciscan tertiaries attempted to
reduce the hierarchical tendencies of the medieval church and return to a
nonstratified mutualist community.

The Anabaptist movement (including the Mennonites, Amish, and Hutterites) separated themselves from the dominant Lutheran and Calvinist
traditions in an attempt to establish a truly mutualist community by isolating themselves from the increasingly dominant secular society. Initially
they experienced tolerance; but with growth came repeated persecution,
forcing them to flee to various locations throughout Europe before finally
settling in the United States.

The persecution was not a response to their mutualist ideals but rather to
their rejection of the dominant social structure. Ironically, their theological
accusers often showed admiration for their mutualist ideals and their consistent practice of such ideals.

In the case of the Anabaptists, while their generosity to outsiders was widely recognized and admired, their refusal to engage in civic affairs eventually brought them into conflict with successive governments, repeatedly forcing them to migrate. Their refusal was based on the belief that government was inherently coercive and therefore the antithesis of their vision of community:

> The vision of this community that operates by different rules from the rest of society and government was generally true of Anabaptists from the 16th to the end of the 18th century. They kept out of civic affairs because of the rules that operate there. They were not free, not at liberty to use rules, because in government there is coercion and an imposition on people, things they do not want.[17]

What was not evident to the theologians of each period was the connection between the mutualist ideal, the social structure of each movement, and their respective attitudes toward the dominant social structure, either ecclesiastical or secular. Ernst Troeltsch described the difference between the church (i.e., the dominant ecclesiastical force) and the sects (i.e., mutually based religious communities) in terms of organizational structure and institutional goals:

> The essence of the Church is its objective institutional character . . . for despite its individual inadequacy the institution remains holy and divine . . . its stability is entirely unaffected by the fact of the extent to which its influence over all individuals is actually attained. The Church is the type of organization which dominates the masses; in principle, therefore, it is universal, i.e., it desires to cover the whole life of humanity.[18]

The same bureaucratic structure, legalistic interaction, and universal desire that characterized the church during its reign were then inherited by its secular successor, the state. The monopolization of conflict is illustrative of this succession. For the church, heretical offenses posed the greatest threat to its domination. Consequently, the church exercised absolute control over theological offenses while ignoring interpersonal conflict such as theft, assault, robbery, etc. The state priorities are the reverse. Theological conflict poses little or no threat to the state, while conflicts involving people and property threaten the legitimacy of the state as guarantor of individual rights. Officials of state, therefore, monopolize what they define as conflict, namely, the threat to the individual rights of person and property. In each system (i.e., church-dominated and state-dominated) bureaucrats respond punitively to the perceived threat while allowing the community to retain control of conflict that is not perceived as a threat. Such a punitive response can be viewed as a reaction to fear—fear in each instance that their bureaucratic control will be eroded.

Bureaucracy, it has been argued, is increasingly necessary in our society; it provides consistency and fairness of action because it is based on a set of formal, rational rules that apply to all.[19] Its formality reduces subjectivity, thereby increasing objectivity. Such objectivity will then engender trust in the institution itself. Law and the respect for law are seen as the epitome of this objective bureaucracy. As trust diminishes among individuals, bureaucracies, particularly legal bureaucracies, become more integral to the maintenance of social order and ultimately to the existence of society itself. In this context, law can be viewed as being inversely related to personal trust. With respect to trust, bureaucracy can be viewed as the antithesis of community.

The inverse relationship between bureaucracy and trust explains why mutualist communities, despite their small size, their rejection of power, and their nonuniversal nature, have been seen as a threat by officials of the dominant society, whether ecclesiastical or secular. Ernst Troeltsch identified social structure, specifically the formal bureaucratic elements, as the distinguishing feature between the church type and the sect type:

> Compared with the institutional principle of an objective organism (i.e., the Church), the sect is a voluntary community whose members join it of their own free will. The very life of the sect, therefore, depends on actual personal service, cooperation, religious equality and brotherly love, indifference toward the authority of the State and the ruling classes, dislike of technical law and the oath and the separation of the religious life from the economic struggle by the means of the ideal of poverty.[20]

Conversely, the church type relies on the existing economic and State bureaucratic structures to establish its dominance in the religious realm, while at the same time exerting its influence in the secular realm: "The fully developed Church utilized the State and the ruling classes and weaves these elements into her own life, she thus becomes an integral part of the existing social order; from this standpoint then the Church both stabilizes and determines the social order."[21]

Mennonite theology, for example, argues that the coercion of formal rules, which are the lifeblood of all bureaucratic structures, militates against community. *Gemeinde*, the Mennonite version of community, is guided by only one law, the law of *agape*: "You shall love your neighbor as yourself" (Matthew 22:39b). But this law is not imposed; it is accepted voluntarily. Ideally, the law is internalized as a symbol of the commitment to community. The Mennonites recognize, however, that the community is composed of members who are tempted and sometimes transgress the law; but the Mennonite response to such transgressions is devoid of the coercion and formality that characterize bureaucratic responses to conflict:

> There are means in the Mennonite church to deal with such things (i.e., transgressions) but the rules are different from those which function in the other kingdom (i.e., the bureaucratic realm). The rules are characterized by patience, the complete rejection of violence and coercion, by acceptance, by

forgiveness, by love and repentance. The process of discipline is carried out or, if you like, the administration of law within the community is carried out not by arbitrary rulers or judges but by the community itself and the process itself was accepted voluntarily to begin with. So we do not have an adversarial way of dealing with things in the first place.[22]

For the Mennonites the goal of the process is not the simple adjudication of a conflict or even the mediation between individuals; it is the healing and growth of the entire community. It is a process of restoration, a process that utilizes exclusion only as a means to reconciliation between the transgressor and the community and, equally as important, the community and the transgressor. The resolution of a particular conflict is not dependent solely on the will and energy of the individual transgressor to commit anew to a rigid set of theological or societal rules. Reconciliation, in the Mennonite view, requires the community and the transgressor to actively engage in a process of negotiation concerning the interpretation of the law of *agape*. Contrary to conventional portrayals of the Mennonites and other communitarian religious societies, they are not rigid and inflexible in their approach to transgressions, particularly nonheretical transgressions (i.e., interpersonal conflict). Because of their voluntary nature, their law is internal rather than external, their response to conflict restorational rather than punitive. Their approach to all human interaction, including conflict, is based on the conciliatory assumption of the mutualist model rather than the adversarial assumption that underlies the bureaucratic approach to human interaction.

## Mutuality and Social Ethics

Stanley Hauerwas, in his analysis of the absence of social ethics in liberal democracy, asserts that trust is the basis of true and ethical community: "Trust is impossible in communities that always regard the other as a challenge and threat to their existence. One of the profoundest commitments of a community, therefore, is providing a context that encourages us to trust and depend on one another."[23] He further argues that a social ethic is only found in communities that subscribe to the mutualist philosophy:

A social ethic means we must recapture the social significance of *common behavior*, such as acts of kindness, friendship and the formation of families. . . . Liberalism presupposes that society can be organized without a narrative that is commonly held to be true. As a result, it tempts us to believe that freedom and rationality are independent of narrative—i.e., we are free to the extent that we have no story.[24]

Within the context of liberalism, we are controlled by *atomism* and *contract*.[25] Our unity with others is based almost exclusively on the belief that such an association will advance our own self-interest. In our rational assessment of situations, we are therefore unlikely to enter into a relationship with an individual who is unable, at least theoretically, to advance our own interests. Such an unwillingness on our part excludes those with little power and few assets from engaging in contractual relations, thus creating the social problems (e.g., crime, poverty, unemployment, etc.) that have plagued the liberal democracies. In our unwillingness to involve ourselves personally with such individuals, we have surrendered community control of these problems to the state. "Genuine public policy in such a society cannot exist," according to Hauerwas, "because society is nothing more than an aggregate of self-interested individuals."[26] In reaction to the failures of the contractarian community to adequately address the mounting social needs of its members, we drift toward the organic model which proposes that we create "a community which is greater than the sum of its parts."[27] This bureaucratic community finds a place for each of its members. In such a community, officials of state or of the corporation become the final arbiters of human relations. The contributing individuals (i.e., organs) must provide a function that is deemed worthwhile by the officials or else be defined as having no worth. Those deemed to have no worth are then forgotten, isolated, punished, or killed. The most illustrative example of the assumption of worthlessness is our present criminal elements of neglect, isolation, and retribution. The successful reintegration of anyone into the society is viewed as an aberration. Such success is always attributed to extraordinary individual effort, thereby reinforcing the ideology of individualism which is the foundation of the contractarian model.

The expanding bureaucratic age has enabled us to absorb an increasing number of people who are defined as having no worth, while at the same time functioning at a higher level of societal efficiency. It is efficiency that has become the mark by which we increasingly evaluate ourselves as a society. Ironically, many have questioned the efficiency of a system that successfully reintegrates so few. In a society that is influenced by both the contractarian and organic models, however, the efficiency of bureaucracy is actually measured by its capable management of conflict that could potentially interfere with the pursuit of self-interest by those who have sufficient resources to benefit from 'free' contractual relations.

The mutual model warns against the emergence of efficiency as the primary measure of success of community or society. The appearance of impersonal and indirect relations has necessitated social structures that are determined by power and law; but unless these structures are subordinated to an overarching mutualist philosophy they will in turn increase the isolation and formal nature of personal relations.

"The necessity for the State and for politics arises with the breakdown of the customary community of direct personal relations."[28] The resulting social structure is guided by the assumption of "enlightened self-interest," which is a remnant of the formerly dominant contractarian ideology. "It conceives of the structure of society in terms of law . . . and its maintenance is achieved by power. This yields a mechanical concept of society. Its components are atomic units, inherently isolated and unrelated."[29] Our inherent fear of the monopoly of the state by a self-perpetuating elite has moved us toward an alternative bureaucratic mode, namely, the organic model of society. In the organic model, society has priority over the individual. Appropriate behavior is generally defined as submission to the whole. The individual "must identify himself with his role—his station and its duties—and suppress his impulse to be himself."[30]

Weber identified role identification and suppression of self as the fundamental elements of the bureaucratic ideal type. They are designed to make living with fear as beneficial as possible for individuals whose primary motive, remember, is their own self-interest. This is not to suggest that negatively motivated relations did not occur in mutualist communities, but there must be provisions made within the community to address such self-interest and the fear that nurtures and sustains it. According to MacMurray, the way to begin limiting fear is to meet the basic material needs of all persons. "There must be a relation between the material necessities of life and the beliefs that it holds concerning the proper ordering of life. No society can exist except in a form which provides for the basic material goods of life."[31]

In establishing an intentional mutualist community, we must begin by addressing the structure of economic life. "The forms of economic life are the essential foundation for mutuality. They do not determine the content of mutuality but they do determine its possibility."[32] Even in an intentional mutualist community, persons must cooperate with each other in indirect relations in order to meet the fundamental needs of the community. Economic cooperation itself can be negatively as well as positively motivated. "This cooperation in work establishes a nexus of indirect relations between all members of the cooperating group, irrespective of their personal relations. . . . Such relations are not relations of persons as persons but only as workers; they are relations of the functions each performs."[33] Functionally motivated interaction is the nexus of bureaucratic society. In the Weberian ideal type, personal relations are minimized while functional relations are maximized. The more dominant the functional relations and consequently the more subordinate the personal relations, the greater the efficiency of the bureaucracy. The increasing dominance of functionality as a means of interaction is the hallmark of the organic model. While the organic relationship occupies an important position within the intentional mutualist community, it is subordinated to the "overarching intentionality of the fully personal life."[34] Functionality is replaced by mutuality. "The economic aspect of the personal—the working life—is both intentional and for the sake of personal life. . . . It must be produced, maintained and developed by deliberate effort."[35] As an indirect and therefore negative relation, it must be "justified by the personal life which makes it possible."[36]

## The Subordination of Self-Will

Among the mutualist religious communities, the Hutterites are the best example of the subordination of organic relations to the mutualist intention. Central to the Hutterite way of life is a "community of goods." Private ownership, according to the Hutterites, is against the nature and will of God. When one seeks permanent membership as an adult, one must make a vow that involves making peace with God, the community, and the desire to own property. According to Hutterite doctrine, "whoever cannot give up his private property as well as his own self-will cannot become a disciple or follower of Christ."[37] As a result of their absolute insistence on the subordination of self-will, the Hutterite community has acquired utopia-like characteristics. There are no distinctions between rich and poor, nor are there many distinctions according to occupations, since most jobs' are rotated in an effort to reduce covetousness and the conflict that accompanies it. People never worry about food, clothing, or housing, regardless of their physical or mental capabilities or their age. Members work without incentive for personal gain. Because all their actions are mutually motivated, identity problems and alienation are virtually nonexistent.

Even though other mutualist religious societies do not subscribe to the Hutterite vow of communal property, they all stress the subordination of self-will. Theologically, each of the mutualist communities equates the subordination of self-will with human freedom. The subordination of self-will must be a "matter of spontaneous self-expression in action."[38] Freedom is seen as the basis of morality. Without true freedom, there can be no genuine morality. Such freedom allows us then to enter into communion with others for their own sake, not because of the force of moral law or the coercive devotion to State or society. That is why membership in these mutualist communities is simultaneously voluntary and absolute. If community membership is not fully voluntary, morality is no longer genuine.

Macmurray identifies the existence of three types of morality, only one of which he argues is genuine. He begins with the premise, as do all mutualists, that freedom is bound up with morality. "If our system of morality is based on a false notion of human freedom, we shall get a false morality. If we mistake human freedom for material freedom, we shall get a false morality and it will be false because it is mechanical."[39] Material freedom can only be promoted and maintained through law. The idea of law is inconsistent with the idea of morality. "The root idea of law is consistency and uniformity,"[40] which are necessary for contractual relations but which limit human freedom, thereby producing a mechanical morality. "The more mechanical life becomes, the more it is organized by law, the less human it is."[41]

Macmurray argues than an inverse relationship exists between law and morality (i.e., the more law is in our lives, the less morality there is). With the emergence of such mechanical morality has come a deepening sense of alienation in society. "The more our actions are governed by laws, the less freely we can act, the less room there is for us to think and feel really, and be ourselves."[42]

Our societal response has been to treat the manifestations of alienation (i.e., various social problems—addiction, crime, poverty, etc.) through a morality of self-service and sacrifice. Macmurray argues that such social morality, like mechanical morality, is a denial of human freedom and ultimately a denial of human nature. Social morality treats individuals as a means to an end. Within the context of social morality, service is devoted not to the individual but to society or the state. For Macmurray, "devotion to service inevitably leads to the service of the organization itself."[43] Social morality is based on the assumption that the more highly organized a society, the better it is. "If you make progress or the evolution of society the great goal of human effort, then you are really worshipping social organization. The more intricate and complicated the mechanism of social organization becomes, the more men have to subordinate their human qualities and activities to the mere business of keeping the machine working."[44] As a result, we slowly lose our freedom and become cogs in the machinery. In this way, the ideal of social morality undermines human freedom. We are told it is our duty to serve society, the result being that we identify not with our communion with others but with the job we do in the social organization. Such dedication to duty constitutes a false morality. For a genuine morality to exist, Macmurray insists that "man is a man, the goodness of his life is in its own inner quality, in its own integrity"[45]—not in service to organizations, the state, or society, but in service to others, freely chosen. This he defines as personal morality, the only genuine morality.

In the mutualist scheme, morality is an expression of personal freedom. Real personal freedom can only be exercised in personal relations with one another. Friendship and, by extension, community are the essence of morality. The communitarian religious societies alluded to throughout are the clearest examples of personal morality (i.e., the mutualist model) in action.

In each community there is an absence of both mechanical and social morality. Both theological doctrine and social histories confirm that these religious communities tend to be guided by the central rule of *agape* and rely very little on legality. Their systems of justice are overwhelmingly substantive rather than procedural. Consequently, their resolution of conflict, through a process of reconciliation, is neither routinized nor absolute. Social morality, too, is absent because these communities purposely eschew organization, thereby limiting extensive hierarchies and specialization. The absence of complex organization has a twofold effect on conflict and conflict resolution within these communities. Conflict as the by-product of alienation—much of what we label deviant in today's society would fall into this category—is practically nonexistent in these mutual religious communities because relations are predominantly personal rather than formal, as is the case in highly bureaucratized societies. When conflict does arise, it is defined as a community problem and it remains in its original context. The resolution of conflict is the province of the entire community rather than the exclusive domain of a specialized legal organization. The conflict is not extracted from the community and made legally relevant by an exclusive judicial body; rather, it is addressed substantively, utilizing only the grand directive of *agape* while recognizing the unique character of each and every conflict. Such are the ingredients of reconciliation.

Reconciliation, because of its grounding in the rule of *agape*, is incapable of punishment for punishment's sake, which is the philosophical basis of retribution and deterrence. Through reconciliation, we must identify what is best for everyone for his or her own sake, not for the sake of the community or society. The goal of reconciliation is quite simple: to bring together the estranged elements of the community and restore the original trust among these elements. Among those to be reconciled are the transgressor, the victim, and, most importantly, the community at large. If the community itself does not reestablish trust with the transgressors, they remain isolated and alienated from the community. Much of the failure of our present criminal justice system can be traced to the continued isolation of those labeled deviant. They are not trusted by society and therefore do not trust society, which is the recipe for recidivism. They feel obliged to complete only the formal requirements imposed upon them by the legal bureaucracy. They feel no obligation to regain trust because others no longer trust them, even after the completion of their sentence. They fulfill their legal obligation to regain their individual rights rather than to rejoin their community. Their motive for fulfilling their legal obligation is of no consequence to either legal bureaucrats or to members of society at large.

Conversely, in the process of reconciliation, motive is everything. The first and foremost task of reconciliation is to restore trust. How that is accomplished, through what means, is unimportant. Once trust is reestablished, the reconciliation process is complete. The underlying assumption of reconciliation is that the initial separation of the transgressor from the community is punishment enough for whatever offense was committed. Additional punishment prescribed by the community is seen as only worsening the lack of trust that has ensued from the original conflict. Such is the starting point of reconciliation. Reconciliation repairs the damage of conflict. It restores harmony and balance to the community. It views each person not as an isolated individual protected by individual rights but as a vital member of the community, a community that is constantly adapting and adjusting to the needs of its members, guided only by the directive of *agape*. For reconciliation to become a part of our present-day lives, we must consider the possibility of establishing mutual communities within the midst of contemporary society. The framework for such communities is already in place in the form of mutualist religious communities and some rural communities, but they must be rescued from their drift toward the absolute acceptance of the contractarian view and their increasing subordination to bureaucratic specialization.

## The Mutualist Model as Social Change

The mutualist model is one of four methods for implementing social change, although today we are apt to consider only three: unfettered individualism in the form of libertarianism, revolution, and reform movements. The mutualist model drastically contrasts with each one of these alternatives: it rejects the possibility of meaningful social change through individual actions; it rejects the coercion that is part of the revolutionary ideology in favor of voluntary membership; and it rejects the possibility of meaningful change through reform because of the persistent influence of formalized bureaucratic relations.

Of these four approaches, only the mutualist method is effective in limiting the amount of severity of conflict and resolving what conflict does arise. Unlike individualism (i.e., contractarianism), the mutual method inhibits rather than encourages fear, the fear that leads to conflict. Unlike revolution, the mutual method is able to offer readmittance to transgressors without the fear of being challenged, thereby limiting conflict. Unlike gradual change, the mutual method eliminates the formal relations that contribute to feelings of alienation, thereby also limiting conflict. The mutual approach is the only option in which reconciliation is possible, because only in a communitarian setting is it assumed that "order and discipline cannot come from human law. It is not a matter of punishment imposed by one person's moral force on another against that person's will."[46] Since such correction is absent in mutualist communities, there is no fear of punishment. Mutualists believe that inner pain and sincere remorse will bring the transgressor back to the community. "Exclusion is not an end in itself; it is to help us search and change our lives."[47]

If, through social change, we seek a society guided by reconciliation rather than retribution, we must be willing to consider the possibility of establishing mutualist communities. While such a possibility is rejected as utopian and idealistic, it is important to remember that these communities represent the only true alternative to the two dominant modes of society, the contractarian and the organic. The very reason mutualist communities have existed and still exist is to set an example that members of the dominant society might finally emulate:

Remember, the reason we live in community is not so the individual members can attain the highest degree of perfection. Instead we believe that by living in total community we set an example and that this is the best service we can do for society today, in its fragmented state. We want all those who sigh and groan under the wrongs in today's world to see that full community lived in mutuality is possible.[48]

## NOTES

1. Despite the continued use of the word *community* to describe various types of social grouping, it is important to distinguish between personal nonbureaucratic social groupings: Tonnie's Gemeinschaft, Durkheim's mechanical solidarity—will be referred to as community and contractual bureaucratic social groupings; Tonnie's Gesellschaft, Durkheim's organic solidarity—will be referred to as society.

2. In order to be viewed rationally, a phenomenon must be observable, quantifiable, and open to reanalysis, the most crucial of these being an openness to reanalysis.

3. For an extensive discussion of the ownership of conflict, consult Nils Christie, 1977.

4. In my own experience as a community mediator, I have discovered that disputants, regardless of their relationships, define conflict as a violation of individual rights and are therefore reluctant even to relinquish temporarily their legal leverage in favor of a system that is based on trust.

5. Emile Durkheim (1960) argues to the contrary, but his failure to distinguish between heretical offenses and interpersonal conflict is isolated as a variable. It is quite clear that societies characterized by mechanical solidarity are more restitutive in their approach than those characterized by organic solidarity. The restitutive character is particularly prevalent in intentional communities which include the communitarian religious societies under discussion here.

6. See Frank G. Kirkpatrick, 1986, p. 232.

7. See Stanley Hauerwas, 1981, p. 79.

8. For a detailed discussion of the contractarian and organic models of community, refer to Frank G. Kirkpatrick, 1986. Kirkpatrick argues that the evolution of the western worldview has been dominated by three models of community: the mutualist, the contractarian, and the organic. Each model, according to Kirkpatrick, contains theoretical assumptions about the nature of human beings, the motivations for social relations, and the corresponding social structure.

9. Love in this context refers to the religiously inspired concept of *agape*, the concern for others for their own sake. Such an action initially requires the suppression of self-will in order to fully understand the other as he/she actually is rather than as we perceive them.

10. See John Macmurray, 1961, p. 150.

11. Ibid., p. 150.

12. Ibid., p. 150.

13. Ibid., p. 150.

14. Even in traditionally noncontractual relations such as family and friendship, there is a trend toward more litigious responses to conflict. For a more theoretical discussion of the direct relationship between the increase in the amount of law and the increased levels of stratification, morphology, and organization in a society, refer to Donald Black, 1985.

15. See John Macmurray, 1961, p. 157.
16. Ibid., p. 157.
17. See Walter Klaasen, 1985, p. 17.
18. See Ernst Troeltsch, 1949, p. 232.
19. Max Weber (1947:340) argued that in a bureaucracy "everyone is subject to formal equality of treatment; that is, everyone in the same empirical situation."
20. See Ernst Troeltsch, 1949, pp. 332–33.
21. Ibid., p. 331.
22. See Walter Klaasen, 1985, p. 15.
23. See Stanley Hauerwas, 1981, p. 11.
24. Ibid., p. 11.
25. For a detailed discussion of the importance of atomism and contract to the liberal democracies, refer to Frank G. Kirkpatrick's discussion of the atomistic/contractarian model of community (1986:13–61).
26. See Stanley Hauerwas, 1981, p. 79.
27. See Frank G. Kirkpatrick, 1986, p. 233.
28. See John Macmurray, 1961, p. 192.
29. Ibid., p. 137.
30. Ibid., p. 142.
31. See John Macmurray, 1935, p. 63.
32. See Frank G. Kirkpatrick, 1986, p. 210.
33. See John Macmurray, 1961, p. 186.
34. See Frank G. Kirkpatrick, 1986, p. 211.
35. See John Macmurray, 1961, p. 187.
36. Ibid., p. 187.
37. See J. Hoestedler, 1983, p. 3.
38. See John Macmurray, 1983, p. 203.
39. Ibid., p. 184.
40. Ibid., p. 185.
41. Ibid., p. 185.
42. Ibid., p. 185.
43. Ibid., p. 185.
44. Ibid., p. 197.
45. Ibid., p. 197.
46. See Eberhard Arnold, 1984, p. 127.
47. Ibid., p. 127.
48. Ibid., p. 135.

## REFERENCES

Arnold, Eberhard. 1984. *God's Revolution.* Ed. John Howard Yoder. Mahwah, N.J.: Paulist Press.
Black, Donald. 1985. *The Behavior of Law.* San Diego: Academic Press.
Christie, Nils. 1977. "Conflict as Property." *British Journal of Criminology* 17 (1).
Durkheim, Emile. 1960. "The Two Laws of Penal Evolution." *The Division of Labor in Society.* Glencoe, Ill.: The Free Press.
Hauerwas, Stanley. 1981. *A Community of Character: Towards a Constructive Christian Social Ethic.* Notre Dame, Ind.: University of Notre Dame Press.
Hoestedler, J. 1983. *The Hutterites.* Scottsdale, Pa.: Herald Press.
Kirkpatrick, Frank G. 1986. *Community: A Trinity of Models.* Washington, D.C.: Georgetown University Press.

Klaasen, Walter. 1985. *Peoplehood and Law.* Kitchener, Ont.: Mennonite Central
     Committee, Canada Victim Offender Ministries.
MacMurray, John. 1983. *Freedom in the Modern World.* London: Faber & Faber
     Limited.
———. 1961. *Persons in Relation.* New York: Harper & Brothers.
———. 1935. "The Nature and Function of Ideologies." In *Marxism.* New York: John
     Wiley and Sons.
Troeltsch, Ernst. 1949. *The Social Teachings of Christian Churches.* Glencoe, Ill.: The
     Free Press.
Weber, Max. 1947. *The Theory of Social and Economic Organization.* Tr. A. M. Hender-
     son and Talcott Parsons. Ed. Talcott Parsons. London: Oxford University
     Press.

*Gregg Barak*

---

## F O U R ·

# Homelessness and the Case for Community-Based Initiatives

*The Emergence of a Model Shelter as a Short-Term Response to the Deepening Crisis in Housing*

There are approximately three million homeless people in the United States. Unless immediate action is taken to preserve and expand the supply of affordable housing, then according to a 1988 Congressionally funded study by the Neighborhood Reinvestment Corporation, there will be an estimated 19 million homeless U.S. residents by the end of the century. Federal spending for low-income housing has been slashed by 77 percent, or 25 billion per year since 1981. For every dollar spent on housing in 1988, $44 were spent on defense. By comparison, at the start of Reagan's first term the ratio spent by the U.S. on defense to housing was only 7 to 1 (HOUSING NOW! 1989). And in his first year of office, President Bush proposed bringing the 1989 figure of less than $8 billion to close to $6 billion annually (Naureckas, 1989).

By the late 1980s the U.S. condition of homelessness counted among its three million casualties: men, women, and children of all racial and ethnic backgrounds; urban and rural workers; displaced and deinstitutionalized persons; alcoholics, drug addicts, AIDS victims, the mentally ill; physically abused mothers and their babies, sexually abused teenagers and preadoles-

47

cents, neglected elderly; and migrants, refugees, and veterans. From the perspective of a criminology of peacemaking and the elimination of all predatory behavior, it is not an exaggeration to think of the new subclass of the homeless, including the suppression of their human potential and the perpetuation of their human misery, as the product of a society characterized by gross structural inequality and social injustice (Thomas and O'Maolchatha, 1989). Furthermore and in different terms, the violence of homelessness and the violence experienced by the homeless in the United States should be viewed in relationship not only to the debilitating social formations of a political economy in transition, but to a public policy on low-income housing which is antisocial on its merits and criminogenic in its consequences. Finally, the expanding reality of homelessness associated with these new categories or populations of homeless people, has certainly been one of the more significant domestic policy issues of the late 1980s and the early 1990s.

The social problem of inadequate housing and homelessness can be addressed by a myriad of public policies in general and by HUD–private sector activities in particular. But I suspect that before we get to the kind of proactive domestic-housing policies which are capable of reversing the U.S. trends in homelessness, we will have to arrive at the favorable end of a continuum that reacts to homeless people with extreme kindness and compassion. The need presently exists, however, both to repudiate the other end of the continuum, which reacts to homeless people with extreme cruelty and inhumanity, and to overcome the large middle areas of public indifference and neglect.

Looking at homelessness from a context of an expanding base of poor people in the United States, we could say that the revved up, financially driven economy of the '80s, which supposedly benefitted some two-thirds of the population while one-third were clearly falling behind, may be revised slightly as we move into the 90s. This will be done so that those who were previously viewed as slipping will come to be viewed instead as an expanding group of have-nots, people who are rapidly becoming marginal victims of a changing political economy. In other words, if the sheer numbers of homeless people swell, as has been predicted, and the magnitude of the homelessness condition continues to grow, then sooner or later there will be a public understanding that the prevailing policy—depending primarily on the private sector, supply and demand, and laissez-faire economics—cannot work to resolve the low-income housing crisis in the United States. Until such time as there is public recognition of the need for the development of an alternative approach to homelessness, the response to the housing shortage will continue to be grounded in the provision of temporary rather than permanent shelter.

When we discuss the *new* homelessness of the U.S. postindustrial economy and the homeless have-nots of our affluent society, we do so not merely in terms of their material possessions or deprivations, but also in terms of their psychological, physical, and social well-being or wholeness. And while there are homeless people who are not only strong in body and mind, there are also those victims of homelessness who have lost their sense of purpose and worth, their sense of identity, their will to live. Taken as a whole, homeless people, regardless of their personal condition, find themselves struggling to cope with the numerous indecencies, indignities, and obscenities that envelop their daily existences. On top of these burdens, homeless people are in the position of having to resist further victimization by other homeless persons, by traditional street criminals, and by the more impersonal forces of alienation and detachment. Nevertheless, in spite of all of the adversity, homeless people (joined by the caring activities of others) have been striving to achieve a sense of friendship and community.

This chapter explores the homelessness condition in the United States and the development of one community's model shelter as a temporary or short-term response to the deepening crisis in low-income housing. While it will be concluded that such community-based responses (1) provide necessary services to the homeless, (2) help to establish the kind of ideological view of homelessness which is conducive for the implementation of a subsidized permanent housing policy, and (3) can arguably prevent further victimization as well as criminalization, these responses will also be regarded as counterproductive solutions in that they contribute to the kind of U.S. domestic policy which tends to avoid structural approaches to structural problems. In the postmodern era, social problems such as homelessness, sexual assault, or drug abuse are politically constructed, ideologically articulated, and media-produced events (Barak, 1988). At the same time, these mass mediated phenomena, surrounded by discourses and value-laden attitudes, create an arena for studying the contradictions of the dominant policies of social control found in the United States today. In turn, these relations allow us to study those groups, organizations, and programs which challenge the prevailing ideologies of bourgeois domestic policies. In short, these policy struggles reveal the necessary kinds of interplay between what have been labelled "reformist reforms" and "structural reforms" (Gorz, 1964). The former refers to actions which help to reproduce the prevailing political and economic arrangements; the latter refers to actions that threaten the status quo (Barak, 1980).

Less generally, this study of homelessness demonstrates the possibility of creating progressive, humanistic alternatives to the existing public practices of a not-caring capitalist welfare system in crisis. Profiled as a positive alternative to the repressive, bureaucratic, and punitive responses typically associated with impoverishment is the experience of Hesed House, a homeless shelter in Aurora, Illinois. This illustration of a reformist reform further demonstrates how community responses to homelessness, while satisfying the human need to develop collective forms of crisis intervention, can also be associated with more fundamental attempts to bring about structural reform. In brief, Hesed House represents one viable strategy for organizing responsiveness to the ongoing struggle against the reproduction of violence, victimization, crime, punishment, and social injustice.

The rest of this chapter is grounded in a changing political economy. It is divided into three parts plus a conclusion: the first attempts to provide an overview and analysis of the problem of U.S. homelessness; the second describes the response of a predominantly working-class community with a small affluent population to the cracks in its social-service delivery system, especially as these had been related to the need of providing shelter for homeless people on a mass scale; and the third critiques such responses and discusses the long-term implications of the lack of a national program specifically designed for the purpose of eliminating homelessness in the United States.

## Fiscal Crisis, Homelessness, and the Social Construction of Public Action

The changing worldwide political economy of the 1970s and 1980s has historically recorded both the end of the postwar boom in the development of U.S. transnational capital and the decline of U.S. hegemony in international relations, each coming to pass during the so-called Vietnam era (Sherman, 1976; Mandel, 1980; Berberoglu, 1987). These changing global realities have had the effect of contributing to what now appears to be a permanent U.S. fiscal crisis brought about by overproduction and the downward turns in the business cycle (Batra 1987). In addition, this crisis has been fueled by the rise to world prominence of the European and Asian economies coupled with the effects of the transnational corporate expansion abroad on the domestic economy. For example, these structural transformations in the global and U.S. economy produced the most severe recession since the 1930s by 1974. The U.S. economy sunk into another recession by 1979 and into a much deeper one in 1982. Current economic trends suggest the strong possibility of a coming crash by the early '90s which may prove to be much worse than any previously (Batra, 1987; Berberoglu, 1987).

For example, the capacity utilization in manufacturing or the ups and downs of the business cycle during the past twenty years reveals that the general trend in business activity is in a downward direction, as each peak in the cycle is lower than the one that preceded it (Economic Report 1987). Data on unemployment rates tell a similar story. In the 1971, 1975, and 1982 recessions respectively, the "official" government unemployment rates at their heights were 6.0, 8.5, and 9.7 percent. It should also be noted that the unemployment rate was higher in two of the three succeeding recoveries: 5 percent in 1973 and 5.9 percent in 1979. By the end of 1989, the unemployment rate had officially dipped to about 5.2 percent. However, it can be argued that in addition to the traditionally hidden unemployed, there had been a growth in the number of underemployed persons during the '80s. These factors combined with the lowering of wages at the bottom end of the income scale have had the effect that a greater number of both employed and unemployed persons are unable today to afford the rising costs of U.S. housing.

Throughout this period of "adjustment," real wages of workers continued to decline with a net loss of 16 percent in income between 1974 and 1984 (Berberoglu, 1987). The weakening American domestic economy has contributed to a decline in workers' purchasing power and a record number of bankruptcies among small businesses and family farmers. Additional problems associated with the 1980s, and foreshadowing things to come in the 1990s, included the highest recorded trade and budget deficits in U.S. history. With respect to the former, trade deficits rose from $9.5 billion in 1976 to $124 billion in 1985. With respect to the latter, buttressed by military expenditures which doubled between 1980 and 1986 and which tripled since the mid 1970s, the annual budget deficits have climbed from $54 billion in 1977 to $221 billion in 1986. And by 1986 the total federal debt was $2.1 trillion, up from $709 billion in 1977 (Berberoglu 1987). By the end of the eighties, however, the debts had begun to decline a bit and appeared to some economists to be leveling-off.

The current debts are also a by-product of the large tax cuts enjoyed by the rich and corporate America during the Reagan administration. Tax breaks and other favorable governmental policies, such as deregulation, not only allowed corporate profits to reach new heights over the past two decades, but also accounted for significant lost revenues. For example, total corporate profits between 1970 and 1985 increased from $74.7 billion in 1970 to $117.6 billion in 1980 to $280.7 billion in 1985 (Berberoglu, 1987). At the same time and to help manage the fiscal crisis, cutbacks in the welfare state generally and in low-income housing programs particularly increased throughout the '80s. When Carter left office in 1980, $32 billion a year was being authorized for low-income housing. Eight years later, when Reagan's administration came to an end, the number of dollars spent on low-income housing had been reduced to about $8 billion. Even if a severe depression in the global and U.S. economies does not occur by the early 1990s as Batra predicts, current trends not only suggest an exponential growth in the number of homeless people, but the potential intensification of class struggle around the issues of the "crimes of the poor" versus the "crimes of the affluent." Unless significantly altered domestic and economic policies are adopted by the state, class conflict and the various expressions of tensions and antagonisms are bound to increase.

Homelessness and the homeless are typically attributed to four factors: (1) individual characteristics such as alcoholism, mental illness, and the lack of marketable skills (Arce, 1983; Bassuk, 1984; Kondratas, 1984); (2) family disruption involving runaway children or elderly persons who lose family support (Crystal, 1984; Freeman and Hall, 1987); (3) institutional

policies affecting dependent populations such as deinstitutionalization of
the chronically mentally ill (Bassuk, 1984; Lamb, 1984; Kondratas, 1984);
and (4) market forces related to housing affordability (Freeman and Hall,
1987; Hopper et al., 1987; Kasinitz, 1987) such as tightening of the low-
income housing market (Bassuk, 1984), rising mortgage interest rates,
declining wages, or job shortfalls.

Although all four contributing factors to homelessness must be addressed by social policy, the fourth, market forces related to housing
affordability, is particularly instructive since it reveals the fallacy of the
meanspirited argument that large numbers of families remain homeless
because of personal traits rather than structural circumstances. Furthermore, if the recent and projected downward economic trends discussed
above continue, the number of U.S. residents vulnerable to homelessness
should increase significantly, especially since we do not seem to be approaching the problem in terms of the root socioeconomic cause. In other
words, it is safe to conclude that we are presently only experiencing the tip
of the homeless iceberg.

In one national study of families with children, for example, real income
declined by 34 percent between 1973 and 1984 for those families in the
lowest income quintile (Danzinger and Gottschalk 1985). Also, in the state
of New York, Hirschl (1987: 14) found that "of the 535,800 households
below the 75 percent poverty level, 421,500 are renters. Of these renters,
77.3 percent pay more than 50 percent of their income in rent. . . . [I]f
income drops for one of these households by more than 50 percent for any
given month, housing costs alone could swamp the household budget."
Using the number of 1983 New York State households below the 75 percent
poverty level and the number of poor households which spend more than
half their incomes on housing costs, Hirschl (1987) calculated that the ratio
of people who are not currently homeless but who are economically vulnerable to homelessness (884,400) compared to homeless people living in
shelter facilities (20,210) was 44 to 1.

Hirschl's (1987) vulnerability thesis is not that housing affordability is the
only cause of homelessness, nor does it predict that those who are economically vulnerable to homelessness will, in fact, become part of the homeless
population. His thesis is that reduced housing affordability is the single
most important condition for the persistence of a large homeless population. Moreover, in terms of economic vulnerability, 80.7 percent of persons
vulnerable to homelessness in New York State are in families (Hirschl,
1987). This finding is consistent with other estimates indicating that the
number of homeless families in the United States is increasing at a faster
rate than the number of homeless individuals (National Coalition for the
Homeless 1986). In the city of New York, for example, the number of
homeless families increased from 800 in 1981 to 4,500 in 1986; and among
these homeless families were 11,000 children (Hirsch, 1987: 8). These
trends in housing affordability and in homelessness generally, in combina-

tion with the other economic trends, suggest that the slowly expanding number of homeless persons in the United States is not an aberration or temporary phenomenon of the "prosperous" eighties, but rather·a normative outcome of a welfare state in crisis, an outcome which will undoubtedly contribute to a dramatically larger homeless population in the '90s.

How the homeless populations of the 90s are to be portrayed will depend in large part on the kind of popular consciousness that develops about the criminalization and victimization of people. More specifically, the formation of a crime and victim consciousness is a dynamic, ongoing process subject to the indeterminate outcomes of cultural, political, and economic struggles as organized interests try to successfully identify and label certain acts or things as "protected by" and "against" the law. More fundamentally, crime, criminalization, and victimization, as well as organized interests, are products of structural changes in the political economy. Consequently, in the immediate future, definitional struggles over the crime problem in the United States should change both as social divisions widen and as racial tensions build in response to the developing global political economy and the intensification of class conflict. And while global and, in turn, domestic economic changes are influencing definitional debates in the areas of both "suite crimes" and "street crimes," the present analysis is only concerned with the social construction of the latter forms of criminality. In particular, the rest of this section addresses the issue concerning the contradictory characterization and identification of homeless people as either criminals or victims and how these social constructions are related to the formation of public policies to meet the needs of the homeless.

The struggle for social justice, as epitomized by the modern welfare state, is the product of decades of class conflict and of political efforts by ordinary Americans to gain some control and stability over their lives in the face of massive disruptions (Block et al, 1987). As the various divisions between the haves and the have-nots widen worldwide, and as more U.S. residents are marginalized by the introduction of new technologies and the new international division of labor, increasing numbers of poor and homeless persons are destined to become subjects of new forms of social control. Whether these forms of social control will be repressive or liberative will depend, in part, on the dominant views regarding the plight of the homeless and the condition of homelessness. If the prevailing ideological views associated with the rise of the bourgeoisie remain triumphant over a postbourgeois alternative in the United States, then the poor and the homeless are likely to be viewed as members of a newly emerging dangerous class; and their status and behavior are likely to be stigmatized or even criminalized. Conversely, should an alternative, postbourgeois ideology rise into ascendency, then it would be more likely that the homeless would be viewed as victims of the contradictions of capitalist accumulation.

Historically, the poor and the homeless have often been viewed by those more fortunate as a dangerous class and have been held liable for societal ills like sin, uban disorder, crime, disease, and poverty. As early as four-teenth- and fifteenth-century England, for example, the bourgeoisie were successful in having the poor and the homeless criminally sanctioned for idleness, vagrancy, and migrating; and their punishment consisted of forced labor or indentured servitude (Chambliss, 1964; Thompson, 1975; Shelden, 1982; Michalowski, 1985). And according to the still dominant bourgeois ideology, crime is limited to behavior proscribed by the criminal law and blamed on individual offenders instead of on structural circum-stances. The bourgeois solution to crime has always served to protect and reproduce the unequal distribution of wealth, power, and property. On the other hand, a postbourgeois ideology of social control assumes that crime is often a consequence of social injustice and economic inequality; and there-fore, a solution is called for that addresses the alienating, dehumanizing, and marginalizing social relations of the political economy.

Today, in any event, those laws (i.e., disorderly conduct, curfew) which remain on the books of most jurisdictions, and the identification of va-grants and homeless people as both criminals and a threat to the social order, reflect the state's need to control, regulate, or surveil the marginal classes of capitalist development. Such laws also reflect the need of the state to sustain class control in general and to resist a more fundamental reordering of domestic priorities and practices based on the expansion rather than the contraction of the welfare state. In short, just when the U.S. ideological opposition to the welfare state has never been so intense, the need to reform and restructure it has likewise never been so strong.

The Reagan cutbacks and the recession of 1982 not only proved to be a catalyst for the rising rates of U.S. homelessness, but for the politicalization of the problems of the homeless and for the growth of public consciousness concerning the needs of the homeless (Hombs and Snyder, 1983). In other words, the formation of public policies in response to homelessness cannot be separated from the prevailing views regarding the homeless; the various policies and views interact with each other to form the public action that is ultimately deemed worthy of support. The two brief illustrations which follow represent the opposing tendencies on the homelessness-response continuum as reflected in the different underlying assumptions concerning the homeless.

In Arizona, as late as the mid-1980s, the homeless had often become objects of law enforcement and subjects for criminalization (Aulette and Aulette, 1987). In a state where general assistance was not available to homeless people, where few shelter beds or soup kitchens existed, and where the unofficial policies of Tucson were to run the homeless out of town, homeless people had been known to be verbally harassed and physically abused by the police. The homeless were also subject there to handcuffing, arresting, and being charged with criminal trespass, squat-ting, and loitering. The Tucson police had even gone so far as to harass people for trying to feed themselves and for constructing shelter—by arresting them, respectively, for the "crimes" of possessing glass (i.e., a peanut butter jar) and carrying a concealed weapon (i.e., cardboard cutters) (Aulette and Aulette, 1987). In this vignette, the criminalization of the homeless repeats the kind of treaab03tment and punishment that victims of increased marginalization, unemployment, and poverty have experienced since mass migrations of laborless people started during the emergence of commercial capitalism some five centuries ago (Chambliss, 1964; Michalowski, 1985). It also reflects the U.S. ideologies of laissez-faire and rugged individualism, dating back to the late nineteenth century, which have helped to reinforce the legitimacy of the free-enterprise system.

On the other hand, in Aurora, Illinois, some state emergency assistance was available for the homeless through the Township Office. Moreover, in addition to decentralized efforts to feed, clothe, and shelter the homeless in this city, there was also a centralized shelter facility due to the efforts of a coalition of religious groups, human service workers, and concerned citizens. This facility, organized in the mid-1980s, provides the homeless not only with a well-designed shelter for singles and families, but also with a soup kitchen, a food pantry, a clothes closet, and a day shelter for those with or without shelter. During cold winter nights, when temperatures often drop below zero, police can be observed picking up homeless people and driving them to one of the community's shelters as a matter of policy. This vignette reveals a city consciousness that developed not only an appreciation for the plight and victimization of people experiencing the homelessness condition, but a public policy toward the homeless which was nonrepressive and humane. This nonviolent alternative response to the homeless of Aurora reflects the twentieth-century ideological values of the Judeo-Christian ethic as expressed in the welfare state and the notion of social security for all. The Auroran response also foreshadows the possibility of developing a postbourgeois future of greater community: corporate and state responsibility for victims of structural problems.

The next section provides a brief history of the origins and early development of Hesed House, a succinct account of the philosophy of Hesed, and an assessment of Hesed House's success and potential as a model shelter for the homeless.[1]

## Aurora's Hesed House: A Model Response for Providing Temporary Shelter

In 1985 Aurora was a city of 85,000 located approximately 40 miles west of Chicago in the heart of the Fox River Valley, where one of the Midwest's largest shopping malls provided many low-paid service jobs to formerly employed Caterpillar workers and a substantial revenue base to an otherwise postindustrialized, slumping economy. According to the 1980 census, the population was 10 percent black, 18 percent Hispanic, and 70 percent white. Throughout most of the 1980s, Aurora's unemployment rate hovered around 10 percent. Because its employment base was dependent on blue-collar industrial manufacturing jobs, it was hard hit by the nation's transformation into a service/information-oriented economy and by the 1979–80 and 1982 recessions.

What this meant for a number of people working and living in Aurora was that they were becoming socially dependent for their daily survival. Beginning in the early '80s, middle-class Aurorans either knew somebody or were experiencing their own need for some kind of life-support services. Many formerly middle-class families were, in short, becoming members for the first time in what some economists began referring to as the "new poor" in the United States.

In response to the impoverishment of a growing number of people in Aurora during the late '70s and into the '80s, several private agencies were established to address the numerous problems associated with a locally depressed economy in transition. In particular: the Aurora Area Interfaith Food Pantry was organized in 1981; the Aurora Soup Kitchen and Clothes Closet, two distinct projects, began in 1982; Public Action Deliver Shelter (PADS) started in 1983; and PADS A.M. opened in 1985. All of these groups have demonstrated a unique model of ecumenical interchurch and inter-agency cooperation in a city where there are perhaps more churches per square mile than anywhere else in the United States. As of January 1986: the food pantry was serving 11,000 persons each month with participation of about 40 churches and 300 volunteers; the soup kitchen was serving 1,300 meals per month through the efforts of 350 volunteers; the collective and distribution network for clothing was serving about 1,600 persons each month and involving 30 volunteers; and the overnight emergency shelter was housing 70 guests nightly and serving 5,500 meals monthly, with a list of more than 100 volunteers.

It is important to point out that both organizationally and politically PADS became the driving force of advocacy for the homeless in Aurora. And although there was an overlap among people who worked in more than one of these community responses, it was those people specifically connected to PADS who fermented a movement which advocated that all people should be entitled to food and shelter—including alcoholics, fire victims, drug abusers, the mentally ill, and the unemployed. This philoso-phy, in conjunction with a strong and politically oriented PADS board of directors, accounted for the fact that PADS was viewed negatively by some very influential people in business, government, and healthcare, who were doing their best not only to shape Aurora's community responses to the homeless and needy, but to define the problem in the first place. Even-tually, it was the PADS perspective and conceptualization of the problem which prevailed over the view shared by the chamber of commerce and the previous city administration.

From its inception in 1983, the PADS ideology was to establish and provide a nonrestrictive shelter for homeless men, women, and children.

The Salvation Army and one other fundamentalist organization had provided limited and restricted emergency shelter care. Many of Aurora's homeless population preferred to sleep outdoors, even during the coldest months of winter. The earliest goal of PADS, therefore, was to reach those homeless who were not being served by traditional means. This open-door policy with respect to the homeless population of Aurora—open to the marginal, the deviant, even the dangerous—was greeted with a mixture of unity, fear, and hostility.

Congregations of the cooperating churches, for example, enjoyed giving alms to the poor but not the sharing of *their* church facilities with those desperate people. Nonetheless, the seven participating churches that came together in the formation and operation of PADS had a surplus of church-attending and nonattending volunteer workers who served the needs of Aurora's homeless population. Meanwhile, community leaders and others feared that an unrestricted shelter for the homeless would attract all the outcasts from Chicago and the surrounding areas who would come running to settle in Aurora. And so for a short time, about 30 months, these politicos attempted to sweep the problem of Aurora's homeless under the bridges of the Fox River. From 1983 to 1985, when PADS began documenting the problem for government and public consumption, many sympathetic journalistic accounts appeared in both the local and national media; and a number of provocative discussions occurred, privately and publicly, between the advocates for the homeless and the powers that be in Aurora. Before long, the coalition of social-service providers, churches, and grassroots organizers—along with their natural constituencies and volunteers—were able to shape Aurora's policy on the homeless. For instance, there was the mayoral election of April 1985, where the Democratic candidate narrowly defeated the Republican candidate by less than half of one percentage point, in what was supposedly a nonpartisan election—thanks, in part, to the backing of a loosely constructed Hesed network which easily accounted for some five percent of the vote. Eventually, the city administration—from the planning department to the police department, as well as the chamber of commerce—joined what was to become the Hesed House bandwagon in celebrating such a high-minded and community-based enterprise that benefitted all Aurorans.

Back in 1984, Hesed House had been legally incorporated and the idea of the board of directors was to secure a central location where the shelter, food pantry, soup kitchen, and clothes closet could deal with the needy more effectively. Aside from the problem of transportation involved in getting from one site to the next, there was the problem that, in spite of the strong volunteer support, there were inadequate cooking facilities, no bathing and laundry facilities, and less than enough space for an expanding population of needy people. A remedy was sought in coordinating organizations already linked by mutual efforts to serve the poor. The objective was not only to join like-minded groups, but to assist existing service-providers in meeting the evolving needs of powerless people with multiple problems. And the providing of hospitality and care, along with the eventual awareness that Hesed House (the *place*) was a symbol of commitment and advocacy for the very poor, did help to establish a bridge to self-reliance for the homeless of Aurora. Because Hesed's efforts linked advocacy to those direct human services addressing "the root causes of injustice," they helped to "promote the empowerment of the suffering and oppressed by standing in solidarity with their struggle and by encouraging them to act in their own behalf" (Hesed House By-laws, 1987).

In November 1985, Hesed House entered into a long-term agreement with the city of Aurora to occupy a vacant municipal incinerator building, centrally located. In sum, this community-based initiative created a private nonprofit-public partnership and included reasonable rent with an option to buy. While the city agreed to maintain the mechanical systems, Hesed House agreed to pay an estimated $400,000 for the necessary renovations to make room both for a short-term, year-round living facility and for the other supporting services. By the fall of 1987 Hesed House had met these goals and was embarking on the next phase of its development.

### PHILOSOPHY

From the Hebrew scriptures, *hesed* is translated sometimes to mean "mercy," other times to mean "pity," but more often to mean "steadfast and enduring love." And José Miranda, the liberation theologian, has translated *hesed* as "interhuman compassion." Rosemarie Lorentzen, the executive director of Hesed House, has noted, however, that "all of our English translations lack the dimension of action that the Hebrew word implies. The Hebrew talks of *doing hesed* with someone, and *hesed* is frequently associated with the word 'mispal' or 'justice.' It implies liberating self and others."[2]

According to the Hebrew scriptures, the unreserved commitment to the weak, the poor, and the oppressed is identical to an absolute sense of justice. As Lorentzen points out, *hesed* is, in fact, "love-justice" and calls for action on behalf of the poor and oppressed. In this sense, *hesed* calls on people to "practice what they preach," to reach out in a love that seeks justice, to proclaim the good news, to do *hesed*. In doing *hesed*, Lorentzen explains how people are required to go beyond "the instinctual human impulse to reach out to those in need because it responds even when the other hasn't earned it or doesn't deserve it, or has abused it in the past. In attempting compassion we step inside the life of another and find ourselves changed in the process." Once inside the other person, a subject is then supposedly able to rebel at the daily assaults on the poor and to search for ways to eliminate the causes of their oppression. In the meantime, the person doing *hesed* is also engaging in the "ministry of hospitality"—in the provision of caring, humane encounters. The spirit of hospitality, properly experienced, will not only protect people from the outside elements, but it will also remove the stigma of charity as handouts, which is viewed as very damaging to human dignity.

Lorentzen sums up the problems of the poor and class struggle this way: The "causes of unemployment, homelessness and other dimensions of poverty are complex." She continues: "A great deal of creativity will be needed to find systemic solutions, the persistence will be required to combat certain opposition. The doing of *hesed*, however, can keep our dreams alive while we work together to create a new and better world."

Finally, and most concretely, Aurora's *hesed* has been a movement of people in a small Midwest city concerned for the dignity, survival, and reclamation of those homeless, hungry, and hopeless folks who were not being served by the more conventional social-service agencies. Hesed House is a place for the operation of a multiversity of human services, rendered to those people who need them most, when they need them, through the combined efforts of staff, volunteers, and supporting churches and friends of *hesed*.

## PROGRAM ASSESSMENT

During the United Nations International Year of Shelter for the Homeless in 1987, the Certificate of Special Recognition was awarded to Hesed House by the Illinois legislature, while the U.S. Department of Housing and Urban Development (HUD) and the State Department jointly made Hesed a part of the Model Project Awards Program. Hesed had lived up to the theme of HUD's program—Housing America: Freeing the Spirit of Enterprise—by demonstrating "successful participation in an exemplary community effort to improve the shelter and neighborhoods of the Nation's poor and disadvantaged."

In referring to the action of hesed workers in his nominating letter, the recently elected mayor of Aurora underscored the importance of the private/public initiative in developing a centralized site for servicing the homeless and needy:

> I believe their strong volunteerism, coupled with the City's willingness to forego revenues by offering them use of surplus property, have resulted in an extensive, compassionate and inexpensive safety net for our community. Part of Hesed House's success is due to its reliance on the private sector and efficient use of resources. (Pierce, 1986)

The Office of Policy Development and Research for the International Year of Shelter for the Homeless used six criteria for rendering its decisions about who would and would not be recipients of HUD's Model Project Awards Program for 1987. The enumerated criteria were as follows:

1. Explore, test or demonstrate existing or new ways and means of improving the shelter and neighborhoods of low-income families

through use of local initiative and with the involvement of the private sector;

2. Serve primarily low-income people, particularly those incomes at or below the poverty level;
3. Contribute to or result in a clear and visible improvement in the shelter or neighborhoods of low-income people before 1987;
4. Contain features in support of lower income families that can be replicated in other locations within the country or in other nations;
5. Lead to affordable improvements for many rather than major improvements for a few;
6. Seek a practical balance between what is desirable, attainable, and affordable by lower income people themselves and the nation as a whole.

Here is the city of Aurora's Community Development Department's (CDD) assessment of Hesed House in relation to these criteria, as the assessment appeared in the CDD's nomination of Hesed House for the HUD Award.

1. In Hesed House's case, private sector volunteers, utilizing a minimum of government assistance, have developed an extensive service delivery system that provides needed emergency shelter for the homeless. By having a permanent location for the shelter in combination with other basic need services, the homeless can be better assisted and their problems addressed. By utilizing a vacant surplus building, the City is foregoing revenue rather than incurring new costs to alleviate the problem of homelessness.
2. . . . the assistance provided is so modest and so basic that it is by nature geared to only the lowest of low income households.
3. By being able to provide separate facilities for women and children, the new centralized location has also resulted in a clear visible improvement. In addition, as more support agencies begin offering periodic service at this site, more people who traditionally slip through the safety net will be able to be identified and assisted.
4. The main features of this project are that local government was able to provide a needed component to Hesed House's plans without having to fund an expensive, paperwork laden program; and that the community's volunteers have been efficiently and constructively organized to deliver services for the poor and homeless on a low cost basis.
5. 'PADS' track record indicates that most of those using their shelter do not stay longer than one week. Many stay only one or two nights before a more permanent form of assistance can be provided. Also, since services are minimal, no one client gets major improvement, but rather gets enough help to get out of a cycle of homelessness.

6. Clearly, providing centralized, minimal services for the poor and homeless does not solve their long term needs immediately. What it does do, however, is provide an inexpensive safety net to help needy families get back into society and make it through the interim. The City does not have the revenue to meet all its other police, health and safety needs, and to provide permanent funding for such a safety net. By both interest groups working together, however, a viable alternative has been found.

Without specifically discussing the CDD's assessment of the Hesed House model, I will, in the next section, set forth a general critique of the future problem of homelessness in the United States and also of the Hesed response as a model for possible replication by other cities trying to cope both with the deepening housing crisis and with a worldwide political economy in transition.

## Social Control, Homelessness, and the Nineties

My analysis of homelessness and the homeless is consistent with those analyses of constitutive criminology which have declined "the seduction that either human agents, through choice or predisposition, or structural arrangements at both institutional and societal level, have priority in shaping crime, victims or control" (Henry, 1989). Moreover, this chapter has argued, both explicitly and implicitly, that the response to homelessness emerges as an ongoing outcome of human interaction that constrains and enables the future of both criminal and noncriminal action. It has been further suggested that the social structure and its constituent controlling institutions can be viewed as an arena for criminologists and others to act as human agents in the formation of U.S. public policy on housing and homelessness—can be viewed through the dialectical interaction between class struggle and the discursive language on homelessness, the homeless, victimization, criminalization, punishment, justice, and the *crime and control* talk which helps to reproduce the existing arrangements of social order.

In the mid-1970s, Spitzer (1975: 644) talked about some of the relationships that we have examined in this chapter:

As economic development creates a relative surplus population, groups emerge who are both threatening and vulnerable at the same time. The marginal status of these populations reduces their stake in the maintenance of the system while their powerlessness and dispensability renders them increasingly susceptible to the mechanisms of official control. The larger and more threatening the problem population, the greater the likelihood that this population will have to be controlled by deviance processing rather than other methods.

Of course this is not only happening now with respect to street gangs and illicit drug dealings, but with the hungry, the homeless, and the debilitated. And while I partially agree with Spitzer's analysis regarding the expanded role of deviance progressing for some marginal groups—especially concerning those members of the dangerous or threatening classes who engage in the more common forms of street criminality—the above analysis has also demonstrated the possibility of utilizing other methods for controlling marginalized members of society. In other words, I also tend to agree with Aulette and Aulette (1987) who have argued that not all behavioral forms of marginality will necessarily become subjects of deviant processing.

In the '90s, for example, the reaction to the projected increases in the number of homeless people in the United States has the potential to go in either the Auroran or Tucson direction, or even in both directions. The increasing number of homeless might also prove to be an important vehicle or agent of social change. If instead of regarding the homeless as threatening and criminal, we regard them as victims of a low-income housing crisis in combination with other economic trends, and if we begin to fashion public and private behavior to respond to the changing political economy, then we could foster the kind of planned economic and social development where public welfare does not take a backseat to private enterprise. Such a view holds that the state should be obligated to providing some humane, minimal level of healthcare, childcare, education, food, clothing, permanent shelter, nonviolence, and personal dignity.

However, as the economic problems deepened during the 1970s and 1980s, the welfare state became the target of ideological attacks by reactionaries, conservatives, and even liberals. The common theme of attacks by ideologues of the right has been that "social welfare measures are a drag on the economy, an incentive to immorality, and a cruel hoax on the needy themselves. . . . [I]n the process, even the phrase 'the welfare state' has been discredited. Conservatives employ it as a term of invective, while liberals, the erstwhile advocates of the welfare state, have been hesitant to defend it" (Block et al., 1987: ix).

During the recent so-called bankruptcy of liberalism, with the exception of the Jackson candidacy and the Rainbow Coalition of 1988, liberals and the progressive left have been in a state of retreat while the right wing and the conservative agenda have been ascending ideologically and politically across the country. The prevailing bourgeois ideology and its vision of the future as pastoral-world in which people are expected to live in stable families within stable communities has fallen victim to a very different sociological reality, yet our public policy remains virtually unchanged in dealing with its national or domestic obligations. More importantly perhaps, the utopianism of the right remains ideologically intact as everyone is supposed to work hard and to remain sober, drug-free, and chaste as well. But even this traditional, nostalgic view of gemeinschaft and the rural past—where authority was firmly vested in adults over children, in men over women, and in the wisdom of the Bible over modern science and humanism—is certainly still being scrutinized and resisted in some quarters today.

Nevertheless, if there is poverty and homelessness after the moral and social reformation of U.S. society has occurred, then in the prevailing "back to the future" bourgeois outlook, "it will be dealt with through individual and local charity rather than impersonal government mechanisms" (Ehrenreich, 1987: 191). Therefore, programs like Hesed House are excellent cases for discrediting the ideological attacks against the welfare state by the right. These programs demonstrate that the right's concerns about the dangers of cruel hoaxes on the needy themselves are unfounded. Similarly, these programs can be used by the hesitant liberals in defense of a modern welfare state. As a prototype, the Hesed model may help to disprove the right's incentive to the immorality and dependency argument while demonstrating that collective intervention can be cost-effective. In short, examples like Hesed House provide competing models where shared responsibility replaces individual responsibility for common social problems.

In the United States, at least, an alternative vision of a postbourgeois society has not now been fully developed by academics or intellectuals nor articulated or even contemplated in the mass media; and certainly such a perspective has little if any backing in the social formation of today's public policy. In fact, the traditionally liberal Democratic party, which has been associated with this viewpoint since Roosevelt's New Deal policies and the more recent Great Society programs of the Johnson Administration, has, for the overwhelming most part, abandoned its historic mission and chosen instead to appropriate the language (e.g., family, hard work, too much permissiveness) of the New Right. Unless an alternative vision is developed and unless a progressive, postbourgeois ideological analysis and political program is constituted by the left, widespread poverty and punitive-repressive governmental intervention are likely to occur. More specifically, if a national domestic policy is not developed to address the low-income housing crisis in particular and the fundamentally changing socioeconomic order in general, and if the hardships and suffering associated with impoverishment and homelessness do not decrease, the victims of the existing policies of a minimalist welfare state will most likely be perceived as threatening and in need of deviance processing rather than as unfortunate people in need of a reformed and modernized welfare state.

A fundamental question raised by this analysis is whether the growing number of homeless people in the United States will become subjects of the repressive-penal apparatus of bourgeois social control or of new forms of welfare and community development. To achieve the latter, as in the Auroran example, an effective response to the right must be mounted based on a genuine critique of capitalist culture and on the development of alternative social policies. Nevertheless, HUD's criteria of a model project and even the Hesed House response reveal the contradictions of doing radical community intervention within the context of liberal and conservative reformism.

On the one hand, the Hesed model of social-service deployment represents not only a critique of bourgeois values and society, but a serious effort to develop progressive alternatives to the existing human-service delivery systems. On the other hand, Hesed's liberal reformist and neo-conservative relationship with volunteerism, free enterprise, and the capitalist welfare state, helps to solidify and reproduce the harmful status quo. These contradictory relations and the philosophy of doing *esed* has very real and profound effects in terms of affecting people's psyches and political orientations. While Hesed House is engaged in the struggle for human survival, it is not a revolutionary approach to addressing the problems of housing and homelessness.

Nevertheless, Hesed workers and volunteers are actively participating in a social-service movement of revolutionary potential. Participants in Hesed House had gained some experience in organizing and in coalition building. They had also been in a position to influence public discourse and practice regarding the homeless in Aurora. In a related way, the Hesed model, especially concerning its orientation to the marginal, the deviant, and the truly needy, helped to shape the viewpoint that those homeless people were primarily victims of political-economic forces and repressive policies beyond their individual control. Such realizations help to create an expectation of social change and a willingness to get involved in the struggle against inequality and for social justice. More generally, the widespread advocacy for the poor and powerless can help legitimate their rights to basic necessities while raising the type of alternative consciousness required for the development of a postbourgeois social order.

As for the replicability of Hesed House as a model for other community-based efforts to resist homelessness, it should be stressed that the idea of one central facility "makes sense" in small- to medium-sized cities with populations of less than 100,000. In more populated urban areas with homeless persons in the thousands, a number of strategically located facilities would seem to make more sense for some rather obvious reasons. Two of those reasons are transportation and residential occupancy or density.

More fundamentally, Hesed Houses are not the answer to the escalating problem of homelessness in the United States. Temporary shelters like Hesed House, which provide needy persons and families with the opportunity to "get back into society and make it through the interim," will prove themselves, at best, as providing short-term living facilities, and at worst, as impeding the developing of a more rational and systemic approach to the long-term housing crisis and condition of homelessness. Dialectically, however, the present analysis believes that a connection can be made between the reformist tendencies of the former and the structural tendencies of the latter.

In particular, both HUD's criteria and emergency/temporary shelters fall way short of seriously confronting the growing shortage in affordable housing, especially in the larger urban cities across the country. HUD's approach to the housing crisis, at least through 1989, has been liberal, reformist to the core and has allowed almost exclusively for the needs of the homeless to depend on the outcomes of the prevailing real-estate market, coupled with a reliance on private development, to ameliorate the shortage in low-income housing. HUD's criteria, moreover, does not call attention to the more fundamental need for changing the living conditions of low-income or no-income persons. Poverty is not to be attacked and neither is privilege; both are to be left intact as individuals and families with incomes at or below the poverty level are to be the primary recipients of temporary shelter services. Through local, voluntary, and private initiatives, neighborhoods of low-income families are to be visibly improved through the removal of the eyesore of homeless people sleeping in the streets. Policies which merely hide the problem, instead of those which attempt to come to grips with the underlying causes of homelessness and the housing crisis, are clearly not the policies needed. What is required are public policies to address such concrete relations as the declining wages in the United States, the contraction of low-cost housing construction, the lack of affordable and quality daycare, the deterioration of neighborhoods and infrastructures alike, gentrification, and the escalating rates of property values in this country.

While the U.S. low-cost housing crisis and problems of the homeless vary from city to city, from rural to urban, and from the Midwest and the South to the West and the East coasts, a common feature is the structural nature of the problem as surrounded by an established discourse, ideology, public policy, and economic pattern of development. The solutions, therefore, lie in addressing and changing these relationships. In other words, the solutions to the U.S. homelessness problem will not be found in the development and reproduction of ideal models of shelter such as the one provided by Hesed House. These kinds of necessary emergency/temporary shelters may provide humane short-term alternatives to living in a subway or alley or to selling oneself into sexual servitude, but they do not provide for the development of long-term permanent housing for all U.S. residents. Low-cost and subsidized housing for the working and nonworking poor who can no longer afford to pay the rent must become the ultimate product of the housing-now movement.

The further victimization of the growing number of homeless people and of the violence of homelessness could be significantly reduced, or even ended, if we were prepared politically to challenge the vested interested of property, business, and defense. For example, 1988 expenditures to subsidize low-income housing account for one cent for every revenue dollar collected. Expenditures to subsidize middle and affluent income housing through mortgage interest write-offs also account for one cent of every dollar of revenue collected. By contrast, expenditures for defense/military expenditures account for 82 cents of every tax dollar. These figures are part of the analysis supplied by the Low-Income Housing Information Service (1989) which maintains that the current homelessness problem in the United States could virtually be eliminated if the amount of the subsidy for low-income housing was tripled from one cent to three cents per tax dollar collected.

Moreover, grass-roots efforts such as Project Habitat, a not-for-profit organization, or the congressionally chartered Neighborhood Reinvestment Corporation, provide small scale efforts to refurbish abandoned homes and buildings and to revitalize neighborhoods. These models of private-public initiative need to be expanded with greater governmental, business, and consumer involvement at all levels. In the process, the large scale refurbishing of bandoned properties and the provision of these to the homeless for rent or purchase adjusted to income, even with modest recompense to former owners, would only help to bring about a change in view of the workings of the "invisible hand" of free enterprise; and it would, at the same time, contribute toward the delegitimation of the sanctity of private property at the expense of human beings. In turn, these kinds of developments in response to the current crisis in low-income housing would help to generate the types of values and consciousness needed in the postbourgeois society, a society where the state guarantees all people the right to basic human necessities.

## NOTES

1. This study of Aurora's Hesed House is based on an ethnography of sorts and on a sociohistorical analysis of a participant-observer experience. From the summer of 1983 to the summer of 1985 I was absorbed full time with the problems of Aurora's hungry and homeless. I was also very well connected politically as a community advocate for the poor, youths, and the physically and sexually abused in Aurora. When I moved away from Illinois in August of 1985, I resigned my position as president of the Board of Directors of Aurora Area Interfaith Food Pantry, Inc. At the time, there were some 34 participating ecumenical churches involved in the food pantry, which also worked in association with Chicago area food banks. My being an atheist and Jewish never was viewed as relevant to my serving as president of this predominantly Christian organization. In terms of my political connectedness, I also had turned in my resignations to several boards, commissions, and committees, including: Public Action to Deliver Shelters, Inc.; Hesed House, Inc.; Aurora Township Youth Commission; Aurora Sesquicentennial Commission; Aurora Chamber of Commerce, Government Operations Committee; and Mutual Ground, Inc. a shelter for abused women and children. The point is

that I was well immersed in the public and private affairs of Aurora and was in an excellent position to engage in both praxis and study. This examination—of the needs of the poor and powerlessness in relationship to homelessness, and of the reactions of the Auroran community—not only benefitted from my ongoing research into the housing crisis and the homeless, but also from my four years to reflect on this "experiment" in trying to reduce some of the needless violence and victimization in our society.

2. With respect to the *hesed* philosophy, I am paraphrasing the "teachings" of Rosemarie Lorentzen, the executive director of Hesed House and the backbone of this response to the needs of the homeless in Aurora. Where any quotations appear concerning the philosophy of *hesed*, they are from an undated brief statement written by Rosemarie to introduce volunteers and workers to the concept. In August of 1987, I visited the incinerator site of the shelter just as the finishing renovations were being completed and Hesed House was getting ready to operationalize all facets of the program as conceptualized only a few years earlier. In early 1988, Rosemarie provided me with a small package of materials on all of the accomplishments and developments discussed within this chapter.

## REFERENCES

Arce, A. A. 1983. "A Psychiatric Profile of Street People Admitted to an Emergency Shelter." *Hospital and Community Psychiatry* 34: 812–17.

Aulette, J., and A. Aulette. 1987. "Police Harassment of the Homeless: The Political Purpose of the Criminalization of Homelessness." *Humanity and Society* 11: 244–56.

Barak, G. 1988. "Newsmaking Criminology: Reflections on the Media, Intellectuals, and Crime." *Justice Quarterly* 5 (4): 565–87.

———. 1980. "In Defense of Whom?" *A Critique of Criminal Justice Reform.* Cincinnati: Anderson.

Bassuk, E. L. 1984. "The Homeless Problem." *Scientific American* 25: 40–46.

Batra, R. 1987. *The Great Depression of 1990.* New York: Simon and Schuster.

Berberoglu, B. 1987. "Labor, Capital, and the State: Economic Crisis and Class Struggle in the United States in the 1970s and the 1980s." Paper presented at the annual meeting of the American Sociological Association, Chicago, August.

Block, F., R. A. Cloward, B. Ehrenreich, and F. F. Piven. 1987. *The Mean Season: The Attack on the Welfare State.* New York: Pantheon.

Chambliss, W. 1964. "A Sociological Analysis of the Law of Vagrancy." *Social Problems* 12: 67–77.

Crystal, S. 1984. "Homeless Men and Homeless Women: The Gender Gap." *Urban and Social Change Review* 17: 2–6.

Danzinger, S., and P. Gottschalk. 1985. "How Families with Children Have Been Fairing." Paper prepared for the Joint Committee, United States Congress.

Economic Report. 1987. Economic Report of the President. 1986. Statistical Abstract of the United States.

Ehrenreich, B. 1987. "The New Right Attack on Social Welfare." In F. Block et al., *The Mean Season: The Attack on the Welfare State.* New York: Pantheon.

Freeman, R. B., and B. Hall. 1987. *Permanent Homeless in America Today?* Cambridge: National Bureau of Economic Research, Working Paper No. 2013.

Gorz, A. 1964. *Strategy for Labor: A Radical Proposal.* Boston: Beacon Press.

Henry, S. 1989. "Constitutive Criminology: The Missing Link." *The Critical Criminologist* 1 (3): 9.
Hesed House. 1987. 8th Revision of the Bylaws, January.
Hirschl, T. A. 1987. "Homeless in New York State: A Demographic and Socioeconomic Analysis." Paper presented at the annual meeting of the American Sociological Association, Chicago, August.
Hombs, M. E., and M. Snyder. 1983. *Homelessness in America: A Forced March to Nowhere*. Washington, D.C.: Community for Creative Nonviolence.
Hopper, K., E. Susser, and S. Conover. 1987. "Economics of Makeshift: Deindustrialization and Homelessness in New York City." *Urban Anthropology*. Forthcoming.
HOUSING NOW! 1989. "Homelessness Fact Sheet," April.
Kasinitz, P. 1987. "Gentrification and Homelessness: The Single Room Occupant and Their Inner City Rival." *Urban Anthropology*. Forthcoming.
Kondratas, A. S. 1984. "A Strategy for Helping Amercia's Homeless." *Backgrounder* 431: 1–13.
Lamb, H. R. 1984. "Deindustrialization and the Homeless Mentally Ill." *Hospital and Community Psychiatry* 35: 899–907.
Low Income Housing Information Service. 1989. "Housing, Homeless and Tax Related Legislation During the 100th Congress."
Mandel, E. 1980. *The Second Slump*. London: Verse.
Michalowski, R. 1985. *Order, Law, and Crime: An Introduction to Criminology*. New York: Random House.
National Coalition for the Homeless. 1986. "National Neglect, National Shame, America's Homeless: Outlook, Winter '86–87." Washington, D.C.: NCH, September.
Naureckas, J. 1989. "HUD Versus the Huddled Masses." *In These Times*, 30 August–5 September.
Pierce, D. 1986. Mayor's Letter of Nomination to HUD, 29 January.
Shelden, R. G. 1982. *Criminal Justice in America: A Sociological Approach*. Boston: Little, Brown.
Sherman, H. 1976. *Stagflation*. New York: Harper and Row.
Spitzer, S. 1975. "Toward a Marxian Theory of Deviance." *Social Problems* 22: 638–51.
Thomas, J., and A. O'Maolchatha. 1989. "Reassessing the Critical Metaphor: An Optimistic Revisionist View." *Justice Quarterly* 6 (2): 143–72.
Thompson, E. P. 1975. *Whigs and Hunters: The Origin of the Black Act*. New York: Pantheon.

*Russ Immarigeon*

---

F  I  V  E·

# Beyond the Fear of Crime

*Reconciliation as the Basis for Criminal Justice Policy*

If perceptions of certainty and severity of punishment
influence intentions regarding reoffending, but have little or
nothing to do with subsequent criminal behavior, then it is
unlikely that programs emphasizing the fear factor will be
effective. These programs may seem to hold the promise of
reducing delinquency because they are believed to induce an
immediate intent of avoiding crime; but the context within
which actual decisions to commit crimes are made differ
substantially from the context in which those intentions are
shaped by programmatic experiences.

—Anne L. Schneider (1990)

Have I romanticized these kids, made them more "human" so
the world will understand them and the problem they
represent? That has certainly not been my attention. I have
tried to present the reality behind the newspaper and
television version of teenagers selling cocaine on New York
City streets. Yes, there is violence and death on those streets,
but there are also struggling young people trying to make a
place for themselves in a world few care to understand and
many wish would go away.

—Terry Williams (1989)

The most effective peacemakers are those who have
experienced the healing of their own fears and can now help
lead others out of theirs.

—Jim Wallis (1983)

Criminal justice policy on the relative use of imprisonment and nonincarcerative sanctions in the 1990s is being shaped, initially at least, by perspectives and circumstances that have emerged over the past twenty years. In this period, prison use and the expansion of social control networks has grown at a staggering rate. Between 1970 and 1988, for instance, prison populations in the United States have more than tripled, from 196,441 to 627,402 inmates (Bureau of Justice Statistics, 1988, 1989). Disproportionality has also become a serious factor. The number of women in local jails across the country has increased ninety-three percent between 1983 and 1988 while the male population in these facilities *only* increased fifty-one percent in the same period (Bureau of Justice Statistics, 1990). Nearly one in four African-American men between the ages of twenty and twenty-nine are either imprisoned or under community supervision on any given day (Mauer, 1990). Probation and parole caseloads have also reached record levels, and never in our history have so many probation and parole violators been returned to prison for technical as well as "new crime" reasons.

But changes in how local, state, and federal jurisdictions are reacting to crime are even more telling than these distressing statistics. Simply stated, rehabilitation has been replaced by retribution as the dominant paradigm for criminal justice intervention. Criminal sentences are more generally intended to punish than reform.

However, bubbling under the surface of this significant change are some different perspectives on how criminal sanctions can respond to criminal behavior and victimization. In particular, restitution and reconciliation are concepts that are gaining currency among conservatives and liberals alike. More importantly, studies are finding that reparative sanctions such as restitution and victim-offender reconciliation are more effective at deterring crime than incapacitative and punitive penalties.

In *Deterrence and Juvenile Crime*, Anne L. Schneider recently reported in a national study of six juvenile restitution programs that "restitution is more effective (than probation) in reducing recidivism because it provides the juveniles with immediate and continuing success in the program. In other words, the juveniles can quickly develop a sense of being successful by obtaining employment and beginning to make their restitution payments or perform their community service. The data suggest that this reduces the offense activity during the time they are in the program. The sense of success and the reduced in-program offense rate both enhance the juvenile's sense of citizenship as well as reduced intentions to reoffend and actual recontacts with the court" (Schneider, 1990: 111).

At the same time, a study of the effectiveness of selective incapacitation, a much proposed remedy for escalating crime rates, suggested, like a number of studies before it, that any hope of significantly reducing crime through incapacitation, whether collective or selective, would seem to be remote (Haapanen, 1990: 136–37).

The 1990s began in a state of massive correctional crowding. But as one decade tumbled over into another, policies based on longer sentences and longer periods of time served were cascading out of control. In Minnesota, for example, the number of women incarcerated in what many people feel is our most progressive state on correctional issues increased from approximately 120 to 180 in less than two years.

Nonetheless, despite an escalating drug war complete with steady Bush-Administration volleys for more prisons and more prisoners, strong interests exist for the use of nonincarcerative sanctions. The Judicial Conference of the United States, for instance, in a March 1989 report on the impact of drug-related criminal activity on the federal courts, supported the use of substance-abuse treatment programs, restitution, fines, and electronic monitoring as alternatives to incarceration. The report also requested more funds for pretrial, probation, and defender services staff to prepare and implement alternative sanctions (Federal Judicial Center, 1989: 53–54).

Shortly thereafter, the Police Foundation released the findings of its National Symposium on Community Institutions and Inner-City Crime Project. This project, too, supported alternatives to incarceration. "Judges should continue to tailor sentences to individual offenders rather than rely totally on sentencing alternatives," the report argued. "Judges should use alternatives to incarceration, particularly when the offender is nonviolent. Community service, restitution, drug treatment, and house arrest can be effective sanctions" (Sulton, 1990: 108–9). Other sections of this report supported the use of halfway houses and discouraged returning parole violators to prison when they have not committed a new crime.

At the start of the decade, then, criminal justice policy in the country relies heavily on repressive measures, but there are numerous cracks in this armor. An opening therefore exists to challenge and organize against the prevailing paradigm of justice. The relationship between criminal justice policies and criminology is generally ill-defined and uncertain. Often times, this relationship, or lack of relationship, is glossed over rather than confronted. Rarely is the process studied in organized fashion. Peacemaking criminology has an important role in developing these inquiries. In this essay, I will briefly refer to some directions for this budding perspective.

In "Conflicts as Property," a paper originally given as the Foundation Lecture of the Centre for Criminological Studies at the University of Sheffield in March 1976, Norwegian criminologist Nils Christie vented his suspicion that "criminology to some extent has amplified a process where conflicts have been taken away from the parties directly involved and have thereby disappeared or become other people's property." Both situations were deplorable, he said. "Conflicts ought to be used, not only left in erosion. And they ought to be used, and become useful, for those originally involved in the conflict" (Christie, 1977: 1).

When applied to ordinary criminal cases, Christie's argument suggests that the interests, perspectives, and concerns of both victims and offenders are "disappeared" or lost when criminal justice officials—police, prosecutors, defense attorneys, probation officers, prison administrators, and even reform advocates—speak or act on their behalf. In short, Christie posits that "professionals" (rather than direct participants) seize control and define (or redefine) what has taken place and what must be done about it. Prosecutors, for instance, may be more interested in convictions with stiff penalties than victim restitution while the victim's main concern, to use a simple example, is that she get her purse and its contents returned to her. Defense attorneys, to use another example, may be well-satisfied that a full package of sentencing alternatives that includes restitution, community service, strict supervision, and the like is to the benefit of the clients they represent when, in fact, they may be "widening the net of social control" for their clients to plunge through while perhaps going far beyond the needs of the victims involved.

Damon Runyon, the writer, once touched on part of what Christie spoke about in observations he once made about murder trials. "A big murder trial possesses some of the elements of a sporting event," Runyon suggested. "There is the same conversational speculation on the probable result. The trial is a sort of game, the players on the one side attorneys for the defense, and on the other side the attorneys for the State. The defendant figures in it merely as the prize" (Pollack, 1972: 27).

More to the point, numerous examples of such thievery can be found in almost any courtroom on any day one chooses to attend local criminal proceedings. For the sake of brevity, let me describe only two such instances which I return to later in this essay.

Several years ago, the Vera Institute of Justice was generous enough to allow me to follow a court representative in its community service program through his daily round of work. At one point, we entered the bullpen, a squalid series of short-term holding cells for detained prisoners awaiting a court appearance, to speak with a defendant who was soon to appear before the bench. Earlier, the court rep had identified this one fellow as a likely candidate for Vera's community service program after a brief review of court papers on file in the courtroom. The court rep spoke to the prisoner for less than five minutes but obtained a staggering amount of information about him, including his drug-use history (McDonald, 1986).

At the bench, the court rep asked the court to sentence the defendant to the Vera program. The Vera program consisted of six weeks of unpaid public-service labor at a community work site supervised by Vera staff. A straightforward sentence. But the judge was interested in the offender's drug-use history. He looked first toward the prosecutor, then toward the defense attorney, and asked whether the offender used drugs. Neither one knew. The court rep was not asked, and he did not volunteer what he knew because while the program helps offenders find treatment services for their addictions, such rehabilitative programming is not a formal part of the services they provide. Meanwhile, the defendant, who may or may not have told the court what it wanted to know, was standing several yards away. A certain source of some information. Yet no one asked him.

More recently, a tragic homicide in Tennessee occurred when a drifter assaulted and murdered a well-known. elderly community volunteer. The drifter was soon caught, jailed, and brought to trial. Before his identification and arrest, however, the victim's brother, a Catholic priest, asked, on behalf of the victim's family, that the prosecutor not seek the death penalty in this case. When the drifter was caught, the family met with the prosecutor to repeat their deeply felt request. The woman killed did not believe in the death penalty, and she would not want further violence to result even when she had been the victim of senseless violence.

In a letter to the prosecutor, the victim's family wrote: "The cruelty of her death, as devastating as it is, does not diminish our belief that God's forgiveness and love, as our mother showed us, is the only response to the violence we know. If the suspect is guilty as alleged, it is clear that he is deeply troubled and needs all the compassion that our society and its institutions can offer." Although this was the sense of justice the victim's family wanted pursued by those who represented their interests (the state of Tennessee), the prosecutor nonetheless asked for the death penalty (Loggins, 1989).

Over twenty years ago, sociologist Ned Polsky gave a ground-breaking critique of criminological methods in an essay in his collected works, *Hustlers, Beats, and Others.* Central to Polsky's critique was the charge that "experience with adult, unreformed, serious criminals in their natural environment—not only those undertaking felonies in a moonlighting way, such as pool hustlers, but career felons—has convinced me that if we are to make a major advance in our scientific understanding of criminal lifestyles, criminal subcultures, and their relation to the social system, we must undertake genuine field research on these people" (Polsky, 1967: 117).

In at least one important way, Polsky's critique mirrors Christie's complaints: Both men fault the common characteristic of avoiding the people who criminologists and criminal justice practitioners are supposed to be dealing with—criminals and victims. American criminology has grown dramatically since the days of Polsky's critique, but too little evidence exists that the field has learned very much.

Crime problems, prison problems, and justice problems are rapidly changing. Definitions of what is criminal are altered in a wink of the eye. In the late 1970s and early 1980s, for instance, the National Coalition for Jail Reform coordinated a broad coalition of disparate criminal justice agencies that agreed that public inebriates (i.e., common drunkards) should not be jailed. Within years, however, Mothers Against Drunk Driving and other victim groups helped establish an environment within which legislators swiftly enacted new laws that criminalized and imprisoned hundreds of thousands of drinking drivers. At the beginning of this sea change, restrictive measures, such as loss of license and incarceration, were the most frequently mandated remedies. More recently, victim participation, victim impact statements, and victim testimony are lending a reconciliatory, community-building edge to the form of changing responses to this serious social issue.

Criminologists have not investigated these changes very adequately. More often than not, they are too accepting of whatever "official discourse" permeates from either governmental fund givers or from ideological restrictions. At an international crime prevention conference in Montreal recently, local and national officials from different countries met to examine different strategies toward crime prevention. Western European and Canadian representatives spoke eloquently about getting to the root causes of deviant behavior. The American response, one observer noted, was drugs, drugs, drugs—the implication being that Americans had lost any tangible grasp of even looking under the surface at what the problem was and, thus, what to do about it. Helplessness, not involvement, becomes our response to social problems.

Crime and fear have many associations. Some of these we are well familiar with. Public opinion polls, for instance, commonly tell us that people in our communities fear crime. How widely crime is feared and how this fear affects our lives varies from one period of time to another and from one community to another.

The relationship of crime and fear is not without its ironies. Victimization surveys, for example, frequently show us that people who have not been victims of crime are more fearful of crime than those who have been attacked or robbed. Old people and women, statistically less likely to be victimized than young men, nonetheless have higher levels of fear. It is far less clear, however, how these findings translate into cogent public policy.

One thing is certain. The fear of crime affects more than how we walk down the street, or even whether we walk down the street, at night. The fear of crime affects the way we determine how we as a society respond, as a matter of social policy, to crime. Part of this shameful situation arises because we as criminolgists too frequently avoid many serious issues in criminal justice policy making.

One example. Several years ago, Gottfredson and Taylor reported that legislative policymakers in Maryland thought that their constituency was far more punitive-oriented than they found out was actually the case. No replications of this study have been done, but it is probable that similar findings would be found elsewhere. What these findings suggest is that instead of finding out what people really think and feel, policymakers avoid this issue, avoid it perhaps because they are lazy, because they are too busy, or because they really do not want to know.

The process of finding out what people really think has further complications. The Public Agenda Foundation recently completed both a national survey and a state-specific survey of public opinion on crime and punishment issues. What they, and several other similar surveys, have found is that people's opinions change when given information that educates them about the topic being discussed. In short, people's opinion can change in rather a short time.

These studies successfully uncover social facts that more comfortably fit into criminological thought than in legislative dialogues. Peacemaking criminology needs to bridge this gap.

## Case Study 1: Homeless Man Stabs Supermarket Manager

A forty-year-old Cuban man, homeless, has a job gathering shopping carts from a supermarket parking lot. He gets paid ten dollars a day. One day, the store manager says he only deserves five dollars. Angered, a struggle ensues and the man stabs the store manager in the knee. The man spends four months in pretrial detention. At his sentencing, the judge receives an alternative sentencing plan that provides for literacy training, work, a place to stay, etc. A community agency has a place ready for him.

Instead of making a decision, however, the judge listens to the prosecutor, who wants a three-year prison term, and to the defense attorney, who wants leniency. Since these two professionals are in conflict, the judge, who is leaning toward the community sentence, holds the sentencing over for another month. This "cooling" period allows both professionals to gain something. The prosecutor gets more punishment. The defense attorney gets some rehabilitation for his client. But the main party—the Cuban man—needlessly loses more time in confinement.

This scenario is very common in American courtrooms. It is a classic example of adversary justice at work. Notice, however, the missing pieces. The victim was not involved in any of the courtroom proceedings. Nor was he mentioned in any of the deliberations. His injury was minor and no one thought to ask him what sentence he would like to see imposed. No one asked if the victim and offender wanted to get together to work things out for themselves. The criminal justice system seemed satisfied with the case's outcome, even though it eventually paid for the cost of two attorneys' time and the price of five months' imprisonment.

## Case Study 2: Prisoner Receives Treatment Long After Need Dissipates

Every once in a while a sheriff or warden says that the jail or prison they manage is so overcrowded that they simply would not accept any more prisoners. These correctional administrators know they do not have any legal authority to do this sort of thing; but frequently they are exasperated, and they are seeking dramatic ways to make a point to the general public that they are in dire straits. One remedy to this situation would be to have courts delay the start of a prisoner's term of incarceration until space is available. When space becomes available, then the prisoner can begin to serve time. The Dutch do this; those awaiting incarceration are called "walking convicts." It is a method of planning and it seems to work. In the United States, however, such a remedy would catch only derisive comments and political rejection.

In the United States, offenders are forced to go directly to jail or prison even when suitable space is not available. Are they ever forced to participate in treatment options when space in these programs is not available? Recently, a New York prisoner captured the double standard that exists in sentencing practice in this country:

> It is ironic that while I was at liberty on the streets and sought a residential treatment program for my cocaine addiction I was told there was a waiting list for such programs and I should keep in contact with the referral agency each month until a space for me opened up. I responded that I was severely addicted and needed help right at that moment, that I was not sure where I would be from month to month or what bizarre behavior and crimes my addiction would drive me to or whether I would be alive to benefit from any such program in the future. My will to straighten out was strong at that moment, but there was no help available. Now as a prisoner of the state, I am not only given such a residential program—long after the exigencies of my former condition have subsided due to over four years incarceration—but I am compelled to partake of such a program as a requirement of earned eligibility (a form of early release in New York State) certification. (Anonymous, 1990: 1)

## Case Study 3: Town Protests State Plans for Prison

If a town does not want a prison in its backyard, is it being selfish or reactionary? Or can a town raise legitimate planning issues not only about corrections policy but also about town development? The small New England farm community of New Braintree is still fighting a five-year battle to prevent the Commonwealth of Massachusettes from converting an empty school into a medium-security prison. This case is particularly interesting because, except for local and regional support, the town has received only conservative backing from statewide leaders. Liberal leaders have abandoned a "cause" that in other times would be a natural target for their interests.

In the late 1960's, New Braintree residents battled successfully to close a private landfill operation that was dumping pollutants, with no environmental protections, just behind where the commonwealth is now in the process of building a prison. "For the first time in its history," one resident wrote the local paper, "New Braintree is in danger of losing its wholesome country atmosphere" (Immarigeon, 1987: 16). Sometime afterwards, the town also acted to deny a private investor from building a large mobile-home park because it would have exhausted the town's fragile water supply.

With its history of environmental concern, townspeople were reasonably interested in future state plans when the commonwealth began exploring the possibility of converting the empty school into a jail for drunk drivers. Initially, the townspeople were simply looking for assurances that this facility would not grow into something larger, an institution that would overtax local resources. Townspeople were stopped short by state officials who preferred to stonewall them rather than inform them. Townspeople, who knew a great deal about stone walls, began to dig in deep.

When New Braintree residents found out that the commonwealth was planning to build a prison at the school site located squarely in the middle of town, they felt that their worst fears were realized. Their organization and political mobilization increased. State officials became more surly in the dealings with townspeople. At different points, state representatives either dismissed the inquiries of the residents out of hand or they insisted on telling them that they were concerned about things such as diminishing land values, higher crime rates, etc. They in fact were not concerned. The town eventually sued the commonwealth over violations of its own administrative procedures for starting construction projects. The town lost. The commonwealth seized by eminent domain the land on which the empty school rested and then, with guards posted outside, placed a perimeter fence around the site and started to renovate the facility—even though (at this writing) there were no funds available to actually house prisoners in the prison.

## Case Study 4: Prison Furloughs, the Presidential Campaign of 1988, and More Prison Furloughs

Other articles in this volume comment on the Willie Horton affair. Briefly, Willie Horton skipped the Commonwealth of Massachusetts while on furlough release. This highly successful state program was brought into question when Horton violently assaulted a Maryland couple. A local campaign—started by several Andover housewives who wanted to find answers to some of their questions about why Horton was on the streets—escalated into a statewide initiative to abolish furloughs for all first-degree, and eventually second-degree, murder offenders. As in New Braintree, a central factor in the development of this campaign was the intransigence of executive-branch officials to address citizen concerns directly.

In the Bush-Dukakis presidential campaign of 1988, President Bush used the Horton case for his own political ends. Dukakis himself also chose a political approach to the issue. Instead of defending the program—Massachusetts corrections officials were chomping at the bit to show not only that the program was tightly managed but also that it was benefitting offenders and citizens alike—Dukakis decided to avoid discussing it.

In the wake of this debacle, in state after state, furlough programs were watered down or eliminated. Regardless of the efficacy of individual programs, furloughs became politically incorrect and were increasingly defined as unacceptable in and of themselves.

Ironically, in the midst of many states opting to reject the use of conditional-release programs as preparation for full release, support for prerelease still holds credibility for at least some state policymakers. In Virginia, for example, Governor Baliles's Commission on Prison and Jail Overcrowding argued in December 1989 for greater use of work-release and prerelease programs as a method of reducing recidivism. The commission's final report stated: "By gradually providing greater contact and interaction with society, while retaining considerable control of inmate's time and activity, and by enforcing values of work and responsibility, these options may also serve to reduce an offender's likelihood to recidivate" (Ferguson, 1989: 59).

## Case Study 5: Barlinnie Special Unit

The Barlinnie Special Unit, established in February 1973, is a Scottish prison unit that houses seriously disruptive prisoners. These are men the prison officials have determined are unmanageable elsewhere in the system.

Various factors may have brought about these changes, but several particular items are noteworthy. Prisoners in the Barlinnie Special Unit are given advantages not afforded other prisoners in the system. Especially, prisoners at Barlinnie are allowed a participatory role in deciding routines within the facility. Community meetings are set up to determine appropriate and inappropriate behavior. Early in the experiment, prisoners decided that all forms of violence were unacceptable. Prisoners are encouraged by prison officers and other staff to verbalize aggressive feelings. Prisoners are held accountable for their behavior as well as the behavior of their fellow inmates. Among the benefits they experience are frequent visits from family and friends, the right to work or not work, and the ability to cook their own food.

The only empirical investigation of this unit to date examined the prison and post-unit behavior of the twenty-five men who had participated in this regime by November 1986. Seventy-two percent of this small population had one or more murder or attempted murder convictions. Sixty percent were serving life sentences. Only three prisoners were serving terms of less than ten years. Results of this study suggest that "transfer to the Special Unit results in a significant and substantial change in the number of physical assaults and the level of disruptive behavior within the unit and following transfer from the unit" (Cooke, 1989; Whitmore, 1987).

In this essay, I have used the term criminology in very broad terms. One could reasonably argue that I have included political scientists, corrections administrators, sociologists, criminal justice practitioners, and many others under a single, unclearly defined rubric. This is true. But criminology as a field has become disoriented. Polsky's assaults on the field more than twenty years ago are still applicable today. Criminologists are more ready to see what officially processed data say than to find out what criminals, victims, policymakers, and administrators themselves have to say. Criminology's growth, therefore, does not necessarily mean its expansion as a field of inquiry.

Contemporary criminologists are still too rarely out in the field. Peacemaking criminologists, however, are susceptible to the same mistakes that traditional, radical, and other criminologists have made. In particular, we can become more enmeshed in our visions than in people's real life experiences.

## REFERENCES

Anonymous. 1990. "A.S.A.T.A. Prisoner's Perspective." *Justicia* (February): 1–4.
Bureau of Justice Statistics. 1988. *Historical Statistics in State and Federal Institutions, Yearend 1925–1986.* Washington, D.C.: U.S. Department of Justice.
———. 1989. "Prisoners in 1988." Washington, D.C.: U.S. Department of Justice.
———. 1990. "Census of Local Jails, 1988." Washington, D.C.: U.S. Department of Justice.
Christie, Nils. 1977. "Conflict as Property." *The British Journal of Criminology* 17 (1): 1–14.
Cooke, David J. 1989. "Containing Violent Prisoners: An Analysis of the Barline Special Unit." *British Journal of Criminology* 29 (2): 129–43.
Federal Judicial Center. 1989. "Impact of Drug Related Criminal Activity on the Federal Judiciary." Washington, D.C.: Federal Judicial Center.
Ferguson, Jack H. 1989. *1989 Commission on Prison and Jail Overcrowding.* Richmond: Governor of Virginia.
Haapanen, Rudy A. 1990. *Selective Incapacitation and the Serious Offender: A Longitudinal Study of Criminal Career Patterns.* New York: Springer-Verlag.
Immarigeon, Russ. 1987. "Saving a Small Town." *Boston Herald Sunday Magazine,* 5 July, 4–7, 16–18.
Loggins, Kirk. 1989. "DA Asking Judge to Bar Strobels' Death Penalty View." *The Tennessean,* 7 September.
McDonald, Douglas Corry. 1986. *Punishment without Walls: Community Service Sentences in New York City.* New Brunswick, N.J.: Rutgers University Press.
Mauer, Marc. 1990. *Young Black Men and the Criminal Justice System: A Growing National Problem.* Washington, D.C.: The Sentencing Project.
Pollack, Jack Harrison. 1972. *Dr. Sam: An American Tragedy.* Chicago: Henry Regnery Company.

Polsky, Ned. 1967. *Hustlers, Beats, and Others*. Chicago: Aldine.
Schneider, Anne L. 1990. *Deterrence and Juvenile Crime: Results from a National Policy Experiment*. New York: Springer-Verlag.
Sulton, Anne Thomas. 1990. *Inner-City Crime Control: Can Community Institutions Contribute?* Washington, D.C. Police Foundation.
Wallis, Jim. 1983. *Revive Us Again: A Sojourner's Story*. Nashville: Abingdon Press.
Whitmore, Peter B. 1987. "Barlinnie Special Unit: An Insider's View." In Anthony E. Bottoms and Roy Light (eds.), *Problems of Long-Term Imprisonment*. Brookfield, Vt.: Gower Publishing Company.
Williams, Terry. 1989. *The Cocaine Kids: The Inside Story of a Teenage Drug Ring*. Reading, Mass.: Addison-Wesley Publishing Company, Inc.

# P A R T
# T W O

# Feminist Peacemaking Traditions and Women's Experience

*M. Kay Harris*

---

## S I X

# Moving into the New Millennium

### *Toward a Feminist Vision of Justice*

The approach of the twenty-first century tends to inspire future-oriented thinking. With respect to criminal justice policies and practices, it is disheartening to imagine what the future holds if the current course is maintained. This article argues that moving toward a significantly brighter future requires abandoning conventional frames of thought and practice and adopting a fundamentally different way of thinking and acting. The focus is on exploring what the next century might look like if a feminist orientation toward justice were embraced.

## Conventional Approaches to Criminal Justice Reform

Most proposals for change in policies directed at crime and criminal justice concerns fall within one of two types. Many proposals are developed from a systems-improvement orientation. This orientation takes for granted existing political, economic, and social institutional structures as well as the values that undergird them, assuming that they are proper or, at least, unlikely to be changed within the foreseeable future. Reform proposals generated from a systems-improvement perspective characteristically are framed as if crime were primarily an individual problem best addressed through more effective or more rigorous enforcement of the law. Thus, they focus on trying to find better means of identifying and intervening with individual offenders and of strengthening and increasing the efficiency of existing criminal justice institutions and agencies.

The other familiar way of framing reform proposals involves a broader crime-prevention/social-reform orientation. Reformers with this orientation emphasize the social and economic underpinnings of crime and the need to address them through policies and programs focused on families, neighborhoods, schools, and other institutions. In recent years, advocates of a prevention/social-reform approach have moved considerably beyond the ameliorative strategies of·the 1960s toward proposals for more sweeping social and economic reconstruction, stressing that policies aimed at strengthening families and communities need to be coupled with efforts to promote economic development and full employment.[1] Although they do not excuse individual offenders or ignore possible advances to be made by improving criminal justice practices, these reformers tend to view interventions with identified offenders more as last lines of defense than as promising avenues for reducing crime.

There are significant problems associated with trying to formulate recommendations for the future on the basis of either of these two conventional ways of framing the issues. The systems-improvement approach has the apparent advantage of offering advances in the identification, classification, control, or treatment of offenders and in the operation, efficiency, effectiveness, or accountability of criminal justice agencies. However, this approach ignores the political, economic, and social aspects of crime and has little or nothing to contribute to the overall, long-term development of social life. Furthermore, it offers, at best, only limited, short-term utility in dealing with crime.

Many systems-improvement advocates promise dramatic increases in crime control if only sanctions can be made more frightening, severe, certain, restrictive, or corrective. But such promises lack both theoretical and scientific support. Current knowledge provides little basis for expecting significant reductions in crime through reshaping policies in hopes of achieving greater deterrent, incapacitative, or rehabilitative effects. Other systems-improvement supporters concede that notable increases in domestic tranquility are unlikely to be secured at the hands of crime-control agents, but argue that until more fundamental changes have been made in social relations and policies, there is no alternative but to continue working toward whatever marginal increases in efficiency, effectiveness, or evenhandedness might be achievable.

To date, prevention/social-reform advocates have made scant progress in overcoming the notion that their proposals already have been tried in the War on Poverty/Great Society era and found ineffective. Many who agree that the measures championed by these advocates are prerequisites for dramatic shifts in crime and social relations doubt that the massive changes envisioned are economically or politically feasible. Furthermore, prevention/social-reform advocates have had little influence in ongoing criminal justice policy debates because their recommendations concerning interim criminal justice policies have been meager and uncompelling. They have offered little more than echoes of systems-improvement reform proposals, accompanied by warnings about the risk of simply reinforcing the underclass and increasing the social divisions in society if repressive measures targeted on offenders are pursued too zealously.

Thus, despite widespread dissatisfaction with the results of current policies and their burgeoning costs, it is difficult to find grounds for believing that the future toward which we are heading holds much promise of anything beyond more of the same. If current trends hold the key to seeing what the criminal justice system will look like in the next few decades, we face the prospect of maintaining a punishment system of awesome proportions without being able to expect much relief from the problems it supposedly exists to address.

## Current Trends

Over the last decade, approximately 200,000 beds have been added to state and federal prisons across the United States, increasing their confinement capacity by more than two thirds (Bureau of Justice, *Bulletin* 1986; 1987). In a recent random sample survey of local jails, officials in 44 percent reported that facility construction or renovation was underway (Bureau of Justice, *Compendium* 1986). And despite the fact that at least 22 states had to make spending cuts in their fiscal-1987 budgets and 23 passed or considered increases in gasoline, cigarette, or sales taxes, a review of spending proposals by governors across the country suggests that substantial additional increases in institutional networks are being planned (Peirce, 1987).

If the average annual growth during the 1980s in the number of federal and state prisoners continues through 1987, the nation's prison population will have tripled over the last fifteen years.[2] But the recent expansion of the punishment sector of the system has not been limited to prisons and jails. At the most drastic extreme, there are now more than 1,800 persons awaiting state execution across the United States (*Lifelines* 1987). At the other end of the penal spectrum, the adult probation population has been increasing even more rapidly in the 1980s than the incarcerated population.

As of the end of 1985, the total population under the control or supervision of the penal system has risen to 2.9 million persons, representing fully 3 percent of the adult males in the country.[3] An estimated one in every ten black adult men was on probation or parole or in prison or jail.[4] The proportion of Hispanics under penal control is not fully reported, but the number of Hispanics in the nation's prisons reportedly has doubled since 1980, a rate of growth that could result in Hispanics constituting one-fourth of the incarcerated population by the year 2000 (Woestendiek, 1987).

Not only have the numbers and mix of persons under penal control been changing, but the nature of that experience has been changing as well. For those incarcerated, such forces as overcrowding, de-emphasis on programs and services, mandatory sentences, and other reflections of an increasingly harsh orientation toward offenders have worked to offset gains made through litigation and other efforts to improve the situation of those confined. Idleness, demoralization, isolation, danger, and despair permeate the prison and the jail.

For those subject to nonincarcerative penalties, levels of intervention and control, demands for obedience, and the sheer weight of conditions never have been heavier. As of the spring of 1986, intensive supervision programs were operating in at least 29 states, and an additional eight states reportedly were planning to implement such programs in the near future (Byrne, 1986). Typical requirements in such programs include not only increased contact and surveillance, but also: mandatory restitution and community service obligations; payment of supervision fees, court and attorney costs, and fines; curfews and periods of house arrest; urinalyses, blood tests, and other warrantless searches; and even periods of incarceration. The latest popular addition to these and other nonincarcerative sanctions is electronic surveillance. There are now more than 45 programs in 20 states using electronic devices to monitor the whereabouts of convicted offenders or defendants awaiting trial (Yost, 1987).

## Iron Bars and Velvet Ankle Bracelets: The Need for New Approaches

Many common citizens, scientists, futurists, and leaders are predicting that the next 25 years portend a series of collisions, conflicts, and catastrophes. Recent world experience with increasing interpersonal violence, terrorism, social injustice, and inequality—along with such growing problems as overpopulation, ecological damage, resource shortages, the continuing arms buildup, and the specter of nuclear holocaust—has generated heightened awareness of the need to think globally and much more creatively about the future. To begin to adequately envision what criminal justice should look like in the year 2012, we need to step outside of the traditional ways of framing the issues and consider approaches that transcend not only conventional criminological and political lines, but also national and cultural boundaries and other limiting habits of the mind. At the same time, "focusing on the principles and tools of punishment" can help us "understand the most prevalent way we have chosen to relate to each other in the twentieth century" (Sullivan, 1980: 14).

Just as the velvet glove only thinly cushions and screens the iron fist, it is important to recognize that "the velvet ankle bracelet" and its ostensibly more benign brethren "community penalties" are facilitating the diffusion and expansion of social control through the penal system and augmenting the iron bars rather than replacing them. With little fanfare or protest, we have come to accept levels of state intrusiveness into individual lives, remarkable in a society that professes to value liberty. The nature and direction of the bulk of changes undertaken in the criminal justice system in recent years are such that the most pressing tasks in the coming years necessarily will involve damage control. Massive efforts will need to be devoted to coping with, undoing, and trying to ameliorate the effects of the present blind, determined push for greater punishment and control. Pursuing a more hopeful future requires exploration of alternative visions of justice.

A number of movements, models, and philosophies in various stages of development have arisen in response to the critical problems of the day, ranging from those focused on world order or global transformation to pacificism or peace studies, reconciliation, humanism, feminism, and a wide range of other visions of a better world and a better future. While few have been focused on criminal justice problems, they offer a rich resource for a fundamental rethinking of our approach to crime and justice.

In seeking to escape the fetters on my own thinking and aspirations for the future, I have found much of value in a number of orientations. Indeed, I have been struck by the common themes that emerge across a variety of perspectives with a wide range of labels. This suggests the possibility of articulating a new direction for the future by drawing from many orientations and avoiding attaching any label to the values and concepts discussed. Such an approach would help prevent burdening the ideas with unnecessary baggage or losing the attention of people put off by the images any particular school of thought raises in their minds. For me, however, the most significant breakthroughs in thought and hope came when I began to apply myself to considering what the values and principles of one particular orientation—feminism—would mean in rethinking crime and justice issues. Thus, the rest of this article shares ideas that emerged from this path of exploration, a path that continues to hold increasing meaning and inspiration for me and one that I hope will attract interest from a variety of people who otherwise might not devote attention to these issues. At the same time, it is my hope that people who find themselves more attuned to other orientations, or who see feminism differently, may find it useful to consider how the values described fit with theirs and what a future based on these values might look like, no matter what terms are used to describe it.

## Values Central to a Feminist Future

Feminism offers and is a set of values, beliefs, and experiences—a consciousness, a way of looking at the world. Feminism should be seen not merely as a prescription for granting rights to women, but as a far broader vision. There are a number of varying strands within feminist thought, but there are some core values that transcend the differences. Among the key tenets of feminism are three simple beliefs—that all people have equal value as human beings, that harmony and felicity are more important than power and possession, and that the personal is the political (French, 1985).

Feminist insistence on equality in sexual, racial, economic, and all other types of relations stems from recognition that all humans are equally tied to the human condition, equally deserving of respect for their personhood, and equally worthy of survival and of access to those things that make life worth living. This is not to argue that all people are identical. Indeed, feminism places great emphasis on the value of difference and diversity, holding that different people should receive not identical treatment, but identical consideration. Feminists are concerned not simply with equal opportunities or equal entitlements within existing social structures, but with creating a different set of structures and relations that are not only nonsexist, but also are nonracist and economically just.

In the feminist view, felicity and harmony are regarded as the highest values. Viewing all people as part of a network on whose continuation we all depend, feminists stress the themes of caring, sharing, nurturing, and loving. This contrasts sharply with an orientation that values power and control above all else. Where the central goal is power, power conceived as "power over" or control, people and things are not viewed as ends in themselves but as instruments for the furtherance of power. Hierarchical institutions and structures are established both to clarify power rankings and to maintain them. The resulting stratifications create levels of superiority and inferiority, which carry differential status, legitimacy, and access to resources and other benefits. Such divisions and exclusions engender resentment and revolt in various forms, which then are used to justify greater control.

Feminists believe that it is impossible to realize humane goals and create humane structures in a society that values power above all else. A major part of feminist effort involves better identifying and confronting characteristics and values—the political, social, economic, and cultural structures and ideologies—that are not conducive to the full realization of the human potential in individuals or society, the negative values that underlie stereotypes, rationalize discrimination and oppression, and serve only to support the groups in power.

Feminist belief is that the personal is the political, which means that core values must be lived and acted upon in both public and private arenas. Thus, feminists reject the tendency to offer one set of values to guide interactions in the private and personal realms and another set of values to govern interactions in the public worlds of politics and power. Empathy, compassion, and the loving, healthy, person-oriented values must be valued and affirmed not only in the family and the home but also in the halls where public policymaking, diplomacy, and politics are practiced.

## Modes of Moral Reasoning

Research on moral development and on how people construe moral choices has identified two orientations that reflect significant differences (Gilligan, 1982; April 1982). In a *rights/justice* orientation, morality is conceived as being tied to respect for rules. It is a mode of reasoning that reflects the imagery of hierarchy, a hierarchy of values and a hierarchy of power. It assumes a world comprised of separate individuals whose claims and interests fundamentally conflict and in which infringements on an individual's rights can be controlled or redressed through rational and objective means deducible from logic and rules.

In a *care/response* orientation, morality is conceived contextually and in terms of a network of interpersonal relationships and connection. This mode of reasoning reflects the imagery of a web, a nonhierarchal network of affiliation and mutuality. It assumes a world of interdependence and care among people, a world in which conflicts and injuries can best be responded to by a process of ongoing communication and involvement that considers the needs, interests, and motivations of all involved.

At present, the care/response mode, with its emphasis on contextuality, relationship, and the human consequences of choices and actions, tends to be viewed as representing a lesser stage of moral development—less broadly applicable—than the rights/justice orientation, with its emphasis on standards, rights, and duties (Scharf et al., 1981: 413). This tendency to contrast and rank the differing modes of reasoning has limited the moral and conceptual repertoires with which problems are approached in the worlds of government, science, and world power. Devotion to peacekeeping and nonviolent conflict resolution often are dismissed as irrelevant or less important than devotion to the "rules of the game" or abstract notions of rights and responsibilities. Thus, the potential contributions of a care/response orientation to dealing constructively with the major global crises of security, justice, and equity have hardly begun to be tapped (Reardon, 1985: 89–90).

There is a need for a massive infusion of the values associated with the care/response mode of reasoning into a wide range of contexts from which they have been excluded almost entirely. It would be a mistake, however, to try to simply substitute a care/response orientation for one focused on justice and rights. Especially at present, when there are such vast differences in power among people, we are not in a position to trust that the interests of the less powerful will be protected in the absence of rules designed to insure that protection.

Studies by Carol Gilligan suggest that although most people can and do understand and use both modes of reasoning, they tend to focus more on one or the other in confronting moral issues.[5] In her research, the mode of reasoning around which people tended to center was associated with gender. Men were more likely to employ a rights/justice orientation and women were more likely to reflect a care/response orientation, although responses from women were more mixed than those for men. Given the capacities of both men and women to use both modes of moral reasoning, and because there is no reason to believe that differing emphases or priorities in moral reasoning are inate or biological (see Bleier, 1984), we have an opportunity to explore more fully the contributions each can make to resolving moral dilemmas of all kinds.

Thus, the challenge involves searching for a more complete vision of justice and morality, a vision that encompasses concern for process and outcomes, as well as principles and rules, and for feelings and relationships, as well as logic and rationality. We need to labor to find ways of more fully integrating abstract notions of justice and rights with contextual notions of caring and relationship in both public (political) and private (personal) realms.

## The Criminal Justice Context: The Dilemmas of Defense and Protection

The criminal justice system provides a clear picture of the challenges ahead. In the criminal justice arena, there is no attempt to disguise the fact that the goal and purpose of the system is power/control. The stated goal is control of crime and criminals, but it is widely recognized that the criminal justice system serves to achieve social control functions more generally. Law is an embodiment of power arrangements: it specifies a set of norms to be followed—an order—and also provides the basis for securing that order coercive force. Coercive force is seen as the ultimate and the most effective mechanism for social defense. And once the order to be protected and preserved is in place, little attention is given to whether the social system to be defended is just or serves human ends.

It is important to bear in mind that penal sanctions, like crimes, are intended harms. "The violent, punishing acts of the state . . . are of the same genre as the violent acts of individuals. In each instance the acts reflect an attempt to monopolize human interaction to control another person as if he or she were a commodity" (Sullivan, 1980). Those who set themselves up as beyond reproach define *the criminal* as less than fully human. Without such objectification, the routine practice of subjecting human beings to calculated pain infliction, degradation, domination, banishment, and execution clearly would be regarded as intolerable.

Feminist analysis of the war system can be applied to the criminal justice system; the civil war in which we are engaged—the war on crime—is the domestic equivalent of the international war system. One has only to attend any budget hearing at which increased appropriations are being sought for war efforts—whether labeled as in defense of criminals, communists, or other enemies—to realize that the rationales and the rhetoric are the same. The ideologies of deterrence and retaliation; the hierarchal, militaristic structures and institutions; the incessant demand for more and greater weaponry, technology, and fighting forces; the sense of urgency and willingness to sacrifice other important interests to the cause; the tendency to dehumanize and objectify those defined as foes; and the belief in coercive force as the most effective means of obtaining security—all of these and other features characteristic of both domestic and international so-called defense systems suggest not just similarity, but identity. People concerned with international peace need to recognize that supporting the "war on crime" is supporting the very establishment, ideology, structures, and morality against which they have been struggling.

We are caught in a truly vicious cycle. Existing structures, institutions, relations, and values create the problems that we then turn around and ask them to solve—or rather, control—using the very same structures, forms, and values, which in turn leads to more problems and greater demand for control. We all want to be protected from those who would violate our houses, our persons, and our general welfare and safety; but the protections we are offered tend to reinforce the divisions and distorted relations in society and to exacerbate the conditions that create much of the need for such protections. The complicated issues surrounding self-defense—whether in an immediate personal sense (as when confronted by a would-be rapist or other attacker), in a penal policy sense (as when deciding how to deal with known assaulters), or in even broader terms (as when confronted by powers and structures that seem bound to destroy us)—vividly illuminate the dilemma.

Sally Miller Gearhart vividly describes the dilemma surrounding trying to work toward the future we dream of while living in the present world by citing a science fiction work, *Rule Golden,* in which Damon Knight wipes violence from the face of the earth by having every agent feel in his/her own body and physical action what she/he delivers. "Kick a dog and feel the boot in your own rib: commit murder and die yourself. Similarly, stroking another in love results in the physical feeling of being lovingly stroked" (Gearhart, 1982: 266). Such imagery highlights:

> . . . the necessary connection between *empathy* and *nonviolence*, [the fact that] *objectification* is the necessary, if not sufficient component of any violent act. Thinking of myself as separate from another entity makes it possible for me to "do to" that entity things I would not "do to" myself. But if I see all things as myself, or empathize with all other things, then to hurt them is to do damage to me. . . .
>
> But empaths don't live if the Rule Golden is not in effect. Our world belongs to those who can objectify . . . and if I want to protect myself from them I learn to objectify and fight back in self-defense. I seem bound to choose between being violent and being victimized. Or I live a schizophrenic existence in which my values are at war with my actions because I must keep a constant shield of protectiveness (objectification) intact over my real self,

over my empathy or my identification with others; the longer I keep up the shield the thicker it gets and the less empathic I am with those around me. So every second of protecting myself from violence makes me objectify more and ensures that I am more and more capable of doing violence myself. I am caught always in the violence-victim trap. (Gearhart, 1982: 266)

Clearly, the standard approach in recent years has been to seek more control—more prisons, more time in confinement for more people, more surveillance and restriction of those not confined. Our willingness to cede greater and greater power to the institutions of social control is a reflection of a desperate society. But "no amount of police, laws, courts, judges, prisons, mental hospitals, psychiatrists, and social workers can create a society with relative harmony. The most institutions can do is to impose the appearance of relative harmony . . ." (French, 1985). To the extent that we acquiesce to continuing escalation of social controls, agents of the state, we reduce correspondingly the prospects for the kind of safety that cannot be achieved through force.

It will not be easy to escape from the cycle in which we find ourselves swirling. Legitimate concerns for safety and protection pose difficult dilemmas for feminists. How can we meet the serious and all-too-real need for protection against violence without violating our peaceful values and aspirations? How can we respond effectively to people who inflict injury and hardship on others without employing the same script and the same means that they do? How can we satisfy immediate needs for safety without elevating those needs over the need to recreate the morality, relations, and conception of justice in our society?

As Marilyn French has put it, "The major problem facing feminists can be easily summed up: there is no clear right way to move" (French, 1985). However, we can expand the conceptual and practical possibilities for change in criminal justice by re-examining our assumptions and expectations.

[W]e need to begin picturing the new order in our minds, fantasying it, playing with possibilities. . . . An exercise in first stepping into a desired future in imagination, then consciously elaborating the structures needed to maintain it, and finally imagining the future history that would get us there, is a very liberating experience for people who feel trapped in an unyielding present. . . . [S]ocieties move toward what they image. If we remain frozen in the present as we have done since World War II, society stagnates. Imaging the future gives us action ideas for the present. (Boulding, 1987)

## Emerging Guides for the Future

Identifying values central to feminist belief does not automatically yield a specific formula for better responding to crime and other conflicts, or for resolving the dilemmas with which we are confronted. Indeed, feminists do not see the best way of moving toward a more positive future as involving primarily analytic and abstract efforts to describe specific structures and processes. Such approaches almost never encompass any explicit element of human relations or affective, emotional content, and few display any cultural dimension (Reardon, 1985: 89–90). "We need theory and feeling as rough guides on which to build a next step and only a next step: flexible, responsive emotional theory capable of adjusting to human needs and desires when these create contradictions" (Reardon, 1985: 89–90).

Feminist values do offer, however, some beginning guides for approaching the future. A key standard to help in making choices is to ask: What kinds of behavior and responses will achieve the goal of the greatest possible harmony? Thus, the task is not to discover how to eradicate crime, but to discover how to behave as befits our values and desire for harmony.

Acceptance of human equality and recognition of the interdependence of all people requires rejection of several current common tendencies. We need to struggle against the tendency toward objectification, of talking and thinking about crime and criminals as if they were distinct entities in themselves. We also need to reject the idea that those who cause injury or harm to others should suffer severance of the common bonds of respect and concern that bind members of a community. We should relinquish the notion that it is acceptable to try to "get rid of" another person, whether through execution, banishment, or caging away people about whom we do not care. We should no longer pretend that conflicts can be resolved by the pounding of a gavel or the locking of a cell door.

A feminist orientation leads to greater awareness of the role and responsibility of society, not just the individual, in development of conflict. This suggests that individuals, groups, and societies need to accept greater responsibility for preventing and reducing those conditions, values, and structures that produce and support violence and strife. Removing the idea of power from its central position is key here, and this requires continually challenging actions, practices, and assumptions that glorify power, control, and domination, as well as developing more felicitous alternatives.

Commitment to the principle of equality means striving for interactions that are participatory, democratic, cooperative, and inclusive, characteristics that are incompatible with hierarchy, stratification, and centralized decision making. Thus, rules, which often are substituted for sensitive, respectful engagement of persons in cooperative problem solving, should not be regarded as sacrosanct. And because people learn from the nature of the processes in which they participate, as well as from the objectives of those processes, we should give greater attention to what the process teaches and how it is experienced.

It may be difficult to imagine how some conflicts could be resolved amicably. Especially while we are in the process of transition, we have to contend with all of the effects that our present structures, values, and stratifications have had on people. Thus, we are unlikely to reach soon a stage in which we can expect never to feel the need to resort to exercising control over another person. But we can greatly reduce our current reliance on repressive measures, and we should aim to move continually in the direction of imposing fewer coercive restraints on other people.

Indeed, we need to question and rethink the entire basis of the punishment system. Virtually all discussion of change begins and ends with the premise that punishment must take place. All of the existing institutions and structures—the criminal law, the criminal-processing system, the prisons—are assumed. We allow ourselves only to entertain debates about rearrangements and reallocations within those powerfully constraining givens. We swing among the traditional, tired philosophies of punishment as the weight of the inadequacies of one propels us to turn to another. We swing between attempting *to do something with lawbreakers*—changing, controlling, or making an example of them—and simply striving *to dole out a just measure of pain*. The sterility of the debates and the disturbing ways they are played out in practice underscore the need to explore alternative visions. We need to step back to reconsider whether or not we should punish, not just to argue about how to punish.

We may remain convinced that something is needed to serve the declaratory function of the criminal law, something that tells us what is not to be done. We may conclude that there is a need for some sort of process that holds people accountable for their wrongful actions. We may not be able to think of ways to completely eliminate restraints on people who have done harmful things. But we should not simply assume that we cannot develop better ways to satisfy these and other important interests as we try to create our desired future.

While we are in the transition process, and where we continue to feel that it is necessary to exercise power over other people, we should honor more completely certain familiar principles that are often stated but seldom fully realized. Resort to the restriction of liberty, whether of movement, of association, or of other personal choices, should be clearly recognized as an evil. Whenever it is argued that it is a necessary evil, there should be a strong, nonroutine burden of establishing such necessity. And where it is accepted that some restriction is demonstrably necessary, every effort should be made to utilize the least drastic means that will satisfy the need established. Thus, we should approach restriction and control of others with trepidation, restraint, caution, and care.

In addition, we should recognize that the more we restrict an individual's chances and choices, the greater is the responsibility we assume for protecting that person and preserving his or her personhood. We should no longer accept the routine deprivations of privacy, healthful surroundings, contacts, and opportunities to exercise choice and preference that we have come to treat as standard concomitants of restriction of liberty. Such deprivations are not only unnecessary but also offensive to our values and destructive to all involved.

These principles make it apparent that we should abandon imprisonment, at least in anything like the way we have come to accept the meaning of that word. There is no excuse for continuing to utilize the dungeons of the past nor for replicating the assumptions, ideology, and values that have created their newer, shinier, more modern brethren, those even now being constructed on an astonishing scale. While tiers of human cages stacked one upon another are the most apparently repugnant form, all institutions erected for the purpose of congregate confinement need to be acknowledged as anachronisms of a less felicitous time.

How should we deal with people who demonstrate that, at least for a time, they cannot live peacefully among us unrestrained? Although the answers to that question are not entirely clear, feminist values suggest that we should move toward conceiving restriction of liberty as having less to do with buildings, structures, and walls and more to do with human contacts and relations. Few if any creatures are dangerous to all other creatures at all times, especially to those with whom they are directly and closely connected on an ongoing basis. Perhaps we can fashion some variant of jury duty and of citizens standing up for one another in the tradition of John Augustus, in which a small group of citizens would be asked to assume responsibility for maintaining one person safely for a period of time. A range of compassionate, constructive, and caring arrangements needs to be created. And we should not allow the most difficult cases to stand in the way of more rapidly evolving, better approaches for the rest.

At the same time, we need to stop thinking about issues related to how best to respond to those who caused harm as if they were totally separate from, or in competition with, issues related to how best to respond to those who have been harmed. There is not a fixed quantity of compassion and care, or even of rights, that will be diminished for those who have been victimized as they are extended to those who victimized them.

Many of these ideas may seem foreign, naive, or beyond our abilities. If they seem foreign, that may be because the ideas of care, community, and mutuality seem foreign. If these dreams for the future seem naive or out of reach, that may be because we have lost confidence in our capacity to choose, to recreate relations, and to realign priorities. It may be tempting to conclude that no efforts in the directions suggested here will be worthwhile, that nothing can be done until everything can be done, that no one can confront crime humanely until everyone is willing to do so. And it is true that we will never approach making such a vision reality if we focus only on issues of criminal justice. Our energies must be focused on the full panoply of global-peace and social-justice issues. But when we turn our attentions to criminal justice, we should choose and act according to the values and aims we seek more generally and not to increase division, alienation, bitterness, and despair. And every day, we should try to act as we believe would be the best way to act—not just in the future, but in the present.

What is advocated here is radical, but hardly novel. It simply echoes themes that have been heard through the ages, if rarely lived fully. We should refuse to return evil with evil. Although we have enemies, we should seek to forgive, reconcile, and heal. We should strive to find within ourselves outrageous love, the kind of love that extends even to those it is easiest to fear and hate. Love frequently is seen as having little relevance outside the personal realm. Yet the power ethic has failed to serve human happiness. To have a harmonious society, we must act in ways designed to increase harmony, not to further fragment, repress, and control. There is no other way. The means and the end are the same.

## NOTES

1. A collection of articles that well exemplifies this approach is assembled in a book designed to provide an update of the report of the National Commission on the Causes and Prevention of Violence, commonly referred to as the Eisenhower Commission after its chair, Milton S. Eisenhower. See *American Violence and Public Policy: An Update of the National Commission on the Causes and Prevention of Violence*, ed. Lynn A. Curtis (New Haven: Yale University Press, 1985).

2. In 1972, there were 196,183 state and federal prisoners. See Mullen et al., *American Prisons and Jails, Vol. I: Summary and Policy Implications of a National Survey* (Washington, D.C.: U.S. Department of Justice, 1980). At year-end 1986, there were 546,659 state and federal prisoners according to the Bureau of Justice *Statistics Bulletin*, "Prisoners in 1986," May 1987. If the average annual growth rate of the 1980s of 8.8 percent continues through 1987, the total will exceed 590,000 state and federal prisoners.

3. These numbers are reported only for males, presumably because men make up most of the correctional population. See "Criminal Justice Newsletter," 16 January 1987, p. 5. It should be noted, however, that the number of women in state prisons has more than doubled since 1981, up to 26,610 from 11,212 in 1981; and the rate of growth in the population of female prisoners has been faster in each of those years than that of male prisoners. See Peter Applebome, "Women in U.S. Prisons: Fast-Rising Population," *New York Times*, 15 June 1981.

4. Given that nearly 87 percent of the adult correctional population was male and 34 percent was black, an estimated 850,000 adult black men were under correctional control at year-end 1985 according to the Bureau of Justice *Statistics Bulletin*, "Probation and Parole 1985," January 1987. The Census Bureau estimates that there were 8,820,000 black adult male residents in the United States at midyear 1985. See U.S. Bureau of the Census, *Estimates of the Population of the United States, by Age, Sex, and Race: 1980 to 1986*, Current Population Reports, Population Estimates and Projections, ser. P-25, no. 1000, p. 24. At year-end 1985, there were approximately 1,617,492 white adult males under some form of correctional control, out of approximately 72,780,000 white adult male residents in the United States, representing a correctional control rate for white adult males of about 1 in 45. Neither the Bureau of Justice nor the Census Bureau data report separate figures for Hispanics or other specific ethnic or racial groups.

5. This discussion is based on an oral presentation by Carol Gilligan at the Community College of Philadelphia in April 1984. See also other Gilligan works cited in this article.

An earlier version of this essay appeared in the 1987 fall-winter volume of the *Prison Journal* of the Pennsylvania Prison Society, a special edition on "The Future of Corrections," pages 27 to 28.

## REFERENCES

Bleier, Ruth. 1984. *Science and Gender: A Critique of Biology and its Theories on Women*, New York: Pergamon Press.

Boulding, Elise. 1987. "Warriors and Saints: Dilemmas in the History of Men, Women, and War." Paper presented at the International Symposium on Women and the Military System, Siuntio Baths, Finland, 22–25 January. On file with author.

Bryne, James M. 1986. "The Control Controversy: A Preliminary Examination of Intensive Probation Supervision Programs in the United States." *Federal Probation* 50: 9.

Bureau of Justice. 1986. "Prisoners in 1985." *Statistics Bulletin* (June).

———. 1986. "Prisoners in 1986." *Corrections Compendium*, November-December 1986.

French, Marilyn. 1985. *Beyond Power: On Women, Men and Morals*. New York: Summit Books.

Gearhart, Sally Miller. 1982. "The Future—if There Is One—Is Female." In Pam McAllister (ed.), *Reweaving the Web of Life: Feminism and Nonviolence*. Philadelphia: New Society Pub.

Gilligan, Carol. 1982. *In a Different Voice: Psychological Theory and Women's Development*. Cambridge: Harvard University Press.

———. 1982. "New Maps of Development: New Visions of Maturity." *American Journal of Orthopsychiatry* (April).

*Lifelines*. Newsletter of the National Coalition Against the Death Penalty. January-February 1987, p. 8.

Pierce, Neal. 1987. "Prisons Are Proving Costly to the States." *The Philadelphia Inquirer*, p. 11a.

Reardon, Betty A. 1985. *Sexism and the War System*. New York: Teachers College Press, Columbia University.

Scharf, Peter, Lawrence Kohlberg, and Joseph Hickey. 1981. "Ideology and Correctional Intervention: The Creation of a Just Prison Community." In Peter C. Kratcoski (ed.), *Correctional Counseling and Treatment*. Monterey, Calif.: Duxbury.

Sullivan, Dennis. 1980. *The Mask of Love: Corrections in America (Toward a Mutual Aid Alternative)*. Port Washington, N.Y.: Kennikat Press.

Woestendiek, John. 1987. "An Influx of Hispanics is Challenging the Prisons." *The Philadelphia Inquirer*, p. 1a.

Yost, Pete. 1987. "Electronic Alternative to Prison is in 20 States." *The Philadelphia Inquirer*, p. 5a.

*Susan Caringella-MacDonald and
Drew Humphries*

---

S  E  V  E  N

# Sexual Assault, Women, and the Community

*Organizing to Prevent Sexual Violence*

The late 1970s witnessed sweeping changes in rape laws as state legislatures sought to improve reporting, do away with "double victimization" (Holmstrom and Burgess, 1978), and increase rape convictions. Virtually all states enacted sexual assault statutes designed to increase the number of cases moving through the courts and to reduce disparities in the disposition of rape and other assault cases. The sexual assault statutes so rapidly and broadly enacted had, however, mixed results (Caringella-MacDonald, 1988). In some criminal justice areas and some jurisdictions, the statutes made significant progress. Some research has found, for instance, that under reform, rates of arrest have been enhanced (Marsh, Geist, and Caplan, 1982), that prosecutorial filing of felony charges has increased (Polk, 1985a; Marsh, Geist, and Caplan, 1982), that conviction rates have grown (Marsh, Geist, and Caplan, 1982) and that parallels in the rates of charging, plea bargaining, and attrition in sexual and other violent assault cases have materialized (Caringella-MacDonald, 1985; Galvin and Polk, 1983). Research has additionally found that victims' experiences have improved under rape reform statutes (Marsh, Geist, and Caplan, 1982).

On the other hand, research has simultaneously shown that police unfounding rates have not diminished (Marsh, Geist, and Caplan, 1982), that police clearance rates have failed to increase (Polk, 1985), that prosecutor case filing has remained unaltered (Chappell, 1982; Loh, 1981), that victim credibility is still discriminatorily questioned (Caringella-MacDonald, 1985; Marsh, Geist and Caplan, 1982; Chappell, 1982), and that conviction rates have not grown as reformers had envisioned (Polk, 1985; Loh, 1981; Clark and Buchner, 1982). Similarly, research has found that sexual assault cases are reduced (through charging and plea bargaining decisions) to a greater extent than other violent assaults (Caringella-MacDonald, 1985). Moreover, discriminatory requirements, such as those relating to corroboration, resistance, and the admissibility of past sexual activity/evidence, have been found to persist in a de facto manner despite legal reforms (Caringella-MacDonald, 1985; Clark and Buchner, 1982; Osborne, 1984; Hayler, 1985; Marsh, Geist, and Caplan, 1982; Bienen, 1983).

This research on the effects of rape-reform statutes is limited in its focus on criminal justice. In addressing how the criminal justice system processes rape cases, research has neglected the effects of statutory reform on individuals at risk for rape and on communities facing the problem of sexual violence. Reforms were inspired by efforts to increase the protections afforded to individual women. Yet, the issue of how sexual assault reforms have impacted on individual-level options as women think through the problem of rape remain unexamined. And though new legal statutes may hold the potential for speeding apprehension and processing of felons, it is reasonable to ask whether advances in processing have improved the quality of options open to communities as they attempt to deal with sexual violence. Relatedly, it is important to ask what community-level efforts can now contribute, given both the successes and the failures of legislative reforms.

In concentrating on these overlooked areas, this essay argues that statutory reform has not altered the range of coping options open to women, nor has it significantly improved the quality of options open to communities confronted with the problem of rape. Communitywide organizing against sexual violence, however, holds promise for further progress in abating the problems of sexual assault.

In suggesting that community organizing can at least partially compensate for the shortcomings for statutory reform, the essay concentrates on three questions: First, what choices are now available to individuals at risk for sexual violence? Second, how can communities organize to address the problems of sexual violence against women? And third, what are the prospects for community contributions in the areas of individual options, legislative failures, and protections for women?

The discussion of individual options is based on conversations among college-age women and on surveys of attitudes toward rape. The discussion of community options is based on a program designed to redress sexual assault in Kalamazoo, Michigan. Using the decisions many women may make about rape to identify some previous unconsidered limits of statutory reform, the essay suggests that communities faced with rape crises would do well to follow the course which the Kalamazoo Task Force on Violence is now charting.

## The Victim and Sexual Assault

From a woman's position, the problem of rape can be broken down into a series of questions: "What precautions am I willing to take to prevent rape?" "What would I do if confronted by a rapist?" "If raped, what am I going to do?" "Do I report the rape, and if so, do I then prosecute the assailant?" In listing these questions, we are not suggesting that all women ask themselves all the questions or even that the process of working them out yields similar answers. For some women, the rape question may revolve around changing lifestyles and prevention; for others it may involve resistance and prosecution; and for some the fear surrounding rape may preclude coming to terms with any of these questions. What we are suggesting is that the range of options open to women is limited by conceptions of safety, by rape myths and de facto legal practices, and even by the theory on which statutory reform has rested.

### PREVENTION

The first question a woman may ask is, "What do I do to prevent rape?" It is a matter of personal safety, and it comes down to a woman thinking about the precautions she might take. But precautions, despite reform, are still a matter of fear and faith. Sexual assault is still the crime women most fear.[1] And an old, but suspect *quid pro quo* suggests that compliance with sex-roles stereotypes will decrease the chances of sexual assault. It is not surprising that the precautionary measures that come most readily to mind are the ones that confine women to traditional roles. They include limiting the time, place, and circumstances of social activities. They involve suppressing details of speech, dress, comportment, or lifestyle that could be construed as sexually provocative. Legal reforms clearly did not broaden the range of precautionary measures available to women concerned about rape. Statutory revisions then failed when considering prevention options. Other newly recommended group activities and self-defense tactics have emerged to supplement older warnings against going out alone at night and strangers. But even so, prevention is still the responsibility of the individual at risk, and it unfortunately continues to take shape as repressive restrictions on personal conduct and expression.

### RESISTANCE

At some point a woman may wonder what she would do if confronted by a rapist. She may ask, "Would I try to stop the assault or would I submit?" The resistance question does not yield simple answers, but recent findings help clarify some of the confusion. Data show that alertness to the risk of sexual assault and resistance can stop an attack. Elias (1985) reports that when women resist they have a greater chance of stopping the rape although they face a higher probability of being injured. Bart and O'Brien (1985) confirm these findings on resistance—the greater the number of resistance measures employed, the greater the probability of stopping the rape—but they show that resistance is not necessarily correlated with injury. A Canadian study (Quinsey and Upfold, 1985) confirms the effectiveness of yelling and screaming in halting sexual assaults, and like the Bart and O'Brien investigation, it finds no connection between injury and resistance. This research suggests that positive associations found in earlier studies reflect a different causal order, namely that injuries lead to resistance rather than the other way around.

In considering the resistance question, it is well to note that the utilities of resisting may go beyond halting sexual assault. For instance, Elias (1985) reports an Israeli study that urges resistance on the grounds that it may be the only factor which preserves a sense of personal dignity during the rape as well as through its aftermath, including through legal proceedings. Additionally, resisting may be crucial to preserving a sense of control and may lessen the victim's sense of guilt about her role in the assault.

Although recent research can help clear up misconceptions about resistance and injury, rape myths and de facto legal practices still make resistance the test of whether a crime has occurred. Consider, for instance, the "rape is impossible" myth. This myth refers to the claim that any woman can stop a sexual attack. It has significant implications for the standards defining consent and force under the older rape and now newer sexual assault statutes. Under older rape statutes, the standards functioned according to the following logic: If, as the myth claims, a woman can stop an attack, then overt acts of resistance are the measure of both force and nonconsent, the elements which define the crime. But if a woman who can stop an attack takes no overt action to resist, then her *acquiescence* justifies the conclusion that the man used no force, the women consented, and hence, no crime took place.

Unfortunately, this rape myth and the importance it places on resistance ignore the central feature of the rape situation, namely, the paralyzing effects of violence, weapons, surprise, or male physical strength on the victim's capacity to resist. Taking the incapacitating effects of male violence on women into account, it is easy to see that consent cannot be inferred from the failure of a victim to resist. And yet resistance, despite statutory reform, is still taken as an indicator of nonconsent (Osborne, 1984). It is a factor used to determine the merits of rape charges, and it continues to make resistance the precondition for exercising one's legal rights.

Though this discussion might lead someone to see resistance as a more attractive option, recent survey evidence reemphasizes the complexity of the question. A Rhode Island survey reports that junior high school students agreed that some circumstances justify male force.[2] Spending money on a date, already having had sexual intercourse, dating over a period of six months, and marriage were said to make it acceptable for a man to force a woman to kiss him or to force her to have sexual intercourse with him. The persistence of such beliefs in dating situations has implications for the resistance question. Seemingly, these young men expect a return on their investment of time and money in a date. Judging from the survey finding, many young women also feel the investment obligates them to fulfill their date's sexual expectations. What can we say about this *bargain?* Once a young woman accepts a date, she apparently consents to the bargain. Should she then attempt to renege, her protest may be seen as violating the basic agreement and then serve to justify the use of force. Under these circumstances, resistance then may be translated into provocation and operate to escalate the attack.

Injury, personal dignity, legal rights, and sexual bargaining are all elements which have to be taken into account in deciding whether and when to resist. The resistance question is difficult to answer definitively because of the above discussed factors but additionally because, although reform statutes have removed resistance requirements in many states, they have not fundamentally altered the choices available to women in rape situations. Put differently, in addition to the criminal justice discretion, which can and has operated to preclude the realization of reform objectives, are an array of practical difficulties, myths, and other obstacles that confront women dealing with sexual violence. Because of this, expansion of the options open to women in this and other areas is by no means guaranteed by even full implementation of the reform objectives.

## REPORTING AND PROSECUTION

Another set of questions that a woman may contemplate concerns reporting an incident and pursuing a case through the criminal justice system. What we know about the decisions affecting whether a victim reports sexual assault suggests that myths about women's complicity in sexual assault and about false accusations are powerful deterrents to reporting. Similarly, persecution rather than prosecution through the criminal justice system hinder victim reports. When women question their role in or responsibility for an assault, they tend to avoid defining it as rape or worry about themselves being put on trial rather than the assailants. This is true for both "classic rape" (Williams, 1984) as well as date and acquaintance rape (Shortland and Goldstein, 1983). And so, despite procedures which were hoped to make it easier for rape victims to come forward, the under-reporting of rape remains inordinate.

For those who do report, the next question concerns whether to follow through with legal charges. What do we know about the women who press charges? Lizotte (1985) maintains that pursuing rape is unique enough to require a separate explanation. Elias (1985) also contends that women who press charges are unusual, and he goes on to report that those who press charges are motivated either by a strong sense of revenge or by the belief that their efforts will help protect other women.

In deciding the prosecution question, some consideration has to be given to outcome. The prospects of winning, i.e., seeing the assailant behind bars, may have increased under reform statutes in some jurisdictions (Marsh, Geist, and Caplan, 1982) but are nonetheless low and unlikely to increase much further. As is generally known, and shown by Galvin and Polk (1983) in California, most case attrition occurs before filing a rape case as a felony. Hereafter, evidence (Polk, 1985b) shows that the rate of custodial sentences imposed on rape defendants is comparable to that of robbery and assault.[3] Approximately 6 percent of the convicted rapists receive custodial sentences. Since the 6 percent figure meets the standard of comparability, it is taken as a sign of success. But viewed by a victim thinking about pressing charges, the 6 percent figure means that most will not see their assailants incarcerated. Moreover, victims' chances are not likely to increase even with renewed efforts in this direction. The incarceration of 6 out of 100 rape defendants seems to have exhausted the criminal justice system's capacity and priority.

In deciding whether to press charges, attention also has to be given to personal costs. There are any number of victim characteristics that are not legally relevant to rape, but which help define the victim as "good" or "legitimate" in conventional terms. The victim's behavior and lifestyle before and during the assault affect the likelihood of prosecution (Chandler and Toney, 1981; Meyers and LaFree, 1982). Evidence of drinking, drug use, or sexual activity before or during a marriage has lead jurors to doubt defendant's guilt in cases where consent is at issue (LaFree and Reskin, 1985). Emotional expressiveness of the victim affects outcomes; emotionally controlled victims are seen as having less aversion to the rape (Calhoun et al., 1981). Factors relating to the issue of consent can be raised on cross-examination, and this means that any woman whose case comes to trial puts her character up for public examination. Moreover, although many states have even strictly limited the admissibility of character/reputation evidence through legal reforms, victims continue to be questioned about past sexual and other activity to impugn their character. Reforms here simply facilitate sustained objections when victims are on the stand (Caringella-MacDonald, 1985). The costs of exposure and prolongation of indignities can be extremely, even prohibitively high. It is not surprising then that women who urge prosecution are unusual. They have weighed the minimal prospects of seeing their assailants behind bars against the potentially high personal costs of prosecution and have still decided to proceed legally. Without a strong sense of revenge or altruism, it is difficult to see how women might decide in favor of prosecution.

So far we have argued that the range of options open to women coping with rape are limited by misconceptions about safety, myths about sexual compliance, resistance, etc., and by legal practices. But even if we could demystify safety, correct rape myths, and bring court officers to heel, flaws in the theory behind statutory reform run counter to efforts to increase these options.

Originally, proponents of reform sought to redress difficulties and discrimination in criminal justice processing and thereby both improve victims' experiences and enhance the conviction rate for rape defendants. In addition to nonreporting and the inordinate levels of attrition owing to police clearance and unfounding rates, prosecutorial denials, and court acquittals, is the problem of the theory underlying reforms. A key to understanding the limited impact of rape reforms on options for women confronted with rape lies with the unexamined connection between protection and punishment. The point of increasing conviction rates in rape cases has been to incapacitate convicted rape defendants and to deter would-be rapists, thereby making the community safer to women.

It is difficult, however, to take incapacitation seriously when available evidence (Polk, 1985b) indicates the criminal justice system incarcerate only about 6 percent of the convicted rape defendants, and when we know that most all inmates will be released back into society at some point. It is noteworthy that increasing prison terms for rapists to meet incapacitation objectives is also problematic for victims. As many reform advocates recognized (Snider, 1985) longer sentences make juries reticent to convict. Incapacitation, then, at best, has a minuscule capacity to increase protections for women.

It is equally difficult to take general deterrence seriously. Deterrence theory rests on the simplistic and frequently erroneous notion that rapists will rationally calculate the costs of punishments, like prison, and then decide against committing a rape on this basis. General deterrence holds, for example, that in restraining the would-be rapist from committing sexual assault, punishment will provide greater protection for women. Currie (1985), in summarizing critics of general deterrence, points to the absence of evidence confirming a connection between punishments and crimes of violence. He argues that deterrence can be more effectively practiced informally, within communities, subcultures, and personal networks where the personal costs of violating norms that would protect women can more readily be made prohibitively high. But even if punishment were actually to deter the would-be rapist, the limited capacity of the criminal justice system to impose custodial sentences would still minimize increases in protection for women.

In effect, punishing rapists cannot increase protection for women, nor can statutory reforms which make convictions easier to secure expand the coping options open to women. Once incapacitation and deterrence are distinguished and clarified, the punishment of rapists is bound to disappoint expectations about individual protection. Punishing rapists may seem a salient concern when discussing both legal reform and individual options, but it recedes when the framework is broadened to consider community level options to address sexual violence.

## The Community and Sexual Assault

Most communities have resources for mobilizing against sexual violence, and in many instances communities have provided some compensation for scant protections provided women. Communitywide Take-Back-the-Night marches, for instance, have helped in offering an alternative to fear and to the self-imposed repressions that allegedly promise safety. Rape crisis centers are additional and clear examples of how communities can mount supplemental assistance for victims. Direct support through counseling and hand holding through criminal justice processes provide dire services to victims. Many sexual-assault centers attempt community education as well, to dispel myths and disseminate reliable information about rape. Communities additionally, through rape-crisis programs or otherwise, have devised watchdog programs where citizens monitor the treatment of victims through the criminal justice system. Monitoring processes can help to sensitize police and criminal justice personnel to victims' needs.

The development and maintenance of such programs demonstrate that communities have and can impact on particular needs relating to sexual violence and its victims. But community efforts have been either fragmented, one-shots—like Take-Back-the-Night marches or awareness weeks—or relegated to a single agency—like a rape-crisis center—that is perpetually understaffed and underfunded given the burden of responsibility for sexual assault education, prevention, protection, and so on. Simply put, efforts to coordinate programs on a communitywide basis have not materialized. Such efforts would, however, have high payoffs.

Since communities can clearly contribute different kinds of solutions, organizing communitywide efforts holds the promise of more effective and efficient resolutions. A community united against sexual violence can pick up where legal reforms have left off, i.e., can potentially help to rectify criminal justice processing problems and begin to enhance individual level options through community-based education and prevention programs.[4]

In Kalamazoo, Michigan, a newly formed task force has taken steps to mobilize the community against violence. The task force is significant in going against the trend to rely on criminal justice solutions, and it opens up new ways of preventing violence, especially against women. Although it is too early to evaluate the task force's accomplishments, it is not too early to draw some lessons from its formative stages. As citizens in other communities raise questions about the adequacy of conventional responses to the problem of rape, the lessons learned in Kalamazoo will come to have greater generality.

## A Tragedy in Kalamazoo

In November of 1987, a student at Western Michigan University (WMU) was found dead. She had been raped and murdered. She had been jogging around the track at WMU's athletic field early one evening when she was approached, attacked, and killed by a stranger. In responding to the student's death, newspapers, television, and the university all reinforced debilitating fears about rape. The public discussion which followed warned women about strangers and told them to avoid going out alone at night. It intimated that women who disregard these warnings would be considered complicit in sexual attacks. It supported the perception that rape is an isolated problem amenable to security and criminal justice solutions. The public discussion justified the standard security measures taken by the university, i.e., improving campus lighting and increasing dormitory security. It legitimated the police search for an assailant as the appropriate solution to the incident.

The response dictated by public discourse distressed many. Some faculty and community leaders began to define the responses as part of the problem. In reinforcing rape myths and in relying on shortsighted solutions, the official response had ignored the pervasiveness of the problem and the depth of concern about it. The rape-murder and the official and public reactions all jointly served to trigger an atypical and promising response.

Women Committed to Stopping Violence Against Women and Men Committed to Stopping Violence Against Women were among the first WMU groups to react. Women and men met separately to talk about fears, experiences, and needs. The Women's Advisory Committee, another WMU group, brought individuals and groups together to discuss building a peaceful campus community. A campus-based organization, Grassroots, brought University groups together with representatives from Kalamazoo community agencies. And finally, a communitywide group, already organized to plan Kalamazoo's first Take-Back-the-Night march and rally, stood ready to respond to this trigger event.

These different coalitions suffered some significant threats to their survival during the initial crisis period. The demands of multiple organizations, each with a growing list of projects, had within weeks following the tragedy dissipated volunteers' energy. Fewer and fewer people showed up at meetings, and those who did turn up took on less and less responsibility. The fact that so many groups were doing something diffused responsibility and relieved the community of having to do anything. And what is more, the police solved the case. The police had arrested a suspect, and the media soon dropped its coverage of the case. A returning sense of security replaced the fear that had earlier galvanized the community. The problem of sexual assault was on the verge of being forgotten as a tragic but containable, isolated incident.

## HOW THE KALAMAZOO TASK FORCE ON VIOLENCE ORGANIZED

What enabled the coalitions to weather the threats to their survival were the successful efforts of some few people to organize against sexual violence on a communitywide basis. Coalition organizers learned that the Kalamazoo County Criminal Justice Commission had made education and prevention a priority for 1988. Taking advantage of a community group priority, organizers submitted a proposal to the commission for a countywide *Task Force on Violence against Women*. Organizers called upon the commission to spearhead the task force effort, to appoint representatives from the community, and to support the effort to reduce violence against women.

Official recognition, crucial for the task force's ability to get anything done, came however at a price. The commission wanted the task force to address the broader problem of violence and to avoid the exclusive interest in violence against women which community-university coalitions had proposed. In the end, the commission charged the task force with looking into violence but conceded that violence against women would receive special attention.

The commission set the task force term for two years and appointed 23 members. Members are drawn from the groups and coalitions that had initially reacted to the rape-murder: the commission and criminal justice agencies, social- and crisis-service agencies, elementary and higher education, the media, religious organizations, and state and local government.

The task force benefited immediately from the commission's official recognition. First, the task force solved problems that had limited the effectiveness of the original coalitions. Focusing the efforts of fragmented groups had proved difficult, but a single task force improves coordination. Getting volunteers to do what they say they would had also been a problem, but it goes without saying that official appointment improves accountability among members. By the same token, getting sexual assault recognized as a public problem had been dependent on a dramatic event that the media could exploit. The fact that the public and media are invited to task force meetings helps to increase the visibility of problem. Visibility and the ongoing character of the task force's work make it more difficult for the community, including the media, to dismiss sexual assault as an isolated set of incidents. Finally, official recognition can carry funding advantages. If/when government officials allocate funds to the task force, they can be seen as responsible to the electorate.

A second set of immediate benefits derive from the task force's composition. The task force began with a broad rather than narrow constituency. Appointing criminal justice personnel, social-service workers, and community organizers to the task force made it difficult for anyone to dismiss the task force as simply a feminist or radical group (Note, 1983). The inclusion of males, many of whom hold powerful positions in the community, brought considerable clout to an issue that has been seen as a "women's issue" (Note, 1983). Furthermore, appointing members with differing views enriched planning and coordination. To plan effectively, the task force requires a comprehensive and multisided definition of the problem. But this is not enough. To coordinate effectively, the task force needs an understanding of how government and community agencies can cooperate to address the problem. Understanding similarities in the problems as well as in its causes and solutions gives people who may be scattered among different and frequently competing government agencies a framework for cooperative action (Poole and Theilen, 1985).

And finally, the task force, in drawing on a wide constituency, profits from its ties to community resources. The "weak ties" (Granovetter, 1973) that characterize the relationships between appointed task force members also link members of different groups closer together and counteract previous separation and fragmentation (Granovetter, 1973; Shapiro, 1987). Weak ties can also encourage the membership to exploit their stronger ties to coworkers and colleagues. Task force members, in remaining tied to their jobs or program, are in a strong position to mobilize the status and expertise of professionals or the time and commitment of coworkers and volunteers on behalf of the task force (Wharton, 1987). In other words, as members involve more and more people in task force work, they mobilize resources necessary for formulating and especially for implementing recommendations (Brilliant, 1986).

## PROBLEMS AND PROSPECTS IN KALAMAZOO

It would be naive to assume that the task force is without problems. Its size and composition are obvious trouble spots. The 23 members which make up the Task Force are too many for an efficient work process. But then, 23 people are too few to represent a community with a population of a quarter million. Complicating matters further, the bias toward persons with agency affiliations leaves the task force open to criticism of elitism (Brilliant; 1986). But more to the point, the opposing views and priorities of members lead inevitably to tension and conflict.

Criminal justice practitioners vie with social workers and progressives over whether the focus and priority ought to be offenders and punishment, victims and supportive intervention, or community and prevention. Some task force members have defined the problem narrowly as psychological and verbal violence, others widely as economic violence and militarism, and still others are worried about drugs. In like fashion, strategy suggestions range from addressing sexist language in the schools to making domestic assault a felony or to redressing economic and political inequalities. Similarly, some members want to target curriculum and educational institutions while others are more interested in the family, the church, self-esteem, or social structures.

In order to resolve its differences, the task force must compromise. In its initial sorting stages, the task force has not resolved differences in an all-or-nothing manner. It has, instead, opted for middle-ground compromise such as according secondary status to violence against women. Even middle-ground compromises of this sort are not free of risk however. Such compromises often relegate causes and other features of a problem that are the most important to finding solutions to the background. And because doing something is preferable to doing nothing, compromises frequently bear results too watered down to matter. Many may be placated or co-opted because of the appeal of the group doing something (Bellah, 1985), but this raises a question about whether actions that appease so many are too compromised to justify the effort.

In spite of such problems, the guidelines adopted by the task force give reason for optimism. Forged in creative, often frustrating sessions, guidelines call for a broad understanding of the problem and hence, broadly based resolutions. They envision an authority both to recommend and to participate in implementing recommendations and an organization designed for accomplishing its tasks.

Task force guidelines give priority to the broadest understanding of the problems of violence, icluding violence against women. They call for a full delineation of the types of violence and related interventions. In this fashion, they give significance to the way culture, for example, contributed to violence as well as to violent forms of behavior. They rest on the principle that a macroscopic rather than microscopic view of violence provides the best grounding for making recommendation. The task force's guidelines are that violence and violence against women are rooted in economic, social, and sexual inequality. By emphasizing root causes of violence, guidelines add weight to the belief that the task force can avoid compromising its original objectives while settling disputes arising from difference in member priorities. A broad rather than myopic view of violence can facilitate continuity in approaches and enhance the potential effectiveness of interventions.

In addition, guidelines call for implementing as well as recommending solutions to the problem of violence. The task force has taken an unusual and exemplary step in planning on implementation. Because the task force intends to follow its recommendations through implementation, there are grounds for believing that recommendations will be heeded. There is no need to belabor the point that recommendations made by countless commissions have gone unheeded. Perhaps because implementation is a concern, guidelines on strategies and program development are pragmatic. They are consistent with the tendency for groups to narrow projects in order to carry them out. They encourage beginning with short-term projects which promise tangible success and then moving on to longer-term, more ambitious projects. As the list of successes increases incrementally, the task force's legitimacy and claims on governmental and community resources ought also to grow.

And lastly, guidelines call for subcommittees which enable a few people to accomplish much. Guidelines, by breaking the work of the task force into specialized topics, encourage members to enlist outsiders with relevant skills and resources in the task of identifying and solving problems. In this fashion, subcommittees expand their own constituencies and assist in making the task force's claim on representing the community more credible. Moreover, the guidelines increase efficiency through a division of labor and ensure coordination. In requiring each subcommittee to meet, study, and make recommendations, they give the task force authority to assess subcommittee recommendations, approving them or suggesting alternatives, prior to developing a plan for implementation. While maximizing the task force's constituency, guidelines still provide for centrally coordinated planning and implementation.

A broad understanding of violence, pragmatic attention to implementing recommendations, and an efficient and responsive organization—these are among the reasons for believing that the Kalamazoo task force may be able to alter the options open to women in responding to sexual violence. And yet much remains to be seen. Though middle-ground compromises have to date resolved conflicts, the long term effects of compromise remain to be seen.

Although changes in the laws on sexual violence have fallen short of reformers' expectations, it is worth remembering that reforms have equipped women with new and necessary tools with which to mobilize the criminal justice system against sexual violence. In arguing that these laws have not expanded the options open to persons at risk for rape, we are not therefore repudiating reform. Rather, we are suggesting that community efforts such as those undertaken by the Kalamazoo Task Force on Violence against Women can now supplement the legal reforms of the past. Although we have delineated more actual and potential drawbacks to such community-based efforts, the prospects for overcoming certain reform failures and for providing women greater options and protections are encouraging.

Organizing communities to deal with the problem of sexual assault has been made easier by the 1970s rape-reform movement. Legal reforms were facilitating because they enhanced awareness about the extent and the causes of sexual violence. Shared knowledge and conceptions regarding the pervasiveness of sexual assault and the violent rather than strictly sexual nature of attacks make cooperative work and strategic intervention more viable undertakings. Legal reforms, then, have opened up some options and possibilities to communities, as is in evidence in the Kalamazoo task force.

What the community can contribute in the area of sexual violence and protection is potentially great. For instance, communities can organize watchdog groups and even research groups to monitor and then insist on implementation that mirrors reform objectives to correct for the failures discovered with the criminal justice processing of sexual assault cases. But perhaps more importantly, the community can offer an alternative response to law and order, criminal justice solutions. Communities are filled with experts from a variety of fields that can come together to bring a variety of perspectives to bear on the problem. Such wide experience and perspective can yield creative and broad strategies not only to protect victims, but additionally to reduce sexual violence by beginning to address deeper-level causes. Education and myth dispelling in early school years, for example, has been a frequent part of the dialogue about rape prevention on the Kalamazoo task force. In-service training for criminal justice officials, as well as the media, have also been targeted for intervention in Kalamazoo. Groups working together in this fashion to bring about attitude change hold the potential for opening up new options for women.

Individual options can be enhanced by improved criminal justice processes in terms of reporting and prosecuting choices; but significantly, they can also be enhanced by communitywide posturing regarding the violence directed against women. If a community is educated, aware and knowledgeable, and intolerant of sexual violence, informal social networks may grow increasingly effective in deterring the abuse of women. And, as Currie (1985) has argued, informal social controls have perhaps greater impact than formal sanctioning on deterring individual behaviors. If any sexual violence at all is prevented in a community, women have no options in making choices about rape prevention and protection.

Yet, just as reform fell short of stated goals, so too can we anticipate that communities will fall short in fully resolving the problems of sexual violence. Addressing root causes may become easier to discuss, but it is unlikely that it has become any easier to intervene at such depths. However, a community organized against sexual violence is one that is intolerant of the gender attitudes and practices that place women and others at risk. This means that the community level is important as it can both empower and transcend individual and legal avenues of recourse. As the legal reform movement paved an easier road for communities, perhaps community efforts can pave an easier path for individual women.

## NOTES

1. The fear of rape may account for women's greater fear of crime, i.e., the possibility of rape makes the consequences of crime more serious for women than for men (Hindelang, 1978: 48–59). The fear of rape is striking among young urban women (Warr, 1985), but more comprehensive research (Oretega and Myles, 1987) shows that age, gender, and race interact so that some groups are in double and triple jeopardy.

2. The Rhode Island survey was reported by Associated Press and reprinted by Ann Landers, "Students' Views on Rape, A Shock to Baffled Reader," *Philadelphia*

*Inquirer,* July 17, 1988. Some 1,700 sixth to ninth graders who attended a Rhode Island Rape Crisis Center's assault-awareness program at schools across the state were polled. The results are presumably from the pretest rather than the post-test.

3. In California, court fillings have increased, but the probability of conviction has remained the same though a general trend toward institutional sentences coincides with the custodial sentencing rate for rapists (Polk, 1985a).

4. We wish to thank Dorie Klein for making the point that victims may be more interested in civil than in criminal litigation and that community programs need to be made aware of such interests. Community efforts could be made responsive to citizen views that some proponents of statutory reform have tended to overlook, such as interests in collecting damages through civil processes. Victims may seek, for example, to recover from the costs of medical treatment and the loss of income due to time away from work. They may seek legal remedies for employers who discriminatorily discharge persons victimized by sexual assault. Or they may want to use the law to force employers and business owners to take steps ensuring safety and security.

## REFERENCES

Bart, Pauline, and Patricia H. O'Brien. 1985. *Stopping Rape: Successful Survival Strategies.* New York: Pergamon Press.
Bellah, Robert. 1985. "Populism and Individualism." *Social Policy* (Fall) 30: 33.
Bienen, Leigh. 1983. "Rape Reform Legislation in the United States: A Look at Some Practical Effects." *Victimology: An International Journal* 8: 139–51.
Brilliant, Eleanor L. 1986. "Community Planning and Community Problem Solving: Past, Present, and Future." *Social Service Review* (December): 568–89.
Calhoun, Lawrence G., Arnie Cann, James W. Selby, and David L. Magee. 1981. "Victim Emotional Response Effects on Social Reactions to Victims of Rape." *British Journal of Social Psychology* 20(1): 12–21.
Caringella-MacDonald, Susan. 1988. "Parallels and Pitfalls: The Aftermath of Legal Reforms for Sexual Assault, Marital Rape and Domestic Violence Victims." *Journal of Interpersonal Violence* 3(2): 174–89.
————. 1985. "The Comparability in Sexual and Non-sexual Assault Case Treatment: Did Statute Change Meet the Objective?" *Crime & Delinquency* 31 (April): 206–22.
Chandler, Susan Myres, and Martha Toney. 1981. "The Decision and Processing of Rape Victims Through the Criminal Justice System." *California Sociologist* 4: 155–69.
Chappell, Duncan. 1982. "The Impact of Rape Reform Legislation." Paper presented at the American Society of Criminology.
Clark, Toni F., and Deborah Buchner. 1982. "Critical Issues in the Prosecution of Rape: A Cross-jurisdictional Study of 17 United States Cities." Paper presented at the American Society of Criminology, Toronto, Ontario.
Currie, Elliot. 1985. *Confronting Crime: An American Challenge.* New York: Pantheon Books.
Elias, Robert. 1985. *The Politics of Victimization: Victims, Victimology, and Human Rights.* New York: Oxford University Press.
Galvin, Jim, and Kenneth Polk. 1983. "Attrition in Case Processing: Is Rape Uniform?" *Crime and Delinquency* 20 (1): 126–54.
Granovetter, Mark S. 1973. "The Strength of Weak Ties." *American Journal of Sociology* 78 (6): 1360–80.

Hayler, Barbara. 1985. "Rape Shield Legislation: How Much Difference Does it Make?" Paper presented at the Society for the Study of Social Problems, Washington, D.C.

Hindelang, Michael, Michael Gottfredson, and James Garafalo. 1978. *Victims of Personal Crime: An Empirical Foundation for a Theory of Personal Victimization.* Cambridge, Mass.: Ballinger.

Holmstrom, Lynda Lytle, and Ann Wolbert Burgess. 1978. *The Victim of Rape: Institutional Reactions.* New York: Wiley & Sons.

LaFree, Gary D., and Barbara F. Reskin. 1985. "Jurors' Response to Victim's Behavior and Legal Issues in Sexual Assault Trials." *Social Problems* 32: 389–407.

Lizotte, Alan. 1985. "Uniqueness of Rape: Reporting Assaultive Violence to Police." *Crime and Delinquency* 31 (2): 169–90.

Loh, Wallace. 1981. "Q: What has reform of rape legislation wrought? A: Truth in criminal labeling." *Journal of Social Issues* 37: 28–52.

Marsh, Jeanne C., Alison Geist, and Nathan Caplan. 1982. *Rape and the Limits of Law Reform.* Boston: Auburn Publishing House.

Meyers, Martha A., and Gary LaFree. 1982. "Sexual Assault and its Prosecution: A Comparison With Other Crimes." *Journal of Criminal Law & Criminology* 73: 1282–1305.

Note. 1983. "A Battered Women's Network." *Practice Digest* 6 (1): 19–22.

Oretega, Suzanne T., and Jessie L. Myler. 1987. "Race and Gender Effects on Fear of Crime: An Interactive Model with Age." *Criminology* 25: 133–52.

Osborne, Judith A. 1984. "Rape Law Reform: The New Cosmetic for Canadian Women." In C. Schweber and C. Feinman (eds.), *Criminal Justice Politics and Women: The Aftermath of Legally Mandated Change.* New York: Haworth Press.

Polk, Kenneth. 1985. "Rape Reform and Criminal Justice Processing." *Crime & Delinquency* 31 (2): 191–205.

———. 1985b. "A Comparative Analysis of Attrition of Rape Cases." *British Journal of Criminology* 25 (3): 280–84.

Poole, Dennis L., and Gary Theilen. 1985. "Community Planning and Organization in an ERA of Retrenchment: Structural and Educational Approaches to Serving Human Need." *Journal of Social Work Education* 3 (Fall): 16–27.

Quinsey, Vernon L., and Douglas Upfold. 1985. "Rape Completion and Injury as a Function of Female Resistance Strategy." *Canadian Journal of Behavior Science* 17 (1): 40–50.

Shapiro, Ben Zion. 1987. "The Weak-tie Collectivity: A Network Perspective." *Social Work With Groups* 9 (4): 113–25.

Shortland, R. Lance, and Lynne Goldstein. 1983. "Just Because She Doesn't Mean it's Rape: An Experimentally Based Causal Model of the Perception of Rape in Dating Situations." *Social Psychology Quarterly* 45 (3): 220–32.

Snider, Laureen. 1985. "Legal Reform and Social Control: The Dangers of Abolishing Rape." *International Journal of the Sociology of Law* 13: 337–56.

Warr, Mark. 1985. "Fear of Rape Among Urban Women." *Social Problems* 32 (3): 238–50.

Wharton, Carol S. 1987. "Establishing Shelters for Battered Women: Local Manifestation of a Social Movement." *Qualitative Sociology* 10 (2): 146–63.

Williams, Linda S. 1984. "The Classic Rape: When Do Victims Report?" *Social Problems* 31: 459–67.

*Larry L. Tifft and Lyn. Markham*

---

## E I G H T

# Battering Women and Battering Central Americans

*A Peacemaking Synthesis*

Until recently, two pervasive violent crimes, the battering of women and the battering of Central Americans, have remained outside the sphere of crime and criminological inquiry.[1] With a few exceptions (e.g., Enloe, 1983, 1985; Barak, 1986; Straus, 1983; Ferraro and Johnson, 1983; Jordan, 1988), these crimes have been conceptualized and analyzed as entirely separate phenomena. As a consequence, many critical similarities and connections between them have not been adequately explored: (1) The nature of battering women and the nature of battering Central Americans is essentially similar; (2) the social and cultural structural sources of these forms of battering are essentially similar; (3) the social processes and vocabularies for accepting and defending these behaviors are essentially similar; and (4) the issues that need to be addressed in ending violence and initiating peacemaking processes are essentially similar.

To disclose that the nature of these behaviors is similar and also to locate the structural sources of these crimes, in both the accepted economic decision-making and the gender arrangements of social life in the United States, questions the legitimacy of these arrangements and the social order. Recognizing that violence, intimidation, exploitation, dependency, and diminishment have their genesis in the core value and everyday social arrangements of our society is a powerful awakening to the realities of structured suffering and the necessity for both personal and social structural change.

Initiating personal and structural (peacemaking) change processes requires: an understanding of the nature of the behaviors which result in harm and suffering, an examination of the essential structural sources of these behaviors, and an understanding of the social processes and vocabularies for accepting and defending these behaviors and sources. We hope our exploratory synthesis helps to initiate these processes.

## Battering Women

In our most intimate relations we expect love; and we are expected to love, nurture, and empower one another. Yet, violence and violent interaction patterns also are generally accepted and thoroughly woven into the fabric of these intimate relationships. Rates of child abuse, sexual abuse and incest, battering, marital rape, and abuse of elderly parents indicate that violence is a fundamental and pervasive pattern of experience among family members in the United States (Van Hasselt, Morrison, Bellack, and Hersen, 1988; Pagelow, 1988). We are much more likely to be victimized both psychologically and physically by an intimate family member than by a *stranger*.[2] Many U.S. couples experience violence at some point in their marriages, and most parents with children report that violence occurs in the course of "caring" for *their* children (Straus, Gelles, and Steinmetz, 1980). This chilling reality makes it clear that certain patterns of family life actually foster and maintain violence. And this systematic violence can only be understood in the context of a society in which many accept and even encourage violence as a means of resolving conflict, creating dependency, and establishing dominance (Straus, 1973; Hotaling and Sugarman, 1986; Bowker, 1983; Dobash and Dobash, 1979; Flitcraft and Stark, 1978; Horton and Williamson, 1988; Martin, 1981; Schechter, 1982; Brock-Utne, 1985; Wardell, Gillespie, and Leffler, 1983; Pagelow and Johnson, 1988; Breines and Gordon, 1983; Tifft and Sullivan, 1980; Lobel, 1986).

The battering of women by men can consequently be understood in the context wherein men have historically established a tradition of social approval for and, in fact, a legal right to control their property—their wives (Pleck, 1987; Pagelow, 1988a; Schechter, 1982; NiCarthy, 1984, 1986; Taub and Schneider, 1982; Davidson, 1977; Saline, 1984). Though most of the formal laws supporting a husband's right to physically discipline and punish his wife have been abolished in the United States (Saline, 1984: 82), traditions of male entitlement and hierarchy linger. Traditions of entitlement are ceremonially embedded in the promise to "honor and obey." They are concretely rooted in economic and gender structures that diminish and marginalize women. Many men continue these traditions of entitlement, using that amount of force and coercion considered necessary to maintain and establish dominance over their wives or partners (Schechter, 1982; Pagelow and Johnson, 1988; Ptacek, 1988, 1988a).

## RECOGNIZING AND DENYING THE REALITY OF BATTERING WOMEN

The incidence of battering is very difficult to discover primarily because of *dissensus* over what actions, with what meanings, constitute battering.[3] In addition, physical aggression by husbands toward wives is under-reported in both official reports and in victimization surveys. In the United States, national victimization surveys indicate that 15 percent of married couples report one or more acts of physical wife assault during the 12 months prior to the interview (Straus et al., 1980; Straus and Gelles, 1986; Feld and Straus, 1989). Estimates of violence over the course of marital relationships indicate that as many as 50 percent of women are physically assaulted by their husbands (Russell, 1982; Straus et al., 1980; Feld and Straus, 1989; Walker, 1979). Couples who are dating but not living together and couples who are unmarried and living together are believed to experience even higher rates of violence (Morrell, 1984; Stets and Straus, 1989; Pirog-Good and Stets, 1989).

Cross-cultural research on family violence (Campbell, 1985; Levinson, 1988; Straus, 1983a) suggest that there is an association (1) between intra-family violence and societal violence (Steinmetz and Lucca, 1988; Mas-umura, 1979; Lester, 1980; Yllö, Straus, 1983a; Levinson, 1988: 488); (2) between violence in one family relationship and violence in other family relationships (E.g., rare or infrequent wife beating is associated with rare or infrequent physical punishment of children [Levinson, 1983]); (3) between intrafamily violence and specific family organizational arrangements (E.g., child abuse occurs infrequently when there are multiple adult alternative caregivers [Levinson, 1988: 488], and wife battering occurs less frequently when partners share household and financial decision-making [Levinson, 1988: 452; Yllö, 1983; Hornung, McCullough, and Sugimuto, 1981]); and (4) between male dominance patterns maintained through violence and specific cultural circumstances (E.g., wifebeating may be infrequent in cultures wherein other cultural and normative practices function to severely control women and to keep them in an inferior position [Campbell, 1985: 183], and violence undertaken to assert male dominance is frequently precipitated by real or perceived challenges to the batterer's possessions, authority, or control [Dobash and Dobash, 1983]).

Not surprisingly, the battering of women has only recently received public recognition as a social problem in the United States. As this recognition requires a radical restructuring of how intimates and the taken-for-granted structures of the society are perceived, it has been met with considerable resistance. Recognition requires an acknowledgement that the core values and interaction patterns—patterns which form the foundation of our social and cultural structure-hierarchy, gender superiority, property-possession, and domination—foster, reinforce, and regularly *produce the battering of women* (Gil, 1977; Flitcraft and Stark, 1978; Brock-Utne, 1985). An idealized or romantic view of family life; proscriptions against state intervention into the alleged sanctuary of the home; the belief that if wife battering existed, it was either episodic or the result of individual pathology (Pagelow, 1984; Pleck, 1987): these have, as well, impeded the recognition of battering as a public policy issue. But denying that reality and recognition of battering is centrally a reflection of gender politics. Women have most often been the victims of violence, and defining this violence against women as a private matter of "personal trouble" has maintained the subordination of women to men (Stanko, 1988: 86; Lobel, 1986). It is not surprising then that battering has become an issue of public policy largely through the consciousness-raising, organizing, and lobbying efforts of women (Tierney, 1982; Schechter, 1982; Pence, 1988).

### BLAMING WOMEN

Responses to battering taken by persons outside the women's movement have frequently isolated and blamed the victim, mystified the structural sources of battering, and advocated the maintenance of the traditional patriarchal family (Dobash and Dobash, 1988). In fact, some writers and media have even tried to shift the focus of violence within the family to violent women; and they thus create the *reality* that there is a "battered husband syndrome" (Langley and Levy, 1977; Steinmetz, 1978) of a magnitude equal to that of the problem of battered wives.[4] This assertion has been strongly refuted (Pleck, Pleck, Grossman, and Bart, 1978). And most researchers conclude that public policy should primarily focus on battered women because: husbands more frequently both repeat their violence and inflict the more injurious forms of violence (Makepeace, 1983); battered women are infrequently reported as having initiated violence—their violence more often being perceived as fighting back and self-defense (Saunders, 1988); and women's needs for empowerment and safety have been defined as greater.

However, focusing on women and/or blaming women for being victimized has frequently led many psychologists, counselors, social workers, and physicians to respond to battering on an isolating case-by-individual-case basis. Many times these professional transformed "battered" women into "mentally disturbed" women, believing they were battered because either they "had deficiencies" (Flitcraft and Stark, 1978) or they "had asked for it." Other times these professionals defined battering as an interpersonal dispute (with one or both persons to blame) and intervened on the belief that mediation or intervention could restore harmony and preserve the family (Martin, 1981a: 190). Such interventions, however, have failed either to reduce victimization or to generate harmony; for restoring harmony frequently meant adjusting women to their *place* and perpetuating arrangements which foster a continuance of the feelings of injustice, dependency, and repression (McGrath, 1979: 16).

Most states have not legislated domestic violence or mate abuse as a specific criminal offense (Lerman, Livingston, and Jackson, 1983), and decision-making within the criminal justice system have frequently defined these batteries as mutual violence or as private matters.[5] The police have regularly not arrested the assailant, discouraged women from pressing charges, and believed that legal action would either serve no useful purpose or increase the likelihood of future battering (Goolkasian, 1986). Similarly, prosecutors have not pursued prosecution (U.S. Commission on Civil Rights, 1982). As a consequence, the culture of superiority/domination-inferiority/dependency has been officially reinforced (Martin, 1981a: 194), male-dominant power relations normalized, and the battering of women denied both a social structural and political context (Dobash and Dobash, 1988).

The frequently asked question "Why do women stay in violent marriages or relationships?" also reflects a blaming-the-victim approach. Though this question may elicit important information for understanding and counseling women and for creating options and opportunities for them to meet their needs outside these relationships, we should be asking the public policy question: "What is it about marriage and our society that keeps women captive in violent marriages or relationships?" (Martin, 1981a: 195–96). The historically accepted beliefs that women are the property of their husbands and that violence is legitimate certainly contribute to this captivity. But public policies also have made alternative living arrangements for women both insufficiently available and extraordinarily tenuous. Moreover, gender socialization and sex-role expectations are often overwhelming. Incorporated into our culture's philosophy, science, morality, and law, gender inequality is obscured by calling it "natural" or "normal" (Martin, 1981a: 196; Stanko, 1985). Most young persons are socialized to act out sex-based, dominant-subsmissive scripts that significantly contribute to the acceptance of and the experiencing of battering behavior in their intimate relationships.

### INDIVIDUAL AND RELATIONAL SOURCES OF BATTERING

Research designed to discover the social relational context or correlates of battering indicates that "official" battering frequently occurs within a family context of social isolation, a lack of community affiliation, a high degree of stress, an acceptance of traditional sex-role and gender expectations, and low access to outside resources. Many women are literally imprisoned in their households, terrorized with fear for their safety and that of their children. In these isolating and demoralizing circumstances, many women develop an uncertainty as to what is happening to them. Alternately they feel that their situation will improve or that they can do nothing about it. Those women who are battered more frequently and those who stay longer in these violent relationships seem to become convinced that whatever problems anyone in the family is experiencing is their fault. Frequently she tries harder to please, to help, to act as a buffer between her partner and the outside world (Wetzel and Ross, 1983: 425). In time, her focus of life becomes him: her identity, her existence, her fate, her needs become defined in terms of him. Even her attempts to leave seem dominated by the powerful hook that she is needed and is the only one to ever understand him (Wetzel and Ross, 1983: 425).

In the context of social isolation, of partner-identity focus, and of few perceived and real options, many battered women acquiesce. Barriers to escape this physical and psychological imprisonment are entrenched not only by gender socialization, emotional commitment, isolation, and the absence of tenable redefining catalysts (Ferraro and Johnson, 1983; Peterson-Lewis, Turner, and Adams, 1988), but also by the structural circumstances of sexism in the wages market, the denial of prior skills development, inexperience with independence and autonomy, the financial burdens of child care, the emotional burden of depriving her children of a father, and religious condemnation.[6]

Research designed to discover the individual correlates of men who batter women (Hotaling and Sugarman, 1986; Hastings and Hamberger, 1988; Hamberger and Hastings, 1986, 1988a; Dutton, 1988, 1988a) indicate that these men are frequently emotionally dependent in their relationships, express negative emotion through anger, and possess diminished self-esteem (Pagelow, 1984). They frequently hold traditional and sex-stereotyped values, subscribe to rigid sex-role definitions (men as superiors and women as inferiors), and believe that there is societal approval of battering—that women need to be controlled, to be put in their place (Watts and Courtois, 1981: 246). These men are frequently jealous (Bowker, 1983; Davidson, 1978; Dobash and Dobash, 1979), do not recognize the real effects of their violence, have been exposed to violence as a child either as a witness of parental violence or as a victim of child abuse (Browne, 1987; Hamberger and Hastings, 1988; Hotaling and Sugarman, 1986), and often demonstrate severe stress reactions when pressured by work, family, or financial matters (Watts and Courtois, 1981: 248; Sonkin, Martin, and Walker, 1985: 42–46; Newman, 1979: 145–46; Hotaling and Sugarman, 1986). This list of descriptive correlates has, however, been derived from research incapable of determining whether these attributes are antecedents, concomitants, or sequelae of battering. Some research suggests that these correlates may be linked to persons experiencing relational discord, e.g., low self-esteem, low comparative assertiveness, high levels of stress, inadequate and ineffective communication skills (Gondolf, 1985; Roy, 1982; Coleman, 1980; Neidig, Freedman, and Collins, 1985). Stark and Flitcraft

(1988: 307) conclude that these correlates appear to be descriptive of men in the United States generally rather than of men who batter women or violent men specifically.

Furthermore, individual correlates research on the "different and strange" batterer deflects attention from the structural contexts of battering (Pence et al., 1984: 478–79) and extracts these men and their behaviors from their interrelational meaning contexts (Stets, 1988; Berkowitz, 1983; Denzin, 1984, 1984a; Breines and Gordon, 1983; O'Toole and Webster, 1988). This research does not tell us why so much violence by men is directed toward a selected specific target—women—within a specific selected context—the household (Schechter, 1982: 210–11; Goolkasian, 1986: 4; Fagen and Wexler, 1987). Correlates indicating that the batterer was under stress, involved in substance abuse, angry, out of control, emotionally inarticulate, or unable to communicate his needs serve: to deny that many men handle stress and anger in other ways (Schechter, 1982; Ptacek, 1988, 1988a); to remove the batterer from responsibility for his acts (Martin, 1981: 197); and to deny the fact that men who batter know very well what they are choosing to do. So, in fact, do those women who batter their partners. Battered lesbians report that many batterers are both excellent communicators of their needs and skillful "terrorists" who choose violence as a tactic to control and secure partner compliance (Hart, 1986: 24; Lobel, 1986: 5).

## STRUCTURAL SOURCES OF BATTERING

That battering is choice-behavior and that these choices are made in a larger structural context are facts often denied by those whose research has taken an individual or interactional focus. Our structural approach to the sources of battering asserts that battering is behavior chosen within the context of hierarchical power arrangments. The battering of women by men is thus located in specific power, gender, economic, and legal structures.[7] It is directly related to the condition of women wherein equality and dignity, equal access to resources, and equal status have been refused (Flitcraft and Stark, 1978; Taub and Schneider, 1982; Pharr, 1986). According to Gil (1977), battering is directly related to the fact that we have shackled our physical and emotional lives to economic arrangements that foster use-values, profit, and personal accomplishment more than collective accomplishment and whole persons.

Others have concluded that violence against women (e.g., battering and rape) has always been an instrumental foundation of men's power (based on some combination of male physical "superiority" and propensity for aggressiveness) and has been as pervasive as patriarchy itself—unchanging and omnipresent. This perspective, however, seems to imply that women are the victims of a "sick sex" (males). It also seems to perpetuate the falsehood that patriarchy, male dominance, and domination itself are immutable. Furthermore, it leaves us without an exploration of how male violence contributes to the processes of domination and denies the reality that economic, religious, legal, sexual, ideological, and physical mechanisms of men's control of women have operated differently both historically and cross-culturally (Pleck, 1987; McGrath, 1979: 19).

Today, the U.S. family has lost many of its prior activities. It has become a rarefied emotional environment primarily concerned with consumption, "emotional restoration," companionship, and initial child care. Driven by capitalist economic transformation and their own conscious activity, women's experience and identity is no longer fully constrained and privatized within the family. Drawn into the wages market, women have challenged patriarchal dominance and enhanced their legal and economic independence (McGrath, 1979). At the same time, women's waged labor has come into conflict with traditional demands on women's time, attention, and work in the home and has called into question both sex-based divisions of labor and the prerogative of male superiority (Flitcraft and Stark, 1978; McGrath, 1979). Confronted with the failure of social institutions to uphold many forms of male dominance—and experiencing the anxiety of not only different versions of what women ought to do, but different versions of what they themselves ought to do—some men have attempted to reconstitute their authority through battering. The contexts in which battering frequently occurs suggest its social significance, its relationship to sex-based divisions of labor, and the changed situation of the family. Battering incidents frequently occur in places that are isolated from outside intervention (McGrath, 1979: 21–22). They frequently involve conflicting expectations of what women should think and do, and they frequently cluster around "women's work" (e.g., pregnancy, child care, housework, and sexual activity). But what is really at issue is freedom of choice, autonomy, and the chance to develop as fully unique human beings (Pharr, 1986).

Theoretical perspectives and intervention strategies derived from the women's shelter movement provide insight into how some processes of domination operate in our society today. If we are to end violence against women, we will have to work for equality on all fronts (Pharr, 1968: 35) and to understand that inequality between the sexes is culturally generated and perpetuated by both institutional structures and sex-role and gender socialization (Stanko, 1985). Two most significant components of these latter processes are homophobia (fear and hatred of homosexuality) and heterosexism (the use of sexual identity for dominance and privilege) (Pharr, 1986a). Pharr (1986: 35) elaborates:

> From the time we are very young, we are taught that there are different proper behaviors expected from each sex, and though the women's movement has worked hard to raise consciousness about these differences, these behaviors are still enforced in a child's life. We still see young boys encouraged to be directive, self-asserting, career-oriented, and young girls taught to

be accommodating, pleasing, indirect, and family-oriented (with perhaps a career thrown in on the side).

Women are taught that to be directive, self-assertive, career-oriented is not to be womanly, feminine, acceptable to men—and therefore they might lose what little power and privilege that has been granted them. The myth is that for a woman to maintain roles—to be a pleaser, a giver, a nurturer, a supporter who demands little for herself—is to be repaid with a man to provide authority over her life, financial security, decision-making, and direction. To eschew roles is to be cut adrift, to be without order, to be out of proper boundaries, to be someone who gets in the way of the flow of society and the acceptable routined order of relationships. The person who thinks that she should be able to accomplish whatever she is capable of instead of what is expected of her is a threat to society; she has stepped out of line. To know no artificial sense of boundaries gives a heady sense of freedom, a sense of release, of joy, and once one knows it, she has to be intimidated if she's to get back in line again; she must be controlled. She must be taught that she will suffer significant losses if she stays out there in those free, open spaces.

It is not by chance that when children approach puberty and increased sexual awareness that they begin to taunt each other by calling these names: "queer," "faggot," "pervert." Children know what we have taught them, and we have given clear messages that those who deviate from standard expectations are to be made to get back in line. The best controlling tactic at puberty is to be treated as an outsider, to be ostracized at the time when it feels most vital to conform. Those who are different must be made to suffer loss. It is also at puberty that misogyny begins to be more apparent, and girls are pressured to conform to societal norms that do not permit them to realize their full potential.

To be a lesbian is to be perceived as someone who has stepped out of line, who has moved out of sexual/economic dependence on men, who is woman-identified. A lesbian is perceived as someone who can live without men, who is therefore (however illogically) against men. A lesbian is perceived as being outside the acceptable routinized order of things. A lesbian is perceived as someone who has no societal institutions to protect her and who is not privileged to the protection of individual males. A lesbian is perceived as someone who stands in contradiction to the sacrifice heterosexual women have made. A lesbian is perceived as a threat.

Lesbian-baiting is an attempt to control women by calling them lesbians because their behavior is not acceptable, that is, when they are being independent, going their own way, fighting for their rights, demanding equal pay, saying no to violence, being self-assertive, bonding with and loving the company of women, assuming the right to their bodies, insisting upon their own authority, making changes that include them in society's decision-making; lesbian-baiting occurs when women are called lesbians because they have stepped out of line. It is successful when women in their fear jump back in line, dance whatever dance is necessary for acceptability . . .

Homophobia keeps us from stepping out of line, getting into the movement for freedom. . . . It is used to disempower women and keep us vulnerable to violence and abuse. To work against homophobia and heterosexism is to work against violence against all women.

Homophobia, heterosexism, rape and rape myths, battering, and violence against women must be seen as strategies used to disempower women, to control women's freedom. They accompany male socialization patterns which expect men to devalue all that is feminine in themselves, to devalue and objectify the women in their lives, and to eventually marginalize or relegate them to a status of commodity, sex object, violence object, or servant (Leonard, 1983).

Understanding the structural contexts and processes of domination that foster battering underscores our collective involvement in violence-producing values and patterns of interaction. Our social and cultural structure produces violence and must be changed if we are to reduce the amount of suffering in our lives. Working with those who batter and those who are battered must be combined with strategies designed to alter the values and arrangements that foster violent behavior and the acceptance of battering.[8]

### The Essence of Battering

The recent literature on lesbian battering (Hart, 1986; NiCarthy, 1986; Lobel, 1986; Marie, 1984) shatters the sufficiency of the male-character/male-dominance/patriarchy perspectives on violence against women. Battering within intimate lesbian relationships turns our focus to the essence of what is involved in *battering as a social phenomenon*, whether the battering involves persons of the same or different sex.[9] Male dominance is only one form of dominance. Male battering is only one form of battering. The literature on lesbian battering directs our attention to the acceptance of hierarchy and dominance and to the social interaction patterns which enforce these relationships (Lobel, 1986).

This literature, as well, provides us with a comprehensive and insightful conceptualization of battering as a social phenomena. Hart (1986; 19):[10]

Battering is a pattern of violent and coercive behaviors whereby one person seeks to control the thoughts, beliefs or conduct of an intimate partner or to punish the intimate for resisting their control.

Individual acts of physical violence, by this definition, do not constitute battering. Physical violence is not battering unless it results in the enhanced control of the batterer over the person battered. If the battered partner becomes fearful of the batterer, if this partner modifies behavior in response to the assault or to avoid future abuse, or if this partner intentionally maintains a particular consciousness or behavioral repertoire to avoid violence, despite the preference not to do so, that person is battered.

The physical violence utilized by batterers may include personal assaults, sexual abuse, property destruction, violence directed at friends, family, or pets or threats thereof. Physical violence may involve the use of weapons. It

. . . [may be] coupled with non-physical abuse, including homophobic attacks on the victim, economic exploitation, and psychological abuse.

A person who finds herself controlled by the partner because of fear of violence may be battered even if that person has not been physically assaulted. If the intimate has threatened her with physical violence or if the partner is aware that merely menacing gestures intimidate her because of a past history as a primary or secondary victim of violence, this person is battered. The person is battered who is controlled or lives in fear of the intimate because of these threats or gestures.

In determining whether violence is battering, the number of assaults need not be telling. The frequency of the acts of violence may not be conclusive. The severity of the violence may also not be determinative. . . .

Battering is the pattern of intimidation, coercion, terrorism or violence, the sum of all past acts of violence and the promises of future violence that achieves enhanced power and control for the batterer over the partner.

Rather than extracting violent acts from their relational meanings, sequences and histories, this conceptualization focuses on the different meanings and consequences that specific behaviors have in both a relational and social structural context. This conceptualization asserts that the scope of behaviors and tactics involved in battering ranges far beyond physical violence and may include sexual violence (Kelly, 1988), psychological violence, emotional violence (Denzin, 1984), isolation, and intimidation (Pence, 1985: 24–25; Dziggel, 1986; 66–68). It places battering in an international context and recognizes that differing tactical/behavioral patterns may well be associated: with differing motivations, e.g., displaying power, expressive anger, validation of self (Gondolf, 1985: 320; Gondolf, 1988; Gondolf and Fisher, 1988; Ptacek, 1988, 1988a) and with differing "causal" dimensions (Bowen and Sedlak, 1985: 3–4; Gondolf, 1985: 319; Gondolf, 1988, 1981; Dutton, 1988, 1988a; Shields and Hanneke, 1983; Hotaling and Sugarman, 1986; Carter, Stacy, and Shupe, 1988; Shields, McCall, and Hanneke, 1988; Caesar, 1988). Understanding differing batterer's tactical/behavioral patterns provides context for understanding the meaning that specific acts or episodes of violence have and provides context for understanding the full impact that specific acts or episodes of violence have upon the victim (Denzin, 1984; Lobel, 1986).

Like men who batter women, women who batter women seek to achieve, maintain, and demonstrate power over their partners in order to maximize the accomplishment of their own needs and desires. Lesbians batter their intimate partners because this violence is perceived as an immediately effective method to gain power and control over them (Goolkasian, 1986: 4; Hart, 1986: 20; Lobel, 1986; Stets, 1988; Ptacek, 1988). These women, like others who batter, desire control over the resources and decision-making processes in family life that power exercise brings, and that violence can assure, when control is resisted. The same elements of hierarchy, power, ownership, entitlement, and control that exist in many non-lesbian relationships exist in some lesbian relationships. Like men who batter women, some women who batter women have learned that battering works in achieving partner compliance (Hart, 1986a; Marie, 1984). But they have also learned that compliance does not engender peace in their relationships. Moreover, many lesbian communities have not yet developed value and social-arrangement alternatives to hierarchy, ownership, violence, domination, and superiority which would more effectively foster and encourage peace and establish peacemaking processes and strategies for conflict resolution (Lobel, 1986; Dietrich, 1986).

Hart concludes that battering is chosen behavior premised on the following beliefs (1986: 25):[11]

1. Those persons who choose to batter believe that they are entitled to control the partner and that the partner has an obligation to acquiesce in this practice.
2. Those persons who choose to batter believe that violence is permissible. (They believe they can live with themselves and conclude that they are ethical/moral persons even if they choose violence against the partner.)
3. Those persons who choose to batter believe that this violence will produce the desired effect or minimize a more negative occurrence.
4. Those persons who choose to batter believe that this violence will not unduly endanger them. (They believe that they will neither sustain physical harm nor suffer legal, economic, or personal consequences that will outweigh the benefit achieved through the violence.)

This is the essence of battering.

## Battering Central Americans

The United States government's policy toward the peoples of Central America parallels the behavior patterns of those who batter women and reflects the essence of battering. The peoples of Central America have been subjected for a long time to patterns of U.S. violence, exploitation, and intimidation. Central American resistance to this dependency and control has been consistently met with economic destabilization campaigns, psychological warfare, terrorism, political coups, low-intensity warfare, and invasions. A comprehensive policy strategy of intimidation, violence, and repression has been rationally designed to maintain and enhance U.S. control over this region of the Western Hemisphere (Morley and Petras, 1987; Barry and Preusch, 1988; Kornbluh, 1987; Klare and Kornbluh, 1988; Walker, 1987; NARMIC, 1987; Sklar, 1988; LaFeber, 1983). U.S. policymakers have consciously decided (1) that the U.S. is entitled to control Central America and that the peoples of Central America are obligated to acquiesce in this power exercise; (2) that violence is permissible, and policymakers can live with themselves and conclude that they are ethical/moral persons and that these policies are ethical/moral even if they involve violence; (3) that the use of violence, intimidation, and threat of violence will produce the desired effect or minimize a more negative one; and (4) that the policy of violence and control will not unduly endanger the United States, and the country will neither sustain physical harm nor suffer legal, economic, or political consequences that will outweigh the benefits achieved through this violence.

## THE ACCEPTANCE OF VIOLENCE AND THE ENTITLEMENT TO USE IT

The United States claims entitlement to the peoples and nations of Central America and demands that they acquiesce to this domination. No region of the world has been subjected to U.S. domination over a longer period of time. From the Monroe Doctrine, through the Roosevelt and Truman correlates, to the creation of the National Security State (N.S.S.)[12] and the Reagan Doctrine (Falk, 1989), the United States has exploited Central America for cheap labor, for the extraction of precious resources, for cash-crop importation, for economic "growth and expansion," and for the freedom of elite economic interests to operate without constraint (Herman, 1982: 9; LaFeber, 1983; Chomsky, 1985: 43–85; Barry, Wood, and Preusch, 1983; Barry and Preusch, 1988; Falk, 1989). In country after country, military regimes and dependent tyrannies (Herman, 1982: 2) have united with the U.S. government and U.S.-based corporations to establish "a politically stable investment climate" and to "develop" these countries as joint ventures. Systematically supplied by the U.S. security establishment (Huggins, 1987) with the latest training and modern technology for torture and interrogation, "improvement in the investment climate" has been achieved by the destruction of popular organizations, the torture of labor and peasant organizers, and the killing of priests engaged in social reforms (Chomsky, 1985: 158). It is, in fact, the function of N.S.S. terrorism to decrease popular participation, to neglect to develop state policies that would meet people's needs, and to "freeze" the arrangements or structures that have generated this condition (Herman, 1982: 84). A prime feature of the National Security State is a reliance on pure force—the use of secret police and the employment of systematic terror, torture, and disappearance. N.S.S. efforts to rally popular support have been both half-hearted and ineffectual "precisely because the ideology and organization of the N.S.S. aims at depoliticizing a restive and threatening majority" (Herman, 1982: 26). In consequence, the peoples of Central America have been perceived as "mere costs of production" (Herman 1982: 84) or as "oxen" in the words of Somoza, the Nicaraguan N.S.S. dictator until 1979.

"Growth and development" has been accomplished at enormous cost. Income distributions have skewed in the direction of greater inequality and an increasingly large number of people are kept in a state of extreme deprivation. Widespread hunger, chronic disease from poverty and social neglect, high rates of infant mortality and stunted growth, wage control and marginalization, and a huge reserve of structurally unemployed and uncared for people are some of these direct human costs. Virtually every indigenous attempt to bring about some reformative change has been met with U.S.-supported N.S.S. violence—torture, detention centers, the missing, death squads, strafing and gutting mountain villages with defoliants, crop destruction—and thus both indirect and outright slaughter.

Implicit in the U.S. "growth and development" model, and the National Security States created to enforce it, is planned, permanent immiseration and expected reactive protest. Most forms of dissent and popular organizing are defined as subversive, retrospectively creating a self-perpetuating mechanism of permanent terror and justifying N.S.S. repression (Herman, 1982: 112). Spiritual violence is also implicit in U.S./N.S.S. policies to assure "growth and development." But this violence is invisible in most corridors of Washington where everyday suffering, exploitation, and battering are accepted and defended. Chomsky (1985: 8) quotes Jeanne Kirkpatrick, a major architect of Reagan Doctrine:

> Traditional autocrats [the ones we do and should support, Kirkpatrick explains] leave in place existing allocations of wealth, power, status, and other resources which in most traditional societies favor an affluent few and maintain masses in poverty. But they worship traditional gods and observe traditional taboos. They do not disturb the habitual rhythms of work and leisure, habitual places of residence, habitual patterns of family and personal relations. Because the *miseries of traditional life* are familiar, they are bearable to ordinary people who, growing up in the society, learn to cope, as children born to untouchables in India acquire the skills and attitudes necessary for survival in the miserable roles they are destined to fill.

There is no doubt that the "miseries of traditional life" have increased as a result of U.S./N.S.S. policies, and that resistance to this *destined* suffering has been viewed as a justification for an escalation in the tactics of State repression. But such a perspective denies that the United States is responsible for this suffering and misery; and it denies that the roles which Central Americans are destined to fill are, in fact, the chosen, direct result of U.S./N.S.S. planning (Chomsky, 1985a).

For example, the Alliance for Progress was developed by the Kennedy Administration partly out of fear that the "Cuban example" might inspire others to undertake similar resistance. Alliance funds were given to U.S. corporations and to indigenous oligarches who controlled banks, mercantile businesses, and prime tillable land (LaFeber, 1983: 154); U.S. investment increased; and economic "growth" occurred in Central America. However, indigenous production shifted from subsistence crops to export crops and every country in Central America lost the capacity to feed its citizenry (Chomsky, 1985: 46). In addition, during most of the period (1960–65) a substantial proportion of Alliance funds went to military regimes which had overthrown constitutional governments. By 1965, with almost half of the population of Central America under military rule, a significant portion of Alliance aid was going, not to assist "free men and free governments" (Alliance language), but, rather, to hold in power regimes to which the people had lost their freedom (Hanson, 1967: 1). The substantial growth of military forces trained for internal repression was a natural component of the Alliance which helped to make such repression necessary (Chomsky, 1985; LaFeber, 1983: 184).

U.S. geopolitical or "Grand Area" planning strategies provide an historical context for understanding such specific policies for Central America as the Alliance, the creation of the National Security State, the U.S. war on El Salvador, the U.S./Contra war on Nicaragua, and the "drug wars." The Grand Area, as one planner put it, was to be the region that is "strategically necessary for world control." The geopolitical analysis held that the Grand Area had to include at least the Western Hemisphere, the Far East, and the former British Empire. It was also to include western and southern Europe and the oil-producing regions of the Middle East; in fact, it was to include everything, if that were possible. Detailed plans were laid for particular regions of the Grand Area and also for international institutions that were to organize and police it, essentially in the interests of subordination to the needs of U.S. economic elites (Chomsky, 1985a: 50). Officially and publicly, we are told that U.S. policies are designed to foster human rights and democratization and also to aid people by raising their standard of living and improving their quality of life. Spokespersons for the government also state that U.S. policies are designed to protect us from domination and any possible form of "communism" (Lamperti, 1988). The rhetoric may shift from human rights (Carter) to anti-terrorism (Reagan), but whatever the legitimation language, the real goals and interests of U.S. geopolitical policy are revealed in U.S.-policy planning documents (Chomsky, 1985a). Chomsky (1985: 48) quotes George Kennan, then Head of the U.S. State Department Planning Staff:

> We have about 50% of the world's wealth, but only 6.3% of its population. . . . Our real task is to devise a pattern of relationships which will permit us to maintain this position of disparity without positive detriment to our national security. . . . We will have to dispense with all sentimentality. . . . We need not deceive ourselves that we can afford . . . the luxury of altruism and world-benefaction. . . . We should cease to talk about vague and . . . unreal objectives such as human rights, the raising of the living standards, and democratization. The day is not far off when we are going to have to deal in straight power concepts. The less we are hampered by idealistic slogans, the better.

Though we are thoroughly socialized not to consider "true costs" (Sullivan, 1987), policies and straight power maneuvers employed to maintain the disparity between *them* and *us* carry severe costs, both material and moral. It is far from clear that *we* benefit materially from a national commitment to "maintain this position of disparity" by force—a commitment that entails global confrontation with the constant threat of nuclear war, an economy driven by military production, the loss of jobs to regions where *we* have implanted National Security States to ensure starvation wages and miserable living conditions, and the loss of thousands of lives (Chomsky, 1985: 49). Morally, we cannot dismiss the issues of human rights, democratization, and meeting human needs from an appraisal of U.S. policy. A careful review of the historical record suggests that U.S. policy in Central America and elsewhere has "sought to destroy human rights, to lower living standards, and to prevent democratization, often with considerable passion and violence" (Chomsky, 1985: 49; Falk, 1989).

Commitment to democracy, human rights, and people's needs is often in conflict with foreign policies established to promote and secure U.S.-based corporate investment and to guarantee our entitlement to a disproportionate share of the world's wealth—what Chomsky (1985: 47) calls the "Fifth Freedom."[13] According to Chomsky (1985: 50–51), governments that take meaningful steps toward democracy tend to become more responsive to domestic needs, thus threatening U.S. control of the "human and material resources" that must be under U.S. command if the disparity is to be maintained. U.S. policy must, therefore, regularly oppose democratization steps in much of the world (NARMIC, 1987) in order to ensure that the Fifth Freedom will not be threatened. In rhetoric, we are always defending ourselves from an Evil Empire, currently Iraq. In reality, the enemy is the indigenous population which attempts to use their national resources for their own purposes. Those who attempt to thwart our policy goals may not originally be Evil Empire allies—they have often been church-based groups or even advocates of capitalist democracy—but they are frequently left with few options but to turn to the Evil Empire for aid and protection against the multitude of diverse tactics of violence that the United States unleashes against them. According to Chomsky (1985: 51), it is U.S. strategy when the Fifth Freedom is threatened in its domain to resort to subversion, terror, or direct aggression to restore it, declaring the target of these actions a subversive member or client of the Evil Empire and acting to make this required truth a reality.

There is no doubt that U.S. violence, whether institutionalized in fiscal policies of immiseration (Barry and Preusch, 1988), N.S.S. terror, or direct warfare, has been defined by U.S. policy officials as both permissible and acceptable. Acceptance has been expressed: in economic rhetoric—"investment strategies to help developing nations"; in political rhetoric—"making the world safe for democracy"; and in national interest or national defense rhetoric—"to defend our national security." Most essentially, U.S. violence has been presented as rational and legitimate behavior based on an unquestioned U.S. entitlement to control the territory, its resources, and its peoples.

## Maximizing the Benefits of Choosing
## Violent Policies

The strategies of violence, N.S.S. terror, and economic dependency have until recently had the desired effects of maintaining the disparity, controlling the hemisphere, and discounting the costs suffered by Central Americans. But when the desired effects have not been so successfully or directly forthcoming, U.S. strategy has shifted to disallow "a good example" (Harrington, 1981). The current war in El Salvador and the U.S./Contra war in Nicaragua illustrate the strategy of minimizing negative effects. From the perspective of U.S. policymakers, the most negative outcome—the threat of a good example—would be Nicaraguan or El Salvadoran autonomy, nondependency, political nonalignment, self-determination, and an economy oriented to meeting the nutritional, health, literacy, and spiritual needs of the citizenry (Collins and Rice, 1985; Chomsky, 1985: 217–24; Barry and Preusch, 1988).

U.S. strategies in Indochina provide a prior historical context for understanding the war on El Salvador and the battering of Nicaragua. In Indochina, U.S. strategies of massive destruction and those which necessitated a survival-compelled alignment with the U.S.S.R. were activated to successfully prevent the threat of a good example for others to follow. According to Chomsky (1985: 70–71; 1985a), it is a mistake to describe the Vietnam War simply as a U.S. defeat. In fact, the United States achieved its major objectives. When a strategy of military conquest seemed failed (1970), a policy of massive devastation was instituted to guarantee that there would be no surviving model of resistance or independence (Bonner, 1984: 59–61). Supporting military coups (Indonesia-1965) and, later, imposing terror-torture states (Philippines-1972) was combined with destroying the National Liberation Front in South Vietnam and independent forces in Laos and Cambodia. This policy ensured that North Vietnam (a U.S.S.R. client) would dominate the region, gave justification for additional hostile actions, and limited the danger that independence and success would "infect" others or have a demonstration effect (Chomsky, 1985a: 54).

In Nicaragua, U.S. policy has been predictable ever since it was recognized that the priorities of the new Nicaraguan government (1979) "meant that Nicaragua's poor majority would have access to, and be the primary beneficiaries of, public programs" (Chomsky, 1985: 72). A policy of low-intensity warfare (Klare and Kornbluh, 1988), economic destabilization and fiscal exclusion (Barry and Preusch, 1988), directed terrorism, and finally "Communist-block" dependency has been instituted to ensure that no successful social and economic development would take place. If a marginal and impoverished nation could begin to utilize its own limited resources to undertake programs of development geared to the needs of its citizenry, then others may ask: Why not us? The contagion may spread, infecting others ("exporting revolution"); and before long, U.S. policies concerned with maintaining the disparity and fostering the most favorable conditions for U.S.-based private overseas investment may be threatened in places that really matter (Chomsky, 1985: 82–83).

This right, claimed by U.S. policymakers, to destroy and batter, to create dependency, and to keep Central Americans subordinate, is a painful reality. Many of us face this reality with initial disbelief and denial, for it is difficult for us to see either the United States or ourselves as terrorists, as batterers. Terrorists and batterers are *someone else* (Tifft, 1982). To emotionally experience, to actually witness the destruction, the horror, the reality of destabilization, starvation, torture and death by design, by public planning, is beyond our comprehension.

We therefore create, or accept an already created, apologetic world of fantasy, lie, and ignorance to conceal the truth and continue the cruel reality. It is not merely the structural constraints within which "news" is created as a commodity (Herman, 1982; Parenti, 1986) or the processes active in the manufacture of consent (Chomsky, 1985b: 139–99) that obscure this reality. It is, as well, our acquiescence in these processes and our desire to not know the truth—that U.S. geopolitical planning strategy is a strategy of death and terror practiced by elites who both individually and collectively "benefit" from these patterns of systematic suffering and human diminishment (Chomsky, 1985: 170).

There are, however, cracks in these structures of fantasy, lie, and ignorance. The assessment that dominance, violence, and repression in Central America will not endanger the United States and that the United States will not sustain physical harm or suffer legal, economic, or political consequences that will outweigh the benefits achieved through this violence (battering), especially in El Salvador and Nicaragua, is being questioned. So far, U.S. policymakers have been able to discount the judgments of the International Court for their illegalities against the people of Nicaragua (Falk, 1989). So far, these policymakers and the mainstream media have been able to deflect attention away from the war and killing in El Salvador. So far, they have been able to direct our attention both to the Contragate scandal, a deflection which concedes that it is acceptable to kill as long as the proper elites are included in the creation of the policies of death (Chomsky, 1988: 63–70), and to usurped power by the National Security Council (Shank, 1987). So far policymakers have been successful in blaming those who refuse to acquiesce to terror, to silence, to spiritual death, and to the National Security State. So far, the rhetoric of "communist beachheads" and "red-baiting" has worked (Petras, 1981). So far, U.S. casualties have been minimized due to the strategy of using non-U.S. personnel. So far, economic losses to U.S. investors in Central America and elsewhere have been minimal. So far, the threat of a good example has been staved off, as the U.S. economic embargo and the militarization of Nicaragua have made the economy and the programs designed to meet human needs suffer. So far, the government of Nicaragua has resisted being fully driven into the arms of the Evil Empire, where assuredly few Nicaraguans wish to be embraced. So far, the essential issues and the fundamental beliefs and arrangements of entitlement to batter have rarely been addressed. And yet, the possibility is substantial that the U.S. policy of battering and violence in Central America and elsewhere will be successfully challenged.

## Analysis and Synthesis

Our analysis indicates that the essential nature of battering women in the U.S. family and of battering Central Americans as U.S. policy is similar. Persons who choose to batter women and/or choose to develop and systematically carry out a policy of battering the peoples of a whole region of the world believe they are entitled to control other persons and that it is the obligation of those subjected to these controls to acquiesce. They believe that they are ethical and moral persons, even if they choose to act violently toward others. They believe that violence is acceptable, and they believe that their selection of specific patterns and tactics of violence will produce the effects they desire or at least minimize the effects they do not. Moreover, they believe it is safe violence (Jordan, 1988)—that they will neither sustain physical harm nor suffer legal, economic, or personal consequences that will outweigh the benefits achieved through their violence.

Our analysis indicates that both spheres of battering have common structural sources. These behaviors are embedded in and generated from widely held and deeply accepted values and beliefs which underlie the arrangements of social order in the United States. Both forms of battering are embedded in entitlement/ownership, the acceptability of hierarchy/superiority/domination, and the legitimacy of violence.

Our analysis indicates that within each sphere similar processes are involved in establishing and maintaining arrangements which foster battering. Battering is but one set of processes initiated to establish and maintain hierarchy, control, and dependency. Homophobia, heterosexism, rape and rape myths, gender socialization, gender tracking, gender-based employment practices, and gender-based Supreme Court decisions all involve processes which separately and collectively facilitate the domination and control of women. Racism, cultural stereotyping, cold-war ideological rhetoric, economic "growth and development," inventing reality and "news," militarization, patriotism (the use of national identity for dominance and privilege), and policies designed to suppress the "threat of a good example" all involve processes which individually and collectively serve to control and dominate Central Americans.

### BATTERING SPHERE AND SOCIAL CONTROL INTERCONNECTIONS

The practices of battering Central Americans and battering women are linked. The reality of family life in many U.S. households fosters an acceptance of entitlement, inequality, violence, and hierarchy—the cornerstones of U.S. foreign policy. Childhood socialization processes (Brock-Utne, 1985: 99–110) often socialize young persons for an acceptance of these arrangements and practices in the international sphere, and vice versa.

In many U.S. families, parents create age-based and sex/gender-based arrangements for the division of labor, access to resources, and decision-making. In these families, young persons do not have equal access to family resources, do not have access, or equal access, to information (Pepinsky, 1987) upon which to make decisions, and are not equal participants in family decision-making. They are assigned sex-based identities, opportunities, and tasks and are often spanked or spoken about as if they were not present. Living within these structural arrangements, what must these young persons learn about equality, democracy, human rights, and dignity? What must they learn about the acceptability of violence, the tactics of domination, and sex-based diminishment? While they are experiencing domination, diminishment, and inequality, are they simultaneously taught to utter the words "equality" and "democracy" and to rehearse justifications for controlling others and the use of violence? If so, it is no wonder that U.S. policymakers can so successfully market their commodity—Central American policy—by saying that they are for democratization and human rights while they manufacture human suffering, terror, and dependency. Revealingly, there are policymakers who acknowledge that they consider the peoples of Central America their *children*, their dependents, their possessions. Like *their* children (and perhaps *their* women), these policymakers see the peoples of Central America as not experienced enough, or not knowledgeable enough, to be included in decision-making, or to make their own decisions.

## MILITARIZATION AND THE CONTROL OF WOMEN

In addition to childhood socialization and experience, many other processes link U.S. policy in Central America, ("maintaining the disparity") and world militarization with the control of women. Militarization processes especially have an enormous effect on the lives of women.

Focus on economic-technological-fiscal militarization processes allows us to explore the connections between state military expenditures and operations and global-corporate strategies for "growth and development," and the *true costs* these policies have for people's lives, especially women's lives (Enloe, 1983: 207; Deane, 1988). As we have seen, large military budgets and a fervent anticommunism have serviced U.S.-based capital mobility and expansion. U.S. investment in training and financing military enforcers of these policies and a growing corporate stake in National Security States have been substitutes for much needed investment and renewal at home (Herman, 1982: 210–20). The resultant export of capital and loan funds to the National Security States has accelerated the rate of abandon-ments, closings, and underemployment in the United States. In fact, economic pressures stemming from access to cheap and unprotected labor abroad—and the "defense" required to keep this labor cheap—have caused the policies put in place at home to increasingly converge with those applied under authoritarian conditions in the National Security States. Selective deregulation and subsidies for corporate interests; a renewed emphasis on security and arms; a reliance on extremely tight money (Herman, 1982); an upward redistribution of income and wealth; and sharp cuts in social service budgets illustrate these policies. Those without homes or affordable housing, those without adequate nourishment, those without restorative health and medical care, and others in need (battered women and children) cannot be attended (Deane, 1988) because our collective monies are being spent to finance "defense" and halting "communism" abroad (Herman 1982), i.e., the Fifth Freedom.

This focus, however, leaves unexplored and unchallenged powerful ideological processes that perpetuate militarization and thwart peace: for example, the processes of sex-based hierarchy (Enloe, 1983: 208; Brock-Utne, 1985: 53, 132). From this perspective, militarization is an institutional embodiment of the aggressiveness and violence connected to patriarchy and the very nature of maleness (Enloe, 1983: 209). According to Enloe (1983: 209–10), this perspective:

> . . . insists that military ideologies and coercive manoeuvres be discussed not simply in terms of technology and economics, but in terms of the sexist structure of the social order. Militarism depends on distorted government budgets, but it also depends on the public denial or trivilialization of wife battering, rape, and pornography. Moreover, this approach is valuable for activists insofar as it promotes a more genuinely radical yardstick for gauging the changes that will ensure the long-term elimination of the military capacity to shape public priorities in any society. *It leads to a conviction that 'personal' relations are so basic to the dynamics which sustain the military's grip on social policy that militarism cannot be pushed back so long as dominance, control, and violence are considered 'natural' ordering principles in relations between men and women—i.e., so long as patriarchy is deemed 'normal'.*

Tracing violence, the acceptance of violence, and battering to a male character trait or fundamental quality of maleness, however, has limited validity. First, it implies that there are such traits and that there is something fundamentally *male* (and *female*), aside from physiological and procreative differences. Second, it implies that gender structures are natural and/or essential and, in this instance, that males are somehow more significant than females in creating and maintaining gender realities, identities, and inequalities. Third, this perspective is insufficient in that it leaves unexplored the diverse historical, cultural, and social processes through which sex-based structures are created and reproduced.

From a process-exploring perspective, the continued existence of both militarization and patriarchy depend on specific, observable processes. Focusing on process puts volition and power into our analysis. Some policies and practices are chosen, others are not. Decisions to exercise power over others derive in part from calculations of interest and benefit. This perspective concurs with our assertions: that battering is choice-behavior; that it reflects specific values and social arrangements, that it is created and reinforced through specific values and social arrangements; and that it is created and reinforced through specific social processes.

From this perspective we can explore how the processes that reproduce social relations which enhance militarization, rather than other social structures and beliefs, get repeated generation after generation (Enloe, 1983: 210). We can also examine how these processes are full of contradictions and subject to struggles which make them problematic. For example, women's rights and choices are critical issues for the militarization of the world, for low-intensity warfare (Chardy, 1986; Klare and Kornbluh, 1988), and for nonnuclear capability. Women's choices can pose a threat to military "manpower," maintaining ethnic military power, and patriarchy in general (Kaye,1986). Women making decisions, and specifically women making reproductive decisions, have sent "waves of anxiety down the corridors of defense establishments" (Enloe, 1985). Military planners and strategists are acutely aware that birth rates, especially within the ethnic groups trusted most by national military elites, have decreased in the 1970s and 1980s in most of the NATO-pact nations and in the U.S.S.R. It is no wonder that there are caps on the numbers of non-men and nonwhites in the U.S. military. It is no wonder that the issues of women's privacy and control of procreation are such significant issues in the United States today (Waisbrooker, 1985; Enloe, 1983; C. Cohn, 1987). The values and processes that underlie and support the control of women, that deny women choice, also underlie militarization (Deane, 1988). Militarization is, therefore, likely to continue as long as the control of women's minds and bodies is an accepted male prerogative, a testimony to "manhood" (Enloe, 1983: 8; Brock-Utne, 1985; C. Cohn, 1987), or accepted as natural or normal.

Although militarization processes affect the lives of both men and women, they are especially dependent on the oppression of women (Brock-Utne, 1985: 54, 82–83; Deane, 1988; Enloe, 1983: 17; Enloe, 1985: 8). The International Monetary Fund's standard package of austerity measures imposed on Third World governments has initiated tenuous and contradictory changes in the relations between women and men in these countries. While the expansion of Third World militaries by the influx of military aid and arms sales has brought about changes in what constitutes masculine behavior, investment-attracting cheap labor has been made cheap through feminization. Foreign investment, militarization, and international debt are directly connected with the practices of rape, prostitution, the feminization of labor, and battering (Enloe, 1985: 8).

The militarization of Central America has intensified the denigration and exploitation of women in historically traditional ways: Militarization has affirmed and extended the role of males as sexual exploiters and "protectors." Prostitution remains a mainstay, preserving military organization and occupation (Gottlieb, 1987). Rape and sexual assault have been insistently practiced by male soldiers in Guatemala and Contras in Nicaragua. Guatemalan army commanders have been quoted as saying that killing Indian women and children is part of a deliberate counterinsurgency strategy. Rape and sexual torture often accompany these murders (Enloe, 1985: 19–20).

Often militarization strategies have been coordinated with corporate employment practices to sustain the kind of internationally dependent, militarized society we have come to call a "banana republic" (Enloe, 1985: 12). Within these banana republics, colonially seeded cultures of machismo have legitimized class and ethnic stratifications in ways that the subjugation of women has perpetuated the inequalities among men. Foreign corporate strategies of class ethnic gender-labor utilization have perpetuated low wages and attenuated worker organizing (Enloe, 1985: 12). However, partly because of the growing militarization and its resultant social unrest, and partly out of their own global profits strategies, some of the largest "banana" corporations have cut back their investments and operations in Central America and have moved to other investment zones where the prospects for stability and profit have looked more promising. Corporate abandonment has left many male "banana" workers unemployed and led some previously unemployed female workers to form their own cash-generating cooperatives.

The corporate journeys to "more promising and stable" investment zones has increasingly meant "shopping for the most compliant foreign regime which will then serve up the cheapest female labor force" (Enloe, 1983: 203). Enloe (1985: 201):

> The resulting pattern is one in which women electronics workers in countries such as The Philippines, South Korea, Taiwan, Singapore, and Indonesia are . . . triply militarized. Their labor is exploited so that their governments can go on buying foreign police and military equipment. They live in societies which are made repressive by militarized governments unwilling to confront deep-seated inequities, preferring to rely instead on coercive force and the aid of friendly powers, such as the U.S., to whom they give military bases. They work on products which themselves either have direct military application or are part of a larger corporate profits formula in which defense contracting plays a central part.

Whether women form cash-generating cooperatives or join the triply militarized and feminized labor force, traditional power relations, divisions of labor, and the emotional basis upon which men and women have related have come under enormous pressures to change. This change and resistance to it has been played out not only in places of work, but in the plazas and in thousands of homes (Enloe, 1985: 15).

Fraught with contradiction, the militarization of women has reinforced the cultural supports for hierarchy and domination in one sphere of life (political-economy) while simultaneously undercutting these supports in another (family). Women's procreative choices, women's work, and the low wages women receive for their renumerated work are integral to the profit formulas of global corporations, the militarization strategies of states, and the intergenerational reproduction of the beliefs and arrangements that sustain hierarchical "social order." Yet, the crucial significance of women's choices, contributions, and changed position must either be unrecognized, defined as nonessential, or fought with strategies that include violence and battering if there is to be no successful challenge to these carefully constructed, sex-based hierarchical "social orders" (Enloe, 1983: 3, 56, 110).

## Policymaking Connections

Our analysis indicates that the processes and consequences of militarization in both the global/hemispheric and interpersonal spheres (C. Cohn, 1987) are not well understood. Replacing these processes with the processes of peacemaking will simultaneously require a much greater understanding of these processes (Sullivan, 1980) and an invitation of processes which will empower and enhance the quality of our lives.

The quality of life for many women in militarized, sex-based hierarchical societies (Enloe, 1983: 6, 46) is constrained in enforced dependency. Their labor is essential, but they neither control it nor receive their just rewards from it. They are expected to take their identity from men: to be nurturant, self-sacrificing, and adaptive to the needs and changes men require. If they step out of expectation, resist, or refuse to remain subordinate, they may be labeled "whore," "bitch," or "lesbian' (Cantor, 1983) and perhaps be subjected to isolation, terror, or battering.

The lives of many Central Americans within the U.S. hemispheric "family" are similarly constrained and dependent. Their labor is exploited and they are to be "used to the suffering." They are expected to be responsive and compliant to the needs and changes U.S. policymakers and private powerbrokers require. If they resist, organize to meet their basic needs, or refuse to act as "oxen," they may be labeled "communist," "sub," "revolutionaries," "terrorists," or "dupes of the Evil Empire," and perhaps subjected to fiscal and economic isolation, low-intensity warfare, terror, or driven into the arms of a different N.S.S.-creating superpower (U.S.S.R.).

As a result, people in the countryside are blamed for wishing to eat, for wishing to see their children live to age five. They are blamed for the necessity of disappearances, for the creation of refugees and refugee camps, for human rights violations, and for the necessity of further U.S./N.S.S. torture and battering.

Similarly, women are blamed for wishing to develop their talents, for acting with autonomy, dignity, and self-determination to meet their needs. They are blamed for increasing their partner's feelings of inadequacy and of insecurity, for creating the need for shelters (refugee houses), for the violence they undertake in response, and for the terror, violence, and battering they and perhaps *their* children suffer.

Nevertheless, while these processes deny responsibility for battering, they also represent verbal accounts which explain, defend, and attempt to legitimate battering practices as necessary, appropriate exercises of power. However, when applied to the battering of partners as compared to the battering of nations, these accounts have had different degrees of success or acceptance. Private policy-individual battering accounts within the family (between individual men and women) have been subjected to greater scrutiny. Individual men and women who batter their partners have been less successful in justifying, acceptably explaining, and legitimizing their behavior and its consequences (Pence, 1985; Ptacek, 1988). In the public policy-collective battering sphere, the meaning and reality of this behavior has been much differently presented and contexted (C. Cohn, 1987). Public policymakers have been more successful in presenting their behavior as outside the categories of violence, terrorism, and crime. They have been relatively successful in defining their violence as necessary, defensive, or appropriate, and disconnecting it from any association with either the battering behavior of men who batter women or international terrorism. Unlike the violence of those who batter their partners, public policy-collective battering has been given a different meaning and impact assessment. This is due in part because whereas we can identify with a single victim (with a battered wife or partner), collective death-dealing and battering has, for most of us, been systematically removed from our affective learning (C. Cohn, 1987) and is neither imaginable nor believable in its horror and consequences.[14]

Furthermore, violence in the private policy-individual sphere can be publicly acknowledged because its sources can be individualized. In this sphere, battering can more plausibly be explained as having individual or interpersonal causes or sources. Private policy-individual sphere violence can be examined or explained by constructing individual profiles or typologies of persons who batter or by discovering psychological deficiencies in the batterer. Batterers can be profiled as angry, insecure, emotionally inarticulate, or as having poor self-concepts, or being unable to see the consequences of their actions. These profiles can be supplemented with those of the victims or descriptions of relational pathology or dysfunction (e.g., the dysfunctional family). As a consequence, sources can be located in the nature of radically different assailants, radically different victims, or radically dysfunctional relationships. This location effectively denies and deflects responsibility for this battering from both us and those who choose to batter. It denies that responsibility is both individual and collective, that individuals make choices within structural circumstances and constraints; and it serves to deflect our attention from the structural sources of battering (Albee, 1986).

In contrast, public policy-collective battering has not been examined through research that might disclose the individual and relational correlates of state and corporate policymakers who choose to batter on a "rational" and "strategic" basis and on a systematic scale. If this research were available, would it indicate that these state and corporate policymakers, like their battering-the-partner counterparts, are angry, insecure, emotionally inarticulate persons who have poor or distorted self-concepts and are unable and unwilling to see the consequences of their actions? Would we discover that the values held by these policymakers are similar to the values held by those who batter their partners? Would we find that the values and attitudes held in common concerning the acceptability of violence, entitlement, and inequality are values held by the majority of persons in our society? Would we discover that public policy-collective battering is undertaken in social contexts of isolation, a lack of world-community affiliation, a high degree of stress, and an acceptance of the "traditional values" of superiority and hierarchy? Would we find that the interactive-emotive processes of accepting (and rejecting) violence and victimizations are similar in both spheres (Denzin, 1984; Ferraro and Johnson, 1983)? Perhaps. We are more convinced that supplemental research will attest that both private policy-individual battering and public policy-collective battering have similar structural sources.

If we wish to stop the violence, we will have to explore more fully the similarities and linkages, both between and within spheres of violent action. We will have to become more willing to believe that parents inflict atrocities on their children; that intimates inflict atrocities on their partners; and that elite decision-makers inflict atrocities on their constituents and subjects. We will have to reject the cultural assumption which pairs wisdom, just action, and benevolence with parental, interpersonal, organizational, corporate, and state power. We will have to participate more energetically in peacemaking processes for resolving conflict, creating mutual autonomy and interdependence, and meeting needs in all spheres of interaction.

## NOTES

1. The social harm and appropriation definitions of crime have allowed criminologists to transcend state definitions of crime and to explore those actions which result in considerable suffering whether they are legally proscribed or not: legal appropriations for reasons for state, (e.g., capital punishment, state terrorism/U.S. policy in Central America (Herman, 1987; Shank, 1987; Pfost, 1987; Block, 1989; Scott, 1989); legal appropriations for reasons of profit, e.g., silent killings, unnecessary surgeries (Reiman, 1984; Kramer, 1989; Hills, 1987); legal appropriations for reasons of domination, e.g., marital rape, battering (Schechter, 1982; Fagen and Wexler, 1987; Hotaling, Straus and Lincoln, 1988; Feld and Straus, 1989; Stanko,

1988; Finkelhor and Yllö, 1985; Yllö, 1988). Through these definitions we have begun to determine our own scope of inquiry, to explore structural harms, and to envision and create social arrangements that foster peacemaking (Brock-Utne, 1985: 1–4), self-determination, and the fulfillment of needs. See Kennedy, 1970; Pepinsky, 1976, 1989; del Olmo, 1975; Tifft and Sullivan, 1980; Tifft and Stevenson, 1985; Sullivan, 1980; Quinney, 1979, 1988; Reiman, 1979, 1984; Schwendinger, 1970, 1977; Elias, 1986; Michalowski, 1985; Brock-Utne, 1985; and Gil, 1979, 1985.

2. This statement has considerable validity when our victimization by the stranger is illegal, as in being robbed while walking down the street. We are, however, much more likely to be seriously victimized or harmed by a stranger whose behavior is legal and who appropriates the quality—health, freedoms of choice—and duration of our lives (Reiman, 1979, 1984; Elias, 1986; Kramer, 1989).

3. Definitional *dissensus* concerning what behaviors constitute battering and who is defined as an intimate partner or victim, has impeded both research and public policy formulation and intervention (Margolin, Sibner, and Gleberman, 1988; Bowen and Sedlak, 1985; Strach, Jervey, Hornstein, and Porat, 1986; Weis, 1988; Yllö, 1988). Some definitions have limited battering to the most extreme manifestations of physical violence, and victim inclusion to a select set of battered persons. Benjamin and Adler (1980), for example, define battering as injuries "that are either visible for some period of time . . . or require medical attention"; and Freeman (1979) asserts that a woman is battered "who has suffered persistent or serious physical abuse at the hands of her partner." These illustrative definitions imply that some level of physical or psychological abuse is socially and/or legally acceptable (McGillivray, 1987; Cecere, 1986: 28) and that only some victims are deserving of protection (Merwine, 1987). These definitions exclude the threat of violence, sexual violence (Kelly, 1988), isolation, psychological violence, intimidation, threat of disclosure (Hart, 1986a), and the destruction of personal property or pets (Pence, 1985: 24–25, 32), although these patterns of behavior are frequently experienced by many battered women (NiCarthy, 1986; Lobel, 1986; Hart, 1986a; Dziggel, 1986: 66–68; Pharr, 1986; Marie, 1984; Pence, 1985). Definitions limited to overt physical violence have been charged with creating a distorted, class-based image of battering which has to some extent diverted research, policy, and intervention to a limited set of victims and assailants (Freeman, 1980; Adams, Jackson, and Lauby, 1988; see also Morash, 1986). Definitions which exclude intimates of the same sex (Lobel, 1986) have had similar distortive effects (see Note 9). Most definitions, including those used in most state protection-order laws, limit the victim of battering to the spouse or former spouse or to the cohabitee or former cohabitee of the batterer (Freeman, 1980; Merwin, 1987; Morash, 1986). For legislative limitations, see Lerman, Livingston, and Jackson, 1983; for exceptions, see Goolkasian, 1986. Consequently, many victims are excluded from legal protection. Women who have never lived with the battering partner do not meet protection eligibility requirements in most states (Lerman et al, 1983; Merwine, 1987), and in some states battered women who establish a legal residence separate from the batterer may forfeit civil protection. Lerman (1984) suggests that "domestic violence" should refer to any overt acts, attempts, or threats—including battery, assault, coercion, sexual asssault, harassment, unlawful imprisonment, unlawful entry, damage to property, and theft— where the perpetrator and the victim have or have had an ongoing personal relationship or living arrangement. Terms such as "family violence" and "wife abuse" are consequently rejected as distractive (Lerman, et al., 1984: 67) and exclusionary (Lobel, 1986). See Lerman (1984) for a comprehensive Model State Act which attempts to resolve definitional and other legislative issues. For a further discussion of definitional issues, see McGillivray, 1987; Bowen and Sedlak, 1985; Lobel, 1986; Tifft, 1989; the text; and Note 4. Battering could be defined as inflicted

deficits on an intimate's potential to develop freely and fully (Gil, 1977, 1979; Tifft, 1989).

4. Many researchers (Breines and Gordon, 1983: 511–12; Saunders, 1986: 48; Hart, 1986a; Levinson, 1988) contend that acts of violence or "marital violence events" should be studied in their context and that extreme caution is needed when applying particular labels or meanings to simple counts of acts or events. The initial studies of marital violence were incidence surveys which indicated that husbands and wives committed similar rates of violent acts (Steinmatz and Lucca, 1988). This data led some researchers to label violence by women as "husband abuse" or "mutual combat" and to infer that women were as violent as were men, an inference challenged by many researchers (McLeod, 1984; Stark and Flitcraft, 1988; Pleck, Pleck, Grossman, and Bart, 1978). Incidence surveys, however, do not ascertain either the cultural or interactional context of these acts or the meanings of these acts to the persons involved (Denzin, 1984; Marie, 1984; O'Toole and Webster, 1988). They fail to explore the intention of these acts, e.g., attack or self-defense (Saunders, 1988; Ptacek, 1988); their consequences, e.g., the degree of psychological or physical injury; or the pattern, history, duration (Feld and Straus, 1989; Fagen, 1988a) or extent of these acts (Stark and Flitcraft, 1988). They fail to distinguish between "real violence," clearly understood by all persons, and spurious, playful, accidental, or paradoxical violence (Denzin, 1984). To infer from simple counts of acts that men and women are similarly violent imposes meanings which may or may not be those of the persons involved; and such inference takes these actions out of the power context within which they take place (Breines and Gordon, 1983: 505). Stark and Flitcraft (1988: 312) conclude that "husband and wife abuse appear similar only so long as all acts of force are equated irrespective of their social, historical, and political context and consequence." To infer that the experiences of men who are victimized by violence or a pattern of violence in the home are similar to the experiences of women who are battered is capricious and pernicious (Berk, Berk, Loeske, and Rauma, 1983). The "mutual combat" characterization and the "husband abuse" syndrome equivalency characterization are very crude empirical distortions. According to Stark and Flitcraft (1988: 312), "there are no clinical reports of battering syndrome among men similar to the profile identified among women." An exploration of the meanings of violence and violent acts and their consequences (Marie, 1984) must be undertaken to grasp fully the personal and cultural realities of these experiences (Stets, 1988; Denzin, 1984, 1984a; Lobel, 1986; Levinson, 1988; Campbell, 1985; Ferraro and Johnson, 1983; Ptacek, 1988, 1988a). While most research indicates that women much more frequently report physical battering (Dobash and Dobash, 1977; Straus, 1976; Berk et al., 1983), this may reflect differences as to meaning, propensity to report, and, of course, experience. Even if women's violence against men does not as frequently result in reportable violence, or even if it does not constitute a comparable battering pattern or syndrome, this form of violence should be neither unexplored nor denied nor minimized (Steinmeitz and Lucca, 1988). To focus exclusively on battered women deflects attention from the reality that some women are caught up in domination and control, that our society glorifies violence, and that we need to recognize and change violence-producing sociocultural conditions. Denial, silence, and secrecy regarding any form of violence cannot break the cycle of violence.

5. There is evidence of a trend toward official criminal sanction against batterers and the availability of greater protective measures for a more comprehensive population of victims (Goolkasian, 1986a: 4–5; Micklow, 1988: 411–17). Due primarily to the organizing efforts of battered women's advocates (Schechter, 1982; Pence, 1988: 19; Fagen, 1988)—and following both the Attorney General's Task Force on Family Violence Report (1984) and significant court litigation (Moore, 1985), as well as

Goolkasian's guides for criminal justice agencies (1986, 1986a)—agencies within the criminal justice system have begun to show a clearer responsibility for taking legal action against domestic violence. In fact, the Attorney General's Task Force Report (1984: 22) recommended that "every law enforcement agency should establish arrest as the preferred response in cases of family violence." Legislation in a number of states (Lerman et al., 1983) and policy development in many communities have forced police agencies to define guidelines for arrest practices (e.g., allowing warrantless arrests, shifting responsibility away from the victim in criminal proceedings), have mandated data collection and reporting, have required domestic violence training programs, have provided for victim protection (e.g., pretrial release restrictions) and assistance, and have authorized the use of civil orders of protection. Additionally, they have issued sentencing guidelines intended to give the clear messages that this violence will not be tolerated, that offenders will be held accountable for their battering, and that the needs of victims and other family members will be met (Goolkasian, 1986a: 2–5). A survey of urban police departments serving cities with populations of 100,000 or more found that in June 1986, 46 percent preferred to arrest the batterer in cases of minor domestic assault. This percentage had arisen from 10 percent in 1984 and from 31 percent in 1985. There had been, as well, a decrease in the percentage of these police departments which do not provide any policy guidelines for their officers on how to handle domestic violence—from 50 percent in 1984–85 to 35 percent in 1986. (E. Cohn, 1987: 22). Arrest is not, however, the practice of police departments (Ferraro, 1989), leading many of those who batter to expect few official negative consequences for their violence and leading many victims to the realization that violence against them (against women) is not seen as serious and that there is little reason to report battering to the police. Unfortunately, these messages are infrequently contradicted by agencies which follow the police within the criminal justice process (Sedlak, 1988: 345). For a more comprehensive discussion of the issues and effects of differing police intervention policies, see Sherman and Berk, 1985; Berk and Newton, 1985; Jaffe, Wolfe, Telford, and Austin, 1985; Berk, Newton, and Berk, 1986; Schmidt, 1987; Fagan, 1988; Steinman, 1988; Williams and Hawkins, 1989; Ferraro, 1989; Mederer and Gelles, 1989; and Sedlak, 1988. Criminalization indicates a shift from defining battering as a personal or relational problem to recognizing battering as a violent social problem and an issue of human (women's) rights. Abolishing the spousal exemption in sexual-assault laws has similarly indicated not only that sexual assault is unacceptable violence, but that the issue of consent is meaningful regardless of marital status (Lerman, 1984; 65; Pagelow, 1988a). Furthermore, coordinated community-intervention projects (Pence, 1985) have demonstrated that changing the official policies and procedures of the criminal justice response to battering can undermine, at least, this official and significant reinforcement for the acceptance of battering and violence against women. Attempts to go beyond altering the official criminal justice system's reinforcement of battering are in their initial stages of development (Pence, 1987, 1988a).

6. While members of the clergy are the most frequently contacted—and often the initial "professional" contacted—by battered women, the theological perspective on women's roles advanced by many clergy and religious doctrines inhibits involvement in the problem of domestic violence. In a survey of Protestant pastors, Alsdurf (1985) found support for the claim that pastors hold a patriarchal attitude toward women which results in a "distrustful, even subtly accusatory manner" of response toward victims whom they counsel. A majority of pastors felt that either the abuse must be severe to justify separation or that no amount of abuse justified separation. For a full discussion of the role of the clery and religious ideology in family violence, see Pagelow and Johnson, 1988; Bowker, 1988; and Horton and Williamson, 1988.

7. Taub and Schneider (1982: 123) point out that law has operated directly and explicitly to prevent women from attaining self-support and influence in the public sphere, thereby reinforcing their dependence upon men. At the same time, the absence of law from the private sphere to which many women have been relegated has not only left individual women without formal remedies, but has also devalued and discredited women as a group.

8. For a review of programs which provide support, advocacy, and safety for the victims of battering, see NiCarthy, 1986; Sedlak, 1988; Pence, 1987; Margolin et al., 1988; Sonkin, Martin, and Walker, 1985; and Sonkin and Durphy (1982). Many coordinated community intervention programs have recognized the necessity of altering the social arrangements and cultural values which underlie and foster battering (Pence, 1985, 1987, 1988a). In accord with this, Gil (1977) and Brock-Utne (1985: 72–142) offer extensive recommendations addressing these necessary changes. Straus (1980) has offered the following much more moderate public policy recommendations: (1) making the public aware of the norm of domestic violence and redefining marriage as a relationship where physical force is unacceptable; (2) reducing the government's use of physical force, limiting violence in the mass media, exacting stringent gun control legislation; (3) eliminating physical punishment as a mode of child discipline and defining physical force as unacceptable behavior between children; (4) teaching parents and children nonviolent means to resolve inevitable family conflicts; (5) sponsoring research to discover the social and psychological factors responsible for child abuse and neglect; (6) reducing government programs that encourage geographic mobility and loosen ties to the extended family; (7) eliminating sexism in society; and (8) arranging for full employment for all, ensuring a guaranteed annual income for everyone who is unable to work, and reducing the extent to which society evaluates individuals on the basis of economic achievement.

9. We were unable to locate research on the incidence of battering among gay intimates. Frequently, gay intimates are excluded by the language of domestic violence statutes and from eligiblity for programs aiding victims of battering. Yet, several victim programs for gays have been established. As recently as 1987 there were no programs for gays who were perpetrators of this form of violence. M.O.V.E., a program that offers counseling for gays and straight men who batter, has sought to meet this need in San Francisco. Two premises of this program are that violence is a men's issue and that battering occurs in gay relationships as frequently as in non-gay relationships.

10. Piercy (1976) and Le Guin (1974) illustrate how language is symbolic of our values and social arrangements. If we desire to bring about a society without gender-based hierarchy and without ownership-possessive relations, we must create and foster language which reflects these desires, values, and arrangements. In this quote, "person" and the pronoun "per" replace sex-designating pronoun (e.g., him, her); the "partner" replaces sex-designating and ownership/possession-designating language (e.g., my wife/husband).

11. According to Hart (1986a), there are no personal attributes or circumstances which permit reliable prediction or identification of the lesbian who will batter her intimate partner. The preliminary research indicates that she is (1986: 20–25):

1. Perhaps the partner who is physically stronger, and perhaps not.
2. Perhaps the partner who has more personal power, and greater access to resources, and perhaps not.
3. Perhaps the partner who experienced violence as a child, and perhaps not.
4. Perhaps the partner who is acutely homophobic, and perhaps not.
5. Perhaps the partner who holds contempt for women or who identifies with men, and perhaps not.
6. Perhaps the partner who perceives herself to be victimized by the world and

misused or controlled by the victim, and perhaps not.

7. Perhaps the partner who has anger control or communication problems, and perhaps not.

12. National Security States (N.S.S.) are those states in which military elites have been carefully nurtured and maintained by a superpower security establishment to serve as the enforcer of a policy of economic exploitation. Enforcement of this policy usually requires massive state terror, the threat of terror, and an attempt to destroy all forms of institutional resistance (e.g., unions, cooperative, political groupings). The ideology of these elites and their establishers combines elements of Nazism, pre-Enlightenment hierarchy and inequality, and a disregard for human rights (Herman, 1982: 1–14; Chomsky and Herman, 1979: 1–40).

13. According to Chomsky (1985: 47), a careful look at history and the internal record of planning reveals a guiding geopolitical principle: preservation of the Fifth Freedom by whatever means are feasible. Much of what U.S. governments do in the world can be readily understood in terms of this principle. Infringement of the four official freedoms (of speech, of religion, from want, from fear) in the domain of other states always evokes much agonized concern. But not in our own domain. Here, as the historical record demonstrates with great clarity, it is only when the fifth and fundamental freedom is threatened that a sudden and short-lived concern for other forms of freedom manifests itself, to be sustained only as long as it is needed to justify the righteous use of force and violence to restore the fifth freedom.

14. According to Carl Rogers (1972: 3), nothing better illustrates the flaw at the heart of our culture than *knowing* without *feeling*. Knowing without feeling not only leads to personal and public irresponsibility and indifference, but, as well, to our acceptance of the most incredible atrocities. We have become so successfully compartmentalized in our knowing—thanks in part to our almost exclusively cognitive education—that an atrocity is simply an intellectual term, something we do not feel. Only if we were able to walk through the awful human aftermath of a "protective reaction strike," for example, would we be able to connect our gut-level, emotional, affective knowing to our intellectual, cognitive knowing. The cynical lesson from the Vietnam War seems to have been: If you kill, do it from far away (e.g., from 30,000 feet up) and do not televise it to the people back home. Strategists for many governments have learned this lesson well: South Africa (violent repression-apartheid); United States (bombing Libya, invading Grenada, war in El Salvador); People's Republic of China (demonstrations of 1980); Union of Soviet Socialist Republics (war in Afghanistan); and, following the advice of Henry Kissinger, Israel (repression and apartheid in the "occupied territories").

## REFERENCES

Adams, David, Jann Jackson, and Mary Lauby. 1988. "Family Violence Research: Air or Obstacle to the Battered Women's Movement?" *Response* 11: 14–18.

Albee, George W. 1982. "Preventing Psychopathology and Promoting Human Potential." *American Psychologist* 37: 1043–50.

———. 1986. "Toward a Just Society." *American Psychologist* 41: 891–98.

Aldsurf, Jim M. 1985. "Wife Abuse and the Church: The Response of Pastors." *Response* 8: 9–11.

Attorney General's Task Force on Family Violence. 1984. *Final Report*. Washington, D.C.: U.S. Department of Justice.

Barak, Gregg. 1986. "Feminist Connections and the Movement Against Domestic Violence: Beyond Criminal Justice Reform." *Journal of Crime and Justice* 9: 139–62.

Barry, Tom, and Deb Preusch. 1988. *The Soft War: The Uses and Abuses of U.S. Economic Air in Central America.* New York: Grove.

Barry, Tom, Beth Wood, and Deb Preusch. 1983. *Dollars and Dictators: A Guide to Central America.* New York: Grove.

Benjamin, Michael, and Susan Adler. 1980. "Wife Abuse: Implications for Socio-legal Policy and Practice." *Canadian Journal of Family Law* 3: 339–68.

Berk, Richard A., Sarah F. Berk, Donileen R. Loseke, and David Rauma. 1983. "Mutual Combat and Other Family Violence Myths." In D. Finkelhor, R. J. Gelles, G. T. Hotaling, and M. A. Straus (eds.), *The Dark Side of Families: Current Family Violence Research.* Beverly Hills: Sage.

Berk, Richard A. and Phyllis J. Newton. 1985. "Does Arrest Really Deter Wife Battery? An Effort to Replicate the Findings of the Minneapolis Spouse Abuse Experiment." *American Sociological Review* 50: 253–62.

Berk, Richard A., Phyllis J. Newton, and Sarah F. Berk. 1986. "What a Difference a Day Makes: An Empirical Study of the Impact of Shelters for Battered Women." *Journal of Marriage and the Family* 48: 481–90.

Berkowitz, Leonard. 1983. "The Goals of Aggression." In D. Finkelhor, R. J. Gelles, G. T. Hotaling, and M. A. Straus (eds.), *The Dark Side of Families: Current Family Violence Research.* Beverly Hills: Sage.

Block, Alan B. 1989. "Violence, Corruption, and Clientelism: The Assassination of Jesus de Galindez, 1956." *Social Justice* 16: 64–88.

Bonner, Raymond. 1984. *Weakness and Deceit: U.S. Policy and El Salvador.* New York: Times Books.

Bowen, Gary L., and Andrea Sedlak. 1985. "Toward a Domestic Violence Surveillance System: Issues and Prospects." *Response* 8: 2–7.

Bowker, Lee H. 1983. *Beating Wife-Beating.* Lexington, Mass.: Heath.

———. 1988. "Religious Victims and Their Religious Leaders: Services Delivered to One Thousand Battered Women." In A. L. Horton and J. A. Williamson (eds.), *Abuse and Religion.* Lexington, Mass.: Lexington Books.

Breines, Wini, and Linda Gordon. 1983. "The New Scholarship on Family Violence." *Signs* 8: 490–531.

Brock-Utne, Birgit. 1985. *Educating For Peace: A Feminist Perspective.* New York: Pergamon.

Browne, Angels, 1987. *When Battered Women Kill.* New York: Free Press.

Caesar, P. Lynn. 1988. "Exposure to Violence in the Families-of-Origin Among Wife Abusers and Maritally Nonviolent Men." *Violence and Victims* 3: 49–63.

Campbell, Jacquelyn. 1985. "Beating of Wives: A Cross-Cultural Perspective." *Victimology* 10: 174–85.

Carter, Jack, William A. Stacy, and Anson W. Shupe. 1988. "Male Violence Against Women: Assessment of the Generational Transfer Hypothesis." *Deviant Behavior* 9: 259–73.

Cecere, Donna J. 1986. "The Second Closet: Battered Lesbians." In K. Lobel (ed.), *Naming the Violence: Speaking Out About Lesbian Battering.* Seattle: Seal Press.

Chardy, Alphonso. 1986. "Pentagon's Low-Intensity Conflict Newest Military Tactic." *Detroit Free Press*, 3, October 14.

Chomsky, Noam. 1985. *Turning the Tide: U.S. Intervention in Central America and the Struggle for Peace.* Boston: South End.

———. 1985a. Intervention in Vietnam and Central America: Parallels and Differences." *Radical America* 19: 49–66.

———. 1985b. "The Manufacture of Consent." *Our Generation* 17: 85–106.

———. 1988. *The Culture of Terrorism.* Boston: South End.

Chomsky, Noam, and Edward S. Herman. 1979. *The Washington Connection and Third World Fascism: The Political Economy of Human Rights.* Vol. 1. Boston: South End.

Cohn, Carol. 1987. "Sex and Death in the Rational World of Defense Intellectuals." *Signs* 12: 687–718.

Cohn, Ellen G. 1987. "Changing the Domestic Violence Policies of Urban Police Departments: Impact of the Minneapolis Experiment." *Response* 10: 22–24.

Coleman, Karen H. 1980. "Conjugal Violence: What 33 Men Report." *Journal of Marriage and Family Counseling* 6: 207–13.

Collins, Joseph, and Paul Rice. 1985. *Nicaragua: What Difference Could A Revolution Make.* Second Edition. San Francisco: Food First.

Davidson, Terry. 1977. "Wife Beating: A Recurring Phenomenon Throughout History." In M. Roy (ed.), *Battered Women: A Psychosociological Study of Domestic Violence.* New York: Van Nostrand Reinhold.

———. 1978. *Conjugal Crime: Understanding and Changing the Wifebeating Problem.* New York: Hawthorne.

Deane, Sherry C. 1988. "The Effects of U.S. Military Spending on Women and Children in the U.S." *Madre* (Fall): 18, 30, 40, 42, 50.

del Olmo, Rosa. 1975. "Limitations for the Prevention of Violence: The Latin American Reality and Its Criminological Theory." *Crime and Social Justice* 3: 21–29.

Denzin, Norman K. 1984. "Toward a Phenomenology of Domestic, Family Violence." *American Journal of Sociology* 90: 483–513.

———. 1984a. *On Understanding Emotions.* San Francisco: Jossey-Bass.

Dietrich, Mary Lou. 1986. "Nothing is the Same Anymore." In K. Lobel (ed.), *Naming the Violence: Speaking Out About Lesbian Violence.* Seattle: Seal Press.

Dobash, R. Emerson, and Russell P. Dobash. 1977. "Wives: The 'Appropriate Victims' of Marital Violence." *Victimology* 2: 436–42.

———. 1979. *Violence Against Wives: A Case Against Patriarchy.* New York: Free Press.

———. 1983. "Patterns of Violence in Scotland." In R. J. Gelles and C. P. Cornell (eds.), *International Perspectives on Family Violence.* Lexington, Mass.: Lexington Books.

———. 1988. "Research as Social Action: The Struggle for Battered Women." In K. Yllö and M. Bograd (eds.), *Feminist Perspectives on Wife Abuse.* Newbury Park, Calif.: Sage.

Dutton, Donald G. 1988. "Profiling of Wife Assaulters: Preliminary Evidence for a Trimodal Analysis." *Violence and Victims* 3: 5–29.

———. 1988a. *The Domestic Assault of Women: Psychological and Criminal Justice Perspectives.* Newton, Mass.: Allyn and Bacon.

Dziggel, Cory. 1986. "The Perfect Couple." In K. Lobel (ed.), *Naming the Violence: Speaking Out About Lesbian Violence.* Seattle: Seal Press.

Elias, Robert. 1986. *The Politics of Victimization: Victims, Victimology, and Human Rights.* New York: Oxford University Press.

Enloe, Cynthia. 1983. *Does Khaki Become You? The Militarization of Women's Lives.* Boston: South End.

———. 1985. "Bananas, Bases, and Patriarchy: Some Feminist Questions About the Militarization of Central America." *Radical America* 19: 23.

Fagan, Jeffrey A. 1988. "Contributions of Family Violence Research to Criminal Justice Policy on Wife Assault: Paradigms of Science and Social Control." *Violence and Victims* 3: 159–203.

———. 1988a. "Cessation of Family Violence: Deterrence and Dissuasion." In L. Ohlin and M. Tonry (eds.), *Crime and Justice: A Review of Research, Volume 11, Family Violence.* Chicago: University of Chicago Press.

Fagan, Jeffrey A., and Sandra Wexler. 1987. "Crime at Home and in the Streets: The Relationship Between Family and Stranger Violence." *Violence and Victims* 2: 5–24.

Falk, Richard. 1989. "United States Foreign Policy as an Obstacle to the Rights of People." *Social Justice* 16: 57–70.

Feld, Scott L., and Murray A. Straus. 1989. "Escalation and Desistance of Wife Assault in Marriage." *Criminology* 27: 141–61.

Ferraro, Kathleen J. 1989. "Policing Woman Battering." *Social Problems* 36: 61–74.

Ferraro, Kathleen J., and John M. Johnson. 1983. "How Women Experience Battering: The Process of Victimization." *Social Problems* 30: 325–39.

Finkelhor, David, and Kersti Yllö. 1985. *License to Rape: Sexual Abuse of Wives.* New York: Free Press.

Flitcraft, Anne, and Evan Stark. 1978. "Notes on the Social Construction of Battering." *Antipode* 10: 79–84.

Freeman, Michael D. A. 1979. *Violence in the Home.* Farnborough, England: Saxon House.

———. 1980. "Violence Against Women: Does the Legal System Provide Solutions or Itself Constitute the Problem?" *Canadian Journal of Family Law* 3: 377–401.

Gelles, Richard J., and Murray A. Staus. 1988. *Intimate Violence.* New York: Simon and Schuster.

Gil, David G. 1977. "Societal Violence and Violence in Families." In J. M. Eckelnar and S. M. Katz (eds.), *Family Violence.* Toronto: Butterworths.

———. 1979. *Child Abuse and Violence.* New York: AMS.

———. 1985. "The Political and Economic Contexts of Child Abuse." In E. Newberger and R. Bourne (eds.), *Unhappy Families.* Littleton, Mass.: PSG.

Gondolf, Edward W. 1985. "Anger and Oppression in Men Who Batter: Empiricist and Feminist Perspectives and Their Implications for Research." *Victimology* 10: 311–24.

———. 1988. "Who Are Those Guys? Toward a Behavioral Typology of Batterers." *Violence and Victims* 3: 187–203.

———. 1988a. "The State of the Debate: A Review Essay on Woman Battering." *Response* 11: 3–8.

Gondolf, Edward W., and Ellen R. Fisher. 1988. *Battered Women as Survivors: An Alternative to Treating Learned Helplessness.* Lexington, Mass.: Lexington Books.

Gondolf, Edward W., and David Russell. 1986. "The Case Against Anger Control Treatment Programs for Batterers." *Response* 9: 2–5.

Goolkasian, Gail A. 1986. *Confronting Domestic Violence: A Guide for Criminal Justice Agencies.* Washington, D.C.: U.S. Department of Justice.

———. 1986a. "The Judicial System and Domestic Violence—An Expanding Role." *Response* 9: 2–7.

Gottlieb, Alan. 1987. "The U.S. Presence in Honduras and the Politics of Prostitution." *In These Times,* 16–22 September, p. 2.

Hamberger, L. Kevin, and James E. Hastings. 1986. "Personality Correlates of Men Who Abuse Their Partners: A Cross-Validation Study." *Journal of Family Violence* 1: 323–41.

———. 1988. "Exposure to Violence in the Families-of-Origin Among Wife Abusers and Maritally Nonviolent Men." *Violence and Victims* 3: 49–63.

———. 1988a. "Characteristics of Male Spouse Abusers Consistent With Personality Disorders." *Hospital and Community Psychiatry* 39: 763–70.

Hanson, Simon. 1967. *Five Years of the Alliance for Progress.* New York: Inter-American Affairs Press.

Harrington, Michael. 1981. "The Good Domino." In M. E. Gettleman, P. Lacefield, L. Menashe, D. Mermelstein, and R. Radosh (eds.), *El Salvador: Central America in the New Cold War.* New York: Grove.

Hart, Barbara. 1986. "Lesbian Battering: An Examination." *Aegis* 41: 19–28.

———. 1986a. "Lesbian Battering: An Examination." In K. Lobel (ed.), *Naming the Violence: Speaking Out Against Lesbian Battering.* Seattle: Seal Press.

Hastings, James E., and L. Kevin Hamberger. 1988. "Personality Characteristics of Spouse Abusers: A Controlled Comparison." *Violence and Victims* 3: 31–47.

Herman, Edward S. 1982. *The Real Terror Network: Terrorism in Fact and Propaganda.* Boston: South End.

———. 1987. "U.S. Sponsorship of International Terrorism: An Overview." *Crime and Social Justice* 27–28: 1–33.

Hills, Stuart, L. 1987. *Corporate Violence: Injury and Death For Profit.* Totowa, N.J. Rowman & Littlefield.

Hornung, Carleton A., B. Clair McCullough, and Taichi Sugimoto. 1981. "Status Relationships in Marriage: Risk Factors in Spouse Abuse." *Journal of Marriage and the Family* 42: 675–92.

Horton, Anne L., and Judith A. Williamson. 1988. *Abuse and Religion: When Praying Isn't Enough.* Lexington, Mass.: Lexington Books.

Hotaling, Gerald T., Murray A. Straus, and Alan J. Lincoln. 1988. "Intrafamily Violence, Crime, and Violence Outside the Family." In L. Ohlin and M. Tonry (eds.), *Crime and Justice: A Review of Research, Volume 11, Family Violence.* Chicago: University of Chicago Press.

Hotaling, Gerald T., and David B. Sugarman. 1986. "An Analysis of Risk Markers in Husband to Wife Violence: The Current State of Knowledge." *Violence and Victims* 1: 101–24.

Huggins, Martha D. 1987. "U.S.–Supported State Terror: A History of Police Training in Latin America." *Crime and Social Justice* 27–28: 149–71.

Jaffe, Peter, David A. Wolfe, Anne Telford, and Gary Austin. 1986. "The Impact of Police Charges in Incidents of Wife Abuse." *Journal of Family Violence* 1: 37–49.

Jordan, June. 1988. "Racist & Sexist Violence in Relation to United States Foreign Policy." *Madre* (Fall): 4, 30.

Kelly, Liz. 1988. "How Women Define Their Experiences of Violence." In K. Yllö and M. Bograd (eds.), *Feminist Perspectives on Wife Abuse.* Newbury Park, Calif.: Sage.

Kennedy, Mark. 1970. "Beyond Incrimination: Some Neglected Facets of the Theory of Punishment." *Catalyst* 5: 1–37.

Kirkpatrick, Jeane. 1979. "Dictatorships and Double Standards." *Commentary* 68: 34–45.

Klare, Michael, and Peter Kornbluh. 1988. *Low-Intensity Warfare: Counterinsurgency, Proinsurgency, and Antiterrorism in the Eighties.* New York: Pantheon.

Kornbluh, Peter. 1987. *Nicaragua: The Price of Intervention (Reagan's Wars Against the Sandinistas).* Washington, D.C.: Institute for Policy Studies.

Kramer, Ronald C. 1989. "Criminologists and the Social Movement Against Corporate Crime." *Social Justice* 16: 146–65.

LaFeber, Walter. 1983. *Inevitable Revolutions: The United States in Central America.* New York: Norton.

Lamperti, John. 1988. *What Are We Afraid Of? An Assessment of the "Communist Threat" in Central America.* Boston: South End/NARMIC.

Langley, Roger and Richard C. Levy. 1977. *Wifebeating: The Silent Crisis.* New York: Dutton.

LeGuin, Ursula K. 1974. *The Dispossessed.* New York: Avon.

Leonard, Linda S. 1983. *The Wounded Woman.* Athens, Ohio: Swallow Press.

Lerman, Lisa G. 1984. "A Model State Act: Remedies for Domestic Abuse." *Harvard Journal on Legislation* 21: 61–144.

Lerman, Lisa G., Franci Livingston, and Vicki Jackson. 1983. "State Legislation and Domestic Violence." *Response* 6: 1–28.

Lester, David. 1980. "A Cross-Cultural Study of Wife Abuse." *Aggressive Behavior* 6: 361–64.

Levinson, David. 1983. "Physical Punishment of Children and Wifebeating in

Cross-Cultural Perspective." In R. J. Gelles and C. P. Cornell (eds.), *International Perspectives on Family Violence*. Lexington, Mass.: Lexington Books.

———. 1988. "Family Violence in Cross-Cultural Perspective." In V. B. Van Hasselt, R. L. Morrison, A. S. Bellack, and M. Hersen (eds.), *Handbook of Family Violence*. New York: Plenum.

Lobel, Kerry. 1986. *Naming the Violence: Speaking Out About Lesbian Battering*. Seattle: Seal Press.

Makepeace, James M. 1983. "Life Events, Stress, and Courtship Violence." *Family Relations* 32: 101–09.

Margolin, Gayla, Linda G. Sibner, and Lisa Gleberman. 1988. "Wife Battering." In V. B. Van Hasselt, R. L. Morrison, A. S. Bellack, and M. Hersen (eds.), *Handbook of Family Violence*. New York: Plenum.

Marie, Susan. 1984. "Lesbian Battering: An Inside View." *Victimology* 9: 16–20.

Martin, Del. 1981. *Battered Wives*. San Francisco: Volcano Press.

———. 1981a. "Battered Women: Scope of the Problem." In B. Galloway and J. Hudson (eds.), *Perspectives on Crime Victims*. St. Louis: Mosby.

Masumura, Wilfred T. 1979. "Wife Abuse and Other Forms of Aggression." *Victimology* 4: 46–59.

McGillivray, Anne. 1987. "Battered Woman: Definition, Models, and Prosecutorial Policy." *Canadian Journal of Family Law* 6: 15–45.

McGrath, Colleen. 1979. "The Crisis of Domestic Order." *Socialist Review* 43: 11–22.

McLeod, Maureen. 1984. "Women Against Men: An Examination of Domestic Violence Based on an Analysis of Official Data and National Victimization Data." *Justice Quarterly* 1: 171–94.

Mederer, Helen J., and Richard J. Gelles. 1989. "Compassion or Control: Intervention in Cases of Wife Abuse." *Journal of Interpersonal Violence* 4: 25–43.

Merwine, Connie J. 1987. "Pennsylvania's Protection From Abuse Act: A Decade in Existence Generates Judicial Interpretation and New Changes in House Bill 2026." *Dickinson Law Review* 91: 805–32.

Michalowski, Raymond J. 1985. *Order, Law, and Crime*. New York: Random House.

Micklow, Patricia W. 1988. "Domestic Abuse: The Pariah of the Legal System." In V. B. Van Hasselt, R. L. Morrison, A. S. Bellack, and M. Hersen (eds.), *Handbook of Family Violence*. New York: Plenum.

Moore, Jamie M. 1985. "Landmark Court Decision for Battered Women." *Response* 8: 5–8.

Morash, Merry. 1986. "Wife Battering." *Criminal Justice Abstracts* 18: 252–71.

Morley, Morris and James Petras. 1987. *The Reagan Administration and Nicargua: How Washington Constructs Its Case for Counterrevolution in Central America*. New York: Institute for Media Analysis.

Morrell, Lisa. 1984. "Violence in Premarital Relationships." *Response* 7: 17–18.

NARMIC. 1987. *Militarization, Central America and the U.S. Role*. Philadelphia: NARMIC/American Friends Service Committee.

Neidig, Peter H., Dale H. Freedman, and Barbara S. Collins. 1985. "Domestic Conflict Containment: A Spouse Abuse Treatment Program." *Social Casework* 66: 195–204.

NiCarthy, Ginny. 1984. *Getting Free: A Handbook for Women in Abusive Relationships*. Seattle: Seal Press.

———. 1986. *Getting Free: A Handbook for Women in Abusive Relationships*. Second Edition. Seattle: Seal Press.

Newman, Graeme. 1979. *Understnding Violence*. New York: Lippincott.

O'Toole, Richard, and Steven Webster. 1988. "Differentation of Family Mistreatment: Similarities and Differences by Status of the Victim." *Deviant Behavior* 9: 347–68.

Pagelow, Mildred D. 1984. *Family Violence*. New York: Praeger.

————. 1988. "The Incidence and Prevalence of Criminal Abuse of Other Family Members." In L. Ohlin and M. Tonry (eds.), *Crime and Justice: A Review of Research, Volume 11: Family Violence*. Chicago: University of Chicago Press.

————. 1988a. "Marital Rape." In V. E. Van Hasselt, R. L. Morrison, A. S. Bellack, and M. Hersen (eds.), *Handbook of Family Violence*. New York: Plenum.

Pagelow, Mildred D., and Pam Johnson. 1988. "Abuse in the American Family: The Role of Religion." In A. L. Horton and J. A. Williamson (eds.), *Abuse and Religion*, Lexington, Mass.: Lexington Books.

Parenti, Michael. 1986. *Inventing Reality: The Politics of the Mass Media*. New York: St. Martin's.

Pence, Ellen. 1984. "The Duluth Domestic Abuse Intervention Project." *Hamline Law Review* 6: 247–75.

————. 1985. *The Justice System's Response to Domestic Assault Cases: A Guide for Policy Development*. Duluth, Minn.: Domestic Abuse Intervention Project.

————. 1987. *In Our Best Interest: A Process for Personal and Social Change*. Duluth, Minn.: Minnesota Program Development.

————. 1988. "The Role of Advocacy Groups in Police Reforms." *Response* 11: 19.

————. 1988a. *Batterers Programs: Shifting From Community Collusion to Community Confrontation*. Duluth, Minn.: Minnesota Program Development.

Pence, Ellen, and other contributors. 1984. "Responses to Peter Neidig's Article: 'Women's Shelters, Men's Collectives, and Other Issues in the Field of Spouse Abuse'." *Victimology* 9: 477–82.

Pepinsky, Harold E. 1976. *Crime and Conflict*. New York: Academic Press.

————. 1987. "Information Sharing As A Human Right." *Humanity and Society* 11: 189–211.

————. 1989. "The Nature of Violence." Paper Presented at the Midwest Sociological Society Meetings, St. Louis.

Peterson-Lewis, Sonja, Charles W. Turner, and Afesa M. Adams. 1988. "Attribution Processes in Repeatedly Abused Women." In G. W. Russell (ed.), *Violence in Intimate Relationships*. New York: PMA.

Petras, James. 1981. "White Paper on the White Paper: The Reinvention of the 'Red Menace'." *The Nation* 232: 353, 367–72.

————. 1987. "Political Economy and State Terror: Chile, El Salvador, and Brazil." *Crime and Social Justice* 27–28: 88–109.

Pfost, Donald R. 1987. "Reagan's Nicaragua Policy: A Case Study of Political Deviance and Crime." *Crime and Social Justice* 27–28: 66–87.

Pharr, Suzanne. 1986. "The Connection Between Homophobia and Violence Against Women." *Aegis* 41: 35–37.

————. 1986a. "Two Workshops on Homophobia." In K. Lobel (ed.), *Naming the Violence: Speaking Out About Lesbian Violence*. Seattle: Seal Press.

Piercy, Marge. 1976. *Woman on the Edge of Time*. New York: Fawcett Crest.

Pirog-Good, Maureen A., and Jan E. Stets. 1989. *Violence in Dating Relationships*. Westport, Conn.: Praeger.

Pleck, Elizabeth. 1987. *Domestic Tyranny: The Making of Social Policy Against Family Violence From Colonial Times to the Present*. New York: Oxford University Press.

Pleck, Elizabeth, Joseph H. Pleck, Marlyn Grossman, and Pauline B. Bart. 1978. "The Battered Data Syndrome: A comment on Steinmetz's Article." *Victimology* 2: 680–84.

Ptacek, James. 1988. "How Men Who Batter Rationalize Their Behavior." In A. L. Horton and J. A. Williamson (eds.), *Abuse and Religion*, Lexington, Mass.: Lexington Books.

————. 1988a. "Why Do Men Batter Their Wives?" In K. Yllö and M. Bograd (eds.), *Feminist Perspectives on Wife Abuse*. Newbury Park, Calif.: Sage.

Quinney, Richard. 1979. *Criminology*. Second Edition. Boston: Little Brown.

———. 1987. "Criminology and the Way of Peace." Paper presented at the Annual Meetings of the American Society of Criminology, Montreal, Canada.

———. 1988. "Crime, Suffering, Service: Toward a Criminology of Peacemaking." *The Quest* (Winter): 66–75.

Reiman, Jeffery. 1979. *The Rich Get Richer and The Poor Get Prison.* New York: Wiley.

———. 1984. *The Rich Get Richer and The Poor Get Prison.* Second Edition. New York: Wiley.

Rogers, Carl R. 1972. *Bringing Together the Cognitive and the Affective-Experiential.* Handout 5. La Jolla, Calif.: Center for Studies of the Person.

Roy, Maria. 1982. "Four Thousand Partners in Violence: A Trend Analysis." In M. Roy (ed.), *The Abuse Partner: An Analysis of Domestic Battering.* New York: Van Nostrand Reinhold.

Russell, Diana H. 1982. *Rape in Marriage.* New York: MacMillan.

Saline, Carol. 1984. "Bleeding in the Suburbs." *Philadelphia Magazine* 75: 1.

Saunders, Daniel G. 1982. "Counseling the Violent Husband." In P. A. Keller and L. G. Ritt (eds.), *Innovations in Clinical Practice: A Sourcebook, Vol. 1.* Sarasota, Fla.: Professional Resource Exchange.

———. 1984. "Helping Husbands Who Batter." *The Journal of Contemporary Social Work* 65: 347–53.

———. 1988. "Wife Abuse, Husband Abuse, or Mutual Combat? A Feminist Perspective on the Empirical Findings." In K. Yllö and M. Bograd (eds.), *Feminist Perspectives on Wife Abuse.* Newbury Park, Calif.: Sage.

Schechter, Susan, 1982. *Women and Male Violence: The Visions and Struggles of the Battered Women's Movement.* Boston: South End.

Schmidt, Janell. 1987. "Replication of the Minneapolis Experiment." *Response* 10: 23.

Schwendinger, Herman and Julia. 1970. "Defenders of Order or Guardians of Human Rights?" *Issues in Criminology* 5: 123–57.

———. 1977. "Social Class and the Definition of Crime." *Crime and Social Justice* 7: 4–13.

Scott, Peter D. 1989. "Northwards Without North: Bush, Counterterrorism, and the Continuation of Secret Power." *Social Justice* 16: 1–30.

Sedlak, Andrea J. 1988. "Prevention of Wife Abuse." In B. V. Van Hasselt, R. L. Morrison, A. S. Bellack, and M. Hersen (eds.), *Handbook of Family Violence.* New York: Plenum.

Shank, Gregory. 1987. "Contragate and Counter-Terrorism: An Overview." *Crime and Social Justice* 27–28: i–xxcii.

Sherman, Lawrence S. 1984. *The Impact of the Minneapolis Domestic Violence Experiment: Wave I Findings.* Washington, D.C.: The Police Foundation.

Sherman, Lawrence W., and Richard A. Berk. 1985. "The Specific Deterrent Effects of Arrest for Domestic Assault." *American Sociological Review* 49: 261–72.

Sherman, Lawrence W., and Ellen G. Cohn. 1986. *Police Policy on Domestic Violence: A National Survey.* Washington, D.C.: The Crime Control Institute.

Shields, Nancy M., and Chrsitine R. Hanneke. 1983. "Attribution Processes in Violent Relationships: Perceptions of Violent Husbands and Wives." *Journal of Applied Social Psychology* 13: 515–27.

Shields, Nancy M., George J. McCall, and Christine R. Hanneke. 1988. "Patterns of Family and Nonfamily Violence: Violent Husbands and Violent Men." *Violence and Victims* 3: 83–97.

Sklar, Holly. 1988. *Washington's War on Nicaragua.* Boston: South End.

Sonkin, Daniel J., and Michael Durphy. 1982. *Learning to Live Without Violence: A Handbook for Men.* San Francisco: Volcano Press.

Sonkin, Daniel J., Del Martin, and Lenore E. A. Walker. 1985. *The Male Batterer: A Treatment Approach.* New York: Springer.

Stanko, Elizabeth A. 1985. *Intimate Intrusions: Women's Experience of Male Violence.* London: Routledge & Kegan Paul.

————. 1988. "Fear of Crime and the Myth of the Safe Home: A Feminist Critique of Criminology." In K. Ylló and M. Bograd (eds.), *Feminist Perspectives on Wife Abuse*. Newbury Park, Calif.: Sage.

Stark, Evan, and Anne Flitcraft. 1988. "Violence Among Intimates." In V. B. Van Hasselt, R. L. Morrison, A. S. Bellack, and M. Hersen (eds.), *Handbook of Family Violence*. New York: Plenum.

Steinman, Michael. 1988. "Anticipating Rank and File Police Reactions to Arrest Policies Regarding Spouse Abuse." *Criminal Justice Research Bulletin* 4 (3).

Steinmetz, Suzanne K. 1978. "The Battered Husband Syndrome." *Victimology* 2: 499–509.

Steinmetz, Suzanne K., and Joseph S. Lucca. 1988. "Husband Battering." In V. B. Hasselt, R. L. Morrison, A. S. Bellack, and M. Hersen (eds.), *Handbook of Family Violence*. New York: Plenum.

Stets, Jan E. 1988. *Domestic Violence and Control*. New York: Springer–Verlag.

Stets, Jan E., and Murray A. Straus. 1989. "The Marriage License as a Hitting License: A Comparison of Assaults in Dating, Cohabiting, and Married Couples." *Journal of Family Violence* 4: 161–80.

Strach, Ann, Nan Jervey, Susan J. Horstein, and Momi Porat. 1986. "Lesbian Abuse: The Process of the Lesbian Abuse Issues Network (LAIN)." In K. Lobel (ed.), *Naming the Violence: Speaking Out About Lesbian Battering*. Seattle: Seal Press.

Straus, Murray A. 1973. "A General Systems Theory Approach to a Theory of Violence Against Family Members." *Social Science Information* 12: 105–25.

————. 1976. "Sexual Inequality, Cultural Norms, and Wife-Beating," *Victimology* 1: 54–76.

————. 1980. "A Sociological Perspective on the Prevention of Wife-Beating." In M. A. Straus and G. T. Hotaling (eds.), *The Social Causes of Husband-Wife Violence*. Minneapolis: University of Minnesota Press.

————. 1983. "Ordinary Violence. Child Abuse, and Wife Beating: What Do They Have In Common?" In D. Finkelhor, R. J. Gelles, G. T. Hotaling, and M. A. Straus (eds.), *The Dark Side of Families: Current Family Violence Research*, Beverly Hills: Sage.

————. 1983a. "Societal Morphogenesis and Intrafamily Violence in Cross-Cultural Perspective." In R. J. Gelles and C. P. Cornell (eds.), *International Perspectives on Family Violence*. Lexington, Mass.: Lexington Books.

Straus, Murray A., and Richard J. Gelles. 1986. "Societal Change and Change in Family Violence From 1975 to 1985 as Revealed by Two National Surveys." *Journal of Marriage and the Family* 48: 265–79.

Straus, Murray A., Richard J. Gelles and Suzanne K. Steinmetz. 1980. *Behind Closed Doors: Violence in the American Family*. New York: Doubleday/Anchor.

Straus, Murray A., and Alan J. Lincoln. 1985. "A Conceptual Framework for Understanding Crime and the Family." In A. J. Lincoln and M. A. Straus (eds.), *Crime and the Family*. Springfield, Ill.: Charles C. Thomas.

Sullivan, Dennis C. 1980. *The Mask of Love: Corrections in America—Toward a Mutual Aid Alternative*. Port Washington, N.Y.: Kennikat.

————. 1987. "The True Costs of Things: The Loss of the Commons and Radical Change". *Social Anarchism* 6: 20–26.

Taub, Nadine, and Elizabeth M. Schneider. 1982. "Perspectives on Women's Subordination and the Law." In D. Kairy (ed.), *The Politics of Law: A Progressive Critique*. New York: Pantheon.

Tierney, Kathleen J. 1982. "The Battered Women Movement and the Creation of the Wife Beating Problem." *Social Problems* 29: 207–13.

Tifft, Larry L. 1979. "The Coming Redefinition of Crime: An Anarchist Perspective." *Social Problems* 26: 392–402.

————. 1982. "Capital Punishment Research, Policy, and Ethics: Defining Murder and Placing Murderers." *Crime and Social Justice* 17: 61–68.

————. 1989. *Stopping the Violence: The Battering of Women and Interventions With Men Who Batter Women—A Critical Assessment.* Unpublished M.A. Paper, Central Michigan University.

Tifft, Larry L., and Lois Stevenson. 1985. "Humanistic Criminology: Roots from Peter Kropotkin." *Journal of Sociology and Social Welfare* 22: 488–520.

Tifft, Larry L., and Dennis C. Sullivan. 1980. *The Struggle to be Human: Crime, Criminology and Anarchism.* Sanday, Orkney: Cienfuegos Press.

U.S. Commission on Civil Rights. 1982. *Under the Rule of Thumb: Battered Women and the Administration of Justice.* Washington, D.C.: U.S. Commission on Civil Rights.

Van Hasselt, Vincent B., Randall L. Morrison, Alan S. Bellack, and Michel Hersen. 1988. *Handbook of Family Violence.* New York: Plenum.

Waisbrooker, Lois. 1985. *A Sex Revolution.* Philadelphia: New Society.

Walker, Lenore E. A. 1979. *The Battered Woman.* New York: Harper and Row.

————. 1985. "Feminist Therapy with Victim/Survivors of Interpersonal Violence." In L. B. Rosewater and L. E. A. Walker (eds.), *Handbook of Feminist Therapy: Women's Issues in Psychotherapy.* New York: Springer.

Walker, Lenore E. A., and Angela Browne. 1985. "Gender and Victimization by Intimates." *Journal of Personality* 53: 179–93.

Walker, Thomas. 1987. *Reagan Versus the Sandinistas: The Undeclared War on Nicaragua.* Boulder: Westview Press.

Wardell, Laurie, Dair L. Gillespie, and Ann Leffler. 1983. "Science and Violence Against Wives." In D. Finkelhor, R. J. Gelles, G. T. Hotaling, and M. A. Straus (eds.), *The Dark Side of Families: Current Family Violence Research,* Beverly Hills: Sage.

Watts, Deborah L., and Christine A. Courtois. 1981. "Trends in the Treatment of Men Who Commit Violence Against Women." *The Personnel and Guidance Journal* 60: 245–49.

Weis, Joseph G. 1988. "Family Violence Research Methodology and Design." In L. Ohlin and M. Tonry (eds.), *Crime and Justice: A Review of Research, Volume 11: Family Violence.* Chicago: University of Chicago Press.

Wetzel, Laura, and Mary Anne Ross. 1983. "Psychological and Social Ramifications of Battering: Observations Leading to a Counseling Methodology for Victims of Domestic Violence." *The Personnel and Guidance Journal* 61: 423–28.

Williams, Kirk R., and Richard Hawkins. 1989. "The Meaning of Arrest for Wife Assault." *Criminology* 27: 163–81.

Yllö, Kersti. 1983. "Sexual Equality and Violence Against Wives in American States." *Journal of Comparative Family Studies* 14: 67–86.

————. 1984. "The Status of Women, Marital Equality, and Violence Against Wives." *Journal of Family Issues* 5: 307–20.

————. 1988. "Political and Methodological Debates in Wife Abuse Research." In K. Yllö and M. Bograd (eds.), *Feminist Perspectives on Wife Abuse.* Newbury Park, Calif.: Sage.

*Walter S. DeKeseredy and*
*Martin D. Schwartz*

---

N I N E

# British Left Realism on the Abuse of Women

## A Critical Appraisal

Over the past 20 years, critical criminologists have made an important contribution and corrective to mainstream criminology by examining elite deviance or "crimes at the top" (Box, 1983; Goff and Reasons, 1978, 1986; Pearce, 1976; Smandych, 1985; Snider, 1980; West and Snider, 1985). However, during this same period many radicals ignored the causes and possible control of working-class victimization (Lea and Young, 1984), preferring to explain away both the crime and the extent of working-class concern with it. Certainly there are exceptions to this broad and sweeping generalization, chief among them being the critical studies on violence against women, children and ethnic groups (e.g., Breines and Gordon, 1983; Dobash and Dobash, 1979; Pearson, 1976; Russell, 1982, 1984, 1986; Schechter, 1982). However, the general "abstentionist position" (Boehringer et al., 1983) of failing to acknowledge working-class crime has allowed right-wing politicians in several countries to manufacture ideological support for "law and order" policies that are detrimental to the powerless and preclude the development of a socialist society (Taylor, 1982). Moreover, the left's failure to take working-class victimization seriously has contributed to the right's hegemonic control over knowledge about crime and policing (MacLean, 1988).

British left realists have attempted to provide a response to both the left's tendency to neglect victimization among the disenfranchised and the conservatives' draconian social-control strategies. Sometimes called radical realism, the response is a critical discourse that attempts to explain predatory street crime and propose short-term, socialist policies to control it.[1] Nevertheless, this important movement in critical criminology has been criticized for a variety of reasons which will be outlined later. Since perhaps the most problematic is the feminist critique, the primary purpose of this essay is to describe and evaluate British left realism on a key variant of feminist research—the abuse of women. The authors will: (1) briefly describe the history and basic principles of British left realism, (2) articulate the strengths and limitations of the radical realist position on female victimization, and (3) provide suggestions for further research and policy development.

## Left Realism in Britain

There are various versions of the history of British left realism. Some contend it is a response to the violent summer riots of 1980 and 1981 in Britain's inner cities (Taylor, 1988). Others (e.g., Young, 1988) maintain that it naturally evolved from a dissatisfaction with the direction of radical criminology in Britain. Either way, there is no doubt that British left realism is a major response to the harsh law and order policies of the Thatcher government. Moreover, it can only be understood in the context of both academic criminology and the complex interests of the Labour Party (Taylor, 1988). It will only be possible to summarize these contexts here, but a more thorough history can be found in MacLean (1988), MacLean (1989), or DeKeseredy and Schwartz (1989).

In the late 1960s and early 1970s, many British scholars were radicalized into the New Left. Many deviance and criminology courses were taught by instructors affiliated with the National Deviancy Conference, and radicals were able to establish "powerbases" in various polytechnics, universities, and institutions of higher education (Young, 1988). Since members of the left realist cohort were able to work in close proximity to each other (e.g., Middlesex Polytechnic and the University of Edinburgh), it is not surprising that they were able to develop a united school of thought. An important political step came when critical criminology began to influence Labour Party thinking in the early 1980s when:

> . . . a new wave of young Labour politicians, many of them schooled in the New Left Orthodoxy of the sixties, were brought into power in the inner-city Labour strongholds. They—and in particular the police committee support units which they brought into being—became important political focuses for the ideas and concerns of radical criminology. (Young, 1988: 170)

At a time when the British Home Office was progressively gaining ideological control over the agenda of mainstream criminological research (Hood, 1987), these alliances gave left realists the opportunity to work through Labour controlled local government offices. In the 1980s, confronted with an oppressive Thatcher government and a right-wing popular press determined to capitalize on racist and class-based crime fears, radical realists struggled to develop progressive anticrime strategies which could be placed immediately into action. The Thatcher government's crushing defeats of the Labour party on the national level made it seem even more necessary to work on specific and detailed projects with local Labour Borough Councils.

In sum, wider academic and political forces have indirectly contributed to the construction of a united left realist perspective in Britain. Since the major tenets of this school of thought have been thoroughly described elsewhere (Kinsey, 1989; Kinsey et al., 1986; Lea and Young, 1984; Matthews and Young, 1986; Young, 1986), only a summary of four of its most important principles will be presented here.

First, predatory street crime is a significant social problem for the working class. Left realists oppose the argument that crime is primarily the product of moral panics or societal reaction. Street crime predominantly victimizes working-class neighborhoods.

Second, the left realist project includes an explanation of street crime and its control that is more complex than the earlier radical theories which stated that the causes of working-class crime are simply poverty and unemployment (Young, 1986) and which rejected the value of any mainstream criminological formulations. In contrast, left realist theory includes four principal variables: the victim, the offender, the state, and the community (Jones et al., 1986). This explanation draws from both Marxist and traditional criminological approaches such as subcultural theory, victimology, strain theory, and select ecological theories (Matthews, 1987); and it tries to bridge macro- and micro-levels of analysis.

Third, left realists advocate the use of both quantitative and qualitative methods, although they reject "abstract empiricism."

The local survey is, in fact, considered to be the most suitable mode of inquiry (MacLean and DeKeseredy, 1990). Left realists have conducted local surveys on victimization, fear of crime, and perceptions of the police (Jones et al., 1986; Kinsey et al., 1986); and more will be conducted in the future.

Fourth, left realists propose short-term anticrime strategies that both challenge the right-wing law and order campaign and take seriously working-class communities' "well founded fear" of street crime (Hanmer and Saunders, 1984). Examples of these initiatives are (1) demarginalization, (2) preemptive deterrence, (3) democratic control of policing, and (4) community participation in crime prevention and policy development (Lea and Young, 1984).

As might be expected, left realism has attracted extensive criticism. Left realists have been attacked for their failure to address the power of police subcultures to undermine progressive reform (Gilroy and Sim, 1987), their concentration on street crime to the virtually total neglect of elite deviance, and their apparent lack of concern for economic crime-control policies (DeKeseredy, 1988; Schwartz and DeKeseredy, 1990). They have been attacked by the British left over their discussions on race and crime (Bridges and Gilroy, 1982; Gilroy, 1982, Sim, Scraton, and Gordon, 1987), as well as by scholars in several countries on their community crime-control measures (Cohen, 1985; DeKeseredy, 1988; Hunt, 1982; Lowman, 1987) and even on their use of the concept "crime" (Hulsman, 1986; Steinert, 1985). Their worst critics have gone so far as to accuse the left realists of accommodating the Thatcher government's draconian social-control policies (Gilroy and Sim, 1982).

These issues and the radical realist responses are complex and require extensive discussions, but it is beyond the scope of this essay to do them justice. Here, our major concern is the British left realist position on woman abuse, a topic that has not been adequately addressed in previous evaluations.

## Left Realism and Women Abuse

The tendency of most "new," "critical," or "radical" criminologists has been to rely primarily on class-based analyses of crime and its control. Simply by virtue of their principal mode of inquiry, many critical scholars clearly exemplify a "gender-blind" approach to criminological studies (Gelsthorpe and Morris, 1988). For example, as demonstrated by Messerschmidt (1986), some of the most widely cited radical works ignore gender, sexuality, and women (see, e.g., Chambliss, 1975; Greenberg, 1983; Gordon, 1971; Spitzer, 1975; Taylor, Walton, and Young, 1973).

Despite significant attempts by feminist scholars to sensitize mainstream and critical criminologists to the gender-blind nature of their teaching and research (e.g., Bertrand, 1969; Carlen and Worrall, 1987; Heidensohn, 1968; Klein, 1973; Leonard, 1982; Millman, 1975; Morris, 1987; Smart, 1976), most criminologists still turn a blind eye to those concerns (Daly and Chesney-Lind, 1988; Gelsthorpe and Morris, 1988; Heidensohn, 1987).

The one major exception to this dominant tendency is research on male violence against women (Daly and Chesney-Lind, 1988; Gelsthorpe and Morris, 1988). Various types of feminist discourse (e.g., liberal, radical, and socialist feminist) are clearly evident in the theoretical and empirical literature on the physical, sexual and psychological victimization of women. Certainly these feminist concerns had an impact on British left realist thinking. In fact, according to Thomas and O'Maolchatha (1989), these researchers were among the first critical criminologists to recognize the importance of feminist inquiry. The influence of feminist victimology on left realism is articulated by two of its main proponents, Matthews and

Young (1986: 2): "The limits of the romantic conception of crime and the criminal were brought home forcibly by the growing feminist concern during the 1970s. Discussions around this issue served to reintroduce into radical criminology discourse neglected issues of aetiology, motivation and punishment." Unfortunately, this influence never penetrated to the deeper levels of discourse, and at times seemed even worse—extensive lip service only. These critiques will be covered in more detail later; but first, one way to examine the influence of feminist theory is by evaluating left realist empirical research on woman abuse.

## Local Crime Surveys and Woman Abuse

With certain exceptions, radical criminology has historically repudiated the use of quantitative modes of data gathering and analysis (Phipps, 1986). This rejection of empiricist methods has, together with other factors, contributed to the development of a right-wing monopoly over knowledge about victimization (MacLean and DeKeseredy, 1990). In the United Kingdom—without alternative sources of information on the frequency, causes, and consequences of victimization—the public, politicians, the media, and a substantial portion of the academy have generally been dependent on data gleaned from state sponsored national studies such as the British Crime Survey (BCS) Chambers and Tombs, 1984; Hough and Mayhew, 1983, 1985).

Although the BCS has provided some much needed data on victimization, it has a number of shortcomings. It is not helpful in studying particular communities, and none of the Home Office reports include a comprehensive gender-specific analysis (Jones et al., 1986). According to Hough and Mayhew (1985: 35), "For rape, the BCS can say little except that in comparison to crimes such as burglary, the risks of rape—and particularly of rape committed by strangers—are very low."

In response to criticism of the BCS and because of their desire to construct short-term anticrime strategies superior to those employed by the Thatcher government, left realists maintained that local crime surveys conducted by independent bodies provide a more focused approach than national studies. They also stated that the four-way interaction of victim, police, offender, and community that underlies the social construction of crime can be examined (Jones et al., 1986; MacLean, 1988). Left realists further argued that local studies are essential for establishing democratic reviews of police activities and community involvement in crime control and policy development (Jones et al., 1986; MacLean and DeKeseredy, 1990).

The Islington Crime Survey (ICS) (Jones et al., 1986), conducted in the London Borough of Islington, was the first major inner-city crime study to be based on left realist arguments (MacLean and DeKeseredy, 1990). Other London boroughs modeled their own surveys after it, including Haringey

(Gifford, 1987), Newham (Harris et al., 1987) and Hammersmith (Painter et al., 1989). More are planned and some are in the process of completion, including a second sweep of the ICS (MacLean and DeKeseredy, 1990).

One of the reasons the ICS was developed was to move beyond the BCS's limited analysis of gender issues. For example, it included measures of: (1) perceptions of risk; (2) fear of crime; (3) avoidance behaviors (e.g., precautions taken to reduce the risk of victimization); (4) rates of criminal and noncriminal violence (e.g., sexual harassment); and (5) the impact of domestic assault and rape. Based on the data gleaned from these measures, Jones et al., (1986: 182–83) argue that:

> The ICS has shown that not only are women more fearful than men but they have very good reasons for this. An examination of the criminal forms of violence directed specifically against women showed that there was a high level of both physical and psychological injury sustained by women very frequently. This survey illustrates that women receive very little institutional support of a satisfactory nature and must take responsibility for their own protection as a consequence. This means that they must engage in more avoidance behaviors than men which restricts them in their activities more often, especially at night.

The ICS findings contribute to a better understanding of woman abuse than those obtained by the BCS; for example, the ICS shows that female victimization is not a rare occurrence (Walklate, 1989). Nevertheless, some key feminist issues are ignored by the ICS even though its authors claim to have been heavily influenced by feminist contentions.

Although a major feminist concern is the relationship between patriarchy and various types of woman abuse, a rigorous analysis of how patriarchy perpetuates and legitimizes female victimization within working-class families is clearly not evident in the ICS and other radical realist writings (Taylor, 1988). According to two prominent feminists (Gelsthorpe and Morris, 1988: 103), this is a "startling omission."

Since left realist surveys such as the ICS did not examine the power accorded males in patriarchal capitalist societies, they remain somewhat similar to "mainstream" surveys on woman abuse (e.g., Straus et al., 1980; Straus and Gelles, 1986). Moreover, realist criticisms of conventional or conservative woman-abuse studies are not really distinct from other critiques (Edwards, 1989).

In sum, left realists have not adequately integrated feminist concerns into their empirical work, but instead their empirical agenda is dominated by a class-based analysis which views female victims as "honorary members of the core working class" (Taylor, 1988: 22). British left realism, according to Edwards (1989: 19):

> . . . has failed to learn from feminist scholarship and campaigns, or else deliberately ignored this considerable body of thought and action. If left

realist criminology is to be saved from the inevitable redundancy of its classical position it must take woman's issues and campaigns and the writings of radical women academics on women's issues seriously.

This is not to say that local surveys cannot be valuable, but that to reach the stated objective of a socialist feminist understanding of woman abuse, left realist surveys should pay much more attention to societal and familial patriarchy. Perhaps North American quantitative studies on the relationship between patriarchy and the physical abuse of women can help as partial models for the development of future new realist projects (Smith, 1989; Yllö, 1983, 1984).

Sample surveys have important strengths. However, some feminist researchers (e.g., Breines and Gordon, 1983; Dobash and Dobash, 1979; Dobash and Dobash, 1983) argue that quantitative, empiricist methods are problematic because they (1) are reductionist, (2) tend to be ahistorical and (3) remove violence out of its larger cultural and structural context. Moreover, others maintain that surveys which employ closed-end measures obstruct an adequate understanding of what sexual assault, physical violence, and psychological abuse mean to the victims themselves (Bograd, 1988; Kelly, 1988). This is not to say that quantitative methods should be abandoned in favor of alternative techniques, but rather that a variety of measures is often more useful. For example, Dobash and Dobash's context-specific method (1979, 1983) may hold the potential for bringing the realists closer to bridging the gap between micro- and macro-level analyses of woman abuse (DeKeseredy, 1989).

Another shortcoming of left realist empirical research and crime control measures is that it does not pay attention to their own precept that working-class people are victimized from all directions in capitalist societies (e.g., Young, 1986). Both the surveys and crime control measures deal primarily with predatory street crimes committed against working-class people rather than crimes of the powerful or elite crimes committed against women. There are many victimizations of women in this society other than street crime. For example, many women are injured or killed in the workplace (Chenier, 1982; Reasons, Ross, and Patterson, 1981) and are victims of unnecessary surgery (Goff and Reasons, 1986). Others are physically and psychologically harmed by pharmaceutical companies (Dowie and Marshall, 1982; Ellis, 1987). Many women are victims of other types of economic crimes committed by corporations (Goff and Reasons, 1986).

If, as left realists argue (Jones et al., 1986: 6), local crime surveys are central to the formulation of "humane policies which accurately reflect people's needs, which are guided by facts and which can be monitored effectively," then the development of better local crime studies which include the concerns of feminist scholars and victimization by elites must be included in order to construct effective policy initiatives aimed at controlling and preventing woman abuse.

Realist criminology's neglect of major feminist critiques and concerns is also evident in their proposals for change. Thus, a critical appraisal of their strategies to curb male violence against women is warranted here.

## Confronting Woman Abuse: The Left Realist Position

The issue of the proper reaction of the state to the concerns and fears of women is one where feminist critiques and socialist critiques are often at odds, making it difficult to develop a socialist feminist critique (Schwartz, 1988). Unfortunately, the usual method of debating in this literature is to note how important feminist concerns are but then forget them for the rest of the discussion (Edwards, 1989).

A problem for a feminist analysis is that virtually all of critical criminology and radical criminology has had little to offer women who are regular victims of violence or who live in regular or constant fear. Although left realist victimization studies make it clear that women have a high fear of crime, they never make it explicit that women's fear of crime is closely connected to a fear of men. As noted above, the problem of gender relations and male power gets lost in left realist discussions in the midst of extensive work on the problems of improving policing in the community (Gelsthorpe and Morris, 1988).

Further, a primary feminist criminological concern is the effect of patriarchal structures on the relations between men (Daly and Chesney-Lind, 1988). Many theorists are becoming concerned that it is unproductive to attempt to describe violence by the powerless without taking into account the position and power accorded men in a patriarchal system, and that an attack on the sexual division of labor is an essential element to ending violent street crime (Messerschmidt, 1986). Of course, one would not wish to argue that the causes of violent crime can only be found in capitalist social relations, which can easily be seen in cross-cultural studies (Schwartz, 1988; Levinson, 1989). However, in current capitalist systems it is an essential factor and one ignored in most radical work.

Perhaps the most difficult problem of all is the issue of what the state can do to protect women, at least under the current social order. Left realists are like many other radicals in looking forward to a state reduced in power. However, some radicals want the state expanded in power in order to take positive measures to reduce structural and economic inequality (Lynch and Groves, 1989); Matthews, 1987). The problem is when theorists like the left realists are in favor of both—reducing the state power most of the time, except when they want to increase the state power.

The most complicated place where this takes place is the question of what to do about violence towards women. Many liberal and radical feminists have responded to women's fears with calls for exceptional or high punishment under the current system for men who victimize women (e.g., Box-

Grainger, 1986; Gregory, 1986). Among liberal feminists, the call is no doubt due to a belief in the value of the criminal justice system in deterring and punishing men (Schwartz and DeKeseredy, 1988). For radical and social feminists, however, any such call is a difficult one and involves walking an extraordinarily fine line between the development of equity for women as a temporary measure and, on the other hand, the support of right-wing power structures and oppressive systems.

The problem is most serious for a left realist or a radical criminologist feminist who would like to call for an end to the current oppressive Thatcher/Reagan/Bush criminal justice system, with a single exception for rapists and woman batterers, for whom we not only need to keep this oppressive system in operation but further need to increase the punishments within it. Illogical as this might sound, this is exactly what left realist feminists (Box-Grainger, 1986) and left criminology feminists (Radford, 1987; Kelly and Radford, 1987) are doing.

It is most difficult to see just what these increased punishments would do, as the theorists remain rather vague. Some abstract idea of protection for women is often cited (e.g., Box-Grainger, 1986) as if increased punishments have provided more protection for women in burglary and theft. Edwards, however, scores those who cannot tell the difference between male demands for more punishment of rapists and female demands for more punishments of rapists, claiming that left-wing feminist demands (1989:11):

> . . . have been seriously misunderstood. Their demands cannot simply be reduced and equated with right-wing Conservative regulation, since feminists' demands for protection through law and policing and right-wing homogenized efforts toward control derive from very different theoretical conceptualization of the relation of law to the state, and very divergent political standpoints. In the apparent demand for more law and policing in the area of violence against women, feminists are simply urging the same consideration for women victims in the home as has already been given to non-spousal and non-partner victims in the street.

The potential for confusion is obvious. If radical criminologists are having trouble with the distinction, one can have some sympathy for the lawmakers and the rapists who will be asked to understand it.

Unfortunately, this fine line of distinction is one which the left realists have had trouble walking. One of the central features of the entire left realist plan of the 1980s has been the proposal for minimal policing, taking the police out of social-work concerns and limiting their intervention in the community to the very minimum required. One exception to this, Kinsey et al. suggest, is to follow the feminist arguments by providing "much more vigorous and thorough" policing in "domestic disputes" (1986: 205). After carefully explaining that minimal policing means nonintervention and that such is the wish of the community, one of the first examples they report is a place for increased "vigorous" policing even if it is against the community's wishes. One can imagine the disdain of the left realists if a Chief Constable had recommended as a solution to "domestic disputes" a "much more vigorous and thorough" policing!

## Alternative Systems

The related arena where the claims of the left realists are open to attack involves the nature of the society, the state, and the law. If you agree that one cannot avoid a criminal justice system much like our current one in complex modern society (Hirst, 1986), with the police unavoidably situated as the principal agency of intervention (Boehringer et al., 1983) and with the criminal law seen as the embodiment of the people's views, then the left realist approach to attempt to restructure the system to make it act better or more in line with socialist ideals makes excellent sense.

Those who disagree with this point of view do so because they believe that a justice system can be devised on systems other than the repression and control of individuals by a powerful state mechanism. Those who disagree the most tend to be the radical and anarchist criminologists who firmly believe that demands for more punishment for criminals will only make matters worse (Pepinsky, 1986; Davidson, 1986). Even while agreeing that left realism has many good points, such theorists fear that it is doomed to reproduce (perhaps on a smaller scale) the very structures of capitalist society which currently imprison us and our patterns of thought and action. The problem for these dissenters is that while they are sure that increased intervention is a problem, many cannot locate an alternative to policing which can provide at least some protection to women from the predatory hordes of men who populate society.

Finding alternatives to the current system which are attractive to feminists has not yet been successful. Although many socialist criminologists have been sensitive to the fact that the law embodies class interests, "it is the precise juncture of bourgeois and male interest which constitutes the corner-stone of women's experience and corresponding oppression" (Edwards, 1989: 13). Marxists have found it simple to argue that laws are made either directly or indirectly to benefit the members of the capitalist or ruling class, but they have only rarely noted that their conceptions of ruling class has in fact been "male members of the ruling class." As Schwartz and Slatin note (1984: 252):

> Feminist analysis alerts us to the necessity of considering that such men have a gender interest in their dominant position. To expect that such men consciously or unconsciously write laws which invariably serve the short-run or long-run interests of capital, but do not similarly incorporate their gender interests into these formulations, is a blindness or naivete equal to any idea that capitalism is a natural condition of humankind.

The difficulty is to develop a new system which will incorporate women's interests in justice, particularly since the development of an equivalent school of thought on feminist justice is only just beginning. Kay Harris, who has been attempting to develop such a perspective, asks one of the primary questions (1987: 34): "How can we respond effectively to people who inflict injury and hardship on others without employing the same script and the same means that they do?" Susan Edwards, while noting that there are many left-wing feminists who can be seen as loosely aligned with left realism in that they believe in increased state repression of certain offenders, points out the importance of remembering that feminist scholarship is divided on these issues, with many feminists "deeply ambivalent about engaging with the law to bring about broader social change" (1989: 15).

There are a number of reparations and conciliation-based strategies which are in great need of examination, but there are very few feminist or abolitionist-based theorists who have been able thus far to match either mainstream criminology or left realist criminology in the construction of detail for proposed justice systems. As Stanley Cohen has noted (1985: 131): "It still makes sense to say that mutual aid, good neighborliness and real community are preferable to the solutions of bureaucracies, professionals and the centralized state . . . [I]t should not be impossible to imagine a way of stopping the relentless categorization of deviants." While it should not be impossible to imagine such a system, it thus far has not yet been done; and when it is done, it will be very difficult to work out.

One interesting avenue for combining the interests of abolitionists and peacekeeping criminologists and the feminist criminologists is the recently popularized notion of a law based on mediation, mutual aid, and reconciliation (Quinney, 1988). Certainly there are serious drawbacks to such proposals which must be carefully considered, including any tendency to serve the needs of the bureaucratic state more than the community, to legitimize the state system, neutralize class conflict, widen the net of social control, and widen the definition of deviance (Selva and Bohm, 1987). Yet, this nation has the implication of being the very solution many feminists may be seeking: the ability to widen the net of social control without invoking the harsh and retributive criminal justice system.

One of the major contributions of feminist theory has been to develop "an appreciation of the under-representation of women's everyday experiences, exploitation and appropriation, and sexual and physical violence against them, in the public debate" (Edwards, 1989: 13). In many ways, women have remained outside the protection of the criminal justice system, because the very form of particularly male behavior which is most fear-inducing is not against the law. Many criminologists have noted that women's fears seem irrational—that even though rape rates are fairly low, the fear that women have to walk in their neighborhood streets can remain high. This is because the behavior which induces a fearful state in wide numbers of women is often not rape itself, but leers, suggestive comments, being followed for blocks down the street, being yelled at from cars, phone calls, being "hit on" in restaurants and bars, and other forms of harassment (Radford, 1987). These behaviors are either not against the law or else so "minor" that virtually any police force will ignore them. Yet, as Kelly and Radford point out (1987: 242): ". . . at the time women are being followed/flashed at/harassed they do not know how the event will end. It is only in retrospect that such events can be defined as 'minor.' " Just as obviously, similar behavior by those who are or have been lovers or husbands is similarly excluded from the purview of the law (Schwartz and Slatin, 1984; Quarm and Schwartz, 1985).

This brings up a fascinating possibility. The worst fear of many radical criminologists such as Selva and Bohm is widening the net of social control. Left realists are similarly afraid of net-widening because they presume that this means more arrests and police powers (Kinsey et al., 1986). At the same time, some of the left-wing feminists are calling for such increased police powers because they are having trouble envisioning an alternative strategy which does not result once again in the marginalizing of women's concerns and fears.

In fact, if the net-widening was used in the manner called for by peace-making criminologists, anarchist Marxists, penal abolitionists, and others who call for a law based on mutual aid and reconciliation, it would speak to many feminist interests more than any program of increased penalties for law violators. There is no reason to believe that higher penal sentences under the current system would reduce violence against women (Daly and Chesney-Lind, 1988). Instead, a program of reconciliation, reeducation, and mutual aid by a caring community would offer the greatest hope of ending the "little rapes" of women in the community. It might not actually reduce the real rape rate, and this would have to be a continuing item of high urgency for radical criminologists. However, if fear is related more to harassment than to rape, and expanding the net of social control could bring in the male harassers to begin a process of stopping their harassment of women, this might in the long run do more to demarginalize women than many other criminology proposals. It would not solve the overall structural problems of a society which encourages the victimization of women by promotion their marginalization economically and politically, but it could do its small part to provide some of the equity that some radical feminists feel will only come from the increased use of penal repression (e.g., Box-Grainger, 1986; Edwards, 1989).

Of course, careful attention will have to be paid to the fact that peacemaking solutions are only useful as part of a package which includes structural change in society, or such solutions may indeed render conflict individual and deny structure (Selva and Bohm, 1987). Further, such proposals will not end the victimization of women by corporate and governmental entities, and some imaginative proposals will be needed to bring nonrepressive solutions into this arena also (e.g., Schwartz and Ellison, 1982). Yet they are bound to be more useful than repressive measures, whether they are packaged as right-wing law and order policies, left realist community control, left-wing feminist calls for equity, or whatever. It may be that, as Edwards suggests, it is important for us to keep in mind that the identical proposals by right-wingers and feminist theorists should not be confused because they originate in different theoretical positions. As suggested earlier in this paper, however, it is unlikely that most members of the working class are particularly concerned to make fine distinctions about the nature of their oppressor, as long as they remain so heavily concerned by the fact of their oppression.

## NOTES

1. Although this paper focuses mainly on the British left realist discourse, it should be noted that the left realist writings of United States scholars (Boostrom and Henderson, 1983; Currie, 1985; Currie, 1989; Gross, 1982; Iadicola, 1986; Michalowski, 1983; Platt, 1978; Platt, 1984; Schwartz and DeKeseredy, 1989), of Canadian scholars (Ahluwalia and MacLean, 1986; Alvi, 1986; DeKeseredy, 1988; Lowman, 1987; Lowman, 1989; MacLean, 1988; MacLean, 1989; MacLean and DeKeseredy, 1990; McMullan, 1986; McMullan, 1988), and of Australian scholars (Boerhinger et al, 1983; C. C. J. 1988; Hogg, 1988; Hogg and Brown, 1988) have made important contributions to debates on the causes and control of violent street crime.

## REFERENCES

Ahluwalia, Seema and Brian D. MacLean. 1986. "Racial Biases in Policing: The Case of the Female Victim." In Dawn H. Currie and Brian D. MacLean (eds.), *The Administration of Justice.* Saskatoon: Social Research Unit, Department of Sociology, University of Saskatchewan.

Alvi, Shahid. 1986. "Realistic Crime Prevention Strategies Through Alternative Measures for Youth." In Dawn H. Currie and Brian D. MacLean (eds.), *The Administration of Justice.* Saskatoon: Social Research Unit, Department of Sociology, University of Saskatchewan.

Bertrand, Marie Andree. 1969. "Self-Image and Delinquency: A Contribution to the Study of Female Criminality and Women's Image." *Acta Criminologica: Etudes sur la Conduite Antisociale* 2: 71–144.

Boehringer, Gill, Dave Brown, Brendan Edgeworth, Russell Hogg, and Ian Ramsey. 1983. "Law and Order for Progressives?: An Australian Response." *Crime and Social Justice* 19: 2–12.

Bograd, Michelle. 1988. "Feminist Perspectives on Wife Abuse: An Introduction." In Kersti Yllö and Michele Bograd (eds.), *Feminist Perspectives on Wife Abuse.* Beverly Hills: Sage.

Boostrom, Ron, and J. Henderson. 1933. "Community Action and Crime Prevention: Some Unresolved Issues." *Crime and Social Justice* 19: 24–30.

Box, Steven. 1983. *Power, Crime, and Mystification.* London: Tavistock.

Box-Grainger, Jill. 1986. "Sentencing Rapists." In Roger Matthews and Jock Young (eds.), *Confronting Crime.* Beverly Hills: Sage.

Breines, Wini, and Linda Gordon. 1983. "The New Scholarship on Family Violence." *Signs: Journal of Women in Culture and Society* 8: 453, 91.

Bridges, Lee, and Paul Gilroy. 1982. "Striking Back." *Marxism Today* 26: 34–35.

C. C. J. 1988. *Campaign for Criminal Justice,* Bulletins 1 and 2, Sydney.

Carlen, Pat, and Anne Worrall (eds.). 1987. *Gender, Crime and Justice.* Philadelphia: Open University Press.

Chambers, G., and J. Tombs (eds.). 1984. *The British Crime Survey: Scotland.* Edinburgh: HMSO.

Chambliss, William. 1975. "Toward a Political Economy of Crime." *Theory and Society* (Summer): 167–80.

Chenier, Nancy Miller. 1982. *Reproductive Hazards at Work.* Ottawa: Canadian Advisory Council on the Status of Women.

Cohen, Stanley. 1985. *Visions of Social Control.* Cambridge: Polity Press.

Currie, Elliott. 1985. *Confronting Crime: An American Challenge.* New York: Pantheon.

———. 1989. "Confronting Crime: Looking Toward the Twenty-First Century." *Justice Quarterly* 6: 5–26.

Daly, Kathleen, and Meda Chesney-Lind. 1988. "Feminism and Criminology." *Justice Quarterly* 4: 497–538.

Davidson, Howard. 1986. "Community Control without State Control: Issues Surrounding a Feminist and Prison Abolitionist Approach to Violence against Women." In Herman Bianchi and Rene van Swaaningen (eds.), *Abolitionism: Toward a Non-Repressive Approach to Crime.* Amsterdam: Free University Press.

DeKeseredy, Walter S. 1988. "The Left Realist Approach to Law and Order." *Justice Quarterly* 4: 635–40.

———. 1989. "Dating Violence: Toward New Directions in Empirical Research." *Sociological Viewpoints* 5 (1). Forthcoming.

DeKeseredy, Walter S., and Martin D. Schwartz. 1989. "British and Left Realism: A Critical Comparison." Paper presented at the annual meeting of the American Society of Criminology, Reno, Nevada.

Dexter, L. A. 1958. "A Note on Selective Inattention in Social Science." *Social Problems* 6: 176–82.

Dobash, R. Emerson, and Russell P. Dobash. 1979. *Violence Against Wives.* New York: Free Press.

Dobash, Russell P., and R. Emerson Dobash. 1983. "The Context-Specific Approach." In David Finkelhor, Richard J. Gelles, Gerald T. Hotaling and Murray A. Straus (eds.), *The Dark Side of Families: Current Family Violence Research.* Beverly Hills: Sage.

Dowie, Mark, and Carolyn Marshall. 1982. "The Bendectin Cover-up." In M. David Ermann and Richard J. Lundman (eds.), *Corporate and Governmental Deviance: Problems of Organizational Behavior in Contemporary Society.* New York: Oxford University Press.

Edwards, Susan. 1989. *Policing Domestic Violence.* London: Sage.

Ellis, Desmond. 1987. *The Wrong Stuff: An Introduction to the Sociological Study of Deviance.* Toronto: Collier Macmillan.

Gelsthorpe, Lorraine, and Alison Morris. 1988. "Feminism and Criminology in Britain." *British Journal of Criminology* 28: 93–110.

Gifford, Lord. 1986. *The Broadwater Farm Inquiry.* London: Borough of Haringey.

Gilroy, Paul. 1982. "The Myth of Black Criminality." In Ralph Miliband and J. Saville (eds.), *Socialist Register 1982.* London: Merlin Press.

Gilroy, Paul, and Joe Sim. 1987. "Law, Order and the State of the Left." In Phil Scraton (ed.), *Law, Order and the Authoritarian State*. Philadelphia: Open University Press.

Goff, Colin H., and Charles E. Reasons. 1978. *Corporate Crime in Canada: A Critical Analysis of Anti-Combines Legislation*. Scarborough, Ontario: Prentice-Hall.

——. 1986. "Organizational Crimes Against Employees, Consumers and the Public." In Brian D. MacLean (ed.), *The Political Economy of Crime: Readings for a Critical Criminology*. Scarborough, Ontario: Prentice-Hall.

Gordon, David. 1971. "Class and the Economics of Crime." *Review of Radical Political Economics* 3: 51–75.

Greenberg, David. 1983. *Crime and Capitalism: Readings in Marxist Criminology*. Palo Alto, Calif.: Mayfield.

Gregory, Jeanne. 1966. "Sex, Class and Crime: Toward a Non-sexist Criminology." In Roger Matthews and Jock Young (eds.), *Confronting Crime*. Beverly Hills: Sage.

Gross, Bertram. 1982. "Some Anticrime Proposals for Progressives." *Crime and Social Justice* 17: 51–54.

Hanmer, Jalna, and S. Saunders. 1984. *Well Founded Fear: A Community Study of Violence to Women*. London: Hutchinson.

Harris and Associates. 1987. *Crime in Newham: The Survey*. London: Borough of Newham.

Heidensohn, Frances M. 1968. "The Deviance of Women: A Critique and an Enquiry." *British Journal of Sociology* 19: 160–176.

——. 1987. "Women and Crime: Questions for Criminology." In Pat Carlen and Anne Worrall (eds.), *Gender Crime and Justice*. Philadelphia: Open University Press.

Hirst, Paul. 1986. *Law, Socialism and Democracy*. London: Allen & Unwin.

Hogg, Russell. 1988. "Taking Crime Seriously: Left Realism and Australian Criminology." In M. Findlay and Russell Hogg (eds.), *Understanding Crime and Criminal Justice*. Sydney: Law Book.

Hogg, Russell, and David Brown. 1988. "Law and Order Politics, Left Realism and Criminology: An Overview." Paper presented at the annual meeting of the American Society of Criminology, Chicago.

Hood, Roger. 1987. "Some Reflections on the Role of Criminology in Public Policy." *Criminal Law Review*: 527–38.

H.O.R.U. 1984. *Research Programme, 1984–1985*. London: HMSO.

Hough, J. Michael, and Pat M. Mayhew. 1983. *The British Crime Survey: First Report*. London: HMSO.

——. 1985. *Taking Account of Crime: Key Findings From the 1984 British Crime Survey*. London: HMSO.

Hulsman, Louk. 1986. "Critical Criminology and the Concept of Crime." *Contemporary Crises* 10: 63–80.

Hunt, Alan. 1982. "Law, Order and Socialism: A Response to Ian Taylor." *Crime and Social Justice* 19: 16–22.

Iadicola, Peter. 1986. "Community Crime Control Strategies." *Crime and Social Justice* 25: 140–65.

Jones, Trevor, Brian MacLean, and Jock Young. 1986. *The Islington Crime Survey*. Aldershot, England: Gower.

Kelly, Liz. 1988. "How Women Define Their Experiences of Violence." In Kersti Yllö and Michele Bograd (eds.), *Feminist Perspectives on Wife Abuse*. Beverly Hills: Sage.

Kelly, Liz, and Jill Radford. 1987. "The Problem of Men: Feminist Perspectives on Sexual Violence." In Phil Scraton (ed.), *Law, Order and the Authoritarian State: Readings in Critical Criminology*, Philadelphia: Open University Press.

Kinsey, Richard (ed.). 1989. *Left Realism and the Prison*. London: Pluto Press.

Kinsey, Richard, John Lea, and Jock Young. 1986. *Losing the Fight Against Crime*. London: Basil Blackwell.

Klein, Dorie. 1973. "The Etiology of Female Crime: A Review of the Literature." *Issues in Criminology* 8: 3–30.

Lea, John, and Jock Young. 1984. *What is to be Done About Law and Order?* New York: Penguin.

Leonard, Eileen. 1982. *Women, Crime and Society: A Critique of Criminological Theory.* New York: Longman.

Levinson, David. 1989. *Family Violence in Cross-Cultural Perspective*. Beverly Hills: Sage.

Lowman, John. 1987. "Rediscovering Crime: Dilemmas of Left Realism." Paper presented at the annual meeting of the Canadian Sociology and Anthropology Association, Hamilton, Ontario.

———. 1989. "Prostitution in Canada: Some Reflections on the Logic of 'Left Regulationism'." Paper presented at the British Criminology Conference, Bristol Polytechnic.

Lynch, Michael J., and W. Byron Groves. 1989. *A Primer in Radical Criminology.* Second Edition. New York: Harrow and Heston.

MacLean, Brian. 1988. "The New Victimology: Political Praxis or Left Unrealism." Paper presented at the annual meeting of the Canadian Law and Society Association, Windsor, Ontario.

———. 1989. "Left Realism and Police Accountability in Canada." Paper presented at the annual meeting of the Canadian Sociology and Anthropology Association, Quebec City.

MacLean, Brian, and Walter S. DeKeseredy. 1990. "Taking Working Class Victimization Seriously." Unpublished manuscript. Carleton University.

Matthews, Roger. 1987. "Taking Realist Criminology Seriously." *Contemporary Crises* 11: 371–401.

Matthews, Roger, and Jock Young (eds.) 1986. *Confronting Crime*. London: Sage.

Maxfield, M. 1984. *Fear of Crime in England and Wales*. London: HMSO.

McMullan, John. 1986. "The 'Law and Order' Problem in Socialist Criminology." *Studies in Political Economy* 21:175–92.

———. 1987. "Epilogue: Law, Justice and the State." In Robert S. Ratner and John McMullan (eds.), *State Control: Criminal Justice Politics in Canada*. Vancouver: University of British Columbia Press.

Messerschmidt, James. 1986. *Capitalism, Patriarchy, and Crime: Toward a Socialist Feminist Criminology.* Totowa, N.J.: Roman and Littlefield.

Michalowski, Raymond. 1983. "Crime Control in the 1980s: A Progressive Agenda." *Crime and Social Justice* 19: 13–23.

Millman, Marcia. 1975. "She Did it All For Love: A Feminist View of the Sociology of Deviance." In Marcia Millman and Rosabeth Moss Kanter (eds.), *Another Voice: Feminist Perspectives on Social Life and Social Science*. Garden City, N.Y.: Anchor/Doubleday.

Morris, Allison. 1987. *Women, Crime and Criminal Justice*. New York: Blackwell.

Painter, K., John Lea, T. Woodhouse, and Jock Young. 1989. *Hammersmith and Fulham Crime and Policing Survey.* London: Middlesex Centre for Criminology.

Pearce, Frank. 1976. *Crimes of the Powerful*. London: Pluto Press.

Pearson, Geoff. 1976. "Paki-Bashing in a North-East Lancashire Cotton Town." In Geoff Mungham and Geoff Pearson (eds.), *Working Class Youth Culture*. London: Routledge and Kegan Paul.

Pepinsky, Harold E. 1986. "This Can't Be Peace: A Pessimist Looks at Punishment." In W. Byron Groves and Graeme Newman (eds.), *Punishment and Privilege*. New York: Harrow and Heston.

Phipps, Alan. 1986. "Radical Criminology and Criminal Victimization." In Roger Matthews and Jock Young (eds.), *Confronting Crime*. Beverly Hills: Sage.

Platt, Tony. 1978. "Street Crime: A View From the Left." *Crime and Social Justice* 9: 26–34.

———. 1984. "Criminology in the 1980s: Progressive Alternatives to Law and Order." *Crime and Social Justice* 21: 191–99.

Quarm, Daisy, and Martin D. Schwartz. 1985. "Domestic Violence in Criminal Court." In Claudine Schweber and Clarice Feinman (eds.), *Criminal Justice Politics and Women: The Aftermath of Equally Mandated Change*. New York: Haworth Press.

Quinney, Richard. 1988. "The Theory and practice of Peacemaking in the Development of Radical Criminology." Paper presented at the annual meeting of the American Society of Criminology, Chicago.

Radford, Jill. 1987. "Policing Male Violence-Policing Women." In Jalna Hanmer and Mary Maynard (eds.), *Women, Violence and Social Control*. Atlantic Highlands, N.J.: Humanities International Press.

Reasons, Charles, Lois Ross, and Craig Patterson. 1981. *Assault on the Worker: Occupational Health and Safety in Canada*. Toronto: Butterworths.

Russell, Diana. 1975. *The Politics of Rape*. New York: Stein and Day.

———. 1982. *Rape in Marriage*. New York: Macmillan.

———. 1984. *Sexual Exploitation: Rape, Child Sexual Abuse, and Workplace Harassment*. Beverly Hills: Sage.

———. 1986. *The Secret Trauma: Incest in the Lives of Girls and Women*. New York: Basic Books.

Schechter, Susan. 1982. *Women and Male Violence*. Boston: South End.

Schwartz, Martin D. 1988. "Ain't Got No Class: Universal Risk Theories of Battering." *Contemporary Crises* 12 (4): 373–92.

Schwartz, Martin D., and Walter DeKeseredy. 1988. "Liberal Feminism on Violence Against Women." *Social Justice*, 15 (3–4): 213–21.

———. 1990. "The Application of Left Realist Principles to North America." *Contemporary Crises*. Forthcoming.

Schwartz, Martin D., and Charles E. Ellison. 1982. "The Use of Criminal Law in Corporate Misbehavior." *Humanity & Society* 6 (3): 267–93.

Schwartz, Martin D., and Gerald T. Slatin. 1984. "The Law on Marital Rape: How do Marxism and Feminism Explain Its Persistence." *American Legal Studies Association Forum* 8 (2): 244–64.

Selva, Lance, and Robert Bohm. 1987. "A Critical Examination of the Informalism Experiment in the Administration of Justice." *Crime and Social Justice* 29: 43–57.

Sim, Joe, Phil Scraton, and Paul Gordon. 1987. "Introduction: Crime, the State and Critical Analysis." In Phil Scraton (ed.), *Law, Order and the Authoritarian State*. Philadelphia: Open University Press.

Smandych, Russell. 1985. "Marxism and the Creation of Law: Re-examining the Origins of Canadian Anti-Combines Legislation, 1890–1910." In Thomas Fleming (ed.), *The New Criminologies in Canada: State, Crime, and Control*. Toronto: Oxford University Press.

Smart, Carol. 1976. *Women, Crime and Criminology: A Feminist Critique*. Boston: Routledge and Kegan Paul.

Smith, Michael D. 1989. "Patriarchal Ideology and Wife Beating: A Test of A Feminist Hypothesis." Unpublished manuscript, Toronto, York University.

Snider, Laureen. 1980. "Corporate Crime in Canada." In Robert A. Silverman and James J. Teevan, Jr. (eds.), *Crime in Canadian Society*. Toronto: Butterworths.

Spitzer, Steven. 1975. "Toward A Marxian Theory of Deviance." *Social Problems* 22: 638–51.

Steinert, Heinz. 1985. "The Amazing New Left and Order Campaign: Some Thoughts on Anti-Utopianism and Possible Futures." *Contemporary Crises* 9: 37–234.

Straus, Murray, and Richard Gelles. 1986. "Societal Changes and Change in Family Violence from 1975 to 1985 as Revealed by Two National Surveys." *Journal of Marriage and the Family* 48: 465–78.

Straus, Murray, Richard Gelles, and Suzanne Steinmetz. 1980. *Behind Closed Doors: Violence in the American Family.* Garden City, N.Y.: Anchor.

Taylor, Ian. 1982. "Against Crime and For Socialism." *Crime and Social Justice* 18: 4–15.

―――. 1988. "Left Realism, the Free Market Economy and the Problem of Social Order." Paper presented at the annual meeting of the American Society of Criminology, Chicago.

Taylor, Ian, Paul Walton, and Jock Young. 1973. *The New Criminology.* London: Routledge and Kegan Paul.

Thomas, Jim, and Aogan O'Maolchatha. 1989. "Reassessing the Critical Metaphor: An Optimistic Revisionist View." *Justice Quarterly* 2: 143–72.

Walklate, Sandra. 1989. "Appreciating the Victim: Conventional, Realist or Critical Victimology." Paper presented at the British Criminology Conference, Bristol Polytechnic.

West, W. Gordon, and Laureen Snider. 1985. "A Critical Perspective on Law in the Canadian State: Delinquency and Corporate Crime." In Thomas Fleming (ed.), *The New Criminologies in Canada: State, Crime, and Control.* Toronto: Oxford University Press.

Ylló, Kersti. 1983. "Using a Feminist Approach in Quantitative Research: A Case Study." In David Finkelhor, Richard Gelles, Gerald Hotaling, and Murray Straus (eds.), *The Dark Side of Families: Current Family Violence Research.* Beverly Hills: Sage.

―――. 1984. "The Status of Women, Marital Equality, and Violence Against Wives." *Journal of Family Issues* 5: 307–20.

Young, Jock. 1986. "The Failure of Criminology." In Roger Matthews and Jock Young (eds.), *Confronting Crime.* Beverly Hills: Sage.

―――. 1988. "Radical Criminology in Britain: The Emergence of a Competing Paradigm." *British Journal of Criminology* 28: 289–313.

*Lila Rucker*

---

T E N

# Peacemaking in Prisons

## *A Process*

If, indeed, our ultimate goal is to live together peaceably as a global family on this planet, situating criminal justice concepts within that context is important. Our mode of thinking, Quinney (1987: 11) suggests, affects the way we live.

The thought of translating such precepts as compassion, care, loving-kindness, and even forgiveness into an actual administrative strategy within the criminal justice system, say, "the correctional bureaucracy," can bring tingles of excitement if we allow ourselves to conjure up images of transforming *correctional* centers into *healing* centers. Infused with genuineness, honesty, and love, these would be places of forgiveness and getting on with life, places where people would be encouraged and enabled to grow beyond their current limitations rather than getting mired down in them. Here, the focus would be on serving the human part of human beings rather than denying it. Here, as Satir envisioned, "the heart and soul as well as the head" would be present and people would feel free to "openly show affection as well as pain and disapproval" (Satir, 1972: 13).

Grounding program in vision, Claassen (1989: 1) contends, is essential. A vision, he writes, "is something that doesn't yet exist and is currently seen only in our imagination. It is rooted in values, spirit, ideas, and ideals. In our imagination we see images of people, programs, interactions, and procedures which incorporate these values and ideals. A vision is a desired state for the future. It is more intuition than linear thinking."

Visions of life-affirming possibilities within the correctional bureaucracy, however, are all too quickly dismissed as irrational as we bring to mind the impossible entanglement of negative forces which are prevalent within the violent reality of our prisons. Here, the norm of hostility, anger, hopelessness, distrust, continual and abnormal physical aggression and sexual assaults, poor health and the spread of diseases, increasing idleness and stagnation, and total loss of privacy (Ingraham & Wellford, 1987) has spawned a life of its own, breeding impotency.

In such a violent context, then, how do we give meaning to our vision? Claassen (1989) suggests that the only way to give meaning to any vision is to give it body, substance, life. Real-life experiences and demonstrations, then, become essential.

It is the thesis of this essay that certain self-help programs which dot the prison population are based on the concept of healing and seek to provide the types of real-life experiences for which Claassen calls. It is my sense that there is much to be learned from such programs and that they set an example for us to consider. Indeed, it is in the very process of atomizing, cutting, and analyzing, Skolimowski argues (1986: 306; see also Quinney, 1987: 11), that objective social scientists lose their capacity for empathy, compassion, and love. Hence, our efforts as criminologists become cold and hardened rather than supple, mechanical rather than vital. Nowhere is this more evidenced than in our prisons.

The purpose of this essay, then, is to analyze one such program, the Alternatives to Violence Project, Inc. (AVP). In keeping with the philosophy that we all have within us the answers to our own questions if we can simply open to them, it is fitting that AVP was born out of the efforts of a group of incarcerated individuals themselves who took the lead almost 15 years ago in a search for alternatives to violence within prisons.

## The Alternatives to Violence Project, Inc. (AVP)

In 1975, the Think Tank, an inmate group in Greenhaven Prison in New York state, "felt the need for nonviolence training in preparation for their upcoming roles as counselors in an experimental program in a Division for Youth institution for under-aged offenders. The Think Tank asked a local Quaker group to provide such training, and this was done (AVP Basic Manual, 1985: A–1)." From Greenhaven Prison, AVP spread to other prisons and to the outside community and is now in 15 states and Canada. The program at Greenhaven Prison is still alive and well.

The format of AVP consists of two three-day-long, intensive experiential workshops. A third session, the Training for Trainers, is offered for participants who demonstrate leadership qualities and who are interested in becoming facilitators. The first of the two workshops, the Basic, focuses on the core components of building community, cooperation, and trust while developing communication and conflict-resolution skills. The second workshop, the Advanced, usually follows some months later and provides in-depth focus on specific issues which contribute to violence (e.g., anger, fear, power, stereotyping, etc.). Group size generally does not exceed 20 participants and there are typically from three to four facilitators who have been trained in AVP principles and techniques of nonviolence. Some of the facilitators are volunteers from the surrounding community, others are incarcerated individuals.

The core philosophy of AVP is one of empowerment, the goal being to "affirm the existence and legitimacy of personal power and to give participants the experience of shared power exercised cooperatively, responsibly and well" (AVP Basic Manual, 1985: C–1).

AVP's conceptualization of power, however, is quite different than that of others. Whereas Huston (1983: 189), reflecting the popular conceptualization of power, contends that the degree to which an individual possesses power is reflected in the degree to which that individual can prevail over another, the AVP conceptualization of power has more to do with creating "win/win" situations and has nothing to do with capacity to coerce others. The idea here is more in keeping with Peck's (1978: 284) conceptualization of spiritual power wherein decisions are made with maximum awareness, with Raven's (1965) conceptualization of informational power wherein sufficient information is provided through clear and nonthreatening communication, and with Rotter's (1966) conceptualization of internal locus of control wherein there is a belief that "I do, indeed, have an impact on my world."

One of the basic tenets of AVP is that there are certain individual and group dynamics that make it possible to transform hostility and destructiveness, aggression, and violence, into cooperation and community (AVP Basic Manual, 1985: A–1). To be sure, social learning theorists have demonstrated that aggression and violence are learned behaviors. They can, therefore, within biological and genetic limitations, be altered by utilizing social learning principles such as modeling (Bandura, 1973: 252). This is of particular significance to a discussion of the transformation of energy within prisons from negative to life-affirming.

Research has demonstrated that utilizing positive responses which are incompatible with the act of violence (e.g., smiling,; state of muscle relaxation; open, clear, direct communication; active listening; the development of trust, etc.) renders the likelihood of aggression and/or violence much more improbable than do negative sanctions such as punishment, shame, or guilt (Ilfeld, 1970: 20). Whereas aggressive-punitive sanctions frustrate the individual and provide negative models to imitate, incompatible positive responses to aggression provide new options and repertoires from which to learn (Ilfeld, 1970: 80).

Teaching nonviolent techniques, therefore, Bandura (1973: 255) contends, "can . . . greatly profit assaultive people. By enlarging their repertory of skills, aggressors achieve greater freedom in meeting present and future problems." Socially adept and verbally skilled individuals, for example, are "able to defuse potentially explosive situations through pacifying moves such as face-saving actions, friendly persuasion, and humor." In keeping with AVP principles of nonviolence such as "risk being creative rather than violent," "use surprise and humor," and "seek to resolve conflicts by reaching common ground" (AVP Basic Manual, 1985), Bandura suggests that:

> . . . verbal skills not only reduce actions productive of violence, they can also help preserve one's integrity and self-esteem in embarrassing situations without having to dispose of antagonists physically. . . . Socially and verbally unskilled persons, (on the other hand), having limited means for handling discord, are likely to become physically aggressive on slight provocation, especially in contexts where violent conduct is viewed favorably.

In keeping with Bandura's thinking, therefore, conflict-resolution skills are an integral part of the AVP program. In general, these skills are comparable to standard communication enrichment programs for individuals in high interdependent relationships who have frequent and strong impact on each other in diverse kinds of activities over a long duration of time (Kelley et al., 1983: 131, 393). More specifically, these skills include "I" statements, active listening, paraphrasing, taking the perspective of another, and six-point problem-solving. Strategies which are utilized to facilitate the repeated practice of these techniques include discussion groups, games, role plays, and paired and group activities, all of which are offered in workshops.

Given the violent context of prisons, however, the pivotal issue becomes one of how to motivate the utilization of nonviolent techniques. How do incarcerated individuals actually move, in other words, from violence to nonviolence, from suspicion to trust, from competition to cooperation, coercion to consensus in the stark reality of prison environments?

Satir (1972: 21) has concluded that the key factor in determining what happens both inside us and between us as individuals is the sense of worth which we each carry around with us. This sense of worth, however, is tied to our sense of connectedness to other human beings. Professional and prisoner alike, our fundamental need is to be understood, to be affirmed. Indeed, Jung has said that schizophrenics cease to be schizophrenic when they meet someone by whom they are understood; the recipient feels that someone values, cares for, and accepts the person that he/she is (Rogers, 1975: 6). Laing has suggested that our sense of identity requires the existence of another by whom we are known (1965: 139). Dramatic health-related effects have been demonstrated to result when a person has been made to know that he/she is cared for and loved, is esteemed and valued, and belongs to a network of communication and mutual obligation (Cobb, 1976: 300). Aspy (1972) has demonstrated that the more others are sensitively understanding, the more likely is constructive learning and change.

The environment within which we exist, therefore, is critical to our functioning capabilities. A competitive atmosphere, Deutsch (1973) suggests, "induces threat, coercion, deception, suspicion, rigidity, and faulty communication" (Linkskold et al., 1986: 99), attributes all of which characterize prisons. A cooperative atmosphere, on the other hand, "induces perceived similarity, trust, open communication, flexibility, concern for the other, emphasis on mutual interests, and attraction between the parties," attributes all of which are fundamental to a healing, nurturant environment.

It is, therefore, a cooperative atmosphere, a consistently conscious endeavor toward community and mutual respect, that is the context within which transformation can begin. Only in an environment of living-kindness, compassion, and genuine caring can a sense of self-worth be nurtured, strengthened, and healed.

## The View from the Circle

It is precisely this type of life-affirming environment within which all AVP activities are couched. From the outset of an AVP workshop, there is something palpably different, something crystal clear and rock solid. Having found themselves in a "seeker friendly" environment (AVP Basic Manual, 1985), participants are enabled to create a true sense of community. In keeping with the AVP philosophy that it is the birthright of each person to live life with dignity and self-respect, participants find that the experiences of each of them are equally valued, that there are no "experts," no credentialed "professionals" with all the answers. On the contrary, and as alluded to above, the leaders represent the AVP belief that individuals have within them the answers to their own questions if they can simply open to them. Encouraging participants, then, to reach down within themselves for those solutions, the workshop leaders simply facilitate that search, offering new techniques, different tools, and a broad range of experiences from which to choose.

It is to this environment that participants come, each with their own individual histories and motivations for being there. Many come initially with hesitation, uncertain of what the concept of alternatives to violence means, much less what it has to do with anything. Due either to a curiosity whetted by fellow inmates' reported experiences with AVP or simply knowing that participation in AVP workshops seems to impress parole boards since participation is on a strictly voluntary basis, some undoubtedly figure that three days spent doing an AVP workshop could be no worse than three days of their regular routine. Everyone seems to come, however, filled with a common desire to fulfill their own ambitions, their own potentialities, hoping, perhaps unconsciously, that this experience might in some way contribute to that end.

The basic premise of AVP, as explained at the outset of each workshop and, indeed, as experienced by all throughout its entirety, is that human beings don't have to be violent with each other, that human violence is not a given, not even in prison. In fact, the spirit which permeates everything that is done reflects assumptions that are quite to the contrary—i.e., that there is always a possibility for an alternative, rather than a violent, response to any action; that we must be willing to set aside old, habitual assumptions that violent or destructive solutions are the only ones possible and be willing to try something different, something creative; that we must believe that a "win/win" solution is possible and that there is something in the person who is challenging us, no matter how hidden it may be, that is willing to join us in seeking such a solution; and, finally, that we must expect the best, not only from ourselves, but from others in our interactions with them (AVP Basic Manual, 1985).

One of the most illuminating aspects of the workshops seems to be the experiences of actually warding off violence simply by utilizing ordinary, yet conscious, actions or reactions. Participants learn from firsthand experience, for example, how it feels to be truly listened to and heard and, conversely, how others react when we listen to them and they are truly heard. Some experience for the first time what it is like to be affirmed by others and appreciated for simply being themselves and, conversely, how others react when they know in their gut that others genuinely affirm them and appreciate their own unique personhood. Participants are enabled to examine in a safe environment the different issues which come up for each of them when they are given a task within a group and are confronted with varying degrees of cooperation and power, either someone else's or their own. They are introduced to and provided practice with techniques of how to communicate with each other in a manner which invites clarity and understanding rather than hostility and misunderstanding, the latter two of which so often lead to violence. Very importantly, participants are confronted with situations in which they are pressed to resolve real-life conflicts nonviolently, thereby providing for themselves the beginnings of a nonviolent experience base with which to offset their far-too-familiar violent experience base.

## The Process

It is enlivening to observe, much less experience, the process at work: affirmation, love, openness, honesty, laughter, respect, diligence, genuineness. At the outset of a workshop, participants seem wary and guarded: Some feign nonchalance with nervous laughter and chatter; others sit cautiously expressionless, arms crossed, registering everything;

others engage in conversation, filling this unfamiliar space with something, anything; still others feign aloofness, exuding an air of superiority. By workshop's end, however, there is a deeply abiding sense of good will that permeates the atmosphere. People look at one another rather than through one another or at the floor. Laughter and joking fill the air. Faces are soft. Eyes sparkle. Smiles abound. Ancient doors have creaked open. Tears spill down radiant cheeks. Heads are on straight; bodies erect. Voices are clear and strong. People approach rather than avoid each other; they connect.

It is an incredible journey participants have shared over the course of the three days together. Having traversed the dry, barren, hostile distances which typically separate them from each other, they have arrived at a fertile, lush plateau where it is more safe to trust and to be open. Immersed in a caring environment in which each individual is consistently treated with dignity and genuine respect, they have been enabled to reveal the caring, human aspects of themselves. They have laughed uproariously in silly games together, worked diligently at serious tasks together, and wept cleansingly in sharing together, risking always new ways of viewing each other. Within this circle, they have felt safe, connected, a part of the whole. Here, there has been no place for rigidity, suspicion, or hostility. Here, there has been no need of threat, coercion, or violence.

## So What's the Big Deal?

The question, of course, from a purely objective perspective, has to do with long-term impact. If our consideration is of new possibilities for administrative strategies within prisons, of what possible significance, we ask, are the effects of three days spent in a nurturing environment relative to the weeks, months, or perhaps years spent in an otherwise violent prison environment?

Their significance, of course, is that of which they are indicative. These individuals have been enabled to create and sustain FOR THREE DAYS a totally nurturing environment in spite of the pathologically violent milieu which surrounds them. In this niche of love, affirmation, and trust, they have been enabled to regenerate, to rest, to discover the caring aspects of each other.

Our work, of course, is to build on their discovery, the process of their discovery, rather than to dismiss it as sweet or superfluous. Such dismissal not only diminishes our sense of the potentiality of human beings but also limits our vision, our ability as professionals to perceive, much less experience, new avenues for growth and change. Indeed, we become habituated to our narrowly objective perspective. Losing sight of the bigger picture and our own place within it, we lose track of our fundamental connections and start thinking and acting in terms of *us* and not *them*.

It is important to be reminded of our connections. Lazoff, for example, contends that all of us, whether inside or outside of prison walls, are engaged in the same thing, really. Each of us, he writes, is simply "seeking to find the place within ourselves which feels at peace with who we are, at peace with the guesses we make as we move through life. . . . [w]e'd all love to stop lying to ourselves, screwing things up, and feeling vaguely incomplete (Lazoff, 1985: xi)."

Peck has suggested that "to be dedicated to the development of the race of which we are a part" is to be "dedicated to 'our' own development as well as 'theirs' " (Peck, 1978:19). Riddle (1982) warns, however, in her feminist analysis of the processes of change, that we can only understand that which we have experienced, that which has meaning. If, therefore, we seek to transform the energy which is prevalent within prisons from violent to nonviolent, we ourselves must draw from such programs as AVP and become engaged in the process of discovery. We ourselves must understand the experience of nonviolence; we must know that of which we speak. As Quinney (1987: 18) observes: "The means cannot be different from the ends; peace can come only out of peace."

## REFERENCES

Alternatives to Violence Project, Inc. (AVP). 1985. *AVP Manual Basic Course*. Alternatives to Violence Project, 15 Rutherford Place, New York, NY 10003.

Aspy, David. 1972. *Toward a Technology for Humanizing Education*. Champaign, Ill.: Research Press.

Bandura, Albert. 1973. *Aggression: A Social Learning Analysis*. Englewood Cliffs: Prentice-Hall, Inc.

Claassen, Ron. 1989. "Vision: Mystical and Practical." *Criminal Justice Network Newsletter* (July-August-September): 1.

Cobb, S. 1976. "Social Support as a Moderator of Life Stress." *Psychosomatic Medicine* 38: 300–314.

Deutsch, Morton. 1973. *The Resolution of Conflict: Constructive and Destructive Processes*. New Haven: Yale U. Press.

Huston, Ted L. 1983. "Power." In Harold H. Kelley et al., (eds.) *Close Relationships*. New York: W. H. Freeman and Company.

Ilfeld, F. W. 1970. "Environmental Theories of Environment." In D. N. Daniels, M. S. Filula, and F. M. Ochberg (eds.), *Violence and the Struggle for Existence*. Boston: Little, Brown and Company.

Ingraham, B. L., and C. F. Wellford. 1987. "The Totality of Conditions Test in Eighth-Amendment Litigation," In Stephen D. Gottfredson and Sean McConville (eds.) *America's Correctional Crisis: Prison Populations and Public Policy*. New York: Greenwood Press.

Kelley, Harold H., Ellen Bercheid, Andrew Christensen, John H. Harvey, Ted L. Huston, George Levinger, Eric McClintock, Letitia Anne Peplau, and Donald R. Peterson. 1983. *Close Relationships*. New York: W. H. Freeman and Company.

Laing, R. D. 1965. *The Divided Self*. London: Tavistock.

Levertof, Denise. 1986. "Invocations of Humanity." *Sojourners* (February): 32–36.

Linkskold, S., B. Betz, and P. S. Walters, 1986. "Transforming Competitive or Cooperative Climates." *Journal of Conflict Resolution* 30 (1): 99–114.

Lozoff, B. O. 1985. *We're All Doing Time*. Hanuman Foundation.

Peck, Morgan Scott. 1978. *The Road Less Traveled*. New York: Simon and Schuster.

Peterson, Donald R. 1978. "Conflict." In H. H. Kelley et al., (eds.), *Close Relationships*. New York: W. H. Freeman and Company.

Quinney, R. 1987. "Criminology and the Way of Peace." Paper presented at the American Society of Criminology Conference, Montreal.

Raven, Bertram H. 1965. "Social Influence and Power." In Evan Dale Steiner and Martin Fishbein (eds.), *Current Studies in Social Psychology*. New York: Holt.

Riddle, D. I. 1982. "Politics, Spirituality, and Models of Change." In Charlene Spretnak (ed.), *The Politics of Women's Spirituality*. Garden City, N.Y.: Anchor Press.

Rogers, C. R. 1975. "Empathic: An Unappreciated Way of Being." *Journal of Counseling Psychology* 5: 2–10.

Rotter, J. B. 1966. "Generalized Expectancies for Internal Versus External Control of Reinforcement." *Psychological Monographs* 80 (609).

Satir, Virginia. 1972. *Peoplemaking*. Palo Alto, Calif.: Science and Behavior Books, Inc.

Skolimowski, Henry K. 1986. "Life Entropy and Education." *American Theosophist* 74: 305–10.

Stanley, Lisa, and Sue Wise. 1983. *Breaking Out: Feminist Consciousness and Feminist Research*. Boston: Routledge & Kegan Paul.

*Fay Honey Knopp*

---

# ELEVEN

# Community Solutions to Sexual Violence

*Feminist / Abolitionist Perspectives*

The issues of feminist/abolitionist perspectives and strategies for controlling and reducing sexual violence, on which I work actively each day, have long been close to my heart.

I write as a Quaker feminist and prison abolitionist, and as a person who has struggled for 50 of her adult years to be a self-determined human being. My views are those social-change perspectives born out of personal resistance primarily to two oppressive forces and institutions I have encountered in my life experiences. These institutions, which I believe are inexorably related, are the oppressive institutions of patriarchy and the oppressive institutions of punishment. Resistance to these two oppressive forces is the mutual social-change agenda binding together the prison-abolition and the feminist movements.

I first outline the social-change process and abolitionist perspective, which provide the context for The Safer Society's work in controlling and reducing sexual violence.[1] Second, I identify some very challenging and often conflicting areas involved in the pursuit of safety, the pursuit of justice, and the pursuit of nonoppressive remedies. Third, I outline some of the primary themes and components of a community-organizing model for reducing and controlling sexual violence.

181

## The Social-Change Process and Abolitionist Perspective

In the United States, public perceptions of crimes and justice come from a variety of sources. Some views are rooted authentically in personal experiences; but, for a majority of people, beliefs about crimes and justice are shaped by a constant bombardment of the media's portrayal of crimes and criminals, by office seekers who exploit fear as a political issue, and by a very well-funded law-enforcement apparatus.

Getting our primary views on justice from such biased sources as the media and law enforcement is comparable to having our perceptions of war, peace, and foreign policy shaped by the Pentagon and its generals. The view we are given is, in fact, a *war model:* persons who commit crimes are seen as the "enemy in our midst"; and solutions offered are more punishments, more weapons, more caging of human beings. But war-model responses to problems that are essentially social, cultural, political, and economic have failed and will continue to fail.

One reason war-model responses fail is because they neglect victim-survivors, leaving them outside the criminal *injustice* process. Victims' needs are not placed at the center of the process; rather, victims most often are used by the prosecution for their own adversarial purposes. Not only is the victim the forgotten person in the process, but, in cases involving sexual victimization the victim is usually the one who is blamed, the victim is the one who is on trial, the victim is the one who must prove that victimization has occurred.

We also know that these war-model responses have failed because offenders' needs for restoration, resocialization, and re-education are rarely considered in the sentencing process. Caging the offender is accepted most often as the "just" response to the commission of a sexual crime; the length of prison punishment is equated with the amount of "justice" to be done.

Prisons *do not work.* They do not reduce crimes; they do not rehabilitate people; they rarely deter; and they fail to protect the public in any enduring way. Imprisonment punishes deeply and expensively in both human and fiscal costs, with damaging effects to both the individual and the community. Prisons punish mainly the poor, the minorities, the powerless, the "losers," the young. Increasingly, prisons are being used to punish women, and to punish them more harshly than ever before.

In states where sex-offender retraining programs are available (see Knopp, 1984), judges are provided an option for sentencing sex offenders to a program offering an opportunity for a lifestyle change. Where alternatives are not available, neither judges, offenders, nor the community are offered options other than the prison or the asylum. Without appropriate alternatives, the caging mentality takes over. In the United States, we have more people imprisoned than ever before[2]; and the number of cages on the drawing boards is expanding beyond all expectations. Such unparalleled expansion only reinforces the war-model belief that more prisons somehow will provide a solution to violent and sexually violent behaviors. As long as the nonsolution of imprisonment is relied upon, the public is relieved of having to make connections between the root causes of antisocial and sexually violent acts and the kind of social-change alternatives that actually could make our communities more just and safe. As long as we use imprisonment as the primary response to sexual crimes, the majority of people can hold on to their mistaken beliefs that there are "criminal types" and "bad seeds" and biological imperatives for people to behave this way.

As long as the primary feminist response to the crime of rape, for instance, is to demand longer, harsher sentences for rapists, we inhibit ourselves from addressing the roots of this behavior. Until we as feminists have a coherent, well-articulated, well-taught analysis to counter the war-model response to criminal sexual behaviors—behaviors that not only are socially and culturally learned, but in fact are supported and perpetuated by societal institutions and practices—we will foster an increasingly caged and punitive society.

In *Instead of Prisons* (Knopp et al., 1976: 150), we reprinted a feminist editorial that said in part:

> If all men who had ever raped were incarcerated tomorrow, rape would continue outside as well as inside prisons. Incarceration does not change the societal attitudes that promote rape. In a society that deals with symptoms rather than causes of problems, prisons make perfect sense. Confronting the causes of rape would threaten the basic structure of society. . . . Prison is vindictive—it is not concerned with change but with punishment. And its real social function is similar to that of rape—it acts as a buffer, as an oppressive institution where a few scapegoats pay for the ills of society. (MacMillan & Klein, 1974)

Mutual education/action strategies on feminist and abolitionist agendas will contribute significantly to a safer and more just society. We will be expending our energies toward controlling and reducing sexual aggression and violence rather than reinforcing and strengthening already extremely oppressive structures.

Prison abolition perspectives are set forth in *Instead of Prisons* (Knopp et al., 1976). This abolitionist publication was designed originally to offer a conceptual foundation and action strategies for facilitating the gradual process of reducing imprisonment while building up a variety of non-repressive alternatives. One of our tasks was to learn good methods for teaching these concepts and becoming involved in the first step of the social-change process,[3] which is *consciousness raising*—"seeing the need for the new." In this case, the perceived need is for a new system of restorative justice based on social and economic justice and on concern and respect for all victims and victimizers, a new system based on remedies and restoration rather than on prison punishment and victim neglect, a new system rooted in the concept of a caring community.

Although people need to conceptualize their own visions of a caring community, The Safer Society Program defines it as a place where "power and equality of all social primary goods—liberty, opportunity, income, wealth, and the bases of self-respect—are institutionally structured and distributed to all members of the community and where the spirit of reconciliation prevails" (Knopp et al., 1976: 10). The Safer Society books, manuals, and workshops help to raise this kind of consciousness. Our primary message is that the sources of antisocial behavior are rooted in the social, political, cultural, and economic structures of society and that solutions must be found there. That does not imply either that persons are not responsible for their behaviors or that we do nothing until the caring community is a reality. It does imply that safer and more just social strategies flow from a social-change agenda advocating social responsibility rather than the traditional crime-prevention/war-model agenda.

If the first step of social change is consciousness raising or seeing the need for the new, the second step is *creativity* or learning how to organize and construct the new. In our case, this means creating a new restorative-justice model in crimes of sexual aggression and violence.

It is extremely difficult to conceptualize a new restorative-justice model when we are dealing with issues of sexual violence. I know this from my own experience. Sexual victimizations make me raging mad. I feel angry, injured, and often vengeful when I listen to the horrendous cases of child and adult sexual abuse that come across our phone and through the mail, or occur in my neighborhood. I try to acknowledge and deal with my anger and then redirect it toward creating a new concept of justice and changing the social conditions that encourage and promote sexual aggression.

In trying to put theories of creativity into practice, many of us in the movement to control sexual abuse are encouraging communities to identify and deal with its root causes. We are moving victim services and offender treatment into a comprehensive perpetrator-prevention framework and forming networks to carry on this work. We are advocating corrective legislation. We are identifying which sexually aggressive behaviors can be handled in the community and which require a controlled environment, and we are trying to implement these and other comprehensive services for both victim/survivors and offenders.

The pressure is always excessive for abolitionists to produce a *plan*, a plan that solves every problem and deals with every criminal act before abolition can be considered. But it is not necessary to have a finished blueprint; it is not necessary to know the last step before taking the first step. The first step toward abolition is to break with the old system and help conceptualize the new.[4]

Though there is no blueprint for abolition, The Safer Society Program offers an "Attrition Model" (Knopp et al., 1976: 62–63) for gradually wearing away the use of imprisonment and simultaneously building a caring community. There are four dynamically interrelated strategies to be pursued, some of which present challenge areas for feminist/abolitionists to consider.

The first strategy is to stop the growth of the prison system, to say "no" to building any more cages. This is called the *moratorium* strategy (64–80).

The second, called the *decarceration* strategy (81–98), is an attempt to get people who are already inside out of jail or prison. For instance, the abolition of bail in the United States would release at least 50 to 60 percent of the jail population. For those involved in issues of sexual violence, community safety, and constitutional liberties, this presents a challenge: Should persons who have been accused and/or have prior histories of sexually violent behaviors, and who have not yet been found guilty, be released to the community before trial? Should they be released with conditions restricting their movement? If so, should such restrictions be enforced? These issues of community safety and preventive detention of sex offenders are serious constitutional- and safety-challenge areas we need to address in our mutual agendas.

A third strategy is one of *excarceration*, which involves moving away from the notion of imprisonment (99–127). There are hundreds of workable and appropriate examples of alternatives in practice currently. They include restitution, fines, community-service work, and dispute and mediation processes. Abolitionists support models of dispute mediation where the conflicting parties and members of their neighborhoods are trained to settle their low- and medium-level conflicts to the advantage of all disputants. Such processes do not determine guilt but determine responsibility for the behavior and how that responsibility will be played out to the satisfaction of the conflicting parties.[5] Clarity does not exist on the limitations of this type of alternative to the court and sentencing processes. Therein lies another challenge area. The National Center on Women & Family Law and other groups contend that dispute resolution, as it is presently practiced, is not beneficial to women in settling any problems involving family violence. They contend it has proved an inappropriate format for these reasons: (1) in such situations women do not have equal bargaining power; (2) few mediators are neutral; (3) mediation does not address or punish past behavior; and (4) communication with mediators often is not confidential.[6]

Seekers of a new justice are challenged: (1) to examine current models of dispute resolution; (2) in consort with the critics of these procedures, to try to determine when and if any type of family violence may be dealt with appropriately through such alternative procedures; and (3) where possible, together to try to construct a just model that can serve fairly all parties involved in family abuse. Proponents of dispute/mediation models should heed the advice of those directly affected and involved in such serious abuses.

The fourth strategy of the Attrition Model is called *restraint of the few*, and it addresses the concerns of feminists and abolitionists more than any of the other strategies. While there is little doubt that the majority of persons now imprisoned could remain in the community if an adequate continuum of alternatives were in place, some persons' behaviors would still present a real threat to public and personal safety. What alternatives, for instance, should abolitionists suggest for persons who have been convicted of very serious sexual crimes? The Safer Society Program focuses energy on this issue because we consider sexual offenses and family violence to be two of the most serious, most neglected, but also the most accepted categories of violent behavior.

In the postconviction phase, The Safer Society Program advocates competent and specialized assessment and evaluation of the sex offender. If the offender chooses the option of re-education and retraining and is considered a good candidate, we advocate residential treatment options. We most strongly advocate early remedial intervention with adolescents at the first demonstration of sexual aggression (Knopp, 1982, 1985).

The principles undergirding The Safer Society Program's abolitionist perspectives on the restraint of persons who present a threat to personal and public safety are (1) that public safety and constitutional rights of victims and offenders be the overriding guiding principles, and (2) that the least restrictive and most humane option for the shortest period of time in the most remedial and restorative environment be applied.

Since 1975, in an effort to understand the issues involved in sexual offenses and to learn how to construct a new restorative justice, I have personally visited hundreds of community-based and residential programs for sex offenders. We have published criteria for assessing risk for community or residential treatment, along with the first study of adolescent sex offenders and their treatment (Knopp, 1982). We have published a study of a range of community-based and residential programs that re-educate and retrain adult sex offenders (Knopp, 1984). We are continually advocating and assisting treatment programs for sex offenders as a Safer Society strategy and publishing self-help manuals (Freeman-Longo and Bays, 1988; Bays and Freeman-Longo, 1989; Bays, Freeman-Longo, and Hildebran, 1990). We are fostering perpetrator prevention strategies for all ages—the young to the elderly. These projects are the logical extension of our abolitionist commitment:

> As abolitionists we are confronted with the struggle between the conflicting forces for change. We are in total agreement with feminist anti-rape worker and other social changer that every effort should be made to apprehend and confront the sexually violent. We share the feelings of outrage experienced by rape victims; we believe that repetitive rapists must be restrained from committing further acts of violence. On the other hand we do not support the response of imprisonment. We challenge the basic assumption that punishment, harsh sentences, and retributive attitudes will serve to lessen victims' pain, re-educate rapists, or genuinely protect society. Not all sex offenders must be restrained during their re-education/resocialization process. But for those sexual violents who do require temporary separation from society— repetitive rapists, those who physically brutalize or psychologically terrorize and men who repeatedly assault children—places of restraint are needed while re-education occurs. Unless these alternatives are developed, there

may be no other choice but the prison or the asylum. Hence the urgency for abolitionists to create programs similar to those we shall cite. (Knopp et al., 1976, 150–51).

By working on behalf of victims, offenders, and a safer society committed to primary prevention of sexual abuse, we hope that we are *building a more caring community,* the all-encompassing strategy of the Attrition Model.

## Challenges in the Pursuit of Safety, Justice, and Nonoppressive Remedies

I have already mentioned some of the following areas that challenge abolitionist and feminist perspectives when we are considering responses to sexual or other violent abuses of women; each reader can no doubt add to this list:

1. Our broadest challenge is to create a feminist/abolitionist perspective on crime and justice and a means of continuing interaction among our social-change movements.
2. To date, there is, unfortunately, only an unjust court system available to validate (1) the fact that a sexual or violent crime against a woman or child has occurred and (2) the role of the victimizer in that transgression. It is still a struggle to get the courts to do that much. While we must be relentless in our efforts to press the courts to deal fairly with all parties prior to conviction, the post-conviction period challenges our creativity. We are challenged to find ways to insure that the court places the victims' needs, the offenders' needs, and the community's needs at the center of sentencing decisions. We must assure that justice is not measured by the amount of prison punishment or pain meted out to an offender to the neglect of the victim/survivor. Using an unjust, repressive structure to provide disempowered women with a sense that justice has been done gives power to a system that is set up to protect the status quo, fundamental to which is male violence against women. To quote Gail Sullivan (1982): "We are thus asking one arm of the patriarchal system to punish some of its members for behavior which is inherent in the social structure." Sullivan also reminds us that the laws are made in the interest of the dominant class—white men—while it is primarily poor nonwhites who go to prison. "If we push for incarceration," she adds, "we legitimize the degradation and destruction of human beings in prisons as a method of social control—and we increase reliance on the patriarchal state to determine who is wrong or guilty."
3. We are challenged to define the limits of the criminal injustice system as a vehicle for bringing justice to disempowered victims. Is

there a positive "iron fist in the velvet glove" role for these systems? Should they be used to help enforce certain decisions? To enforce protective orders in battering cases? To remove assaultive fathers from homes when they won't leave voluntarily? To ensure that offenders will stay in treatment in the community after the "arrest effect" wears off? Are these appropriate roles for the system at this time, or are there other community methods for enforcement?

4. Another challenge is the question of dispute mediation as an excarceration strategy when utilized for disputes involving family violence. Is there a just form of mediation that can be used to handle these disputes to the satisfaction of the victim, the offender, and the community?

5. We are challenged to address the matters of safety and constitutional rights, the issue of preventive detention. If a person has a prior history of sexual offense and has been accused but not convicted of a new violent sexual offense, does he have the right to bail? If he is released, are there alternative methods of supervision or surveillance that will assure he will not commit a similar crime prior to trial?

6. A challenge that is extremely compelling and deserves lengthy deliberation and dialogue is the issue of pornography. In the United States, this relates to First Amendment rights to free speech. This is a social issue that must engage deeply the feminist/abolitionist movement (see Rosenberg, 1989).

## Themes and Components of a Community Organizing Model

I will outline briefly some of the bare-bones themes and components of a community-organizing model for reducing and controlling sexual offenses, though it is important that we strategize collectively when approaching this complex issue.

The Safer Society Program prefers a social-justice prevention model based on community responsibility for one another's safety and on respect for all persons involved in the sexual assault. Thus we suggest the formation of three coordinated task forces or components for communities that wish to control and reduce sexual assaults: a perpetrator prevention/education component, a victim/survivor prevention component, and an offender-restoration component.

## Perpetrator Prevention/Education

A perpetrator prevention/education component should involve *primary prevention* of sexual assault, which means eliminating the social conditions and attitudes that promote and perpetuate assaults. Carolyn Sparks, a feminist and sexual-assault specialist, says that if we are to do this we must first understand and then critique the rules of the patriarchal social organization. We must uncover the social prejudice against women and children that is upheld by institutional laws and policies and, as a result, by popular thought. In its place, she says, we must construct a new set of rules for social relationships, a way in which we can organize society so that women's and children's *status* precludes their being preyed upon. The prevention of sexual violence, then, as we indicated previously, becomes not the traditional war model of crime prevention but truly a movement for social justice (Sparks, 1982).

This approach is validated by research by anthropologist Peggy Reeves Sanday at the University of Pennsylvania (Sanday, 1982), who studied 95 tribal societies and found that 47 percent were free of sexual assault. She compares elements present in rape-free societies (where rape is unthinkable) with rape-prone societies (where rape is common). Commonalities among rape-free societies provide us with this prevention agenda:

1. In the rape-free societies, women are treated with considerable respect, and prestige is attached to female reproductive and productive roles. Women are respected and influential members of the community.
2. Interpersonal violence is minimized and in some cases virtually absent. The peoples' attitude regarding the natural environment is one of reverence rather than one of exploitation.
3. The relationship between the sexes tends to be symmetrical and equal, particularly in terms of power. Female power is valued as much as male power. Decision making is usually by common consent.
4. The source of energy and creativity in the universe is often attributed to a female figure.

In the societies in Sanday's study that were unambiguously rape-prone (17 percent), certain themes are revealed that we must avoid and reverse if we are to control and reduce sexual aggression and violence:

1. In the rape-prone societies, men as well as women view sexual relations in violent terms. Women expect to be hurt, and men believe that their virility is proved through hurting.
2. Rape is a means by which men control women and mark themselves as men.
3. Violence is tolerated, and men and boys are encouraged to be tough, aggressive, and competitive.
4. Women take little or no part in public decision-making and do not figure prominently in religious ritual or thought.
5. The relationship between the sexes is unequal.
6. A man's potential sexual rights over the woman he chooses must be respected. She is considered his property.

Sanday's studies reaffirm the notion that our behavior is not male or female because of anything inherent in human nature. How we behave is programmed culturally; much of what is undesirable must be deprogrammed. Being female or male, says Sanday, is very much a characteristic of the culture in which we live; that is, male nature has not been selected genetically for violence. Male nature is not, as it has been depicted, an everpresent struggle to overcome baser impulses bequeathed by our apish ancestors. *In rape-prone societies, rape is explicitly linked to the control of women and to male dominance.* These perspectives are central to any program geared toward preventing sexual assault. We must learn how to articulate these perspectives and make them operational in creative programs that reflect the values found in rape-free societies.

There are many community programs and educational materials that teach strategies that are designed to prevent victimization. The Safer Society Program advocates teaching children and women that they own and control their own bodies and teaching men that they have the obligation to respect this. Though we must change laws and social policies to do this, there are excellent programs that are teaching these values to male and female children. [7]

## Victim/Survivor Prevention*

A victim/survivor-prevention component should encompass funding for all service, advocacy, and restoration strategies and support systems. In Minnesota, a model for the rest of the country, the legislature appropriates money every two years and funds an entire coordinated network of sexual-assault crisis services throughout the state. There is continual inservice work, consciousness raising, and education about rape and rape prevention in every community. Outreach includes traditionally neglected victim populations: women of color, Native Americans, disabled and elderly, gays, and low-functioning persons. Statewide funding is the key to good victim/survivor services, and it should be guaranteed by earmarked appropriations from legislative bodies.

As we shall see in data included in the following description of the sex-offender treatment component, it is extremely important that young male victims of sexual assault also receive specialized victim services and counseling.

## Offender Restoration

A sex-offender treatment component should involve services to: "hands-off" nuisance offenders (exhibitionists, voyeurs, obscene telephone-calls,

---

*The Safer Society Program focuses on perpetrator prevention in the belief that victims should not bear the primary responsibility for preventing victimization.

etc.); "hand-on passive" offenders (fondlers, frotteurs); and "hands-on aggressive" offenders (rapists). The women's movement and rape-crisis movement has had an important influence on sex-offender retraining approaches by insisting that rape is a crime of anger, power, and violence rather than a crime of sexual passion.

A recent study (Abel, Mittelman, and Becker, 1984) alerts us to the importance of early remedial intervention: (1) The number of sexual crimes committed by a single individual can be extremely high; for instance, 232 child molesters admit to an average of 75.8 victims, each. (2) Single individuals often engage in a wide variety of sexual crimes (50 percent of the men in the study had multiple deviations, including child molestation, incest, rape, and exhibitionism). (3) The onset of these crimes is very early (57 percent of 411 sex offenders studied began their behaviors by age 19). And (4), most strikingly, in a study of 240 individuals who committed 91,000 sex crimes, there was an increase in the average number of victims per offender, from 6.75 when they were under 18, to 380 when they were adults. Says Abel, "If you don't get them early, this is what will happen. Early intervention is effective" (Abel, 1984).

Though rape is a very severe problem, in terms of *incidence*, child molestation is a much more serious problem (Abel, Mittelman, and Becker, 1984).[8] The victim load, according to Abel (1984), falls very heavily on *boys who are molested outside the home*. These figures were larger than incest offenses in the home.[9]

Where programs for sex offenders exist, they are located in the community, in mental health facilities, and in prisons (Knopp and Stevenson, 1989). Risk criteria have been developed by specialists, and good assessment and evaluation procedures are available for determining the suitability of a person for retraining either in the community or in a more controlled residential setting.

One model is a useful example of a nonrepressive alternative: a house in Minnesota devoted exclusively to the treatment of 26 sex offenders—nonprofit, privately owned; providing intensive, excellent care—that includes work with the whole family, with a gradual, monitored easing of the offender back into the community (Knopp, 1984).

Retraining of sex offenders includes for each offender the following: (1) accepting responsibility for their offenses; (2) understanding the sequence of thoughts, feelings, events, high-risk circumstances, and arousal stimuli that make up their *offense cycle* preceding their sexual assaults; (3) learning how to intervene in the offense cycle at its earliest sign by calling upon the appropriate methods, tools, or procedures each has learned, in order to suppress, control, manage, and stop the behavior; (4) learning new prosocial attitudes and behaviors; and (5) testing and maintaining their new, safe life-style in the community with long-range support and monitoring (see Knopp 1984, 1985; Freeman-Longo and Bays, 1988; Bays and Freeman-

Longo, 1989). Retraining may take from one to five years or longer depending on the nature, length, and pattern of the behavior.

Finally, The Safer Society Program keeps a sharp eye on whether programs are retraining offenders into traditional role behavior between men and women or encouraging new, nonpatriarchal roles. This is an important factor; some programs emphasize nonoppressive roles admirably.

If we are going to cooperate with the justice system: It should be a system with which we can feel comfortable. It should be a system that does not require us to abdicate our ethical standards of personal decency. It should be a system that does not retraumatize the victim, a system that places both the victim/survivor and the offender at the center of the restorative process. It should be a system that reduces rather than increases pain; a system that does not co-opt service providers and victim advocates into a pain-increasing stance. We have a right to expect that from a just system, and we have the obligation to work toward that hope—a new justice (Knopp, 1988: 8). We can become creators of a new justice by working on new responses to sexual violence as abolitionists and feminists. Our message must be loud and it must be clear: The victimizer must take responsibility for his sexual crimes. But the community also must examine its responsibility for the behaviors—must uncover the societal roots of sexual violence, understand them, and find ways to reduce the potential for such violence to occur.

## NOTES

1. The Safer Society Program, a national program of the New York State Council of Churches, formerly operated as the Prison Research/Education/Action Project (PREAP).

2. Populations in state and federal prisons nationwide as of June 30, 1989, totalled 673,565; jail populations as of June 30, 1987, were 295,873.

3. Four steps are identified in the social-change process: (1) consciousness raising; (2) creativity; (3) structural continuity for distributing justice; and (4) second-wave consciousness-raising to keep the new system from becoming old, closed, and unchallenged. This process is based in part on concepts advanced by Manfred Halpern, Princeton University.

4. See also Mathieson, 1974, pp. 24–25.

5. Dispute mediation differs from arbitration where disputants give a third party legal authority to render a binding decision.

6. The National Center on Women & Family Law, 799 Broadway, Room 402, New York, NY 10003. Also see "Violence in the Family," *JSAC Grapevine*, January 1987, vol. 18, no. 6 (Joint Strategy and Action Committee, Inc., 475 Riverside Drive, New York, NY 10115).

7. See, for example, the *Child Assault Prevention Project* (CAP), a Division of the National Assault Prevention Center, Box 02005, Columbus, OH 43202, (614)291-2540; and also *Understanding and Responding to the Sexual Behavior of Children: A Perpetration Prevention Project*, Kempe National Center, University of Colorado Health Sciences Center, 1205 Oneida Street, Denver, CO 80220, (303)321-3963.

8. The study reports that rapists (n = 89) averaged 7.5 victims per offender as compared to child molesters (n = 232) who averaged 75.8 victims per offender.

9. Of four types of child molesters studied, the frequency of molestations of young male victims outside the family (mean 278.7) was more than 11 times greater than the frequency against young female victims outside the home (mean 24.9) and more than five times greater than young male victims inside the home (mean 51.3).

## REFERENCES

Abel, G. 1984. Remarks transcribed from taped comments and transparencies at Safer Society Program press briefing, Albany, 7 February 1984.

Abel, G., M. Mittelman, and J. Becker. 1984. "Sexual Offenders: Results of Assessment and Recommendations for Treatment." Unpublished manuscript available from Judith Becker, Ph.D., New York State Psychiatric Institute, Sexual Behavior Clinic, Box 17, 722 W. 168th St., New York, NY 10032, (212)960-5851.

Bays, L., and R. Freeman-Longo. 1989. *Why Did I do it Again?* Orwell, Vt.: Safer Society Program.

Bays, L., Freeman-Longo, R., and Hildebran, D. 1990. *How Can I Stop?* Orwell, VT: Safer Society Program.

Freeman-Longo, R., and L. Bays. 1988. *Who am I and Why Am I in Treatment?* Orwell, Vt.: Safer Society Program.

Knopp, F., et al. 1976. *Instead of Prisons: A Handbook for Abolitionists.* Orwell, Vt.: Safer Society Press.

Knopp, F. 1982. *Remedial Intervention in Adolescent Sex Offenses: Nine Program Descriptions.* Orwell, Vt.: Safer Society Press.

———. 1984. *Retraining Adult Sex Offenders: Methods and Models.* Orwell, Vt.: Safer Society Press.

———. 1985. *The Youthful Sex Offender: The Rationale and Goals of Early Intervention and Treatment.* Orwell, Vt.: Safer Society Press.

———. 1988. "The Safer Society Program and Press." In *Domestic Violence and Nonviolence Peacework* (September). Boston: American Friends Source Committee.

Knopp, F., and W. F. Stevenson. 1989. *Nationwide Survey of Juvenile and Adult Sex-offender Treatment Programs and Models, 1988.* Orwell, Vt.: Safer Society Press.

MacMillan, J. and F. Klein. 1974. *Feminist Alliance Against Rape Newsletter,* September-October.

Mathieson, T. 1974. *The Politics of Abolition.* New York: John Wiley and Sons.

Rosenberg, J. 1989. *Fuel on the Fire: An Inquiry Into Pornography and Sexual Aggression in a Free Society.* Orwell, Vt.: Safer Society Press.

Sanday, P. 1982. "Cultural Factors Related to Sexual Violence." Remarks transcribed from taped address at the Fourth National Conference and Workshops on Sexual Aggression and Prevention of Child Molestation and Rape, Denver, 18 April 1982.

Sparks, C. 1982. "Prevention Strategies and Plans for Action." Remarks transcribed from taped address at the Fourth National Conference and Workshops on Sexual Aggression and Prevention of Child Molestation and Rape, Denver, 15 April 1982.

Sullivan, G. 1982. "A Funny Thing Happened on the Way to the Revolution." *Aegis.*

*Maria R. Volpe*

---

## T W E L V E

# Mediation in the Criminal Justice System

## *Process, Promises, Problems*

Michael Grotville's upstairs neighbor, David
Nunke, has repeatedly played his stereo at
an intolerable level for the last month.
Every time Michael went upstairs to ask
David to turn it down, David was rude to
him. David would tell him to "get lost" and
slam the door in his face. One night,
Michael decided that "enough is enough"
and would not allow David to slam the door
in his face without first turning down the
stereo. When Michael attempted to push
his way into David's apartment to lower the
stereo himself, David pushed him. Michael
fell down the stairs, called the police, and
asked that David be arrested.

Conflicts such as this one are very common. People involved in tense
situations may find that their actions can lead to criminal charges and
further processing by the legal system. At the conclusion of the traditional
adversarial process, one party walks out vindicated, and one is found
guilty. Depending on the intensity of the feelings, the winner may even feel

that the punishment meted out to the other was not sufficiently severe. And, despite the fact that a verdict was rendered, the process never dealt with the real problems. In fact, in a situation such as the hypothetical one presented here, the adversarial process could, in fact, polarize Michael and David even more.

Since the early 70s, the adversarial processing of a wide range of disputes occurring in a variety of contexts, including those involving selected criminal matters, has come under scrutiny in American society. Increasing attention has been given to alternative means of dispute resolution such as negotiation, conciliation, mediation, fact finding, arbitration, mini-trial, rent-a-judge, and ombudsman (Marks et al., 1984; BNA, 1985; Goldberg et al., 1985, Riskin and Westbrook, 1987; Lesson and Johnson, 1988; Murray et al., 1989). Of all of the dispute-resolution processes gaining recognition and acceptance, mediation poses the most promise and the most problems for the criminal justice system. Mediation is a process that enables parties involved in a dispute to work through their differences with the assistance of a third party.

There is growing evidence that there is widespread interest in the use of mediation in the criminal justice system. Varied state legislation has been passed throughout the country introducing mediation in community settings (ABA, 1984); hundreds of programs have been established to process criminal disputes that would otherwise have been handled by the courts (ABA, 1986); victim/offender-mediation programs have been created to bring together convicted offenders with their victims in face to face meetings (Chupp, 1989; Umbreit, 1986, 1989). In addition, a wide range of other efforts and resources have emerged including conferences, directories, educational programs, funding sources, journals, newsletters, professional organizations, service providers, teaching materials, textbooks, trainers, and videos (Volpe, 1989b).

Mediation has been used in two major ways in the criminal justice system. One has been for criminal justice professionals to use mediation skills and techniques as an intervention strategy when they process cases. The second has been for them to refer selected criminal cases to dispute-resolution programs offering mediation services (Volpe, 1989a).

While the formal use of mediation is still in its infancy in the criminal justice system, it is nonetheless evident that it can no longer be ignored by criminal justice professionals, scholars and policymakers. This chapter will address mediation's potential and challenges for the criminal justice system. The next section will briefly consider the theoretical framework against which the mediation process is understood.

## The Adversarial View of the Criminal Justice System

In criminal proceedings, actions reflect an adversarial orientation where it is fully expected that sides will be taken. The state is pitted against the defendant using rules of evidence and procedure. At the end of the legal process, there are verdicts and the determination of innocence and guilt. While there are some departures from the ideal adversarial processing of criminal disputes—for example, in the use of plea bargaining—they too are conducted in the shadow of the adversarial processing of cases.

Criminal justice professionals—including police, legal representation, and court and correctional personnel—are prepared through their education and training to advance this adversarial thinking (Riskin, 1982; Volpe, 1988). The legal system rewards them for complying with explicit and implicit rules theoretically designed to promote due process and the protection of legal rights.

Furthermore, this adversarial mind-set is reinforced by the public, which has certain expectations of criminal justice professionals. For instance, if citizens call the police, they usually expect them to do something. Similarly, if they choose to take their matter to court and file charges against others, they expect judges to make decisions. And, when they go to lawyers, they expect them to act as partisan advocates representing their interests. When verdicts are pronounced, outcomes are measured in punitive terms. It is common to hear questions such as "What punishment did s/he receive?"

In recent years, however, some of the thinking supporting this traditional dispute processing landscape has been challenged. Mediation has emerged as an attractive, kinder and gentler, dispute-processing alternative.

## Mediation and the Criminal Justice System

When criminal disputes are mediated, they are usually transformed into civil matters. McGillis (1986: 4) has noted that this is done "by treating the cases as matters for discussion between the individual disputants and not for processing between the state and the defendant." It is not surprising, then, that the bulk of the criminal matters sent to mediation are considered to be minor in nature. Unlike tort action where the mediation of some large scale, complex civil actions has received widespread praise for reaching mediated agreements, the climate is very different for criminal cases where mediation is introduced with great caution and trepidation. It is hard to imagine a serious, widely reported criminal action going to mediation. James A. Wall (Wall and Rude, 1989: 191) recounts a situation he experienced in 1980 after watching a plea bargaining scene on the television program "Hill Street Blues." Wall questioned why the judge did not mediate between the prosecutor and the defense attorney. In his own words, he states:

> Early the following morning, I posed the question to Larry Schiller, a member of my department who taught business law. His response: "Judges don't mediate in criminal cases."

"Why not?"
"Because it's against the law." (Later we found it is illegal in forty eight states.) "But," he quickly added, "they do mediate in civil cases, if they wish." (1989: 191)

When criminal cases are mediated, they are usually referred to dispute-processing forums using mediation outside of the courts. These programs have varied markedly in sponsorship, size, funding source, philosophical underpinnings, geographical location, etc. (McGillis, 1986: 19–30; ABA, 1986). Generally speaking, it is possible to differentiate between these programs primarily with respect to their relationship to the criminal justice system, i.e., those which are directly connected with local court systems, those which are not, and those which are a combination of the two (Wahrhaftig, 1982; McGillis, 1986: 20–29).

## COURT-CONNECTED DISPUTE-RESOLUTION PROGRAMS

Typically, court-connected dispute-resolution programs receive their referrals from the justice system, serve large geographical areas, use coercion to pressure individuals to use the programs, hold brief hearings, and have high caseloads and large budgets (McGillis, 1986: 21). These programs seek to reduce court backlogs and claim to do so through expedient and cost-effective forums.

## NON-COURT-CONNECTED DISPUTE-RESOLUTION PROGRAMS

Those mediation programs that are not connected with the justice system tend to stress community empowerment (Wahrhaftig, 1982; Shonholtz, 1984). Their goal is not to assist the justice system in better servicing the community or in reducing court backlogs, but in offering a whole new type of justice system. Considerable emphasis is placed on organizing the community and educating citizens to seek out the local mediation program as a first step in dealing with their differences with others rather than going to justice system officials. Typically, these programs serve smaller areas, receive their cases from outside the justice system, do not coerce individuals to use their services, hold longer, informal hearings, and have smaller caseloads and budgets (McGillis, 1986: 21).

## COMPOSITE DISPUTE-RESOLUTION PROGRAMS

Some of the programs are a mixture of the court-connected and non-court-connected programs. While the court-connected programs tend to be on one end of the continuum and the non-court-connected on the other end, the hybrid programs are in the middle. Hence, they receive cases from the justice system but also encourage individuals to walk in. In comparison with court-connected programs, they are not as coercive, hold briefer hearing sessions, are less formal, and have lower caseloads and budgets (McGillis, 1986: 21).

For the most part, all of these programs use volunteers to mediate disputes between individuals who have an ongoing relationship (ABA, 1986). Despite the informality of these programs, Merry (1989b: 86) has commented that the mediation developing in American society is one where "the mediator comes to resemble the judge in stance and claims to authority, [and] the process of mediation itself acquires some of the symbolic and formal structure of the court. Mediation adopts the form of the court in its use of official documents, its rituals of signing and funding, its self-definition as official, and its construction around the metaphor of the contract."

## Mediation: The Process

Historically, mediation has existed as the dominant process of resolving conflicts in many societies throughout the world (Gulliver, 1979; Merry, 1989b). Mediation has also been used as a favored intervention process in American society by various ethnic and religious groups (Auerback, 1983) including Chinese (Doo, 1973), Jews (Yaffe, 1972), and Quakers (Ordione, 1954) and in labor management relations. Despite this rich past, mediation has not been used extensively as a formal intervention process in American society by the legal system. Overall, it has been only vaguely understood, often confused with arbitration or even meditation.

Mediation is a relatively short-term participatory intervention process that enables disputing parties to resolve their differences with the assistance of a third party, known as a mediator, in an informal, face-to-face, private, and confidential setting (Folberg and Taylor, 1984; Moore 1986; Stulberg, 1987). Unlike arbitrators and judges, mediators do not make a decision for the parties, who are encouraged to speak for themselves and participate without the assistance of legal representation (Cooley, 1986). Although it is generally assumed that the parties will participate in the process voluntarily, this ideal has been less so as parties are increasingly pressured to attempt mediation.

The mediator guides the disputing parties to think through their concerns and to find common ground by helping them to consider relevant information, clarify issues, narrow their differences, generate settlement options, and tailor a workable plan for the future. In order to do so, the mediator must be able to build trust with the parties and listen to their emotions and interests. Since blame, vindication, guilt, innocence, and who is right and who is wrong are not central to the mediation process, the mediator helps the parties to move beyond past incident(s) and consider future arrangements.

Depending on the mediator's style and skill, philosophical perspective, nature of the issues, the parties' past relationship, their negotiation style, and the context within which the mediation occurs, the actual mediation process will vary. Procedurally, for instance, a mediator may routinely separate the parties for a private meeting known as a caucus or, on the contrary, never do so (Moore, 1987). Furthermore, the mediators control the communication flow, amount of time disputants can speak, and the topics that can be addressed and at what point (Silbey and Merry, 1986). While there is no hard and fast rule regarding the number of mediation sessions to be held, the mediation of criminal cases is generally conducted in one session (CDRCP, 1989: 37).

Although mediation is not rights- or rule-oriented, it is nonetheless not undertaken in a vacuum. The mediation of criminal disputes, as is true of other types of substantive issues, is conducted in the shadow of the legal system (Mnookin and Kornhauser, 1979). More specifically, that is, the process and its outcomes are often colored, if not directly influenced, by the legal system, its adversarial nature, and related concerns.

## Mediation: The Promise

Central to the promise of mediation has been the improvement of the delivery of justice. Included among the benefits of using mediation have been the reduction of court backlogs, speedier processing of cases, availability of inexpensive services, empowerment of individuals and neighborhoods, and the opportunity for more appropriate forums than provided by the traditional legal adversarial system. By enabling disputants an opportunity to explore the underlying concerns and creative options, mediation offers them an opportunity to salvage relationships and live more peacefully.

Although the amount of research on the processing of criminal matters through mediation has increased in recent years, it is still limited and often buried in research focusing on community, neighborhood, or interpersonal disputes, some of which may be criminal in nature (Cook, et al., 1980; Davis, et al., 1980; Felstiner and Williams, 1980; Harrington, 1985; DRAC, 1979; Pruitt and Kressel, 1989). Nonetheless, the results of major evaluation studies that include the mediation of criminal cases are generally positive. Data show that parties are highly satisfied with the mediation process (Cook, et. al., 1980; Davis, et. al., 1980; Felstiner and Williams, 1980), are highly likely to reach agreements (Beer, 1986: 26; CDRCP, 1989: 1), view the agreements as fair (Davis, et al., 1980), and are, when agreements are reached, likely to comply with the terms agreed to (Cook, et al., 1980).

## Mediation: The Challenges

As the mediation process and programs have matured in American society over the last two decades, they have come under increasing scrutiny. While it is generally agreed that mediation can and does work, depending on who is examining it, the concerns vary. Since mediation has been used in very diverse contexts, the vast amount of literature regarding this process does not focus on the mediation of criminal cases. In fact, very little has been written exclusively about this type of mediation. The following section attempts to pull together some of the key concerns as they apply to the mediation of criminal matters. Four major areas of concern will be addressed: first, getting disputants to the table; second, concerns about the process itself; third, concerns about mediators; and fourth, implications of mediation for the criminal justice system.

## GETTING DISPUTANTS TO THE TABLE

One of the major concerns confronting those attempting to provide mediation services to disputants involved in criminal disputes is getting disputants to agree to participate in the process. Resistance to mediation manifests itself in a number of ways (Volpe and Bahn, 1987). In general, mediation programs have not experienced large caseloads. This has often been attributed to a variety of reasons. Merry and Silbey (1984: 154) comment that "by the time they are willing to turn to others for help with their problem, the parties no longer wish to settle the dispute by discussion and negotiation." In reflecting on the usage of the Community Dispute Settlement program in suburban Philadelphia, Beer (1986: 37) remarked that "usually those who reach mediation have tried several tactics before they phone CDS. The police, the mayor, the principal, the district court—anyone who might have an answer has heard their complaints."

Other reasons cited include availability of other informal dispute processing mechanisms, the disputants' lack of knowledge about mediation programs, and also the resistance of the gatekeepers of the criminal justice system. Police, prosecutors, judges, and other criminal justice system actors are often reluctant or uneasy about referring cases, particularly those which are criminal in nature, to mediation programs. Many of them are evaluated by very traditional criminal justice measures such as arrests, convictions, or trials. Therefore, sending a case to a mediation program that may result in a dismissal is alien to their world. Others may feel that mediation does not provide a just outcome.  ·

Furthermore, disputants are often unwilling to go to mediation regarding criminal disputes. For the victims, there are a wide range of reasons including fear in meeting with those who perpetrated crimes on them, concerns over possible outcomes, and not wanting to see the perpetrator again (Smith, 1988: 125–26). For instance, mediation is not a process that easily addresses revenge and retaliation since the parties are encouraged to reach their own agreements. The likelihood that they will *both* agree to substantial punishment is virtually nonexistent. Peachey (1989: 307) remarks: "In many situations, mediation simply cannot deliver the kind of outcome desired by one of the parties. Disputants sometimes desire revenge or they want their position to be vindicated by a third party (preferably someone in authority). It does not take long for these individuals to realize that mediation cannot deliver the kind of justice they desire." Furthermore, mediation programs and legislation often allow for charges to be dropped if agreements are reached.

Hence, it is not surprising that caseloads are generally low unless the dispute-resolution programs are court-connected. While mediation is characterized as a voluntary process and one that works best when individuals choose to work through their own differences, the reality is that they are more likely to try mediation if they are pressured, and even more so if they are coerced to go.

Not only is getting the parties to the mediation table a problem, but keeping them there can be equally problematic. Because of the nature of the mediation process, it is highly possible for significant others who might influence one of the disputing parties to disrupt the mediation efforts. For instance, if a mediator separates the disputing parties and meets with them individually, it is possible for the waiting party to make a phone call to a significant other and come back to the session with a markedly different approach. If this were to happen, it could well be that this party might decided to change his/her mind about the terms being worked out at the table. Should an attorney be contacted, s/he may not feel that his/her client's best interests are suitably considered in a mediation process which is directed at finding common ground and encourages the party to reconsider what the attorney has worked out.

## THE MEDIATION PROCESS

Many questions continue to surface about which types of disputes can be processed through mediation. More specifically, which criminal disputes can be mediated? While it is widely agreed that misdemeanor level cases are suitable, there is much less agreement about felony cases. New York is the only state with legislation which enables the courts to adjourn selected felony cases in contemplation of dismissal to local dispute-resolution centers (Art. 215, NYS Penal Law). Much conern has been expressed regarding such issues as child abuse and domestic violence. Yet, numerous programs address one or both of these areas in their caseload (Mayer, 1985, 1989; Marthaler, 1989).

The appropriateness of mediation when there is an imbalance of power between the parties has been raised. Power disparities can be particularly challenging for the weaker party, who may be intimidated, co-opted, or exploited by mediation (Merry, 1989;: 240–43; Davis and Salem, 1984). Unlike the courts where, theoretically, neutral principles are applied to all, mediation strives for a consensual outcome tailored to meet the needs of the parties. Power disparities are, therefore, not necessarily neutralized.

In general, agreements reached in mediation are only as binding as the parties allow them to be. Parties are encouraged to uphold the agreements that they reached. Should one or both of the parties not comply, they are usually encouraged to go back to the program and attempt re-mediation or some adjustment to the agreement. In criminal cases where the court has adjourned the matter pending the successful mediation outcome, non-compliance can result in traditional criminal processing.

The fact that mediation prides itself in being a very informal process which allows disputing parties to share their thoughts behind closed doors also raises questions for those who might be interested in quality control. How does one know what is going on behind the closed doors in an informal, private, confidential setting? Is the mediator being fair, manipulative? (Merry, 1989a: 243–44). If the disputants are in need of legal advice, how can they be assured of such?

Furthermore, unlike the traditional legal system which allows for the collection of information through discovery, mediation does not provide for such a process. Hence, disputants are at the mercy of each other to be honest and to produce accurate, appropriate, and necessary information for a mutually satisfactory agreement to be reached. Mediation programs handling criminal disputes are often run by non-lawyers who may not provide the disputants with legal protections and legal counsel.

## THE MEDIATORS

For the most part, the mediators handling the criminal disputes are volunteers trained by local dispute-resolution programs. In recent years, questions have been raised about the nature of the education and training received by mediators in general (*Dispute Resolution Forum*, 1989). To date, there has been no uniformity in training or credentials for those desiring to mediate in the United States. Some of the emerging legislation is beginning to address this concern. For example, New York State requires 25 hours of training for mediators in the community-based programs handling minor criminal and civil cases.

## MEDIATION AND THE CRIMINAL JUSTICE SYSTEM: INTERFACING AT WHAT COST?

Proponents of mediation often stress that mediation is less expensive than the traditional criminal justice system. This, however, is difficult to assess due to the limited comparative data. Some show that due to the low volume of cases, mediation is not in fact cost saving. Furthermore, some evidence shows that court backlogs are not affected since the kinds of cases that end up in mediation would either have been dismissed or not entertained at all by the courts (Cook et al., 1980).

Numerous authors—including Tomasic (1982), Abel (1982), Harrington (1985), and Hofrichter (1982)—have questioned whether these programs allow for further expansion of state influence in the lives of individuals. For instance, because dispute resolution programs are readily available and eager to process disputes that occur between individuals with an ongoing relationship, such individuals can become unnecessarily entangled in an official informal process. They argue that many of these cases would probably have been dismissed by the courts.

Many of the new ventures using mediation solicit their funding and resources from sources outside of the criminal justice system. This reliance on soft monies creates uncertainty for many of the programs regarding their future and that of the many so-called minor criminal cases now handled by them.

Incorporating mediation into traditional structures provides great challenges. Can the mediation programs withstand being co-opted by the very system that they were attempting to replace? On the other hand, the institutionalization of these programs is one of the best assurances they will be ensured a sense of continuity (Merry, 1989: 245–47).

Police, prosecutors, and court personnel continue to work in hierarchical organizational environments where ranks are clearly delineated. They are not rewarded for sending cases to mediation programs which are generally perceived as entities quite external to the criminal justice system.

The preceding points suggest that the proliferation of interest in the use of mediation presents both promises and problems for the criminal justice system. It offers the hope that nonadversarial ways of handling criminal matters are possible, and it allows parties to work through their differences while avoiding criminal processing and labeling.

On the other hand, mediation does not readily lend itself for integration into the criminal justice system. It raises uneasy challenges for criminal justice professionals. Resistance arises not only in the need for change in the adversarial view of processing disputes, but also in the perceptions of disputants, legal actors, and not least, the public's notion of justice.

Overall, mediation efforts have been eclectic and often fragmented, evolving in a haphazard manner. Much research needs to be done to address the many questions currently being posed by a process that is currently in its formative stages of acceptance and utilization by the criminal justice system.

## REFERENCES

Abel, Richard L. 1982. "The Contradictions of Informal Justice." In Richard L. Abel (ed.), *The Politics of Informal Justice, Volume 1, The American Experience.* New York: Academic Press.

ABA (American Bar Association). 1984. *Legislation on Dispute Resolution.* Washington, D.C.: ABA Special Committee on Dispute Resolution.

———. 1986. *Dispute Resolution Program Directory, 1986–1987.* Washington, D.C.: ABA Special Committee on Dispute Resolution.

Auerback, Jerold S. 1983. *Justice Without Law? Resolving Disputes Without Lawyers.* New York: Oxford University Press.

Beer, Jennifer E. 1986. *Peacemaking in Your Neighborhood: Reflections on An Experiment in Community Mediation.* Philadelphia: New Society Publishers.

BNA (Bureau of National Affairs). 1985. *Resolving Disputes Without Litigation.* Rockville, Md.: Bureau of National Affairs.

Chupp, Mark. 1989. "Reconciliation Procedures and Rationale." In Martin Wright and Burt Galaway (eds.), *Mediation and Criminal Justice: Victims, Offenders, and Community.* London: Sage.

CDRCP (Community Dispute Resolution Centers Program). 1989. *Annual Report April 1, 1988-March 31, 1989.* Albany: CDRCP.

Cook, Royer R., Janice A. Roehl, and David I. Sheppard. 1980. *Neighborhood Justice Centers Field Test: Final Evaluation Report.* Washington, D.C.: United States Department of Justice, National Institute of Justice.

Cooley, John. 1986. "Arbitration vs. Mediation—Explaining the Differences." *Judicature.*

Davis, Albie M., and Richard A. Salem. 1984. "Dealing with Power Imbalances in the Mediation of Interpersonal Disputes." *Mediation Quarterly* (December): 17–26.

Davis, Robert C., Martha Tichane, and Deborah Grayson. 1980. *Mediation and Arbitration as Alternatives to Prosecution in Felony Arrest Cases—An Evaluation of the Brooklyn Dispute Resolution Center (First Year).* New York: Vera Institute of Justice.

DRAC (Dispute Resolution Alternatives Committee). 1979. *The Citizen Dispute Settlement Process in Florida: A Study of Five Programs.* Tallahassee: Supreme Court, Office of the State Courts Administrator.

*Dispute Resolution Forum.* 1989. Washington, D.C.: National Institute for Dispute Resolution.

Doo, L. W. 1973. "Dispute Settlement in Chinese American Communities." *American Journal of Comparative Law.*

Felstiner, William L. F., and Lynne A. Williams. 1980. *Community Mediation in Dorchester, Massachusetts.* Washington, D.C.: U.S. Department of Justice, National Institute of Justice.

Folberg, Jay, and Alison Taylor. *Mediation: A Comprehensive Guide to Resolving Conflicts Without Litigation.* San Francisco: Jossey-Bass.

Goldberg, Stephen B., Eric D. Green, and Frank E. A. Sander. 1985. *Dispute Resolution.* Boston: Little Brown.

Gulliver, P. H. 1979. *Disputes and Negotiations: A Cross-Cultural Perspective,* New York: Academic Press.

Harrington, Christine B. 1985. *Shadow Justice: The Ideology and Institutionalization of Alternatives to Court.* Westport, Conn.: Greenwood Press.

Hofrichter, Richard. 1982. "Neighborhood Justice and the Social Control Problems of American Capitalism: A Perspective." In Richard L. Abel (ed.), *The Politics of Informal Justice, Volume 1, The American Experience.* New York: Academic Press.

Leeson, Susan M., and Bryan M. Johnson. 1988. *Ending It: Dispute Resolution in America.* Ohio: Anderson Publishing Co.

Marks, Jonathon B., Earl Johnson, Jr., and Peter L. Szanton. 1984. *Dispute Processing in America: Processes in Evolution,* Washington, D.C.: National Institute for Dispute Resolution.

Marthaler, Dennis. 1989. "Successful Mediation with Abusive Couples." *Mediation Quarterly* 23: 53–66.

Mayer, Bernard. 1985. "Conflict Resolution in Child Protection and Adoption." *Mediation Quarterly* 9: 69–81.

———. 1989. "Mediation in Child Protection Cases: The Impact of Third Party

Intervention on Parental Compliance Attitudes." *Mediation Quarterly* 24 (Summer): 89–106.

McGillis, Daniel. 1986. *Community Dispute Resolution Programs and Public Policy,* Washington, D.C.: U.S. Department of Justice, National Institute of Justice.

Merry, Sally Engle. 1989a. "Myth and Practice in the Mediation Process." In Martin Wright and Burt Galaway (eds.), *Mediation in Criminal Justice: Victims, Offenders and Community.* Sage: London.

———. 1989b. "Mediation in Nonindustrial Societies." In Kenneth Kressel, Dean G. Pruitt, and Associates (eds.), *Mediation Research: The Process and Effectiveness of Third-Party Intervention.* San Francisco: Jossey-Bass.

Merry, Sally Engle, and Susan S. Silbey. 1984. "What do Plaintiffs Want? Reexamining the Concept of Dispute." *Justice System Journal* 9: 151–78.

Mnookin, Robert H., and Lewis Kornhauser. 1979. "Bargaining in the Shadow of the Law: The Case of Divorce." *Yale Law Journal* 88: 950–97.

Moore, Christopher W. 1986. *The Mediation Process: Practical Strategies for Resolving Conflict.* San Francisco: Jossey-Bass.

———. 1987. "The Caucus: Private Meetings that Promote Settlement." *Mediation Quarterly* 16: 87–101.

Murray, John S., Alan Scott Rau, and Edward F. Sherman. 1989. *Processes of Dispute Resolution: The Role of Lawyers.* New York: Foundation Press.

Ordione. G. S. 1954. "Arbitration and Mediation Among Early Quakers." *Arbitration Journal.*

Peachey, Dean E. 1989. "What People Want From Mediation." In Kenneth Kressel, Dean G. Pruitt, and Associates (eds.), *Mediation Research: The Process and Effectiveness of Third-Party Intervention.* San Francisco: Jossey-Bass.

Pruitt, Dean G., and Kenneth Kressel. 1989. "Introduction: An Overview of Mediation Research." In Kenneth Kressel, Dean Pruitt, and Associates (eds.), *Mediation Research: The Process and Effectiveness of Third-Party Intervention.* San Francisco: Jossey-Bass.

Riskin, Leonard L. 1982. "Mediation and Lawyers." *Ohio State Law Journal,* 43: 29–50.

Riskin, Leonard L., and James W. Westbrook. 1987. *Dispute Resolution and Lawyers.* St. Paul, Minn.: West Publishing Co.

Shonholtz, Raymond. 1984. "Neighborhood Justice Systems: Work, Structure, and Guilding Principles." *Mediation Quarterly* 5: 3–30.

Silbey, Susan S. and Sally E. Merry. 1986. "Mediator Settlement Strategies." *Law and Policy* 8: 7–32.

Smith, David; Harry Blagg, and Nick Derricourt. 1988. "Mediation in the Shadow of the Law: The South Yorkshire Experience." In Roger Matthews (ed.), *Informal Justice.* London: Sage.

Stulberg, Joseph B. 1987. *Taking Charge, Managing Conflict,* Lexington, Mass: Lexington Books.

Tomasic, Roman. 1982. "Mediation as an Alternative to Adjudication: Rhetoric and Reality in the Neighborhood Justice Movement." In Roman Tomasic and Malcolm M. Feeley (eds.), *Neighborhood Justice: Assessment of an Emerging Idea.* New York: Longman.

Umbreit, Mark S. 1986. *Victim Offender Mediation: Conflict Resolution and Restitution.* Washington, D.C.: U.S. Department of Justice.

———. 1989. "Violent Offenders and Their Victims." In Martin Wright and Burt Galaway (eds.), *Mediation and Criminal Justice: Victims, Offenders and Community.* London: Sage.

Volpe, Maria R. 1988. "Dispute Resolution Education, Training and Critical Issues for Criminal Justice Professionals." *Research in Law and Policy Studies* 2: 265–77.

————. 1989a. "The Police Role." In Martin Wright and Burt Galaway (eds.), *Mediation and Criminal Justice: Victims, Offenders and Community.* London: Sage.

————. 1989b. "Managing Conflict in the Public Sector." *Public Productivity and Management Review* 13 (Fall): 99–106.

Volpe, Maria R., and Charles Bahn. 1987. "Resistance to Mediation Understanding and Handling It." *Negotiation Journal.*

Wahrhaftig, Paul. 1982. "An Overview of Community-Oriented Citizen Dispute Resolution Programs in the United States." In Richard L. Abel (ed.), *The Politics of Informal Justice, Volume 1, The American Experience.* New York: Academic Press.

Wall, James A., Jr., and Dale E. Rude. 1989. "Judicial Mediation of Settlement Negotiations." In Kenneth Kressel, Dean G. Pruitt, and Associates (eds.), *Mediation Research: The Process and Effectiveness of Third-Party Intervention.* San Francisco: Jossey-Bass.

Yaffe, J. 1972. *So Sue Me! The Story of a Community Court.* New York: Saturday Review Press.

# PART
# THREE

# Critical Peacemaking
# Traditions

*Dragan Milovanovic*

T  H  I  R  T  E  E  N

# Images of Unity and Disunity in the Juridic Subject and Movement toward the Peacemaking Community

The nature of subjectivity is central in criminological analysis. There is a crisis, however, in critical criminology over epistemological and ontological suppositions behind theorizing of what is and what may be. Here we would like to explore subjectivity at three levels: the juridic, semiotic, and ontological. We focus on the conceptualization of the subject that has been stabilized since the Renaissance, a subject assumed to be endowed with free will, consciousness, self-reflectiveness, and a construction posited to be determining—in a word, a centered subject. In law we find its reflective form, a subject that is calculable, predictable, and accountable. We would then like to contrast the Nietzschean-Deleuzean with the Hegelian-Kojevean notion of value creation for the purpose of exploring a direction for a *transpraxis*, a humanistic transfiguration of man/woman and for visions for movement toward the peacemaking community.

Hegel has been inspirational in critical criminology even though not often read nor integrated directly in theorizing. His notion of the *Absolute Spirit* and *master-slave* dialectic has been the core from which much critical analysis has stemmed. The latter produces dichotomous value orientations as well as qualitatively distinct desires. The former notion is teleological; social movement revolves around the unfolding of an idea, a telos. This conception was grasped in different forms: by Karl Marx in his notion of dialectical materialism in the form of the thesis-antithesis–higher-synthesis dynamic, and by Max Weber in his notion of a monolithic force of "rationalization." Hegel's master-slave dialectic has been incorporated by Marx in the form of the struggle between the bourgeois and proletariat. In contrast to this has been the postmodernist tradition that relies heavily on the Nietzsche-Deleuze rendition of the master-slave dialectic, "genealogical" analysis, and *pathos*. This is the terrain on which conceptualizations of an alternative form of subjectivity and social formation will develop.

## Subjectivity: Images of Unity and Disunity in the Juridic Subject

The juridic subject, the abstract and formal subject in law with a specified locus of rights respected by the state, rests on certain ontological assumptions. The notion of the "reasonable man/woman" in law endowed with equivalent worth—that is, all are measured by an equivalent standard the criteria of which assumes the existence of free will, a determining, self-conscious subject, and capacity to choose within a limited range of acceptable means to attain some specified end–is the juridic cell of Western democracy. The lurking metaphysical bogeyman is disunity, chaos, unpredictability, uncalculability. Whether we look: at Weber's historical analysis of the transformation from the status contract to purposive contract and its personification, the juristic personality (1978; see also Milovanovic, 1989a); at Pashukanis's commodity-exchange perspective whereby the fetishism of commodity finds its parallel development (homology) in legal fetishism (1980); at Habermas's analysis of the decoupling of the lifeworld from system imperatives and the recoupling in the late 17th and 18th centuries by which purposive-rational action has replaced symbolic communication as the primal form of action, now guided by the steering media of power and money, universalized by the abstraction of equivalence in law (1984, 1987); or whether we look at the current form of the juridic subject as being but the end result of interest balancing, a return to "status," as the "structural interpellation" perspective indicates (Milovanovic, 1987, 1989a)—we note the end result of these analyses is the specification of a subject who is centered, determining, self-reflective, and the focus of a uniform and precise juridical inquiry whenever a transgression is said to occur. Purposive-rational action, then, becomes a value-rational form of action reflected in legal form, where the primal form of conduct is said to be oriented to a rational means-ends calculation, where ends are specified as given.

We look deeper into this metaphysical realm and note that what lies beyond the formally espoused criteria for the juridic subject is the value of calculability, predictability, order, and accountability. But this has had a political economic development. Consider Weber's classic study of the relationship between rationality and free will (1975: 120–34). "Irrationality," Weber tells us, should be equated with "incalculability." Many, Weber tells us, connect freedom of the will with incalculability. The latter point, however, belies everyday facts, according to Weber:

> Every military order, every criminal law, in fact every remark that we make in conversation with others, 'counts' on the fact that certain impressions will penetrate the 'psyches' of those for whom they are intended. They do not depend upon the absolute unambiguity of these impressions in every respect and in every case. But they do depend upon a calculability which is sufficient *for the purposes* which the command, the law, and the concrete utterance are intended to serve. (Weber, 1975: 121)

Through some further ingenious arguments, Weber attempts to show that human conduct is intrinsically calculable and hence determinable. Generally, he tells us, it is assumed that the more incalculabe (uninterpretable) an action is, the more freedom of the will, or freedom of action, that person must have had. However, it is the converse that is true (Weber, 1975: 128). Starting with the idea that subjects make empirical generalizations of activity—that is, subjects can objectify observed experiences (perceptions) in means-ends chains (e.g., they can abstract into concepts and laws)—then, given a particular end, we may apparently conclude whether the subsequent mean chosen is rational, is based on empirical generalizations of whether it furthers that end. Hence, the greater the freedom of the will for Weber, the more determinable is the choice arrived at and the more calculable is the subject said to be. Hence calculability for Weber stands for predictability. Rational conduct, then, hinges on the ability to objectify perceptions into empirical generalizations. And elsewhere Weber tells us it is precisely because subjects orient themselves to maxims that their behavior is predictable (Weber, 1975: 105–16).

What Weber overlooks, however, is that empirical generalizations are narrative constructions (see also Jackson, 1985, 1988). Language, we argue, provides a metatheory of action and subjectivity. Consider Nietzsche:

> To ordain the future in advance . . . man must first have learned to distinguish necessary events from chance ones, to think causally, to see and anticipate distant eventualities as if they belong to the present, to decide with certainty what is the goal and what the means to it, and in general be able to calculate and compute. Man himself must first of all have become *calculable, regular, necessary.* (1968a: 494)

Elsewhere, Nietzsche tells us—his "universal law"—that for a human to be healthy s/he must have certain horizons within which to exist (cited in Love, 1986: 53). These horizons are provided by language itself. In a brilliant, be it a provocative polemic, Nietzsche tells us in *Twilight of the Idols*, in implicit and anticipatory contrast to Weber's analysis, that "four great fictions" are perpetuated in language itself. Language provides us with the fiction (1) that the actor is separate from the action, (2) that with this distinction causality can be attributed to the actor by the emphasis on a presumed determining consciousness, (3) that specific causes then can be attributable to particular events, and finally (4) that it is freedom of the will that animates the process. Thus Weber, confronted with the dilemma of the relationship between freedom of the will and rationality, falls trap to semiotic fictions. This fetish animates his whole edifice. Nietzsche would tell us that Weber correctly objectified the myths presented to us in language, and the legal form is but a further objectification of these myths, these fictions, hence a double objectification. Thus is posited the juridic subject who is formally free, equal, endowed with proprietorship interests, and who is further a mathematical locus of calculability, predictability, determinability, and accountability. Consider Nietzsche:

> Our "understanding of an event" has consisted in our inventing a subject which was made responsible for something that happens and for how it happens. We have combined our feeling of will, our feeling of "freedom," our feeling of responsibility and our intention to perform an act, into the concept "cause."

In contradistinction, for the Hopi Indian studied by Whorf, the world is seen in terms of "eventing," the coming to be and the passing away of phenomena (1956: 147). As Nietzsche would tell us, "there is no 'being' behind doing, effecting, becoming; 'the doer" is merely a fiction added to the deed—the deed is everything" (1968a: 481). In the Weberian construct, the fictions implicit in language have been completed in the juridic sphere. They stand as fetishes, as idols that are henceforth worshiped.

It was particularly during the development of the capitalist mode of production that the "decoupling" phenomena—e.g., a time where the "lifeworld" and its locus of signifiers and its synchronic connection with the internal dynamics of systems, mediated by "communicative action" in the production of meaning, are separated; whereby new "steering media," based on money and power, structure the relationship and are now constitutive of meaning construction (see Weber, 1978; Habermas, 1984, 1987)—produced a strengthening of this fiction as several forces in combination developed assuring the fiction's permanent status (Weber, 1978; Milovanovic, 1983, 1988, 1989a). Thus, purposive-rational action attained a value-rational anchoring (Habermas, 1984, 1987) because of a confluence of forces that all were predicated on the existence of semiotic fictions already there. It was the arrival of the new forms of control, the discipling mechanism (Foucault, 1977), that were to produce a more ubiquitous and omnipotent form for disciplining bodies in the social formation, producing subjects of docility and utility. Language is but the primal disciplining mechanism.

Individual difference may vary from an established criteria; but, beyond a certain point, variation is constitutive of deviance in the legal sense. But difference is the essence of being human, and to subsume subjects to equivalent standards is to pass over the inherent differences (i.e., abilities, needs, potentials, temperamental traits, etc.) which represent the uniqueness of each person (see, also, Lee, 1959). Formal equality, then, may be indeed an ideal toward which Western democracies choose to tend, but it does not in itself assure the realization of social values. In fact, it is a fetish well in tune with the needs of capital logic. Weber, Pashukanis, Habermas and others have well argued that notions of the juridic subject are inherently connected with capital logic. The notion of the juridic subject, then, has no existence outside of the political economic domain. It does not tell us in any ontological sense how subjects really think, choose, and act. It only posits their equivalence in order to make them predictable, calculable, and accountable. Thus we have an algebraic $x$, the subject as signifier, who is filled in with a signified, content (e.g., legally specified attributions). This signified, historically, has undergone movement; its anchoring is inherently politically economic in nature. Making subjects equivalent under the law, then, is a utility principle serving precise functions; it is not reflective of humanistic being in the world, nor does it necessarily assure maximal fulfillment of social values.

## Subjectivity: Images of Unity and Disunity in Discourse

Postmodernism—or my appropriation, the post-Frankfurt school—has stipulated the idea of the *decentered subject*. The rediscovery of Freud's early writing and its rendering a linguistic read has ushered in the psychoanalytic semiotic framework (see also Silverman, 1983; Metz, 1982). The "I" of an utterance, of a statement, is not, according to Nietzsche, Benveniste, Lacan, Deleuze and Guattari, and many in the postmodernist tradition, the same as the "I" of its production (Milovanovic, 1990a, 1990b). Consider Lacan's classic statement "I am lying." Clearly two planes are implicated: the statement, and its production.

Language provides fictions on at least two levels. First, following Nietzsche—and for further empirical support, we may borrow from the seminal works of Whorf on the Hopi Indian (1956)—language provides a fiction that the subject is analytically separatable from action. The basic grammatical structure of subject with predicate, verb and object, implies a controlling subject. Consider, however, the Hopi. Rather than describing an observed action of running by the words "he is running," the Hopi use one word, "running," a statement that assumes the unity of actor and act; in other words, we have action and no more. Second, the form of language in use is constitutive of subjectivity. Lacan (1977), integrating the works of Saussure, Levi-Strauss, Benveniste, and Freud, has indicated that language can be conceptualized along two main axes, the metaphoric and the metonymic. The metonymic, the diachronic dimension, stands for syntactical structures; the metaphoric, the actual potential storehouse of signifiers. Signs, for Lacan, are composed of the duality: signifiers, the acoustic-image; and signifieds, the concepts referred to. The two axes are constitutive of meaning. As an utterance unfolds, both axes are drawn from—each word chosen has many other possible substitutable words (the metaphoric/synchronic dimension); and each word, signifier, must be placed in a specific sequence for grammatical correctness (the metonymic/diachronic dimension). Together in this signifying chain, a sequence of signifieds is mobilized providing meaning to the narrative construction. A signifier, according to Lacan's classic definition, then, is a subject for another signifier and no more. Since signifiers can also be defined as the presence of an absence, then subjects too, in their utterances—by the use of personal pronouns to represent themselves in their absence—are implicated in this process; that is, the subject much like the signifier, with the entrance into language, finds itself constituted in nonreferential signifying chains (e.g., the Real is not being reflected; signifiers only refer to other signifiers which in turn refer to other signifiers, etc.). The "I" of a statement, of an utterance, represents the subject in its absence. The producer of the statement, in other words, is absent in the utterance itself. The subject is a signifier and can be defined as the subject for another signifier in a signifying chain. Thus subjectivity is intricately connected with language. In sum, language produces fictions, the subject of discourse is but a signifier; the signified, the producer of the statement remains hidden. And this was indeed Freud's early discovery, particularly in his *The Interpretation of Dreams* (1900).

Weber's ambitious project in defining social action is a surface explanation defining the play of signifiers. Signifiers are elevated, in his framework, to the level of the "real" overlooking the complex, dynamic processes that appear under the bar of the classic signifier/signified duality. The narrative constructions that the "rational" subject is said to construct in the process of developing generalizations, which in turn are the basis of "rational" mean-ends calculations, are devoid of signifieds, the essences of being itself. The play of signifiers is a play of the presences of absences. The subject has disappeared from the scene, replaced by a fetish. In law, this classic fetish appears in the *persona* of the juridic subject.

We can see, then, that language always already provides the material, the form, from whence the world is divided in certain ways. Whorf, explaining the differences between the standard Indo-European and the Hopi language, has told us that "each language is not merely a reproducing instrument for voicing ideas but rather is itself the shaper of ideas, the program and guide for the individual's mental activity, for his analysis of impressions, for his synthesis of his mental stock in trade. . . . We dissect nature along lines laid down by our native languages" (1956: 212–13). Further, certitude is a linguistic fiction. Consider Whorf's discussion of how we express mass nouns—"homogenous continua without implied boundaries"

(1956: 140) such as milk, water, sand, etc. We make use of a binomialism whereby we preceed the mass noun by a particular concrete form (i.e., a glass of water, a cup of milk). Distinctions, differences, are, in Western cultures, therefore marked by this "linguistic binomialism," by the form-plus-formless formula always already existing in language. This, however, does not exist in the Hopi language. Whorf implies that with the coming of the industrial revolution and its need for precise measurements, a new form of expression of amorphous entities materialized. This adds to semiotic fictions along Nietzsche's lines, particularly the idea that specifically discrete objects exist rather than "dynamic quanta" in relationship.

What neither Whorf nor Lacan, nor indeed Nietzsche, does, however, is to situate discourse in a political economy. Elsewhere, we have argued that different discourses, linguistic coordinate systems, exist with specific discursive subject-positions; and the creation of reality and the constitution of subjectivity is based on assuming a position within these spatiotemporal coordinates (Milovanovic, 1988a, 1990a 1990b). We extend this argument by indicating that in the advanced forms of the capitalist mode of production, what gives the appearance of unity is indeed the disciplining mechanism, particularly legal linguistic coordinate systems. That is, since the signifier is the presence of an absence, and following Lacan and Deleuze and Guattari, since signifiers are imprisoned in the flow of signifying chains, so, too, the legal subject is centered in the legal linguistic coordinate system which anchors the perpetual flow of signifieds under the signifiers. The "anchoring" (Lacan, 1977) is not arbitrary. It is a politically determined phenomena. Thus, the "I" of legal discourse is captured in legal signifying chains that have no reference to specific signifieds, to beings, but rather to their representation, the "I" of discourse. The "reasonable man/woman in law," then, is an arbitrary construct, but one well suited for the imperatives of capital logic. The availability of substitutable parts in the machinery of capitalism assure its smooth functioning. The well-oiled machine finds metaphors aplenty. It is this that Weber struggled with, which finally was made manifest in his statement of despair, coined the "loss of freedom" and the "loss of meaning" in the new age, the iron cage of capitalism.

Two recent explanatory mechanisms have been presented for this constituting process. Althusser (1971) has used the concept of "interpellation," by which he means a "hailing" whereby the subject, in responding to the hail ("Hey you there!"), inserts him/herself in a particular discursive subject-position. This also entails being placed in a constellation of circumscribed signifiers from which to draw, and hence being at the mercy of its implications (e.g., connotations), of its anchored signifieds. The notion of "suture" (Lacan, 1977) is the other element of this process. Here, according to the psychoanalytic semiotic framework, narrative constructions inevitably present gaps which must be smoothed over, sutured as in a surgical tie. What is mobilized in this process is desire, a response to lack. The Freudian, as well as the Lacanian edifice, rests on a stipulated constantly aroused lack and the subsequent mobilization of desire, and on the search for discharge of psychic energy, a return to homeostasis, a negation of lack. Materials (signifiers) that are indeed borrowed in order to present coherent stories in narrative constructions are circumscribed by the discourse one finds one self in, or inserted in. Reality construction, and so, too, subjectivity, is constituted by these dynamics, and interpellation and suture provide the key explanatory dynamics. In sum, the subject perceived as determining, in control, self-reflective, "free," and calculating, is a fiction, a product of signifying practices.

In late capitalism, what Deleuze and Guattari refer to as the "post-signifying regime" (1987: 111–48), a new ubiquitous but yet elusive point or origination of interpellation has developed, one separate from people as such. These "points of subjectification,"—constituted, we add, by capital logic, technological imperatives, and the phallocentric order—produce a self-referential self-system, in which the subject of the statement becomes more and more the subject of its production, a recursivity that produces the dynamics of hegemonic domination that is devoid of controllers as such. Deleuze and Guattari refer to this as the "doubling of the subject." In the post-signifying regime, the glorification of the centered subject is a celebration of a fetish, a creation of political economic forces.

## Subjectivity: Images of Unity and Disunity— Ontological View

We would like now to examine two prominent views of the relation of values to subjectivity. The Hegel-Kojeve master-slave examination must be compared with Nietzsche-Deleuze for an explication of value creation, desire and subjectivity. It is our thesis that the former is inherently homeostatic. In fact, it was in France, during the latter part of the 1960s and 1970s, that Nietzsche was to supplant Hegel and become the basis of post-modern thought. In order to progress further in our struggle for developing the vision of an alternative order, we must come to terms with this critical and as of yet not fully explored difference between the two classic perspectives on the master-slave dialectic (See also Strong, 1975; Love, 1986; Deleuze, 1983; Bogue, 1989; Kojeve, 1969: 16–30; Nietzsche, 1966).[1]

The Hegelian-Kojevian thesis of the master-slave dialectic has it that each, the master and the slave, finds him/herself in a position of value creation vis-à-vis the other. Each needs the other in order to define and validate self. The master morality is created by the master stipulating "I am good, therefore you (the slave) are bad." The master delights and attains satisfaction in the consuming, the negating, of the things produced by the slave for him/her. The master's existence is mediated by the other, the slave, who gives recognition to him/her. Thus the desire for recognition emerges out of this dialectic. But the master seeks recognition without in turn giving recognition to the slave. The slave, in contrast, must negate a negation.

S/he says "He (the master) is bad (not good), therefore I am not not-good." This is a double negation, a negation of a negation, that produces a positive. The slave recognizes the master, but attempts to negate him/her. The master sees the slave as a thing, an animal; thus the master is recognized by a thing or an animal. The slave recognizes someone (the master) who in turn does not recognize him/her. After the victory of the master over the slave, then, desire for recognition is intricately connected with being recognized by this thing, this animal, and not by another person. Since satisfaction rests on recognition by the other, the master will never be satisfied. It is only for the slave, or the person who has passed through slavery, has overcome slavery, that satisfaction is possible at all (Kojeve, 1969: 16–30). The master cannot go beyond what s/he is, cannot progress further, cannot change. The master has risked everything to attain the position of master and this is the end point. S/he does not produce, does not work but consumes, negates what is produced by the slave. Thus satisfaction is purely negative, beyond attainment. But work is what transforms, concretizes, educates. And the slave must repress immediate consumption desires in order to work. The slave transcends him/herself through work. S/he gains recognition in the objects produced. The objects created are affirmations of self, a projection of inner desire which then reaffirm the producing, working self. Subjects realize themselves through the products produced. And thus, the Hegel-Kojeve thesis has it that "the future and History . . . belong not to the warlike Master, who either dies or preserves himself indefinitely in identity to himself, but to the working slave" (Kojeve, 1969: 23).

The Nietzsche-Deleuze schema is quite different. Whereas Hegel's philosophy of value creation was essentially centered on a "negation of a negation," for Nietzsche it was centered on a philosophy of affirmation (Bogue, 1989: 15, 18). The master (noble) and the slave (base) indeed find themselves in struggle, in establishing differences. The master's existence is based on an active and affirmative value-creating way of being; the slave on a reactive and negative way. The master sees him/herself as good and the slave as base, as not good; therefore the master affirms his differences from the slave in calling him/herself good and the slave bad. The slave, however, resents the master, and defines the master as bad. The slave, similarly to Hegel-Kojeve, says "He is bad (not good), therefore I am not not good." And to establish difference, to gain value is to do a double negation, a negation of a negation, which creates a positive. The slave must react and negate in order to create value. The master only needs to affirm and act on his/her defined differences from the slave. For the master, everything is positive in the premise, and the negative exists in the conclusion of the syllogism. The master's philosophy is an active negating. For the slave the premise is negative and only through reaction and negation in the form of a negation of a negation does a positive appear (Deleuze, 1983: 120–21; Bogue, 1989: 16–18). Everywhere, Nietzsche tells us, we find the slave morality victorious over the masters'. For Nietzsche, unlike Hegel, it is the master morality that is affirmative. In reality, however, the master and slave morality is found in various combinations in everyone and is not necessarily defined by economic status (Nietzsche, 1966: 204; Strong, 1975: 239).

In *The Genealogy of Morals*, Nietzsche explains the development of the slave morality and its various instances—"bad conscience," "ressentiment," "guilt," and the "ascetic priests"—all subsequently incorporated in other forms by such thinkers as Freud, in his *Civilization and its Discontents*, and as Weber, in his "The Social Psychology of World Religion" (Strong, 1975: 239). History, for Nietzsche-Deleuze, is one of the triumphs of reactive forces that only produce a will to nothingness. His parable of the lamb and the bird of prey is illuminating (see Strong, 1975: 243–45; Deleuze, 1983: 122–23; Bogue, 1989: 26–27). The lamb, faced with the constant threat of the eagle swooping down to take one of its own, starts questioning the apparent motives of the bird of prey. It asks why should the eagle do so for the lamb and his/her companions pose no problems for the eagle. The lamb, after comparing the eagle's to its own behavior sees the eagle as consciously doing its acts, and hence, evilness is attributed to it. Thus the eagle is seen as capable of calculating and making decisions. Given this, the lamb reasons, the eagle could have acted otherwise than it did. The lamb, in other words, is coming up with a uniform criteria by which both the eagle and lamb should operate. But the eagle does not abide by these standards. Because of continued suffering experienced by the lamb, the lamb attributes evilness to the bird of prey. Thus, for Nietzsche, the real "cause" is the suffering by the lamb. The lamb's whole project becomes one in which he tries to develop a system by which the eagle will stop doing its presumedly conscious act. This parable attempts to bring out the thought processes taking place in slave morality. To come to an understanding of his/her suffering, the slave (lamb) develops increasingly sophisticated tricks to deal with the attributed evilness of the eagle (master). Here, too, lies the paralogism behind "ressentiment," namely the fictions that (1) the actor can be separated from his/her act, (2) the actor is attributed with consciousness (i.e., ability to do otherwise than what he does) and hence blameworthiness, and (3) freedom of the will animates the process. The masters are increasingly frustrated by the trickeries of the lamb and eventually take on the same form of thought as the slave; they seek reasons for the slave's activities. Slave morality increasingly predominates. With the slave's developed thought process appears, increasingly, "ressentiment," the bad conscience and ascetic ideals, the triumph or reactive forces (nihilism, the will to nothingness)—the core themes of Nietzsche's *On the Genealogy of Morals*. In fact ressentiment at a certain point is essential for the slave: "[w]e can guess what the creature of *ressentiment* wants: he wants others to be evil, he needs others to be evil in order to be able to consider himself good" (Deleuze, 1983: 119). Thus, "in order to exist, slave morality always first needs a hostile world" (Nietzsche cited by Deleuze, 1983: 119).

The basis of a good self-identification only comes about by a contrast to a posed badness in existence. Only through a negation of the negation—that is, reaction and negation—can a positive value develop.

The best that this society can produce is the "higher man," the "last men" (as opposed to Nietzsche's ideal transfigured subject, the "overman"). This is the end point; no further evolution can take place according to Nietzsche. The "higher men" discussed in *Thus Spake Zarathustra* are the ideals toward which genealogical development tends (see also Deleuze, 1983: 164–66). Much like the "cheerful robots" of C. W. Mills, the "higher men" are nothing but affirmative and perpetual yea-sayers (Nietzsche, 1960; Strong, 1975: 278). The "higher men" are unable to play, laugh, dance, and gamble (Nietzsche, 1960: 319–32; Strong, 1975: 278; Deleuze, 1983: 170). They lack the ability to experience, experiment, learn, practice, internalize, transcend: all necessary elements in the process of developing into the "overman," a qualitatively new way of being, thinking, experiencing, marked by a new constituting dynamic—the "eternal return." Here is celebrated multiplicity, chance, and becoming (Deleuze, 1983: 189–94; Bogue, 1989: 30–34).

## Transpraxis and the Peacemaking Community

We are reaching the beginning of a journey. We shall speculate on what we may find along the way. We shall feel vindicated if we contribute to a new orientation that eventually leads to humanistic change in society. But speculation based on existing highly insightful analyses is necessary in order to make the quantum leap, the transcendental step to what may be. As Albert Einstein once said, we not only must have the fortitude to gather data, compare insightful analyses, integrate the disparate materials, and draw out implications; but at some point, we must be able to take a giant step, sometimes itself being purely intuitive and unverbalizeable, in order to create a new absolute postulate from which researchable hypotheses will be developed and tested. Much post-Renaissance thought has been caught, imprisoned, in a paradigm that resists allowing quantum leaps to what may be. Postmodernist theorists have told us to leave yesterday behind and to develop new tools of analysis. Nietzsche has been central and inspirational.

In some ways Nietzsche's and Marx's analysis of the development of the subject and society overlap (see also Love, 1986). For both, the subject needs to externalize itself in objective form, a form which subsequently reflects subjectivity and contributes to its determination. For both, fetishes, false ideologies, and idols come to dominate man/woman in their activities. And, too, for both, productive activity is essential for value creation. For Marx, socialism will be a step toward the higher form of society, communism. Here, under socialism, bourgeois forms and notions would still prevail, such as the formal equality principle in law, given best idealized expression in the Fourteenth Amendment to the U.S. Constitution . (Here, the "equal protection clause" states equally situated should be equally

treated.) At best, gross disparities in treatment would be somewhat allevi-
ated. However, submitting all, regardless of inherent differences, to a
similar yardstick is intrinsically repressive. The fetishistic equivalence principle, brought about by commodity exchange, renders all uniform, calculable, and predictable. The narrow horizon of bourgeois law will still exist
(Pashukanis, 1980). For Nietzsche, the development of the "higher man"
would coincide with Marx's "dictatorship of the proletariat" phase (see also
Love, 1986: 107). But for both theorists, previous forms of domination still
exist, be they in inverted form. What has been reconstituted are the forms
of domination (see also Henry and Milovanovic, 1990; Bannister and
Milovanovic, 1990; Milovanovic and Thomas, 1989; Milovanovic, 1988a).
The "higher men," for example, passively affirm new value positions. What
is still needed is a movement to the beyond. For Marx it was the communist
subject, for Nietzsche the "overman."

Marx tells us that in the higher forms, communism, the guiding principle
would be "from each according to his [or her] abilities, to each according to
his [or her] needs." The existence and continuation of differential abilities
and needs is central in this schema. Man/woman would not be perceived as
intrinsically static, predictable, calculable, isolated, and reducible to juridic
subjects in law. Rather, man/woman would be comparable to use-values,
floating signifiers, with a plurality, a multiplicity of potential signifieds that
only find temporary anchorings.

For Nietzsche the key lies with the development of the "overman." Let's
briefly trace Nietzsche's thinking on the state of subjectivity. The essence of
the subject lies in the notion of the "will to power." This concept must not
be confused with commonsensical notions of the existence of some self-
conscious and determining agent striving to fulfill some desire for power.
Rather, the world and the subject are "dynamic quanta" in complex and
intricate relations to other dynamic quanta. In truth, no stable entities exist.

The will to power has two dimensions: First, the will to power is characterized by either being affirmative or negative; and second, the quality
aspect of will to power is made up of either active or reactive forces
(Deleuze, 1983: 53–54; Bogue, 1989: 22). "Forces," Bogue tells us, "are mere
instruments of the will to power" (1989: 22). The will to power indicates an
inner force that orients becoming. "To impose upon becoming the character
of being—that is the supreme will to power" (Nietzsche, 1968c: 330). Or, as
Bogue tells us, "the will to power is a kind of inner centre of force, a power
of becoming active or reactive, whose quality is either affirmative or negative, and it is manifested as the affectivity of force, the power of being
affected" (1989: 23). The will to power is the source of value and meaning
for the subject; it is an organizing principle that orders the drives. The
subject, then, is an ordered plurality of drives that exist only in relation to
other ordered plurality of drives in a dynamic flux of becoming, a becoming
rooted in *pathos*. "[N]o things remain but only dynamic quanta," Nietzsche
informs us, "in relation of tension to all other dynamic quanta; their
essence lies in their relation to all other quanta, in their 'effect' upon the

same" (1968c: 339). A stable subject, the centered subject, again, is pure semiotic fiction. The play of differences in this schema constitutes values and meaning.

The metaphysics, the ontological basis, of healthy being can be described (Deleuze, 1983; Bogue, 1989). A healthy, normally functioning being can be conceptualized as a conglomeration of forces, a multiplicity of forces arranged in a dynamic ordering of "dynamic quanta" in relation to yet other loci of dynamic quanta; some of these forces are active, some reactive (Bogue, 1989: 25–26; Deleuze, 1983: 111). The "will to power" is the orienting principle; force is its instrumentality. Thus we may have either an affirmative becoming-active force and an affirmative becoming-reactive force or a negative becoming-active force and a negative becoming-reactive force (see figure 1 below). Force, dualistically conceptualized as either "active" or "reactive," can be further operationalized; the former signals action and direction, the latter restriction and subordination. Each subject has both tendencies. One, however, becomes more dominant. Should, for example, the reactive forces predominate, the subject will be no more than what his/her immediate environment dictate: in the passive sense, in so much as s/he will be monolithically determined by the existing constellation of forces in a unique articulation; in the active sense, in so much as the very attempts and/or success in change are either negating of what is or reconstituting of the given form of domination. Here, new values will not be created; the subject merely responds to and negates values already in existence. The healthy subject, on the other hand, actively carries through his reaction; s/he "acts his reaction" (Deleuze, 1983: 111; Bogue, 1989: 26).

For the Nietzsche-Deleuze schema, an additional component of a healthy subject is the power of forgetting. Anticipating Freud (e.g., the pleasure principle tending toward hallucinatory satisfaction; the reality principle delaying action until a suitable object is found in the external world), the subject dominated by reactive forces cannot forget; s/he reacts to mnemic traces in the psychic apparatus. These sensations with their affects stay within reach of consciousness and become the basis of reaction. The active forces are constantly overwhelmed by the affective mnemic traces. Although necessary, mnemic traces now become the basis of reaction, or "ressentiment." Objects experienced, or even experiences themselves, are felt as oppressive and painful, arousing feelings of resentment—ressentiment (See Strong, 1975: 245–50). As Deleuze tells us, "the man of *ressentiment* in himself is a being full of pain: the sclerosis or hardening of his consciousness, the rapidity with which every excitation sets and freezes within him, the weight of the traces that invade him are so many cruel sufferings" (1983: 116). Here the subject is dominated by the spirit of revenge. The healthy state, on the other hand, is one in which there exists a positive dependence on a certain forgetting in order for the active forces to respond (not merely react) to external sense data (Bogue, 1989: 26; Deleuze, 1983: 112–14). This power of forgetting is a positively adaptive force—

similar to Freud, who tells us that the organism must temporarily suspend immediate satisfaction in order to find more suitable objects which will create more genuine satisfaction than hallucinatory forms. Where the power of forgetting starts to disappear, charged mnemic traces intrude into the conscious sphere and the forces of reaction dominate the forces of action (Deleuze, 1983: 114). As in the previously provided schema—Nietzsche's parable of the lamb and the bird of prey—when reactive forces dominate, the stage is reached where nihilism, the will to nothingness, bad conscience, and the ascetic ideal predominate. Slave morality has replaced master morality (Bogue, 1989: 26; Deleuze, 1983: 64–66, 111–19, 124–26, 144).

By ranging the will to power according to whether the dominant aspect is affirmative or negative, and the force aspect as either active or reactive, a two-by-two table can capture the possible ideal-type relationships.

Figure 1. Transpraxis

|  | | |
|---|---|---|
| Affirmative | Master (Noble) — — — — Overman Communist man/ woman | Higher man Praxis |
| Negative | Transpraxis | Slave (Base) |

Will to power

We should also point out in advance that this static depiction cloaks a more dynamic one that can be conceptualized as:

Figure 2. Dialectics, Intersubjectivity, and Change

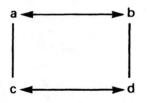

Figure 2 depicts that values, based on differences, are created only in relationship. In fact it was Lacan who best portrayed the decentered subject in terms of dualistic and dialectical inter- and intra-subjective relationships that are constitutive forces of subjectivity, portrayed in his quatrilateral subject of "Schema L" (1977: 192–94). One of the constitutive relationships is the *moi-l'autre* dimension (the ego-other dualism). Here the ego is caught in imaginary relationships where the other is perceived as a mirror reflecting being. Thus the relationship is constituted by floating *imagoes* as well as signifiers. The Nietzsche-Deleuze schema, too, indicates that subjectivity is centered on dualistic relationships, where values are created from the dialectical play between the elements.

From figure 1, the master's (noble's) will to power is affirmative and the connected force is active. Thus we have an affirmative becoming-active. For the slave (base), the will to power is negative and reactive. Here we have a negative becoming-reactive. Value is created by a negation of a negation, a homeostatic, conservative resolution. This is typified in the Lacanian construct of desire where the organism responds to lack by negating it and no more: this is its ideal end point.

The "higher man" is characterized by an affirmative will to power but a reactive force, an affirmative becoming-reactive. Presently constituted societies can do no better than produce the *higher man*; s/he is its upper limit. Here, no new values are being created. Previous forms of domination are re-created as in the "dictatorship of the proletariat" phase stipulated by Marx and Engels. The form of domination itself remains the same, be it now in the hands of the victorious proletariat. Consider Deleuze:

> [T]he higher man remains within the abstract element of activity, he never raises himself, even in thought, to the element of affirmation. The higher man claims to reverse values, to convert reaction into action. . . . But reaction will never become action without this deeper conversion: negation must first become a power of affirming. (1983: 170)

Here also is the predominance of yea-sayers, "worshipers of the ass," donkeys and camels, according to Nietzsche. (In the same vein, C. W. Mills has referred to the twentieth century bureaucrat as the "cheerful robot.") They say "yes" to everything with a smile. An inversion exists, but with previous forms themselves still intact (e.g., the "narrow horizons of bourgeois thought" as in the formal equality principle being given greater force). Praxis often means rediscovering the previous forms of domination in existence and applying these to the new situation, sometimes quite clearly, sometimes inadvertently (see also Henry and Milovanovic, 1990; Bannister and Milovanovic, 1990; Milovanovic and Thomas, 1989; Milovanovic, 1988a). Consider, in a different context, Goffman's classic study of "secondary adjustments" of inmates in a mental hospital (*Asylums*, 1961). Often the inmates would incorporate psychotherapeutic language and make use of it as a form of leveling differences between staff and inmate. What is being reconstituted, while even providing a measure of relief, is a hierarchical form of domination. Or consider the new form of exorcism that has arisen on the Left. Often in their haste to get from here to . there, would-be reformers, driven by reactive forces, ressentiment, search out the evil in all that appear before them, even, if need be, constructing it and attributing it to the person they confront, a construction which then becomes the basis of hostile attacks. "I shall find the evilness within you, even if I have to create it, which will then be the basis of my attack." The evil construct is often of the would-be reformer's making, and alas s/he is more often tilting at windmills (see also Groves, 1989). And, finally, according to Nietzsche, there are things that the higher man is incapable of doing: laughing, playing, dancing (Deleuze, 1983: 170; see also Strong, 1975: 277–83).

The lower left-hand corner depicts active negation, the "second stage of nihilism," and with it, the beginnings of the production of new values, a transfiguration brought about by the incipient appearance of the "overman," or man/woman in the communist society as envisioned by Marx and Engels (upper left-hand corner). This, the lower left-hand cell, however, is a transitional stage for Nietzsche, a step toward the "overman." Marx, of course, did not envision this stage in the movement to the "higher forms."

Transpraxis is the beginning of overcoming what is. It appears in incipient form in the second phase of nihilism (Bogue, 1989: 32). What occurs is that the negative will to power separates itself from the reactive forces, becomes an active self-destructive force, an active negation, which is the prelude to the new person, the "overman" according to Nietzsche (Deleuze, 1983: 174; Bogue, 1983: 32) and the "communist person" according to Marx. This is an active negation; that is, it is composed of an active force and a negatively orienting will to power. It is the occasion of a profound break, a transcendence from the will to nothingness, nihilism—bad conscience, ascetic ideals, ressentiment—that characterizes the sphere dominated by reactive forces. A crossing-over of sorts takes place whereby the previous negative becoming-reactive forces undergo a fission; an "active destruction" (Deleuze, 1983: 174) inaugurates the movement toward the "overman." But all this is in movement—the direction: an affirmative becoming-active (upper left-hand cell of figure 1). This is an active destruction of all that had been, in preparation of what can be. It is not a negation of a negation as in the Hegelian script of the master-slave dialectic. It's a "transmutation" and "transfiguration"; in a word, transpraxis. The subject destroys him/herself actively in preparation for new values, a new way of being.

This new way of being, a new form of value creation (figure 1; upper left-hand corner)—the overman and the communist subject—is the "eternal return" of Nietzsche (Nietzsche, 1968c: 544–50; 1960: 150–56, 319–32;

Strong, 1975: 260–93; Deleuze, 1983: 71–73). Core values here are the celebration of multiplicity, chance, and the "being of becoming." This marks the beginning of the peacemaking community. The "eternal return" inaugurates new ways of being; it acknowledges the present as being a continuation of the past-becoming-present, and the future of the present-becoming-future (Bogue, 1983: 30; see also Strong, 1975: 265–73); but only the affirmative becoming-active can undergo the eternal return. It acknowledges difference, celebrates multiplicity, encourages becoming, and glorifies chance—the throw of the dice (Bogue, 1983: 30–31; Deleuze, 1983: 47–49, 186–94). It acknowledges, affirmatively, the play of differences as value creation. The instrumentality, the active force, now is mobilized for the eternal return: ". . . return is the being of becoming, the unity of multiplicity, the necessity of chance; the being of difference as such . . ." (Deleuze, 1983: 189).

Transpraxis, then, is not only a form of action, affirmative action, but is an actively constituted negation, a destruction and transcendence of what was before in preparation of what can be. It transcends notions of praxis which are often still conservative in their undertaking. What is needed is the new person in a peacemaking community. The peacemaking community celebrates: *becoming*—being, dance; *multiplicity*—unity, laughter; *chance*—necessity, play (Deleuze, 1983; Strong, 1975: 278–83).

## NOTES

1. We have essentially made use of a triangulation process in teasing out an understanding of Nietzsche by relying on (1) Nietzsche's texts, (2) the insightful revisionism of Deleuze (1983) as well as the precise secondary analysis by Bogue (1989) and Strong (1975), and (3) my own integration and synthesis of these materials.

## REFERENCES

Althusser, Louis. 1971. *Lenin and Philosophy.* New York: Monthly Review Press.
Bannister, Shelley, and Dragan Milovanovic. 1990. "The Necessity Defense, Substantive Justice, and Oppositional Linguistic Praxis." *International Journal of the Sociology of Law* 18 (1). Forthcoming.
Bogue, Ronald. 1989. *Deleuze and Guattari.* New York: Routledge.
Deleuze, Gilles. 1983. *Nietzsche and Philosophy.* New York: Columbia University Press.
Deleuze, Gilles, and Felix Guattari. 1987. *A Thousand Plateaus.* Minneapolis: University of Minnesota Press.

Foucault, Michel. 1977. *Discipline and Punish: The Birth of the Prison*. New York: Vintage Books.

Goffman, Irving, 1961. *Asylums*. New York: Doubleday.

Groves, Byron, 1989. "Us and Them: Reflections on the Dialectics of Moral Hate." *The Critical Criminologist* 1 (2): 3.

Habermas, Jurgen. 1984. *The Theory of Communicative Action, Vol. One, Reason and the Rationalization of the Society*. Boston: Beacon Press.

———.1987. *The Theory of Communicative Action, Vol. Two, Lifeworld and System: A Critique of Functionalist Reason*. Boston: Beacon Press.

Henry, Stuart, and Dragan Milovanovic. 1990. "Constitutive Criminology." *Journal of Criminology*.

Jackson, Bernard. 1985. *Semiotics and Legal Theory*. New York: Routledge and Kegan Paul.

———. 1988. *Law, Fact and Narrative Coherence*. Merseyside, U.K.: Deborah Charles.

Kojeve, Alexandre. 1969. *Introduction to the Reading of Hegel*. Ithaca: Cornell University Press.

Lacan, Jaques. 1977. *Ecrits: A Selection*. New York: Norton.

———. 1981. *The Four Fundamental Concepts of Psychoanalysis*. New York: Norton.

Lee, Dorothy. 1959. *Freedom and Culture*. New York: Prentice-Hall.

Love, Nancy. 1986. *Marx, Nietzsche, and Modernity*. New York: Columbia University Press.

Metz, Christian. 1982. *The Imaginary Signifier*. Bloomington: Indiana University Press.

Milovanovic, Dragan. 1983. "Weber and Marx on Law: Demystifying Ideology and Law—Toward an Emancipatory Political Practice." *Contemporary Crises* 7: 353–70.

———. 1987. "The Political Economy of 'Liberty' and 'Property' Interests." *Legal Studies Forum* 11: 267–93.

———. 1988a. "Jailhouse Lawyers and Jailhouse Lawyering." *International Journal of the Sociology of Law* 16: 455–75.

———. 1988b. *A Primer in the Sociology of Law*. Albany, New York: Harrow and Heston.

———. 1989a. *Weberian and Marxian Analysis of Law: Structure and Function of Law in a Capitalist Mode of Production*. Aldershot, U.K.: Gower Publishers.

———. 1989b. "Post Modernism and Critical Criminology." *The Critical Criminologist* 1 (3). Forthcoming.

———. 1990a. "Re-Thinking Subjectivity in Law and Ideology: A Semiotic Perspective." In D. Currie and B. MacLean (eds.), *Struggles for Equality: Re-Thinking the Administration of Justice*. Toronto: Garamon Press.

———. 1990b. *Law, Semiotics, and Reality Construction*. In progress.

Milovanovic, Dragan, and Jim Thomas. 1989. "Overcoming the Absurd: Prisoner Litigation as Primitive Rebellion." *Social Problems* 36 (1): 48–60.

Nietzsche, Friedrich. 1960. *Thus Spake Zarathustra*. New York: The Modern Library.

———. 1966. *Beyond Good and Evil*. New York: Vintage Books.

———. 1968a. *Basic Writings of Nietzsche*. Ed. W. Kaufman. New York: The Modern Library.

———. *Twilight of the Idols/The Anti-Christ*. Harmondsworth, Middlesex: Penguin Books.

———. 1968c. *The Will to Power*. Vintage Books.

Pashukanis, E. 1980. "The General Theory of Law and Marxism. In P. Beirne and R. Sharlet (eds.), *Pashukanis: Selected Writings on Marxism and Law*. New York: Academic Press.

Silverman, Kaja. 1982. *The Subject of Semiotics*. New York: Oxford University Press.

Strong, Tracy. 1975. *Friedrich Nietzsche and the Politics of Transfiguration.* Berkeley: California University Press.

Weber, Max. 1975. *Roscher and Knies: The Logical Problems of Historical Economics.* London: Collier Macmillan Publishers.

———. 1978. *Economy and Society.* Two volumes. G. Roth and C. Wittich (eds.). Berkeley: University of California Press.

Whorf, Benjamin. 1956. *Language, Thought, and Reality.* New York: John Wiley and Sons.

*Susan L. Caulfield*

---

## F O U R T E E N

# The Perpetuation of Violence through Criminological Theory

### *The Ideological Role of Subculture Theory*

> It can be readily understood that, in the
> desire to examine and utilize apparently
> more precise categories, scholars might
> overlook the degree to which their own
> scientific behavior is determined by the
> same political conditions which gave rise to
> legal definitions in use. But this is
> insufficient for explaining why conventional
> political categories have succeeded in
> superseding all other ethical, as well as
> professional, criteria for defining the nature
> of crime.
> —Schwendinger and Schwendinger
> (1970)

As Schwendinger and Schwendinger (1970) pointed out two decades ago, theorists must be both aware of and cautious about the role of the state, and state institutions, in the definition of crime.[1] Traditional theorizing about crime may often have unforeseen and harsh consequences for both criminologists and others. I ask why, and whether traditional theories, particularly subculture theories, serve the purposes of theorists or of the state.

In his essay on "Objectivity and Liberal Scholarship," Chomsky (1969) notes how both a highly restrictive ideology and increased professionalization have led to social scientists acting *not* as independent and responsible critics of state practices, but, rather, as agents of the state. A highly restrictive ideology is one that, for instance, promotes freedom of expression but actually rewards (e.g., through funding, tenure, etc.) only certain perspectives. The effect of professionalization is manifested in an adherence to technique, to methods, rather than, for instance, to more qualitative approaches. Combined, the ensuing ideology almost demands an adherence to proscribed methods and may, in fact, depend on those methods for the preservation of the ideology itself.

The main thrust of this essay is to examine the types of theories or perspectives that are perpetuated by criminologists and to ask the criminologist to put forth only theories or perspectives that seek to identify harms such that those harms can be reduced. I argue that the current perpetuation of harm-producing theories is antithetical to the criminologist's role and should be avoided in the future. In particular, subculture theory will be examined regarding the ideological role it plays and the subsequent perpetuation of violence it promotes.

## The Use of Subculture Method

The identification of subcultural groups in our society has taken on a role far beyond that originally intended by criminologists. It can be assumed, if only for the sake of argument, that the original identification of subcultural groups was designed to detect the criminal element in order to fashion solutions to crime. Unfortunately, the use of subcultural identification, through the proliferation of such theories in criminology, has taken on a legitimacy due merely to its existence in the literature. This legitimacy then allows for the use of subcultural identification that goes far beyond objective etiological purposes. In particular, the state and the criminal justice system rely heavily on the identification of subcultures. One need look no further than the moral panics that have surrounded the "war on drugs." Moral panics are a tool of the state whereby an issue (generally a "crime") can be elevated to a status where the public demands that something be done to the group that perpetuates this act. The events surrounding the behavior spiral increasingly upwards in significance until the public feels threatened. What was once acceptable behavior becomes intolerable due to images of monsters and devils committing various sins (see Becker, 1963). These monsters and devils must, of course, meet certain criteria—such as being at the lower end of class, race, and gender hierarchies. State agents involved in such behavior—e.g., the CIA drugs-money-guns connection (see Marshall et al., 1987)—are not viewed as monsters; their involvement is not even recognized as such by state officials.

The key to this signification spiral, then, is the identification of a group of people engaged in this and other horrible behavior; that is, the subversive minority (see Hall et al., 1978, for elaboration). Due to the legitimacy of subcultural method, the state can easily point to a group that can be used to serve the overall purposes behind a moral panic, primarily an increase in "law and order." Furthermore, the fact that it is generally a member of the government who ultimately points the.finger, the process is further steeped in legitimacy, no matter how unwarranted the charge may be.

## MISUSE OF THE METHOD

The proliferation of subculture theories by criminologists has resulted in the bastardization of a method for the use of those in positions of power, because of an overreliance on the techniques rather than on the implications of using the technique. The identification of subcultures is now used as empirical evidence of violent people in our society. As Chomsky noted in his analysis of intellectuals, "behavioral scientists who believe themselves to be in possession of certain techniques of control and manipulation will tend to search for problems to which their knowledge and skills might be relevant, defining these as the 'important problems' " (1967: 25). Basing research on the ability to apply a method clearly narrows the range of behavior that can be explored. This is especially true when the method, here subcultures, is defined such that it excludes certain groups from consideration, since there must be some type of cultural demarcation. (This, of course, excludes from consideration those who have the "quintessential characteristics" of the dominant culture, such as federal agents and those from the middle and upper social classes.)

What follows is an analysis of how people are labeled as violent and how this labelling serves an ideological purpose to the extent that it removes attention from other, more violent, people or groups. Ultimately, what results is the conception of a false reality of violence and the perpetuation of a discipline of approach that has serious ramifications for the people in this society. In discussing theory, Gouldner notes how "myths are woven into the total view of social reality, deeply, but invisibly, by the entire structure of language and conceptualization" (1970: 49). The very language of subculture theory is used to create a false conception of reality, as witnessed by the extensive use of it in a moral panic process. While the ideas put forth carry beyond nationally created boundaries, the United States will serve as a key example of the harmful effects that result from the use of subcultural method.

While subcultures cannot exist in a society that has no dominant culture, the use of subcultural method still persists and grows. The identification of criminal or deviant subcultures in this society clearly has ideological underpinnings. Groups are labeled as subcultures because such labeling creates the illusion that we are all part of the same group. This clearly has implications for notions of consensus and playing a role in the same game, necessary beliefs for the perpetuation of the U.S. political-economic system. However, while it is necessary that such groups be viewed as part of the overall culture, it is also necessary that they be seen as deviant or criminal members in order that the state may take action against them. Often times, the behavior engaged in by these groups is neither deviant or criminal. Instead, the behavior is viewed as threatening by those in positions of power.

One subcultural group that is evidence of this is the Committee in Solidarity with the People of El Salvador (CISPES). CISPES is a grass-roots organization trying to draw attention to the plight of people in El Salvador and bring some form of relief to these people. CISPES has not been documented as having committed any criminal acts. To the contrary, CISPES actively demonstrates against what it views as criminal acts, that is, United States policy in Central America (e.g., support for Duarte and his death squads).

United States policy in Central America has been a continuing display of long-term intervention in other countries in the name of democracy and anticommunism. However, as Chomsky (1985) notes, the United States is actually seeking global hegemony in order to preserve the freedom to rob and to exploit (see also Chomsky, 1988; Herman, 1982; Moyers, 1988). U.S. intervention in Central America, then, is not in the name of freedom or safety for the people of the United States but is, instead, designed to benefit those with political and economic power. Evidence of this purpose goes beyond current practices in Central America. Similar events have taken place in Chile, Guatemala, Vietnam, and elsewhere, and often because of the needs of multinational corporations with interests in those countries (Chomsky, 1985, 1987; Elias, 1986; LaFeber, 1984).

Because of the long held economic interests that multinationals have had in Central America, any action that questions the legitimacy of U.S. intervention becomes a cause of concern for those doing the intervening. This concern translates into the "pulling of political-economic strings" and police action against the groups who question U.S. policy. These latter groups become labeled as subversives, as a type of criminal subculture. As Chomsky (1985: 251) states: "Separatism, *subcultures* . . . acceptance without awareness of the doctrines of the state religion—these are among the many reflections of the Western system of fragmentation and ideological control (emphasis added)." The use of subcultural identification, then, serves as ideological role of separating the "good guys" from the "bad guys" and advocating investigation and prosecution of the latter.

History shows us the effects of U.S. intervention in Central America and elsewhere. U.S. placement of puppet regimes in Third World countries not only lends support to the economic and political ventures of those in power, it also gives near-unbridled discretion to the resident puppet. Lacking any supportive relationship from the populace, dictators have a history of violating human rights and maintaining death squads. Such was the case in El Salvador with Duarte and in Nicaragua under Somoza. It is to these human rights abuses and subsequent abuses at home in the United States that groups like CISPES respond:

> Look what they're doing in El Salvador. People working for democracy and human rights are arrested, tortured, and assassinated by Duarte's death squads. The harassment of CISPES [by the FBI] shows that support for dictatorship abroad can only be maintained by repressing democracy at home. The counterinsurgency war is being fought against the people of El Salvador and against U.S. public opinion. (Zielinski, 1988, quotes Sanbrano)

This is one example of the use of subcultures to identify one group as criminal (CISPES) in order to protect a more criminal group (Duarte, death squads, U.S. government). Not only does such identification create problems for the members of CISPES and their families, it detracts attention away from people or groups who are really committing crimes and hurting people.

In a similar fashion, the people of Nicaragua have been labeled as terrorists due, in part, to their active resistance to United States intervention in their country. The use of the term *terrorist* conjures up images of killers and criminals and ignores the chain of events that led to these people rising up against the forces that seek to put an end to self-determination. Namely, the perpetuation of over forty years of intervention on the part of the United States to maintain the country as a subservient client state of multinational corporate concerns.

It is important to understand that the process of identifying subcultures is similar at both domestic and foreign levels, and at criminal and non-criminal levels. As Tifft and Markham point out, elsewhere in this anthology, the structural conditions that allow for battering Central Americans also allow for battering in the American home. Similarly, the structural conditions and processes that result in Sandanistas being labeled as terrorists in order to gather support for the contra forces, also allow for citizens in this country to be labeled as the true criminals in order to garner support for more law enforcement, more prisons, and less procedural rights. For a case in point, merely examine the ongoing "war on drugs" where the administration hopes to decrease criminals' rights and increase the tactics by which criminals can be located and processed through the criminal justice system.

## IMPLICATIONS OF MISUSING THE METHOD

The labeling of these groups as criminals, subversives, and terrorists serves numerous ideological purposes. First of all, attention is diverted from what the United States government is actually doing. For example, slaughter is conducted in Third World countries under the auspices of anticommunism, whereas the reality is availability of land and labor to multinational corporations. At home, attention is detracted from the Iran-Contra affair while the citizens are inundated with horror stories about drugs.

Moreover, the labeling of these groups as violent creates an atmosphere of support for violent resolution. If a government official states that our borders are not safe due to the dangerous communist influence in Central America then the United States's use of violence against these foes is legitimated. Similarly, at home, if those involved in the selling and using of drugs are portrayed as dangerous individuals, then harsh tactics are required to restore order. History suggests that the U.S. government is not truly interested in identifying the drug subcultures. Merely witness the handling of Manuel Noriega and the handling of the drugs-money-guns connection documented during the Reagan administration (see Marshall et al., 1987, regarding the CIA's role in the trafficking and selling of cocaine). The current administration affects an anti-Columbian, anti-Noriega posture, yet does nothing substantive to curtail this behavior. These latter activities are not the concern of the state, due to the involvement of the state. The state, by necessity, defines its own activities as beyond incrimination and, therefore, must select another group as the target of legal action (Kennedy, 1970).

## Transcending the Perpetuation of Violence

> [T]he dominant expressions of the academic social sciences embody an accommodation to the alienation of men in contemporary society, rather than a determined effort to transcend it.
>
> Gouldner 1970

The process of identifying and reacting to violent groups is not solely the result of criminological theorizing. However, the perpetuation of subcultural theories, and others, lends legitimacy to this process and creates rather than reduces harms. Moreover, when the discipline declares research to be objective and value-free, it ignores the subjective, value-laden nature of its product, namely theories. As Gouldner noted, almost twenty years ago, we must be careful since "conventional methodologies of social research often premise and foster a deep-going authoritarian, a readiness to lie and to manipulate people" (1970: 50).

It is important for the criminologist to see that research has a bearing on the life of the *researcher* as well as on the life of the *subject*. To not see this, especially in terms of subculture theory, is to believe that one is "on the outside of the prison"—one of the good, obedient members of the dominant culture. As Foucault (1977) pointed out, such a belief structure merely serves to legitimate state authority and power, because it is an acceptance of the lines drawn by the state, by the standards imposed by those at the top of the hierarchy. In essence, it supports a hierarchical view of the world, that research is done on, and applied to, those at a lower level than the researcher. Encased within a hierarchy, the work done must fit within the boundaries defined by those who wield power. This may very well be the essence of the problem—criminologists so concerned with state-defined problems, that they cannot see the greater problems of state-created and state-maintained violence, of which the criminologist's work may play a vital role in perpetuating.

In his introduction to *American Power and the New Mandarins*, Chomsky (1969: 6) discusses the role of the intellectual elite in preserving a repressive ideology. He quotes Randolph Bourne, who, in 1917, wrote that the younger intelligentsia are "trained up in the pragmatic dispensation, immensely ready for the executive ordering of events, pitifully unprepared for the intellectual interpretation or the idealistic focusing of ends. . . . They have absorbed the secret of scientific method as applied to political administration." Those, then, who will be instrumental in the fashioning and enacting of policy are clearly linked to the needs of the state. Bourne was addressing how this was a new role for those who would be seen as liberal and radical intellectuals: "They are a wholly new force in American life, the product of the swing in the colleges from a training that emphasized classical studies to one that emphasized political and economic values."

Discussing Vietnam, Chomsky notes that the intellectuals of the 1960s also fell prey to the technical effectiveness of war and in so doing did more to support rather than question the existing power structure and its policies. As Chomsky notes, there is a domestic analogue to the oppresson overseas, evidenced by the oppressive policies used against groups in this country. What follows from this is that the mandarins, the intellectual elite, lend support to domestic policies that serve to oppress or otherwise harm groups of people. The criminological elite play a part in this harm when their practices are more supportive of "high-level methods" (i.e., technology), rather than serious social change. In reference to Bourne's note on the changes in education, there may be little hope for harm-reducing theories if university programs become geared toward professional schooling. Many criminal justice programs are considered professional schools and turn out (graduate) a large number of criminal justice technocrats. While this is a troublesome in itself, what is harder to accept is the continuing dissemination and perpetuation of materials (i.e., theories and research) that are not only harm-producing, but tacit acceptance of state-defined history, state policy—in essence, *state ideology,* an ideology that requires the mistreatment of some in order for the state structure to survive.

In an analysis of methodology as ideology, Gouldner (1970: 50) notes that "research methods always premise the existence and use of some system of social control. It is not only that the information they yield may be used *by* systems of social control, but that they themselves *are* systems of control."

The use of subcultural method is a process that not only harms those who are targeted by the method, but also serves to support the overriding state ideology that calls for more and more social control. This effect of subcultural method has been demonstrated by examining cases in which the method has been used to control those who have not committed criminal activities but, instead, have voiced strong opposition to United States policy, both at home and abroad. The harm that is produced by this methodology is considered antithetical to the purported role of the criminologist who should, it is viewed, seek means by which not only crime can be identified and dealt with but by which harms can actually be reduced. To not address the issue of harm, and how to reduce harm, is to effectively not do anything about the social consequences that both lead to and result from crime.

It is not surprising that criminologists do not generally address the issue of harm, since they are but one part of a larger intellectual elite that serves the needs of the state apparatus. Interestingly, Sutherland's (1939) theory of differential association pointed out, decades ago, that human actors acquire both values and behaviors through a process that involves frequent and intense exposure to, and association with, significant others who promote those values and behaviors. However, in light of the fact that this role has been discussed by scholars for decades, it is viewed as problematic that significant steps have not been taken to change this role. It is the contention herein that the role of the criminologist should adapt both to address the issue of harm and to seek ways to reduce rather than perpetuate harm.

In order to accomplish this, the criminologist must seek nonviolent ways to resolve harms. If criminologists really want to reduce harms and promote peace, then we need to find ways that transcend the subcultural solution. Critics of a peacemaking perspective would posit that it is either this labelling approach or nothing, that we cannot help people unless we first label them as in need of help. This latter contention is based on a tacit acceptance of how the state both defines harm and reacts to harm. Tifft (1979) addresses this issue in his comparison of prospective, rights-based justice and retrospective needs-based justice. The former type of justice, what we currently have, requires an *a priori* establishment of what will be done if *legally-defined* rights are misappropriated. A prospective rights-based approach to justice is based on hierarchy and differentiation. This is evident from historical accounts of crime which outline how crime both derives from state structure and is necessary in order for state structure to exist (Kennedy, 1970). One manner in which this form of "justice" is manifested is through the identification of and reaction to "criminals," hence the state supports and encourages the use of subculture method.

Instead of relying on a system of justice that, by its own definition, serves the needs of the state, Tifft (1979) suggests a process of justice that is retrospective and based on needs. Perhaps such a process would allow us to draw on compassion and help *those who view themselves* as in need of assistance. In addition, such a process would allow us to be more imaginative in our pursuit of harm-reducing theories. Instead of relying on legally-defined behavior, why don't we define harm according to those who view themselves as injured? Such an approach would, of course, encompass many of the behaviors currently examined in criminology. However, it would also allow the theorist a chance to promote peace and well-being through a process that does not create harmful actions.

This process of promoting peaceful solutions to crime and reducing the use of harmful techniques is not easy in the face of structural conditions that seem to thrive on violent resolutions. But why should those who study crime, why should any intellectual, be expected to remove *themselves* from the process of their discipline? The definition of crime, the creation of theories, the policy implications of the work—these are political enterprises. Instead of pledging a nonexistent objective and value neutral tone, perhaps criminologists should be more accepting of their political role. When intolerable behaviors or practices—e.g., racism, genocide, the Vietnam War, U.S. policy in Central America, covert participation in death squads—are discussed, numerous people try to combat these behaviors or practices. Witness the work of Martin Luther King, Jr., who used peaceful means to fight racism in the United States. Witness the work of CISPES, which has used peaceful tactics to work for the people of El Salvador. Witness the peace groups, such as Witness for Peace and the Pledge of Resistance, who rely on peaceful means to affect change. Within the area of crime, however, there are intolerable behaviors and practices abounding. Yet, as "intellectuals" it is not our *given* role actually to question these behaviors and practices. Instead, we are supposed simply to analyze them. Given this kind of structure, how are we supposed to do anything substantive about harms? Peaceful resolution requires action; it is, by no means, passive.

Criminologists are in a position to use peaceful methods within a discipline that both addresses harm and creates harm. How, given what we know of crimes by the powerful, can we as a discipline still see violence as an interpersonal street-problem rather than as a function of state and of state-supported studies? Doesn't such a view do violence to both the recipients of our research and to ourselves? In transcending the problem of methodologies and the misuse of methodologies, we should refocus our attention on peace—on peace rather than on harm. And ultimately we should use our knowledge not for harm, but for peace.

## NOTES

1. The use of the term *state* should not be viewed as a reification of the state but, instead, should be understood as encompassing complex political-economic structures and processes. As Domhoff (1986: 226) has noted:

> "State" is a concept with three levels of meaning. At the most visibile level, the state is a "sovereign political territory." It is a nation-state, such as the United States or France. However, the state as a sovereign political territory is maintained by a "government system" or "state apparatus." This is the second meaning of 'state,' and it includes all aspects of the formal system of government—executive, legislative, judiciary, military, and police. Most important, however, the "state" is a state of mind, and its essence involves a common will on the part of the people within a given territory to unite for the common defense of that territory. The "state," then, is ultimately defined by a common allegiance (patriotism), which is expressed in a willingness to accept the government system and to defend the common territory. The "state" as government apparatus and as a state of mind are thus embodied in the definition of the state as a "sovereign political territory."

These comments demonstrate not the existence of a single entity, but the existence of various processes, and structures,· through which people act for reasons of state.

## REFERENCES

Becker, H. S. 1963. *Outsiders: Studies in the Sociology of Deviance*. New York: Free Press.

Chomsky, Noam. 1969. *American Power and the New Mandarins*. New York: Pantheon.

———. 1985. *Turning the Tide*. Boston: South End Press.

———. 1987. *On Power and Ideology: The Managua Lectures*. Boston: South End Press.

———. 1988. *The Culture of Terrorism*. Boston: South End Press.

———. 1988. "The Ruling Class and the Problem of Power." In F. Lindenfeld (ed.), *Radical Perspectives on Social Problems: Readings in Critical Sociology*. 3rd ed. Dix Hills, N.Y.: General Hall, Inc.

Domhoff, G. William. 1986. *Who Rules America Now?* New York: Simon and Schuster.

Elias, R. 1986. *The Politics of Victimization: Victims, Victimology and Human Rights*. New York: Oxford University Press.

Foucault, M. 1977. *Discipline and Punish: The Birth of the Prison*. New York: Vintage Books.

Gouldner, A. W. 1970. *The Coming Crisis of Western Sociology*. New York: Equinox Books.

Hall, S., C. Critcher, T. Jefferson, J. Clarke, and B. Roberts. 1978. *Policing the Crisis: Mugging, the State, and Law and Order*. New York: MacMillan Press.

Herman, E. 1982. *The Real Terror Network*. Boston: South End Press.

Kennedy, M. 1970. "Beyond Incrimination: Some Neglected Facets on the Theory of Punishment." *Catalyst* 5 (Summer): 1–37.

LaFeber, W. 1984. *Inevitable Revolutions: The United States in Central America*. New York: W. W. Norton and Company.

Marshall, J., P. D. Scott, and J. Hunter. 1987. *The Iran-Contra Connection: Secret Teams and Covert Operations in the Reagan Era*. Boston: South End Press.

Moyers, B. 1988. *The Secret Government: The Constitution in Crisis*. Cabin John, Md.: Seven Locks Press.

Schwendinger, H., and J. Schwendinger. 1970. "Defenders of Order or Guardians of Human Rights?" *Issues in Criminology* 5 (2): 123–57.

Sutherland, E. H. 1939. *Principles of Criminology*. 3rd ed. Philadelphia: Lippincott.

Tifft, L. L. 1979. "The Coming Redefinitions of Crime: An Anarchist Perspective. *Social Problems* 26 (4): 392–402.

Zielinski, M. (1988). "FBI's probe of CISPES exposed." *The Guardian:* 1, 9.

*Peter L. Sanzen*

---

## F I F T E E N

# The Role of Education in Peacemaking

The criminal justice system was established to contribute to peace. United States criminal justice has instead rested on two ideologies, the crime-control and due-process models. Crime control has become the overriding value. But officials in a criminal justice system who focus attention only on crime create a reality that is based upon restriction of behavior, not only of criminals, but of all citizens. Recent examples of this suppression include the consideration of random drug testing of Justice Department employees and Driving-While-Intoxicated checkpoints, both of which require restricting large numbers of innocent people in order to identify a small number of lawbreakers. This excessive maintenance of order isolates and segregates people, and it suppresses their freedom and ability to grow and mature into the peaceful lives necessary for personal and collective safety. In fact, this suppression of people's freedom is a greater obstacle to the control of crime than crime itself is. Suppression reduces the dignity of the person, resulting in increased alienation and, thereafter, a greater urge to control.

This syndrome, which is widespread in the criminal justice system, has extended to criminal justice education as well. But it is through education that this reality might be changed. By shifting the focus of education from the values of control and repression to the values of peace, a change in the justice system could be begun. Crime control is too narrow a focus on criminal justice's role in making peace. Peace means reducing the power that is based on control, domination, exploitation, hostility, and alienation, all of which produce segregation. Peace means increasing people's power to do things *with* others rather than *to* others by building trust, acceptance, respect, love, nurture, and caring—all of which integrate rather than separate people. The concept of peace must be introduced into education, where change can be discussed and analyzed and alternative approaches considered.

Before focusing on what criminal justice education can offer the system of justice and students of justice, consider criminal justice itself and the pervasive ways it reflects the values of control as the means for keeping the peace. From police to prison, the emphasis is on personal submission to the *machinery* of justice. The police, court personnel, and correctional workers focus attention on processing people like machine parts and ignore people's individuality. One of the most frightening and dramatic examples of this distorted focus is the Supreme Court's ratification of the death penalty for sixteen-year-olds to control juvenile crime.

The police system in the United States has historically been evaluated on its ability to control crime even though police do not have the ability to deal with the sources of crime—poverty, illiteracy, inequitable economic opportunity, etc. The police dwelled on the symptom "crime" to the exclusion of preserving freedom and peace as a matter of policy. The belief is that efficient repression works better than affirming a citizen's sense of personal worth.

Efficiency is measured negatively, by how many culprits are taken, vilified, isolated, immobilized, and disenfranchised. While the Bill of Rights is designed to guarantee freedom, for example, police try constantly to circumvent and circumscribe constitutional safeguards. Piliavin and Briar (1964: 212) found in their research on youths: "Compared to other youths, Negroes and boys whose appearance matched the delinquent stereotype were more frequently stopped and interrogated by patrolmen— often even in the absence of evidence that an offense had been committed." In addition, a report by Richard Dehais (1987: 24) for the State University of New York's African American Institute cites studies by Petersilia (1983) and Zalman (1979) which demonstrate that blacks and Hispanics "are more likely than whites to be arrested under circumstances that provide insufficient evidence to support the charges." And those whose cases are not thrown out for lack of evidence have a statistically higher probability of imprisonment and receive longer sentences for such types of crimes as sex, drugs, burglary, and larceny (Dehais, 1987: 36). Former Attorney General Meese and the Justice Department sought more recently to limit the *Miranda* ruling, restrictions on search and seizure, and the rights of minorities and women to justice in the workplace and in everyday life.

The principal result of this approach is to maintain an unjust and coercive system of repression of citizens in both criminal and noncriminal areas. Crime control extends from the repression of crime to repression in general. This creates fear and insecurity in the general public. Devaluation of any group (including criminals) is a devaluation of all citizens and leads to destruction.

Moving into the court system, one finds a continuation of these values. Court workers also offer a sterile, mechanical version of due process. "Due process" emphasizes adversariness at the expense of freedom and dignity. The chief method of operation, plea bargaining, undercuts even adversariness, let alone due process, rather than preserving the freedom, dignity, and personal worth of those who appear before the courts.

Plea bargaining is an extension of police repression. The quest for efficiency treats defendants as components in an assembly line from arrest to disposition. Guilt is presumed and fear of harsh sentences is instilled: anything to encourage guilty pleas.

This approach with its focus on efficiency, guilt, and the mechanical processing of people may be somewhat successful at repressing crime, but it does not create a condition that encourages living peacefully in a free world. As Jonathan D. Casper (1972: 166) says in his book *American Criminal Justice: The Defendant's Perspective:* "[A defendant's] encounters with the law do not teach him moral lessons about how he ought to behave; rather, they reinforce his image of himself as an outsider, as an appendage of the society of which he would so much like to be a member." Corrections is the end of the repressive process. Here even programs designed to be non-repressive are based on repression. Probation and community based correctional workers, for example, must still present their approaches to the community as repressive to be considered as offering viable alternatives. This practice only reinforces the belief that crime in the final analysis can be controlled solely by repressive means, producing an endless sea of people calling for longer prison terms and capital punishment. Our prisons reflect the repressiveness within and around each one of us.

This process most dramatically affects the inmate and the inmate's keepers. The prisoner can only increase self-esteem and self-worth by acquiring power to control others. This inmate becomes a repressor, while division and isolation continue. As in the Wild West, the inmate becomes preoccupied by the next gunslinger's arrival.

Prison staff rely on repression, too, and by so doing increase the inmates' and hence their own insecurity. Even the oppressor's situation is one of fear and insecurity, of constant fear of insurrection and disobedience from out of the captive society.

Finally, the struggle to restore personal order and worth for the ones we call criminal is more difficult because we never refer to them as respected members of society again. They become inmates, prisoners, clients, probationers, parolees, ex-cons, but never a member of a cooperative living arrangement. Their isolation makes transformation to peaceful living more difficult. Sykes's analysis of people in prison underscores this situation. Sykes (1958: 22) states in the *Society of Captives:*

Whatever may be the personal traits possessed by these men which help bring them to the institution, it is certain that the conditions of prison life itself create strong pressures pointed toward behavior defined as criminal in the free community. Subjected to prolonged material deprivation, lacking heterosexual relationships and rubbed raw by the irritants of life under compression, the inmate population is pushed in the direction of deviation from, rather than adherence to the legal norms.

Repression and domination are an issue not only for criminal justice but for all of us in search of a peaceful communal life. The criminal justice system reflects the larger society. Is there an alternative?

One alternative can be implemented in education by making it *peace* education. The teacher can introduce into the critical analysis and description of how criminal justice works a commitment to finding how to make peace. At the core of this peace approach is an emphasis on the values of justice and dignity as requisite to the survival of the human collective. This redefinition requires an understanding that freedom, equality, and justice mean not only due process—procedural safeguards—but also a human process—dignity and personal worth.

The second step in a peacemaking approach is to provide students with an understanding of the context for creating this value system. This implies the necessary understanding of the ability to live freely—a philosophy of freedom that reinforces integration and acceptance. It requires educators to provide a philosophical, sociological, and anthropological examination of the elements that foster cooperative living. With this step, students can begin to understand the basis for the concepts of freedom, justice, and dignity, and begin to develop a focus on civility—living, loving, caring—and not on violence (an eye for an eye). These values are in many ways opposite to the themes of control and punishment that predominate in criminal justice curricula.

In the classroom, we teachers must also examine whether, by our methods, we are teaching repressive or peaceful means of change. The classroom should be the focal point for the breakdown of authoritarian control over our students, allowing instead for active decentralized participation by students in the learning process. Albert Shanker, president of the American Federation of Teachers, supported this notion by addressing the problem of quality in public schools in a 1988 *New York Times* editorial and calling instead for "restructured schools—with a democratic, human face." Coercion in education is no different from coercion in the criminal justice process.

We also need to assist students in breaking down those aspects of themselves that cause conflict—tools of segregation such as prejudice, competition, power, superiority—and help them realize that we all need each other to be whole, regardless of how people have been labeled. The teacher should encourage the students to contemplate and examine their attitudes and beliefs and then help them to connect themselves to others in a cooperative studying arrangement. Students should work in small groups and be encouraged to look both at their actions in terms of the group and at their commitment to each other as the key to an equitable and just life together. This arrangement can promote each student's own health, self-image, and confidence. The student can learn by experience that cooperation leads to stability and the cherished goals of safety and security.

Success in this educational approach depends heavily on a teacher's self-awareness and sense of freedom. This is probably the greatest challenge to the teacher because it requires an inner search for freedom, equality, and dignity. The focus of teaching, then, becomes putting peace, not control, into practice—attending to healing, not repression.

Ultimately the issue is not only one for police and workers in courts, corrections, and the classroom. The issue is for each one of us. Each of us is a miniature criminal justice system—police officer, judge, jury, and correctional officer. Daily existence places us in these roles, whether we be a boss, subordinate, parent, sibling, spouse, lover, friend, or teacher. Our living arrangements leave us open to having a degree of control over other people; it becomes our choice to generate peaceful living arrangements. Disciplining our children—or controlling our lovers, students, or subordinates—is one area in which we can begin moving toward positive transformation of ourselves.

When control and domination of others are our values, we utilize our power in a manner that disconnects us from ourselves and others. Inside as well as outside ourselves, we become destructive. Valuing power for power's sake leads us to devalue the power of human connection.

In the search for order we have developed a system which debases and devalues criminals, children, students, and others by repressive means, simply because of the belief that these means are the most efficient. Efficiency, domination, control, repression are all invoked in the name of security and safety. Marilyn French (1985: 503) elaborates on this idea in *Beyond Power*:

> [A]t every level self is part of group, group part of self. Alastair MacIntyre points to the absurdity of modern notion that extrication from group—family, tribes, village, community, society—means freedom, when in fact one's group identity is intrinsic to one's personal identity, whether we like it or not, whether we admit it or not. Our insistence on individuality, independence, freedom, defined as freedom from bonds to others, has fostered competitiveness and rivalry; together, these values have made modern life a battleground, a noisy, dangerous, filthy, urban nightmare, from which the only relief is isolation and retreat. . . . [O]nly with a sense of our identity with others, of our participation in family, community, or society, can we create a harmonious home, a community in which laws are assented to rather than enforced, in which concord rather than discord predominates.

In the criminal justice classroom, this vision offers a humanizing focus, not the dehumanizing focus of the criminal justice system. This vision offers a way to teach not only the values of human dignity, peace, and harmony, but also the understanding that coercive action and compliance are unnecessary and counterproductive. Perhaps this kind of teaching can lead to change in the criminal justice system itself.

## REFERENCES

Casper, Jonathan D. 1972. *American Criminal Justice: The Defendant's Perspective.* Englewood Cliffs, N.J.: Prentice-Hall, Inc.
Dehais, Richard J. 1987. *Racial Discrimination in the Criminal Justice System: An Assessment of the Empirical Evidence.* Albany: African American Institute, State University of New York.
French, Marilyn. 1985. *Beyond Power: On Women, Men, and Morals.* New York: Summit Books.
Piliavin, I., and Scott Briar. 1964. "Police Encounters with Juveniles." *American Journal of Sociology* 70: 204–16.
Reiman, Jeffrey H. 1984. *The Rich Get Richer and the Poor Get Prison: Ideology, Class and Criminal Justice.* 2nd ed. New York: Macmillan Publishing Co.
Shankar, Albert. 1988. "Teaching to the Tune of a Bullhorn." *New York 7.*
Sykes, Gresham M. 1958. *The Society Of Captives: A Study Of A Maximum Security Prison.* Princeton: Princeton University Press.

*John F. Galliher*

---

# The Willie Horton Fact, Faith, and Commonsense Theory of Crime

## Commonsense Theories and Crime Causation

During the height of protests against the war in Viet Nam, the Nixon Administration sought to define the protests in a fashion "that deflected and obscured the basic issue of the war, perhaps intentionally, by defining the situation in terms of a . . . theory of communication breakdown" (Hall and Hewitt, 1970: 18). This explanation is strongly rooted in American culture. The *solution* for the Nixon administration was to ignore demands to end the war by claiming that all Americans really agreed on the issues and thus the real *problem* was that they merely failed to communicate with one another. Whereas one usually starts with the problem and, in a logical, deductive fashion works toward a solution, the example of communication failure demonstrates that in this case the Nixon administration started with a desired solution and worked back to the problem.

Very similar to this theory of communications breakdown, cultural assumptions about crime and criminals are sometimes referred to as commonsense theories (Hartjen, 1981). These theories are produced as follows: "The meanings members of a culture share . . . can be thought of as a set of rules" (Hartjen, 1981: 438–39). Treating theories in this manner, one is obliged to deal with them as things, "as concrete phenomena to be investigated in their own right" (Hartjen, 1981: 440–41). Thus, "an adequate

245

science of crime involves investigation of the 'methods' used by common-sense actors to produce crime and criminals" (Hartjen, 1981: 442). "[C]ommonsense theories offer descriptions and accounts of the world to actors and thereby provide them with methods for dealing with it" (Hartjen, 1981: 440). These commonsense theories are found in: "detective novels, newspaper reports, television stories, [and] conversations with friends" (Hartjen, 1981: 439). But "Until recently, most criminologists have addressed themselves to questions such as 'What causes crime?' Under the guise of scientific inquiry, they have insisted that the world they see is the world that *must be*" (Hartjen, 1981: 436) without recognizing how their theories are imbedded in culture.

American politics clearly reflects not only theories of communications breakdown, but also commonsense ideas about crime causation. The Bush campaign in the 1988 presidential election used television commercials that drew on a white racism legitimated by a white fear of crime. The commercial featured a middle-class, white couple emotionally recounting the kidnapping, torture, humiliation, and rape experienced at the hands of a black male named Willie Horton (who was often pictured with a menacing scowl). He was a convicted murderer who had been furloughed from prison in Massachusetts by Governor Michael Dukakis, the Democratic candidate. There is a widespread cultural, black-male–savage commonsense theory of crime as reflected in the Willie Horton commercial which is a product of racism and also legitimates racism.

## Academic Criminology and Its Theories

Commonsense theories provide the environment for criminology. The long-term commonsense theory of the black-male savage exists side by side with the intellectual history of Western criminology, and they reinforce and nurture each other. Not only do commonsense theories provide an environment for academic criminology, but criminology in turn feeds back support for biological commonsense theories. An example of such influence of academic theories is found in the Sunday supplement to a local newspaper, where the following true-false question was asked: "The fingerprints of criminals are different from those of law-abiding citizens." The answer, the article indicated, was *true*. "A team of research scientists contrasted the fingerprint patterns and ridge counts of 175 criminals with those of a noncriminal control group. The study showed that the pattern frequency of the fingerprints of the criminal group differed significantly from those of the noncriminal control group" (*Family Weekly*, 1975: 9). Moreover, early in this century Goddard found high proportions of hereditary feeble-mindedness among both European immigrants and delinquents (1917a, 1917b). Such research informed early twentieth-century immigration laws that provided quotas for eastern and southern Europeans and made it impossible for the United States to accept most of those desiring to flee the Nazis (Ryan, 1976).

The theoretical history of criminology includes: Freud and his notion of the id housing a human's animal impulses; Lombroso emphasizing incomplete biological evolution as the cause of crime; and, of course, Goddard's claims of inherited feeble-mindedness as the cause of crime. Thus, theory in criminology is not the same as in the rest of sociology, awash as criminology continues to be with biological positivism. An *American Sociological Review* article on IQ and delinquency published in 1978 favorably cited Goddard's early twentieth-century research on feeble-mindedness (Hirschi and Hindelang, 1977). More recently, two Harvard University professors, political scientist James Q. Wilson and psychologist Richard Herrnstein, in *Crime and Human Nature* (1985), trumpeted biological origins of criminal behavior, as did a recent *American Journal of Sociology* article comparing marauding honeybees to street criminals (Cohen and Machalek, 1988). All this biological positivism has obscured other important early criminology (Beirne, 1987).

This intellectual history allows criminologists to say things that others cannot. For instance, Wilson and Herrnstein recently asserted: "Even to allude to the possibility that races may differ in the distribution of those constitutional factors that are associated with criminality will strike some persons as factually, ethically, or prudentially wrong. We disagree." (Wilson and Herrnstein, 1985: 468). From the evidence they marshal, including black crime rates, these authors conclude that criminal behavior has significant biological causes. "To the extent there are important constitutional factors at work, then programs would have to be tailored to individuals rather than groups, a difficult and painstaking task" (Wilson and Herrnstein, 1985: 492). According to this logic, one's constitutional rights will be dependent upon demonstrating specific biological or genetic traits.

In the sociology of science or the sociology of religion, biological theories would be seen as both ridiculous and dangerous. The academic community would be aghast at any attempt to explain the cultural patterns of behavior in religious groups who marry frequently within the group in terms of a theory that draws even partially on biology. A study claiming to investigate Jewish genes and success in the medical and legal professions would be seen as laughable and even dangerous, as would an analysis of Mormon chromosomes and economic success. Another research topic possibility might be an investigation of genetic inheritance and the born-again experience among fundamentalist Christians. This behavior seems to be as good a candidate as most crime for biological explanations if, like crime, being born again is usually seen as an extra-rational behavior. In short, the substantive material alone does not necessarily make unique demands upon criminologists to consider biological sources of behavior.

## The Hidden Meanings of Theory

Contrary to the claims of those emphasizing biological origins of behavior, empirical evidence does not force a specific theoretical position. To the American Civil Liberties Union (ACLU) and the National Association for the Advancement of Colored People (NAACP) as well as other researchers, arrest and imprisonment rates for black males (not to mention rates of executions) show evidence of racism in two ways. Greenberg and Himmelstein (1969) indicate the massive number of black arrests and convictions reflect racism in the criminal justice system. It has been found that blacks are more likely to be arrested, tried, convicted, and imprisoned than are whites, even when controlling for the seriousness of the offense (Farnworth and Horan, 1980; Spohn et al., 1981–82). It has also been argued that the greater representation of blacks in national crime figures is also a consequence of discrimination in employment. And Geis (1965) has noted that the way crime rates are constructed is a reflection of racism—comparing blacks and whites, but not Catholics and Protestants. This method of construction reflects this same commonsense theory of the black-male savage.

The driving force in any research is what Hughes (1971) has referred to as the major premise, or the underlying reason for conducting the research in the first instance. The major premise of research on the biological causes of crime is that, as Wilson and Herrnstein note above, legal attempts to control crime and delinquency will have to take such factors into account if such factors are found to be positively associated with high rates of crime and delinquency—that is, the civil rights of such alleged biological misfits will have to be abridged. The major premise of any research is typically not made explicit (Hughes, 1971) but nonetheless influences the cultural rules used to generate commonsense theories. The implication is that biological characteristics can legitimately be used to abridge the civil rights of those with such characteristics associated with crime to prevent their crime, even before they have committed such violations, if crime can be demonstrated to be caused by, or correlated with, biological characteristics.

## The Policy Implications of Theory

Since the cultural commonsense theory of the black-male savage is typically unspoken, as is the major premise of studies drawing on biological causes of crime, the folklore of the black-male savage cannot be challenged directly. For example, one starts with support for the death penalty and looks for a commonsense theory to support this position. Both biological commonsense theories and biological criminological theories increase support for the death penalty as a form of pest control since there is no possibility of rehabilitation, and the commonsense black-male–savage commonsense theory increases white demands for retribution. If the commonsense theories provide a supportive cultural environment for the development of biological theories in criminology, the latter, for their part, provide ammunition for the white forces in a race war—since others, without the benefit of the "expert genetic knowledge" of the Harvard behavioral scientists mentioned above, are forced to rely on oblique, coded phrases to express their views or commonsense theories, such as by expressing support for the death penalty as a deterrent or as retribution and by expressing opposition to "forced" bussing. Only Ph.D.s can claim that their computers tell them that blacks are truly biologically inferior. Perhaps it is understandable then that those drawing on biological causes feel compelled to claim to be unbiased scientists, a good example being Wilson's assertion in a *Time* book review (1985: 94) that "this [book] has nothing to do with conservation times. Do not put this book in that framework."

By the same token, feminists should recognize that the premenstrual syndrome is a dangerous explanation to use in attempting to avoid criminal responsibility, whether or not it contains an element of truth. If some females successfully use this defense it is likely that all females will be confined to a second-class status for the foreseeable future and, due to their alleged special irrationality, could be continually excluded from leadership positions. For a handful of women to avoid prosecution, all women will be denied certain human rights.

For those who doubt that racism is really reflected in the Willie Horton scenario and who might be inclined to claim that it represented rather a genuine concern for the victims of rape and other sexual assaults, we can consult the political record again for guidance. During the fall of 1989, after using the Willie Horton commercial in a winning campaign, President Bush vetoed a federal appropriation that would have provided financial assistance for poor women seeking abortions for pregnancies resulting from rape and incest. As one member of Congress observed during the futile attempt of the U.S. House of Representatives to override the veto, if the young woman who was raped by Willie Horton had as a consequence become pregnant and would have required federal assistance with fee payment, President Bush would have demanded that she carry Willie's baby to term. While this story does not really offer compelling proof of the president's motivations, it does at the very least suggest that sincere concern for rape victims was not his only motivation for using the Willie Horton case in his campaign.

As in the Nixon-Administration case, which started with the *solution* of ignoring war protestors and then led to defining the *problem* as communication failure, if one adopts the solution of capital punishment, this appears to be nicely suited to defining the problem as being the unredeemable black-male savage. In other words, if one accepts such a racist, "Willie Horton" theory of criminology or any theory of academic biological positivism, then resolving the problem of criminal behavior through social and economic change—conciliation, mediation, education, compromise, or any other peacemaking strategy—is not possible. Peacemaking is then impossible because only biological solutions such as sterilization, frontal lobotomies, electroshock therapy, and capital punishment seem plausible in addressing problems thought to have biological causes.

## REFERENCES

Beirne, Piers. 1987. "Adolphe Quetelet and the Origins of Positivist Criminology." *American Journal of Sociology* 92 (March): 1140–69.

Cohen, Lawrence E., and Richard Machalek. 1988. "A General Theory of Expropriative Crime: An Evolutionary Ecological Approach." *American Journal of Sociology* (November): 465–501.

*Family Weekly.* 1975. "True or False?" 23 November: 9.

Farnworth, M., and P. Horan. 1980. "Separate Justice: An Analysis of Race Differences in Court Processes." *Social Science Research* 9: 381–99.

Geis, G. 1965. "Statistics Concerning Race and Crime." *Crime and Delinquency* (April): 142–50.

Goddrad, H. H. 1917a. "Mental Tests and the Immigrant." *The Journal of Delinquency* 2 (September): 243–77.

———. 1917b. "The Instincts of the Feeble-Minded." *The Journal of Delinquency* 2 (November): 352–55.

Greenberg, Jack, and Jack Himmelstein. 1969. "Varieties of Attack on the Death Penalty." *Crime and Delinquency* 15 (January): 112–20.

Hall, Peter M., and John P. Hewitt. 1970. "The Quasi-Theory of Communication and the Management of Dissent." *Social Problems* 18 (Summer): 17–27.

Hartjen, Clayton A. 1981. "Crime as Commonsense Theory." *Criminology* 18 (February): 435–52.

Hirschi, Travis, and Michael J. Hindelang. 1978. "Intelligence and Delinquency: A Revisionist Review." *American Sociological Review* 42 (August): 571–87.

Hughes, Everett C. 1971. "Principle and Rationalization in Race Relations" In *The Sociological Eye: Selected Papers.* Chicago: Aldine-Atherton.

Ryan, William. 1976. *Blaming the Victim.* Revised edition. New York: Vintage Books.

Spohn, C., J. Gruhl, and S. Welch. 1981–82. "The Effect of Race Sentencing: A Reexamination of an Unsettled Question." *Law and Society Review* 16: 71–88.

Wilson, James Q. 1985. "Are Criminals Born, Not Made?" Book review. *Time,* 21 October: 94.

Wilson, James Q., and Richard J. Herrnstein. 1985. *Crime and Human Nature.* New York: Simon and Schuster.

*Robert Elias*

---

S  E  V  E  N  T  E  E  N

# Crime Control as Human Rights Enforcement

> Crime threatens the social order in the same way as totalitarianism
>
> —Charles Silberman

> You will not eliminate crime by eliminating poverty, ignorance, poor health, and ugly environments. But it is clear that such conditions are demonstrably responsible for most crime
>
> —Ramsey Clark

> . . . the crimes committed in the name of the state, unfortunately, have . . . been so great that we cannot shun the obligation to examine the grounds of its authority and subject them to rigorous critique
>
> —Robert Paul Wolff

## War and Peace

When the government declares another of its countless wars on crime or on drugs, criminology often provides logistical support for the resulting battles. This happens even though these wars are never won; indeed, we can easily predict that they'll be lost. Why do we pursue predictably ineffective crime policies? Why does criminology so often support those wars, thus promoting its own, professional failure? Instead of making *war*, crime control and criminology should be making *peace*.

The government has perhaps a strategic sense of this, having already appropriated the word "peace": At U.S. military bases, the new motto is "Peace" Is Our Profession. Likewise, in many areas, police officers are now "peace" officers. Nevertheless, military and law-enforcement policies remain virtually the same: they're still pursuing war not peace.

What would crime control or criminology as peacemaking look like? What do we mean by peace? Over the four-decade history of peace studies, peace has come to mean two things: *positive* peace and *negative* peace (Galtung, 1980). We're most familiar with the commonsense notion of negative peace, meaning an absence of violence and war. Here, crime control as peacemaking might resemble conventional crime policy (but with significantly different tactics): fighting crime either to prevent personal violence or to prevent crime "wars" such as those fought among drug dealers or mafia families. Crime policy typically fails to produce this kind of peace, perhaps because officials don't seriously want it (Reiman, 1984), but also because it makes the wrong diagnosis and pursues the wrong strategies (Anderson, 1988; Pepinsky and Jeslow, 1984; Walker, 1985).

In part, crime policy fails because it ignores the second notion of peace. Positive peace describes not what government should prevent, but what government or the society should provide—*justice:* and not just criminal justice, but also political, economic, and social justice. You can't have peace if you don't have justice. Injustice is not merely unpeaceful in itself. It's also the source of further violence and war in any society, and it's the major source of the kind of violence and war we commonly call *crime*.

Most crime results from political, economic, and social injustices that the government or the society has failed or refused to prevent. In some circles, that injustice is called "repression": a violation of human rights. Thus, promoting peace is a matter of the government not merely refraining from its own violence and war (and crime) but providing the conditions to persuade others against launching their own violence and war (and crime). Crime control can be successful only by taking human rights enforcement seriously.

## Conventional Crime Control

Mainstream crime policy uses war purportedly to create peace. Yet as a process, its wars undermine both negative and positive peace: they use violence and rights' violations as their major tactics. The need to win these wars rationalizes the use of illegitimate, but supposedly more effective, methods: We're told the police should no longer be "handcuffed"; rights must be sacrificed; our enforcement and punishments must be more violent. In the long run, crime will decline and peace will reign (President's Task Force, 1982). Yet the peace never comes: criminal violence keeps pace with escalating official violence.

Despite the wars, criminal victimization continues because conventional crime policy either ignores or misdiagnoses crime's sources (Wilson and Hernnstein, 1985). Officials argue that we don't or can't know the causes of crime, or they attribute it to what might better be viewed as crime symptoms. They blame offenders and institutions, even victims. Offender-blaming attributes crime to evil individuals or their inadequate families. Institution-blaming focuses on lax enforcement, inadequate resources, excessive rights, and judicial softness as the causes of crime. Victim-blaming faults victims for not taking precautions sufficient to deter crime. Predictably, crime-control strategies follow from these diagnoses. They're pursued; they fail.

Nevertheless, officials return to these diagnoses and strategies time and again (Elias, 1990b). Criminology largely follows suit, adopting official definitions and perspectives. When officials go to war, criminology goes to war too. When confronting crime, government limits its scope; criminology does so too (Elias, 1985). The diagnoses made of what causes crime necessarily constrict the options for fighting it; make the wrong diagnoses and you'll likely pursue the wrong strategies. Conventional crime policy's repeated failure would seem reason enough to consider alternatives. Better yet, alternative diagnoses and strategies already exist (Brady, 1981; Currie, 1985; Elias, Forthcoming).

## Alternative Crime Policy

### BLAMING THE SYSTEM

An alternative crime policy would wage peace not war. It would begin with a different diagnosis: Crime primarily results not from inherently or inevitably evil offenders, nor from institutional inefficiencies, nor from victim complacency. Rather, it's caused by adverse or destructive political economic, and social conditions that induce crime across the spectrum of classes and races in American society. Instead of blaming offenders, institutions, or victims, this diagnosis blames the system, the existing set of U.S. political and economic arrangements. Inadequacies in the American political economy provide the breeding ground for most crime (Elias, 1986; Quinney, 1980).

The economic system, for example, produces poverty, inequality, homelessness, hunger, and other victimization. It's not surprising that many poor people turn to crime, for economic gain or merely to vent their frustrations (Barlow, 1988; Braithwaite, 1979; Michalowski, 1985; Silberman, 1978; Wideman, 1984). The economy also promotes excessive materialism, competition, and consumerism. To get ahead and keep ahead, middle- and upper-class people commit crime too. If their wrongdoing was measured or enforced like poor people's crimes, it would amount to far more criminality and damage than the conventional crime we worry so much about (Frank, 1985; Green and Berry, 1985; Hochstedler, 1984; Mokiber, 1988; Reiman, 1984).

The political system has its own inadequacies, induced partly by the economic system. Government officials widely commit crimes themselves, usually with little or no accounting, the Iran-Contra episode being only the latest example (Chambliss, 1989; Foraker-Thompson, 1988; Kelman and Hamilton, 1989; Kwitny, 1987; Ratner, 1987; Tushnet, 1988). Access to meaningful political participation is blocked for almost all but the very wealthy. Elections function more to tame the masses than to empower them. Despite talk about getting government off our backs, it steadily centralizes and grows. We're overwhelmed and alienated by our various public and private bureaucracies, including most of our workplaces. Government pays lip service to equality while tolerating or promoting racism, sexism, and classism (Dunbar, 1984; Gross, 1980; Marable, 1983; Parenti, 1988; Russell and Van den Ven, 1984). Whether in its domestic policy or its foreign policy, we learn by the government's official actions, if not by its pious rhetoric, that violence is legitimate (Herman, 1982; Rubin, 1986; Wolfe, 1978).

In practice, we lack both political and economic democracy. Our system produces problems and conditions that breed crime far more than the things we usually blame. Societies with greater political and economic democracy have less crime and victimization. Even nations like those in Eastern Europe or like Cuba, which has little political democracy but greater economic democracy, have much lower crime rates than our nominally democratic capitalism (Clinard, 1978; Los, 1982).

### CRIME AND REPRESSION

But the problems of failed political and economic democracy are the sources of more than merely criminal victimization; the problems are themselves victimization. Human rights advocates would call these problems repression. International law requires nations to prevent or deal with these problems; and nations which fail to do so (particularly if, like the United States, they have the means) are human rights violators. These are crimes against humanity. Repression is crime. Crime is a human rights violation. Crime results from the violation of human rights produced by unjust political and economic arrangements (Meier and Geis, 1978; Reasons, 1982).

Criminals are also victims, and, of course, offenders bear some responsibility for their crimes. But viewing criminals as passive automatons shaped by monolithic forces degrades offenders every bit as much as our conventional criminal process. And recognizing offender motivations does not excuse their crimes. Nevertheless, offenders act within an environment that often makes crime a viable alternative, a likely possibility, even a necessity. It's not an environment of lenience, as "law and order" advocates argue. (The United States has long had one of the world's highest incarceration rates and severity of punishments.) Rather, it's an environment of victimization, which beats people down, robs them of opportunities, and provokes their rage, frustration, and desperation. In response, they attack others; but their victims are much like themselves: Most victims come from the same backgrounds, and many of them have committed their own crimes for similar reasons (Elias, 1986).

It's politically convenient for officials to pit criminals and victims against each other. Protecting victims has justified our growing fortress mentality: increasing government powers and declining individual rights. Yet victim policy does not reduce crime; and arguably, pursuing crime control strategies that routinely fail, even encourage crime, makes victimization even more likely (Elias, 1990c). Successful crime control relies not on promoting victims over offenders, but on recognizing how both are victimized and how the rights of both must be protected. Victims and criminals have the same interest: the protection of their human rights.

Alternative crime control strategies would follow from this diagnosis. It would require us to reduce or eliminate crime's systemic sources. We'd have to significantly restructure our political and economic system, bringing both much closer to democracy and justice. Thereby, we'd be promoting both positive and negative peace: a reduction in the violence the system and its major institutions directly produce, and a reduction in the violence committed by others in the society in reaction to injustice. By pursuing justice, we'd be pursuing peace; and we'd also be reducing the crime that now significantly impedes that peace.

## Resisting Peace

Why does mainstream crime policy, which routinely fails, shun this alternative? It does so because it would clash dramatically with the American system's conventional political and economic practice both at home and abroad. To adopt alternative crime policies, we'd have to pursue crime control that really reduces crime rather than merely overseeing it. We'd have to stop manipulating or blaming victims, and take victimization (criminal and otherwise) seriously. We'd have to reject "democracy for the few" in favor of a more just political economy. We'd have to renounce our isolation from the world community and our rejection of international human rights standards (Chomsky, 1988; Elias, 1990c; Falk, 1981; Parenti, 1988; Reiman, 1984).

### ROGUE SOCIETY

Let's examine, for example, U.S. human rights policy. The United States has long crusaded as democracy's champion at home and abroad. It's held up its own system as the democratic ideal and justified its foreign policy as helping others become more democratic. By now, it's hardly controversial to suggest that in practice the United States does neither. Even the pretensions of real democracy largely evaporated with Jimmy Carter, who at least pursued human rights rhetorically if not very vigorously in practice. Whether it's our increasing poverty, homelessness, inequality, and violence at home, or our promotion of brutal repression abroad, the victimization produced by the U.S. government and our other institutions hardly makes our commitment to human rights credible (Chomsky and Herman, 1979; Goldstein, 1978; Gross, 1980; Klare and Arnson, 1981; Lappe et al., 1980; Scherer and Shepard, 1983; Special Issue, 1989; Weisband, 1989).

The United States is out of step with the world community (Boyle, 1988; Frappier, 1984; Weston, 1987). We pull out of United Nations' agencies while other nations commit themselves more fully. We're practically alone in rejecting the Law-of-the-Sea-Treaty's cooperative exploration of the oceans in favor of competitive exploitation. We defend the unconscionable marketing of infant baby formula while the rest of the world deplores it. We support pariah states like Chile, Israel, and South Africa while the international community condemns them. We increasingly reject and violate international law (and the jurisdiction of agencies like the World Court) while the rest of the world increasingly embraces it. We substitute military intervention for diplomacy when even the Soviet Union has rejected the practice. George Bush asks the U.S.S.R. to intervene in Rumania, and Mikhail Gorbachev says they don't do that kind of thing anymore. A few days later, the United States illegally invades Panama; and the Latin American nations, no lovers of Manuel Noriega, rightfully condemn us.

## HUMAN RIGHTS STANDARDS

Likewise, the United States exhibits a limited commitment to international human rights standards (Claude and Weston, 1989; Forsythe, 1989). By now, the world's nations have recognized, and most have ratified, three "generations" of human rights: political and civil rights; economic, social and cultural rights; and peace, development and environmental rights. The United States has ratified none of these standards. We've even shunned the Covenant on Political and Civil Rights, which comes closest to our narrow human rights definitions. Although this covenant embodies many of the things already in our own Bill of Rights, it adds other rights and, more menacing, threatens to make the rights substantially enforceable and not merely rhetorical. We'd have an international obligation to take these rights seriously. And instead of piecemeal, impermanent, and often unenforced rights protections (Scheingold, 1974), we'd be responsible for more honestly and equitably guaranteeing freedom of expression, political access, privacy, due process for suspects and defendants, and race and gender equality—rights that have instead declined in the last two decades (faster than they can be promoted) and are threatened even further by the recently inaugurated Rehnquist Court (Curry, 1988; Dorsen, 1984; Karp, 1988; Lobel, 1988; Marx, 1988; Pell, 1984; Spence, 1989).

Even more ominous for the American system would be accepting and protecting the second and third generations of human rights. Embracing economic, social, and cultural rights, for example, would force the United States to fundamentally change its political economy, which now acts systematically to deprive these rights for vast portions of the population. We can imagine why officials won't recognize the right to housing, employment, quality education, nutrition, good working conditions, comprehensive healthcare, and social and cultural equality. Similarly, the newest generation of human rights—the rights to peace, development, and a clean environment—also clashes with the American system since this generation would condemn our persistent and far-flung military and economic interventionism, reject our vast nuclear stockpiles, and indict the corporate pollution of our environment.

Human rights covenants are treaties in U.S. and international law. If we were to ratify these treaties, they would become the law of the land under the U.S. Constitution. As such, the rights they contain would be legally enforceable in U.S. courts. We can imagine the threat posed to the American system by suits brought to demand that these rights be protected. Suppose claims were brought by our four million homeless Americans for their housing rights, or by our 60 million illiterates for their educational rights, or by our millions of jobless (50 percent in our ghettos) for their employment rights, or by our 30 million underfed for their nutrition rights, or by our millions of uninsured (50 percent of the population) for their healthcare rights, or by even millions more (such as those living near our 75,000 toxic dump sites) for their environmental rights. Or suppose U.S. citizens or foreigners sued to protect the rights of the millions of people victimized by the repression and economic deprivation our foreign policy exports to nations like El Salvador, Lebanon, Chile, South Africa, and many others?

## RIGHTS AS THREATS

Despite the rhetoric, the United States has been only minimally committed to protecting human rights. The few exceptions are politically motivated, such as the "demonstration elections" we've sponsored to help sanitize our client states (Brodhead and Herman, 1987). When we back away from the endless dictators we've either sponsored or installed, it's only after they've outlived their usefulness (such as Noriega in Panama) or where their popular overthrow is inevitable (such as Marcos in the Philippines). If popular revolution (such as in Nicaragua) threatens to seriously protect human rights and promote real political and economic democracy, we attack it.

A nation which tolerates and even promotes the victimization caused by repression can hardly be expected to respond differently to victimization caused by crime. Wars on crime and drugs, government-backed victim movements, and pious rhetoric about the "forgotten" victim in the criminal process achieve little for crime victims in practice. There's little evidence that officials ever thought they would (Elias, 1983, 1990a, 1990b).

We don't take crime and its victims seriously for the same reasons we don't take repression and its victims seriously; to do so would require fundamental changes in the American system, which would upset its prevailing concentration of power and resources. Undoing that concentration is the only hope for genuinely protecting and providing human rights; and short of that, crime and other victimization will continue unabated. The United States can't achieve peace if it's only willing to fight wars, especially since they're often launched not just against innocent foreigners, but also against its own people. Are U.S. wars, whether against domestic crime or foreign enemies, fought to promote democracy for the many or to preserve democracy for the few?

## TAKING RIGHTS SERIOUSLY

Real crime control would consider rights not as an obstacle but rather as its major objective (Walker, 1982). Now, to fight crime, our "law and order" policy restricts and violates the rights of suspects, defendants, and the public; it further victimizes purportedly to end victimization. Indeed, alternative crime control would promote human rights fully: not just for suspects and defendants, not just to stem a growing police state, but also for the kind of political, economic, and social justice that would significantly eliminate crime's sources in the first place. An effective crime policy would recognize the relationship between criminal victimization and human rights victimization, not treat the two as separate and unconnected, and pursue a joint strategy designed to alleviate them both simultaneously.

How can this be done? We can begin, perhaps, by taking the lead offered by the recently passed United Nations Declaration on the Victims of Crime and Abuses of Power (Lamborn, 1987; U.N. Secretariat, 1980). Here the link has been made, despite U.S. resistance, between crime and repression. Like other declarations, its effectiveness depends first on getting as many nations as possible to ratify it; and the United States should be pressured to do so. Next, the U.N.'s Crime Prevention and Criminal Justice Branch must devise standards for the declaration's implementation; and criminologists, victimologists, and human rights advocates should contribute to this process (Geis et al., 1985). More generally, the United States should be pushed to get in step with the international community: It must ratify the human rights covenants. It must respect the sovereignty of other nations and peoples. It must recognize international law (Bassiouni, 1985; DeCataldo Neuberger, 1985; Hertzberg, 1981; Johnston, 1974, 1978; Lopez-Rey, 1985; Lynch et al., 1988; Schaaf, 1986).

At home, the United States must take human rights seriously, implementing and enforcing them in both the political and economic realms. To do so requires not merely a more just legal system and less criminal government, but fundamental changes in the American system to undo its many obstacles to political and economic democracy. The United States must be held more accountable. Criminology and victimology can contribute by challenging prevailing assumptions about official benevolence and by adopting alternative definitions and perspectives on crime and victimization (Elias, 1986; Snider, 1988).

Of course, these objectives will not come easily. By now it should be obvious that formidable and fundamental changes will be needed to significantly reduce crime. A human rights perspective, however, gives us a new way of approaching the task ahead and, perhaps, a more powerful and symbolically acceptable mechanism for accomplishing it.

No doubt the obstacles will be compounded by official resistance to a substantive human rights movement. Rights will likely remain a threat to those unwilling to relinquish political and economic power, both at home and abroad. Our archconservative Supreme Court and foreign policy will be further impediments to taking rights seriously. Nevertheless, one wonders how long the United States can resist our rapidly changing world. With the walls of repression falling in Eastern Europe, and with incipient signs of democratic renewal in Latin America (despite U.S. policy), now is perhaps a historic opportunity. With renewed determination, perhaps we can launch a real human rights movement, beyond mere rhetoric, which emphasizes substantive protections of all human rights—a movement which will help reduce not only human rights victimization, but criminal victimization as well (Eide, 1986; Kim, 1983).

How can criminology work for peace? It can promote human rights—*justice:* the only effective path to peace, whether in our streets or among our nations (Alston, 1981).

## REFERENCES

Alston, Philip. 1981. "Peace As A Human Right." *Bulletin of Peace Proposals* 11: 319–26.

Anderson, David. 1988. *Crimes of Justice.* New York: Times Books.

Barlow, David E. 1988. "Economic Crisis and the Criminal Justice System." Paper presented at Annual Meeting of American Society of Criminology, Chicago.

Bassiouni, M. C. 1985. "The Protection of 'Collective Victims' in International Law." *New York Law School Human Rights Annual* 2 (Spring): 239–57.

Boyle, Francis A. 1988. "International Law, Citizen Resistance, and Crimes By the State." Paper presented at Annual Meeting of American Society of Criminology, Chicago.

Brady, James. 1981. "Towards Popular Justice in the U.S." *Contemporary Crises* 5: 155–94.

Braithwaite, John. 1979. *Inequality, Crime and Public Policy.* New York: Routledge and Kegan Paul.

Brodhead, Frank and Edward Herman. 1987. *Demonstration Elections: U.S. Staged Elections.* Boston: South End Press.

Chambliss, William. 1989. "State-Organized Crime." *Criminology* 27: 183–208.

Chomsky, Noam. 1988. *The Culture of Terrorism.* Boston: South End Press.

Chomsky, Noam, and Edward Herman. 1979. *The Washington Connection and Third World Fascism.* Boston: South End Press.

Claude, Richard, and Burns Weston (eds)., 1989. *Human Rights in the International Community.* Philadelphia: University of Pennsylvania Press.

Clinard, Marshall. 1978. *Cities With Little Crime.* New York: Cambridge University Press.

Currie, Elliot. 1985. *Confronting Crime.* New York: Pantheon.

Curry, Richard (ed.) 1988. *Freedom At Risk: Secrecy, Censorship and Repression in the Eighties.* Philadelphia: Temple University Press.

DeCataldo Neuberger, Luisa. 1985. "An Appraisal of Victimological Perspectives in International Law." *Victimology* 10: 700–709.

Dorsen, Norman. 1984. *Our Endangered Rights.* New York: Pantheon.

Dunbar, Leslie, (ed.) 1984. *Minority Report.* New York: Pantheon.

Eide, A. 1986. "The Human Rights Movement and the Transformation of the International Order." *Alternatives* 11: 367–402.

Elias, Robert. 1983. *Victims of the System.* New Brunswick, N.J.: Transaction Books.

———. 1985. "Transcending Our Social Reality of Victimization." *Victimology* 10: 6–25.

———. 1986. *The Politics of Victimization: Victims, Victimology and Human Rights.* New York: Oxford University Press.

———. 1990a. "The Conflicting Politics of Victim Movements." *Victimology* 14: 25–37.

———. 1990b. "Wars on Drugs and Crime as Historic Propaganda." Unpublished paper.

———. 1990c. "Which Victim Movement? The Politics of Victim Policy." In Wesley Skogan, et al., *Victims and Criminal Justice.* Newbury Park, Calif.: Sage.

———. Forthcoming. *Taking Crime Into Our Own Hands.* Unpublished manuscript.

Falk, Richard. 1981. *Human Rights and State Sovereignty.* New York: Holmes and Meier.

Foraker-Thompson, Jane. 1988. "Crime and Ethics in Government: Constitutional Crisis." Paper presented at Annual Meeting of American Society of Criminology, Chicago.

Forsythe, David. 1989. *Human Rights and World Politics.* Lincoln, Nebr.: University of Nebraska Press.

Frank, Nancy. 1985. *Crimes Against Health and Safety.* Albany: Harrow and Heston.

Frappier, Jan. 1984. "Above the Law: Violations of International Law by the U.S. Government." *Crime and Social Justice* 23: 1–45.

Galtung, Johan. 1980. *The True Worlds.* New York: Free Press.

Geis, Gilbert, Duncan Chappell, and Michael Agopian. 1985. "Toward the Alleviation of Human Suffering." Dubrovnik: Rapporteurs' Report of the 5th International Symposium on Victimology.

Goldstein, Robert. 1978. *Political Repression in Modern America.* Cambridge, Mass.: Schenkman.

Green, Mark, and John F. Berry. 1985. *The Challenge of Hidden Profits: White Collar Crime as Big Business.* New York: William Morrow.

Gross, Bertram. 1980. *Friendly Fascism.* New York: M. Evans.

Herman, Edward. 1982. *The Real Terror Network.* Boston: South End Press.

Hertzberg, Sandra. 1981. *The Protection of Human Rights in the Criminal Process Under International Instruments and National Constitutions.* Amsterdam: Eres.

Hochstedler, Ellen (ed.). 1984. *Corporations as Criminals.* Beverly Hills: Sage.

Johnston, Stanley. 1974. "Toward A Supra-National Criminology: The Right and Duty of Victims of National Government to Seek Defense Through World Law." In Israel Drapkin and Emilio Viano (eds.), *Victimology: Theoretical Issues.* Lexington, Mass.: Lexington Books.

————. 1978. "Instituting Criminal Justice in the Global Village." In Emilio Viano (ed.), *Victims and Society.* Washington, D.C.: Visage Press.

Karp, Walter. 1988. "Liberty Under Siege." *Harper's Magazine* (November): 53–67.

Kelman, Herbert and V. Lee Hamilton. 1989. *Crimes of Obedience.* New Haven: Yale University Press.

Kim, Samuel. 1983. *The Quest for A Just World Order.* Boulder: Westview.

Klare, Michael, and Cynthia Arnson. 1981. *Supplying Repression.* Washington: Institute for Policy Studies.

Kwitny, Jonathan. 1987. *The Crimes of Patriots.* New York: Simon & Schuster.

Lamborn, LeRoy. 1987. "The United Nations Declaration on Victims: Incorporating 'Abuse of Power'." *Rutgers Law Journal* 19: 59–95.

Lappe, Frances Moore, Joseph Collins, and David Kinley. 1980. *Aid As Obstacle.* San Francisco: Institute for Food & Development Policy.

Lobel, Jules. 1988. *A Less Than Perfect Union.* New York: Monthly Review Press.

Lopez-Rey, Miguel. 1985. *A Guide to United Nations Criminal Policy.* New York: United Nations.

Los, Maria. 1982. "Crime and Economy in the Communist Countries." In Peter Wickman and Timothy Dailey (eds.), *White Collar and Economic Crime.* Lexington, Mass.: Lexington Books.

Lynch, Michael, David McDowall, and Graeme R. Newman. 1988. "Crime in the World System." Paper presented at the Annual Meeting of American Society of Criminology, Chicago.

Marable, Manning. 1983. *How Capitalism Underdeveloped Black America.* Boston: South End Press.

Marx, Gary T. 1988. *Under Cover: Police Surveillance in America.* Berkeley: University of California Press.

Meier, Robert, and Gilbert Geis. 1978. "The Abuse of Power as a Criminal Activity." In Gilbert Geis (ed.), *On White Collar Crime.* Beverly Hills: Sage.

Michalowski, Raymond. 1985. *Order, Law and Crime.* New York: Random House.

Mokiber, Ronald. 1988. *Corporate Crime and Violence.* San Francisco: Sierra Books.

Parenti, Michael. 1988. *Democracy for the Few.* New York: St. Martin's.

Pell, Eve. 1984. *The Big Chill.* Boston: Beacon Press.

Pepinsky, Harold E., and Paul Jesilow. 1984. *Myths That Cause Crime.* Cabin John, Md.: Seven Locks Press.

President's Task Force on Victims of Crime. 1982. *Final Report.* Washington, D.C.: U.S. Government Printing Office.

Quinney, Richard. 1980. *Class, State and Crime.* New York: Longman.

Ratner, Michael. 1987. "Contragate, Covert Action and the Constitution." *Social Policy* (Summer): 43–47.

Reasons, Charles. 1982. "Crime and the Abuse of Power." In Peter Wickman and Timothy Dailey (eds.), *White Collar and Economic Crime.* Lexington, Mass.: Lexington Books.

Reiman, Jeffrey. 1984. *The Rich Get Richer and the Poor Get Prison.* 2d ed. New York: J. Wiley.

Rubin, Lillian. 1986. *Quiet Rage: Bernie Goetz in A Time of Madness.* New York: Farrar, Straus & Giroux.

Russell, D. E. H., and N. Van den Ven. 1984. *Crimes Against Women.* East Palo Alto, Calif.: Frog In the Well Press.

Schaaf, R. W. 1986. "New International Instruments in Crime Prevention and Criminal Justice." *International Journal of Legal Information* 14 (June): 176–82.

Scheingold, Stuart. 1974. *The Politics of Rights.* New Haven: Yale University Press.

Scherer, Jacqueline, and Gary Shepard (eds.). 1983. *Victimization of the Weak.* Springfield, Ill.: C. Thomas.

Silberman, Charles. 1978. *Criminal Violence, Criminal Justice.* New York: Vintage.

Snider, Laura. 1988. "The Potential of the Criminal Justice System to Promote Feminist Concerns." Paper presented at Annual Meeting of American Society of Criminology, Chicago.

Special Issue, 1989. "Domestic Surveillance." *Covert Action Information Bulletin* 31 (Winter): 1–74.

Spence, Gerry. 1989. *With Justice for None.* New York: Times Books.

Tushnet, Mark. 1988. *Central America and the Law.* Boston: South End Press.

United Nations Secretariat. 1980. "Crime and the Abuse of Power: Offenses and Offenders Beyond the Reach of the Law." U.N. Doc. A/CONF/87/6.

Walker, Samuel. 1982. "What Have Civil Liberties Ever Done for Crime Victims? Plenty!" *Academy of Criminal Justice Sciences Today* (October) 4.

———. 1985. *Sense and Nonsense About Crime.* Belmont, Calif.: Brooks-Cole.

Weisband, Edward (ed.). 1989. *Poverty Amidst Plenty.* Boulder: Westview, 1989.

Weston, Burns. 1987. "The Reagan Administration Versus International Law." *Case Western Reserve Journal of International Law* 19: 295–302.

Wideman, John Edgar. 1984. *Brothers and Keepers.* New York: Penguin.

Wilson, James Q., and James Hernnstein. 1985. *Crime and Human Nature.* Cambridge: Harvard University Press.

Wolfe, Alan. 1978. *The Seamy Side of Democracy.* New York: Longman.

*Joseph A. Scimecca*

E  I  G  H  T  E  E  N

# Conflict Resolution and a Critique of "Alternative Dispute Resolution"

Although the study of conflict is most likely as old as antiquity—and Luce and Raiffa (1957) have even claimed that with the exception of love and God, more has been written on conflict than any other subject—systematic inquiry into conflict is a more recent development and is usually traced to the works of Karl Marx (1818–83) and Max Weber (1864–1920). Intervention in conflicts for the purpose of resolving them is an even more recent development, emerging only over the last quarter century. Examples of those who have attempted to systematically study and practice effective methods of conflict intervention are (1) at the *family* level '(Coogler, 1978; Haynes, 1981; Koopman, 1987; Saposnek, 1983); (2) at the *neighborhood* and *community* level (Laue, 1982, 1987; Pompa, 1987; Salem, 1982; Scimecca, 1988); (3) at the *labor-management* level (Blake et al., 1964; Colosi, 1987; Colosi and Berkely, 1986); (4) at the *environmental* level (Bacow and Wheeler, 1983; Bingham, 1985; Richman, 1987; Susskind and Wheeler, 1983; Susskind and Cruikshank, 1987); and (5) at the *international* level (Burton, 1969, 1987; Curle, 1971; Doob and Fotz, 1973; Kelman, 1987; Wedge, 1969, 1970, 1971).

The above mentioned theorists and practitioners along with numerous others are laying claim to the establishment of a new field, that of conflict intervention (Sandole and Scimecca, Forthcoming; Scimecca, In press). As is so often the case with emerging fields and disciplines, confusion reigns.

Little distinction is made between techniques and processes of conflict intervention being used, and very divergent social movements are lumped together under the generic term, "conflict resolution." For example, Richard Hofrichter—whose book *Neighborhood Justice in Capitalist Society* (1987) is one of the best of the radical criticisms of Neighborhood Justice Centers (where mediation services are offered as an alternative to formal court proceedings)—uses of conflict resolution as the descriptive term for what is practiced in these centers. He (Hofrichter, 1987: xxv) writes: "The major objective of conflict resolution . . . is not primarily justice but order-maintenance and problem solving. Formal legal procedures and authoritative judicial making obstruct the capacity to resolve a dispute; they merely impose a solution." This, indeed, may be what goes on in Neighborhood Justice Centers, but to label it conflict resolution points to a lack of understanding by Hofrichter. And he is not alone in his confusion. Conflict resolution has come to mean different things to different people. To the strategist it is the most sophisticated means of deterrence, even a first strike against a potential enemy if this seems necessary to prevent conflict. Resolving conflict for the lawyer is a court determination on the basis of legal norms and legal arguments, even the death penalty in some circumstances. For the industrial negotiator it is a settlement arrived at in a bargaining situation, even if it entails the loss of jobs. For the traditional mediator it involves a possible sense of injustice on the part of weaker parties (Burton, 1988).

In order to add some clarity to this state of confusion, a differentiation must be made between the various types of approaches which have all been subsumed under the general rubric of conflict resolution.

With this in mind, I differentiate between *conflict resolution, conflict management*, and *conflict settlement*, and then show that Alternative Dispute Resolution (ADR), which is the fastest growing phenomena in the legal system today and which is so often confused with conflict resolution, is *not* conflict resolution. ADR predominantly uses either the techniques of conflict management or conflict settlement, and because of this I will argue that the growing criticism of conflict resolution as a new form of social control (see Able, 1982; Cain, 1985; Hofrichter, 1987; Harrington and Merry, 1988) may very well apply to ADR but does not apply to conflict resolution.

## Conflict Resolution, Conflict Management, and Conflict Settlement: Brief Definitions

In differentiating between conflict resolution, conflict management and conflict settlement, I rely on the work of John Burton (1979, 1987, 1988, 1990), who is considered a pioneer by those who see themselves in the field of conflict intervention. Burton defines conflict resolution in direct opposition to conflict settlement and conflict management. For him, conflict resolution entails the use of collaborative problem-solving in a situation where a neutral third party helps the disputants engaged in facilitation or mediation. Conflict resolution is an analytical process that tries to get to the root of the problem. It aims not merely to resolve the immediate conflict but also to provide insights into the generic nature of the problem, thereby contributing to the elimination of the sources and the prevention of other instances in which the conflict might return (Burton, 1988, 1990).

The distinction between *conflict resolution* and *conflict settlement* is that the former brings about an outcome that is self-supporting and stable because it solves the problem which produced the conflict, whereas the latter fosters an outcome which does not necessarily meet the needs of all concerned. A settlement of a conflict is accepted at the time because of the jurisdiction of a court, the superior bargaining power of the opposing party, or some coercive threat that has been exercised by the opposing party or by a third party.

*Conflict management*, for Burton (1979, 1987, 1990), implies that conflict is an organizational problem, one that can be managed by changing conditions within social institutions. For example, an argument between two workers in an agency can be managed by such means as transferring one or the other, changing some of their work conditions, providing more staff help, etc. For the most part, though, no real structural changes in the conditions that produced the conflict are altered. It is their conflict that is managed, not the conflict that is produced by the workplace (Burton, 1987).

It must be pointed out that Burton's definitions are nowhere near universally accepted, not even by those who have collaborated with him. Dennis Sandole, for example—a coauthor and colleague of Burton and coeditor of what is generally considered to be the first comprehensive reader in the field, *Conflict Management and Problem Solving: Interpersonal to International Applications*—uses the terms conflict management and conflict resolution synonymously and states that conflict management is "more comprehensive than conflict resolution" (1987: 4). Yet, if there is to be some semblance of order in the field of conflict intervention, clarity of terms is essential; and, in my view, Burton, by differentiating between the various techniques, moves us further along the road to clarity than anyone else presently writing on the subject. Therefore, relying heavily on Burton, I propose the following differentiation between *conflict resolution, conflict management,* and *conflict settlement:* manner:

> *Conflict resolution* entails the use of collaborative problem solving in a situation where a neutral third party helps the disputants engage in conciliation, facilitation, and/or mediation. The resolution contributes to the elimination of the sources of the conflict.
> *Conflict management* implies that conflict is an organizational problem, one that can be managed by changing conditions within social institutions. No real structural changes occur in the conditions that produced the conflict.
> *Conflict settlement* fosters an outcome which does not necessarily meet the

needs of all concerned but is accepted for the time because of coercion by a stronger party.

## Conflict Resolution as Collaborative Problem-Solving

Conflict resolution, then, as I am defining it, is an interdisciplinary process of analysis and intervention which is concerned with solving problems which result in destructive conflict. It starts from the premise that traditional strategies of bargaining and negotiation, where one party gains at the expense of the other, sometimes "settles" conflicts but does not "resolve" them. A simple example of this can be seen in a family situation. Imagine a husband and a wife in a conflicted situation, and further imagine that the husband has all the resources at his disposal (He works, she doesn't; he controls the money, etc.). He, then, imposes his will upon her and they "settle" their dispute his way. But do they "resolve" it? The chances are that she will harbor resentment; and eventually the conflict will surface again, perhaps leading to greater conflict, maybe even a divorce. How much different is this from a superpower like the United States or the Soviet Union imposing its will on a lesser power?

The origins of conflict resolution as collaborative problem solving can be traced to developments in industrial relations in the 1960s. Conflict in industry had traditionally been handled by forms of bargaining and negotiation where both parties to the conflict or dispute tried to gain as much as they could and give up as little as they had to. Most classical organizational theorists (Mooney and Reiley, 1939; Taylor, 1911) had looked at organizations as closed systems, assuming that conflict was disruptive and detrimental to the organization's functioning. Of the classical organizational and industrial theorists only Mary Parker Follet (1940) recognized the possible constructive possibilities for conflict within organizations. She (Follet, 1940: 30–31) wrote that instead of condemning conflict:

> . . . we should set it to work for us. . . . What does the mechanical engineer do with friction? Of course his chief job is to eliminate friction, but it is true that he also capitalizes friction. The transmission of power by belts depends on friction between the belt and the pulley. The friction between the driving wheel of the locomotive and the track is necessary to haul the train. All polishing is done by friction. The music of the violin we get by friction. We left the savage state when we discovered fire by friction. We talk of friction of mind on mind as a good thing. . . . We have to know when to try to eliminate friction and when to capitalize it, when to see what work we can make it do.

Follet recommended integrative problem-solving rather than suppression as a preferred conflict management tool (Alban, 1987).

It was not until the mid-fifties that the transition took place to what

Robbins (1974) refers to as the "behavioralist's school of organizational behavior," where conflict was viewed as an inevitable and integral aspect of productive organizations. Much of this new view of conflict is attributable to sociologist Lewis Coser, whose book, *The Functions of Social Conflict* (1956), introduced the German social philosopher Georg Simmel (1858–1918) to the American social-science and organizational-behavior literature.

The handling of conflicts lagged about a decade behind this new look at conflict, and not until the mid-sixties was the resolution of conflict in industry thought of in anything but the traditional forms of power-bargaining and negotiation where each side sought to impose its will on the other. But then social scientists and management consultants began to point to the need for some type of cooperative interaction between concerned parties, something they claimed would lead to increased productivity. This represented a real break from the authoritarian model of management, and along with it came the realization that stable solutions to labor-management problems required some type of accommodation to the needs of both sides. Zero-sum solutions, where one party gains at the expense of the other, were seen as ineffective and inefficient. If short-term settlements, and not long-term resolutions, were the only result, the same problems would surface at the next bargaining session. Indeed, oftentimes the subsequent bargaining sessions became more bitter as the party which perceived itself as losing in the previous round of bargaining now sought to make up for its losses and win even more than its adversary had previously won. For those who were studying this process of the acceleration of conflict, the logical next step was to call for decisions which would be made as the result of cooperation among the parties concerned.

In particular, Blake, Shepard, and Mouton (1964) began to take a new approach to conflict and describe divergent techniques for dealing with conflict. They isolated five ways. The first is withdrawal. A second way is to try and smooth over the differences that are seen as the basis of the dispute. Third, one or more parties to a conflict may force a win or lose resolution. The fourth way is the most commonly used approach, that of compromise. These four ways, however, are problematic, in that, with the possible exception of total withdrawal, the conflict will occur again. In order to resolve conflicts so that they will not reoccur, Blake, Shepard, and Mouton (1964) advocated a fifth way: the use of a problem-solving attitude, similar to what had been called for by Follet.

The insights which came from the conflict resolution pioneers in the industrial area were never fully incorporated in labor-management bargaining as evidence by the fact that most collective bargaining still proceeds much the same as it did two or three decades ago. Nevertheless, the rudimentary processes of collaborative problem-solving did spread somewhat, particularly in the international arena. In the mid-sixties, a group of international lawyers at the David Davis Institute in London published a white paper which stated that such traditional conflict-settlement processes and institutions—as judicial settlement, mediation, arbitration, negotiation, and the other means which were a part of the United Nations Charter— were not being used effectively. The lawyers concluded that the major problem was not with the mechanisms available for resolution but was rather an unwillingness on the part of governments to properly use these processes. They called for more effective use of traditional mechanisms of conflict resolution.

The white paper produced a heated debate, with academics at the Centre for the Analysis of Conflict in London taking the position that the traditional means of conflict resolution were not working, not because of any unwillingness to use them but because they were based on false premises. Under the leadership of John Burton, a former Australian Permanent Foreign Se... etary and a participant in the U.N. Charter Conference in 1945, the Centre for the Analysis of Conflict set out to falsify the proposition raised by the Davis Institute that disputing parties were unwilling to cooperate in resolving conflicts. To do so, the Centre began with two hypotheses: (1) parties to disputes would use suitable institutions to resolve conflicts if they were available; and (2) the existing institutions (courts, mediation, arbitration, etc.) were not acceptable to all parties because responsible authorities would not hand over decision making on matters of important concern to an outside body, but they would instead be amenable to trying to resolve conflicts in an exploratory and analytical manner in a neutral setting.

To test this, the Centre advocated a whole new process, one based on the work of Blake, Shepard and Mouton (1964) which would require a neutral and skilled third party. The Centre expanded this to a panel of facilitators who would help the disputing parties arrive at a mutually agreed upon solution to their conflict. Burton and his colleagues are credited with instituting the first "international problem solving workshop," which they labeled "Controlled Communication Workshops" (Burton, 1969). This term referred to the role played by the panel of facilitators who were there to insure that a dialogue free of traditional, zero-sum, power bargaining and negotiation could take place. It was the primary job of the facilitators to insure that acceptable outcomes to the conflicting parties would evolve from the meetings.

The first workshop took place in 1965, when Burton, with the approval of the prime minister of Great Britain, Harold Wilson, invited representatives from Indonesia, Malaysia, and Singapore, countries which were then involved in continuous violent conflict. These governments had previously refused an invitation by Prime Minister Wilson to meet. The panel of facilitators consisted of ten scholars and included one American, the Harvard University international lawyer, Roger Fisher.

The workshop meetings lasted over a week, and after some follow-up by the Centre, all three governments advised the Centre that no further assistance was necessary. Although it is impossible to say that the workshops were directly responsible, fighting between the three parties stopped shortly thereafter.

The Centre for Conflict Analysis continued its research into conflict resolution and the use of problem solving workshops. And in 1966, when the United Nations official in charge of the Cyprus negotiations, the Nobel Peace Prize winner, Ralph Bunche, could not persuade the Greek and Turkish Cypriots to meet together, the Centre asked the conflicting parties to meet, and they did so. Once again, the panel was composed of ten scholars. Three representatives from the social science community of the United States were among the ten: Chadwick Alger of Ohio State University (International Relations), Herbert Kelman of Harvard University (Psychology), and Robert North of Stanford University (International Relations). The Greek and Cypriot representatives requested further meetings, but it was felt at the time that this would interfere with U.N.' procedures. Although no positive conflict resolution results came out of this workshop, it was still important in that valuable research was accumulated (see Burton, 1969). The inclusion of Americans also enabled the techniques in international conflict resolution to spread beyond Great Britain to the United States. Fisher, Kelman, Alger, and North are all considered to be among the leading American conflict intervention scholars; and Fisher's coauthored book, *Getting to Yes* (1981), was not only an immediate bestseller but has also become a valuable handbook for practitioners. John Burton came to the United States in 1984 as a visiting professor at the University of Maryland's Center for International Development; and since 1985, he has been on the faculty at the Center for Conflict Analysis and Resolution at George Mason University. It should be noted, too, that the informal processes developed in the international workshops of Burton and his colleagues has evolved into what is now called "second track diplomacy," which is being taught by the United States Foreign Service Institute (McDonald and Bendahmane, 1987). In this process, informal negotiations are run parallel to formal negotiations and nonofficial representatives of governments can state concerns and offer creative options that they could not in a formal negotiation process.

In the mid-sixties, in a parallel development, Leonard Doob and William Fotz of Yale University, independent of what was occurring in England, began to consider the need for an alternative approach to traditional methods of dealing with border disputes. Their first workshop took place in August of 1969 (Doob and Fotz, 1973). Subsequently, Herbert Kelman (1972, 1982, 1987) began to work out an approach that is a synthesis of Burton's and Doob's technique.

Although the refinement of the practices of collaborative problem-solving has been an important part of the development of what I am calling conflict resolution, *the* most important development has been the undergirding of conflict resolution upon a theoretical base. Burton (1979, 1984, 1990a), along with his colleagues at the Center for the Analysis of Conflict in

London and more recently at George Mason University in Virginia (Burton, 1990a), has been developing a theory of conflict resolution which starts from the premise that there are universal, inviolable, human needs which when thwarted result in deep-rooted conflicts.

## Conflict Resolution and Human Needs

Although a human needs approach to theory has been a part of social science for quite some time—indeed has provided the foundation for the "Goals, Processes, and Indicators of Development" (GPID) project of the United Nations University, which resulted in a major publication, *Human Needs*, edited by Katrina Lederer (1980)—it is the name of John Burton who is most often associated with human needs theory when one speaks of conflict resolution. Burton's human needs theory of conflict resolution draws on the humanistic psychology of Abraham H. Maslow (1954), the sociology of Paul Sites (1973) and Stephen Box (1971), and the sociobiology of Edwin O. Wilson (1975), to formulate a theory of conflict and conflict resolution based on the premise that individuals seek to fulfill a set of universal needs which, when thwarted, result in deep-rooted and protracted conflicts.

In *Deviance, Terrorism and War* (1979: 72–73), his clearest statement to date of his theoretical framework, Burton discusses nine distinct universal human needs. They are:

1. *A need for consistency in response.* Only through consistent responses can there be learning and consistency in behavior.

2. *A need for stimulation.* This is the other side of the coin to consistency in response. The individual must be stimulated in order to learn.

3. *A need for security.* Without security there is a withdrawal from response and stimulation.

4. *A need for recognition.* Through recognition the individual receives confirmation that his or her reactions to stimulation are approved. Recognition also provides the encouragement factor in learning.

5. *A need for distributive justice.* Distributive justice provides an appropriate response or reward in terms of experience and expectations.

6. *A need to appear rational and develop rationality.* This follows from the need for consistency of response. Rationality is a function of the behavior of others. Inconsistent responses invoke irrationality.

7. *A need for meaningful responses.* Unless responses are meaningful to the individual they will be interpreted as inconsistent.

8. *A need for a sense of control.* Control is a defense mechanism; if the other needs are met there is no need for control. Since the other needs are never fully met, the ability to control rather than react to the social environment is consequently a need.

9. *A need to defend one's role.* The individual has a need to secure a role

and to preserve a role by which he or she acquires and maintains recognition, security and stimulation.

The first eight are taken from Sites (1973) and, the last, *role defense*, Burton adds to the list.

By looking to human needs as the source of conflict, Burton offers a radical alternative to traditional means of dealing with conflicts. For him there can be no resolution of conflict without analyzing the underlying issues that generate the conflict. Thus there can be no resolution of conflict unless it takes into consideration the political realities of those parties in conflict. In short, a basic assumption of Burton is that unless the human needs of individuals and groups are satisfied, no matter what form or degree of coercion is exercised, there will be no societal stability. Deep-rooted conflicts are an indication, not only that something is wrong in a society, but also that the conflicts will continue unless the needs are met. Although it is too early to tell what will eventually transpire as totalitarian after totalitarian regime topples in Eastern Europe, from Burton's perspective such political upheavals are the inevitable result of thwarted human needs. Conflict resolution, thus, is much different from conflict management, from conflict settlement, and from that with which it is so often confused—Alternative Dispute Resolution (ADR).

## Alternative Dispute Resolution (ADR)

ADR is best seen as an attempt at reforming the administration of justice in the United States. Sometimes called "Delegalization," it represents a movement away from the formal, adversarial proceedings of the courts toward informal processes.

Although ADR is not, by any means, new—its roots can be traced back to colonial times (Auerbach, 1983) and its more modern form to the mid-nineteenth century (Harrington, 1982; Whiting, 1988)—nevertheless, its phenomena growth raises some exceedingly important questions, perhaps the most important of which is its relationship to societal mechanisms of social control. Before confronting this relationship, however, more background information on ADR is needed.

ADR's beginnings are usually traced to the 1970s (Adler, 1987). A major impetus for its rapid growth was the 1976 National Conference on the Causes of Popular Dissatisfaction with the Administration of Justice, sponsored by the American Bar Association. The conference concluded that alternative forms of dispute resolution, in particular mediation and arbitration, would ease congested courts, reduce settlement time, and minimize costs. The development of Neighborhood Justice Centers (which practiced mediation) and Multi-Door–Courthouse programs (which directed disputants to the most appropriate dispute resolving mechanism: litigation, mediation, or arbitration) were encouraged. Today there are over 350 alternative dispute resolution programs in the United States ranging from community justice centers to the Federal Mediation and Conciliation Center. About a third of these are run by or are closely connected to the courts; another third are connected to the prosecutor's office; and the remaining third are community- or church-based. The number of mediators engaged in this practice has increased from approximately 2,500 in 1976 to well over 20,000 (Sandole, 1985).

ADR, like other terms in conflict resolution, has been very broadly and loosely defined. For example, the National Institute for Dispute Resolution, under the sponsorship of the U.S. Department of Justice, convened an Ad Hoc Panel on Dispute Resolution and Public Policy in 1983 and defined its scope of inquiry as "all methods, practices, and techniques, formal and informal, within and outside the courts, that are used to resolve disputes" (*Administrative Conference of the United States*, 1987: 12). In short, ADR was officially seen as encompassing all of the major processes which are now being used to deal with disputes (*Administrative Conference*, 1987: 44–46). The following were listed:

> *Arbitration.* Widely used in labor-management disputes, where a neutral third party renders a decision after hearing arguments and reviewing evidence.
>
> *Court-Annexed Arbitration.* Judges refer civil suits to arbitrators who render prompt, non-binding decisions. The option is available to return to court if a party or both parties are not satisfied with the decision.
>
> *Conciliation.* An informal process in which the third party tries to bring the disputants to agreement by lowering tensions, improving communications, interpreting issues, exploring potential solutions and in general trying to bring about some sort of negotiated settlement.
>
> *Facilitation.* Where the facilitator functions as a neutral process expert to help parties reach mutually accepted agreements. The facilitator avoids making any substantive contributions.
>
> *Fact-Finding.* Where a fact-finder, drawing on both information provided by the parties and additional research, recommends a resolution of each outstanding issue. It is typically non-binding and paves the way for further negotiations and mediations.
>
> *Med-Arb.* A third party is authorized by the disputants to serve first as a mediator and then as an arbitrator empowered to decide any issues should mediation not bring about a satisfactory settlement.
>
> *Mediation.* A structured process in which the mediator (a neutral third party) assists the disputants to reach a negotiated settlement of their dispute. The mediator is not empowered to render a decision.
>
> *Mini-Trial.* A privately developed method used to bring about a negotiated settlement in lieu of corporate litigation. Attorneys present their cases before managers with authority to settle, and most often a neutral advisor is present (usually a retired judge or another lawyer).
>
> *Multi-Door Center (or Multi-Door Courthouse).* Offers a variety of dispute

resolution services in one place with a single intake desk which screens clients.

*Negotiated Investment Strategy.* A mediation process which brings together federal, state, and local officials and community members to resolve differences, disputes and problems related to the allocation and use of public resources.

*Negotiation.* A process where two parties bargain with each other.

*Neighborhood Justice Center (NJC).* Local dispute resolution centers. Deals primarily with disputes among individuals in ongoing relationships.

*Ombudsman.* A third party employed by an institution to handle the grievances of its employees or constituents. The ombudsman can either be empowered to take action directly or to bring suggestions to those in decision-making positions in the institution.

*Public Policy Dialogue and Negotiations.* Primarily aimed at bringing together representatives of business, public interest groups and government to explore regulatory matters.

*Rent-a-Judge.* Process by which the court can refer a pending lawsuit to a private neutral party for trial, as if it were being tried in a regular court. The verdict can be appealed through regular court appellate system.

If the ad hoc panel's definition of what constitutes ADR is accepted there can be no "alternative" dispute resolution because every conceivable dispute resolution technique is encompassed by the panel's definition. With this in mind, and to sharpen the distinction between Conflict Resolution and ADR, I define ADR as: those processes which are alternatives to the formal legal or court system, in particular, Neighborhood Justice Centers (NCJs) or Community Mediation Centers (CMCs). My definition serves a twofold purpose: first of all, by narrowing the scope of ADR it enables us to differentiate between quite different approaches to conflict, something that both critics and supporters have failed to do; secondly, it enables me to better examine the blanket criticisms of conflict resolution that have been made, thereby differentiating between which criticisms hold for which process or movement.

## Conflict Resolution, ADR, and Social Control

Of all the conflict intervention processes, ADR has generated the most criticism. In particular, ADR has been vulnerable to the criticism that those forms of ADR attached to courts and even non–court-attached Neighborhood or Community Dispute Centers (NDCs and CDCs) are "primarily institutions of state political and social control" (Hufrichter, 1987: xiv). Although there are numerous other criticisms of ADR, ranging from whether it is speedier than formal court proceedings to whether or not the general public prefers it to the formal court structure, it is those criticisms that relate to its being a mechanism for social control that are the most important for understanding whether ADR holds out any real potential for peacemaking. I will, therefore, concentrate only on those specific criticisms that relate ADR to social control.

In searching the literature, I have isolated what I consider to be the six most important criticisms of ADR as a mechanism for social control. I will present these criticisms and argue that, although they may pertain to ADR, they do not hold for collaborative problem-solving conflict resolution.

The first and one important criticism of ADR is that it lacks a reasoned justification that arises out of any broad concept of conflict (Burton, 1990). ADR is simply a number of different processes used by NDCs and CDCs. Indeed, this is why "dispute" as a term is employed rather than "conflict." The justification for using ADR and the processes employed are based more in the legal tradition and in the experience of the individual practitioner than in any theoretical framework. As a consequence, there is an overemphasis on process, unsupported by articulated insights into the generic nature of different disputes. ADR emphasizes the *how* to deal with conflict, and in most instances without any real theoretical justification for *when* and *why* to use conflict intervention techniques. This blind faith in the *how* of the processes, without any understanding of the *when* and *why* (which would be present if ADR had a theoretical foundation), makes it particularly vulnerable to the social control criticism. Collaborative problem-solving conflict resolution, on the other hand, because it is based on a theory of human needs, is anything but social control. The theory states explicitly that thwarted human needs produce conflict and points to the need for social change (Burton, 1990; Scimecca, 1990).

A second criticism of ADR is that like formal law, it is embedded in individualism. As such, the fundamental principle of individual responsibility is seen as the cause of the conflict (Abel, 1982). This focus enhances social control by not looking to inequalities in the society as a reason for conflict. Grievances are trivialized and the basic social structure is not questioned. Insofar as practitioners provide satisfaction with the services they have to sell to clients at one social level or another, it is because these may be adequate for many superficial disputes, such as organizational management problems and some environmental problems. However, their failures, when seemingly superficial problems turn out to have more deep-rooted sources, are not usually recorded. When this becomes apparent, as when a strike is not resolved or when a communal or international conflict escalates into violence and persists, failure is attributed, not to any inadequacy in theory or practice, but either to the alleged inherent complexities of the situation or to the irrational preferences which the individual disputants bring to the conflict. The assumption is that rational individuals should be able to resolve their conflicts, and if they cannot, then the problem lies with them. Here, again, I would support this criticism of ADR; and again, I would argue that it does not hold for conflict resolution. Conflict resolution, by focusing upon human needs and how they are thwarted by social structures, offers a theoretical framework which takes into consideration culture, class, race, and gender (Avruch and Black, In press; Rubenstein, 1990). Quite simply, when social structures and human needs are in conflict, it is the social structures that must change according to conflict resolution.

A third criticism relates to ADRs' emphasis upon misunderstandings as opposed to questions of power and structure (Hofrichter, 1987). ADR has concentrated on particular types of disputes—organizational, industrial, matrimonial, communal, environmental, and others—which do not involve widespread violence, confrontations with authorities, or defiance of legal norms. These conflicts limit the role of the third party to helping conduct discussion and to pointing out the misunderstandings in communication that arise. The underlying assumption is that the parties themselves have sufficient insight into both the nature of their conflict and possible options to find an agreed outcome that will be lasting. All that is required and provided is a process which helps communication between disputants. However, as U.S. Court of Appeals Judge Harry Edwards (1986: 668) reminds us: "It is a fact of political life that many disputes reflect sharply contrasting views about fundamental public values that can never be eliminated by techniques that encourage disputants to 'understand' each other. Indeed, many disputants understand their opponents all too well." Although conflict resolution also seeks to get the parties to understand their problems, it does so not by focusing on miscommunication but by emphasizing an understanding of the nature of conflict and its sources: institutional, human, cultural, and others (Burton, 1988).

A fourth criticism of ADR revolves around the question of neutrality. The supposed neutrality of the third party favors compromise and conceals the fact that values which confirm the existing advantages between unequals is necessarily biased (Laue, 1982). Very few, if any, practitioners of ADR challenge the neutrality position; for them it is an unexamined assumption. As such, their neutrality supports the status quo, no matter how unequal it may be. Conflict resolution, on the other hand, seeks to empower the subordinate party (Laue, 1982). As I have stated elsewhere (Scimecca, 1987; 30): "there are no neutrals in the conflict resolution process . . . all intervenors alter the power configurations between disputing parties, and . . . this alteration should be one of empowerment of the powerless."

The fifth criticism holds that ADR has lost sight of its original purpose: its concern for the poor, for all those who did not have access to the law (Harrington and Merry, 1988). The prime focus of ADR is seen as organizational expansion and as the carving out of profitable jobs for new professionals. Along these lines, it has been argued that the American Bar Association's interest in ADR has less to do with providing alternatives to the law than with opening up new sources of revenue for lawyers. My view of this criticism is mixed because although numerous NDCs and CDCs have been expanding bureaucratically, most others have remained small and have not created many jobs. As for the ABA, although there is no specific data, there is also no reason, given the history of the ABA, to doubt that the criticism is correct. Conflict resolution, by emphasizing the fulfillment of human needs as its main focus, though, remains immune to this criticism.

The sixth and last criticism is that, more than an alternative to courts, ADR represents an alternative to politics and community organizing which lacks any organic connection to communities. Originally conceived to offer justice in communities by those who comprise the community, it has let itself become the province of professionals (Tomasic and Feeley, 1982). Here, too, I have mixed feelings. Although I would like to see grass-roots justice dispensed within communities, I also believe that people who are trained for twelve to forty hours in conflict intervention techniques are nowhere near adequately prepared to resolve conflicts. At best, they can deal with minor superficial disputes—which paradoxically leaves them vulnerable to the criticism that they do not deal with structural issues—and at worst, they can do real harm. Learning how to practice conflict resolution takes years of learning and practice, and this is what professionals are: individuals with advanced knowledge and training. Here I must opt for professionals trained in collaborative problem-solving conflict resolution.

To conclude, I am basically in agreement with those critics of ADR who see it as yet another mechanism for social control. However, I hope that I have made a convincing argument that conflict resolution is very different from ADR in that conflict resolution offers tremendous potential for peacemaking and the establishment of social equality. Although conflict resolution is still in its infancy, it offers an important prospect for peacemaking. And as better and more comprehensive theoretical frameworks are formulated and more and more research is accumulated concerning the causes of conflict and the processes of its resolution, the hope is held out that deep-rooted conflicts and social injustice which characterizes a great deal of the world today, may be altered by the peacemaking possibilities of conflict resolution.

## REFERENCES

Abel, R. (ed.) 1982. *The Politics of Informal Justice*, Vol. I. New York: Academic Press.
———. 1982. "The Contradictions of Informal Justice." In R. Able (ed.), *The Politics of Informal Justice*. New York: Academic Press.
Adler, P. S. 1987. "Is ADR a Social Movement?" *Negotiation Journal* 3 (January): 59–71.
Administrative Conference of the United States. 1987. *Sourcebook: Federal Agency Use of Alternative Means of Dispute Resolution*. Washington, D.C.: Office of the Chairman.
Alban, B. 1987. "The Evolution of Intraorganization Conflict Management: A Synoptic Review." Unpublished paper, George Washington University.

Auerbach, J. 1983. *Justice without Law.* New York: Oxford University Press.
Avruch, K., and P. W. Black. In press. "The Conception of the Person in Conflict Resolution." *Negotiation Journal.*
Bacow, L. and M. Wheeler. 1984. *Environmental Dispute Resolution.* New York: Plenum.
Bingham, G. 1985. *Resolving Environmental Disputes: A Decade of Experience.* Washington, D.C.: The Conservation Foundation.
Blake, R. R., H. A. Shepard, and J. S. Mouton. 1964. *Managing Intergroup Conflict in Industry.* Houston: Gulf.
Box, S. 1971. *Deviance, Reality and Society.* New York: Holt, Rinehart and Winston.
Burton, J. W. 1969. *Conflict and Communication: The Use of Controlled Communication in International Relations.* London: Macmillan.
———. 1979. *Deviance, Terrorism, and War: The Process of Solving Unsolved Social and Political Problems.* New York: St. Martin's Press.
———. 1984. *Global Conflict: The Domestic Sources of International Conflict.* Brighton, Sussex: Wheatsheaf Books, LTD.
———. 1987. *Resolving Deep-Rooted Conflict: A Handbook.* Lanham, Md.: University Press of America.
———. 1988. "Conflict Resolution as a Political System." Working Paper 1, Center of Conflict Analysis and Resolution, George Mason University, Fairfax, Va.
———. 1990. *Conflict and Prevention.* London: Macmillan.
———. 1990a. "The Need for Human Needs Theory." In J. W. Burton (ed.), *Human Needs and Conflict Resolution.* London: Macmillan.
Cain, M. 1985. "Beyond Informal Justice." *Contemporary Crises*, 1985: 335–73.
Colosi, T. R. 1987. "A Model for Negotiation and Mediation." In D. J. D. Sandole and I. Sandole-Staroste (eds.), *Conflict Management and Problem Solving: Interpersonal to International Applications.* London: Francis Pinter. New York: New York University Press.
Colosi, T. R., and A. E. Berkely. 1986. *Collective Bargaining: How it Works and Why.* New York: American Arbitration Association.
Coogler, O. J. 1978. *Structured Mediation in Divorce Settlements: A Handbook for Marital Mediators.* Lexington, Mass.: Lexington Books.
Coser, L. 1956. *The Functions of Social Conflict.* New York: Free Press.
Curle, A. 1971. *Making Peace.* London: Tavistock.
Doob, L. W., and W. Fotz. 1973. "The Belfast Workshop: The Application of a Group Technique to a Destructive Conflict." *Journal of Conflict Resolution* (4) 237–56.
———. 1987. "Conflicts." *International Journal of Group Tensions* (1–4) 15–27.
Edwards, H. T. 1986. "Alternative Dispute Resolution." *Harvard Law Review* (3) 1986: 668–84.
Fisher, R., and W. Ury. 1981. *Getting to Yes: Negotiating Agreement Without Giving In.* Boston: Houghton Mifflin.
Follet, M. P. 1940. In H. C. Metcalf and L. Urwick, (eds.), *The Collected Papers of Mary Parker Follet.* New York: Harper and Brothers.
Harrington, C. 1982. "Delegalization Reform Movements: A Historical Analysis." In R. Able (ed.), *The Politics of Informal Justice.* New York: Academic Press.
———. 1985. *Shadow Justice: The Ideology and Institutionalization of Alternatives to Court.* Westport, Conn.: Greenwood Press.
Harrington, C., and S. E. Merry. 1988. "Ideological Production: The Making of Community Mediation." *Law & Society Review* (4): 501–27.
Haynes, J. M. 1981. *Divorce Mediation: A Practical Guide for Therapists and Counselors.* New York: Springer.
Hofrichter, R. 1987. *Neighborhood Justice in Capitalist Society.* Westport, Conn.: Greenwood Press.

Kelman, H. C. 1972. "The Problem-Solving Workshop in Conflict Resolution." In R. L. Merrit (ed.), *Communication in International Politics.* Urbana: University of Illinois Press.
———. 1982. "Creating the Conditions for Israeli-Palestinian Negotiations." *Journal of Conflict Resolution* (1): 39–75.
———. 1987. "The Political Psychology of the Israeli-Palestinian Negotiations: How Can We Overcome the Barriers to a Negotiated Solution?" *Political Psychology* (3): 347–63.
Koopman, E. J. 1987. "Family Mediation: A Developmental Perspective on the Field." In D. J. D. Sandole and I. Sandole-Staroste (eds.), *Conflict Management and Problem Solving: Interpersonal to International Applications.* London: Francis Pinter. New York: New York University Press.
Laue, J. H. 1982. "Ethical Considerations in Choosing Intervention Roles." *Peace and Change,* (2-3): 29–41.
———. 1987. "The Emergency and Institutionalization of Third Party Roles in Conflict." In D. J. D. Sandole and I. Sandole-Staroste (eds.), *Conflict Management and Problem Solving: Interpersonal to International Applications.* London: Francis Pinter. New York: New York University Press.
Lederer, K. (ed.). 1980. *Human Needs.* Cambridge, Mass.: Oelgeschlager, Gunn & Hain, Publishers.
Luce, R. D., and H. Raiffa. *Games and Decision.* New York: John Wiley and Sons.
Maslow, A. H. 1954. *Motivation and Personality.* New York: Harper.
McDonald, J. W., Jr., and D. B. Bendahmane (eds.). *Conflict Resolution: Track Two Diplomacy.* Washington, D.C.: Center for the Study of Foreign Affairs, Foreign Service Institute, U.S. Department of State.
Mooney, J. D., and A. C. Reilly. 1939. *The Principles of Organization.* New York: Harper Brothers.
Pompa, G. G. 1987. "The Community Relations Service." In D. J. D. Sandole and I. Sandole-Staroste (eds.), *Conflict Management and Problem Solving: Interpersonal to International Applications.* London: Francis Pinter. New York: New York University Press.
Richman, R. 1987. "Environmental Mediation: An Alternative Dispute Settlement System." In D. J. D. Sandole and I. Sandole-Staroste (eds.), *Conflict Management and Problem Solving: Interpersonal to International Applications.* London: Francis Pinter. New York: New York University Press.
Robbins, S. P. 1974. *Managing Organizational Conflict.* Englewood Cliffs, N.J.: Prentice-Hall.
Rubenstein, R. 1990. "Class-Based Conflict Resolution." In J. W. Burton (ed.), *Human Needs and Conflict Resolution.* London: Macmillan.
Salem, R. A. 1982. "Community Dispute Resolution Through Outside Intervention." *Peace and Change* (2-3): 91–104.
Sandole, D. J. D. 1985. "Training and Teaching in a Field Whose 'Time Has Come': A Postgraduate Program in Conflict Management." In C. Cutrona (ed.), *The Elements of Good Practice in Dispute Resolution.* Washington, D.C.: Society of Professionals in Dispute Resolution (SPIDR).
———. 1987. "Introduction." In D. J. D. Sandole and I. Sandole-Staroste (eds.), *Conflict Management and Problem Solving: Interpersonal to International Applications.* London: Francis Pinter. New York: New York University Press.
Sandole, D. J. D., and I. Sandole-Staroste (eds.). 1987. *Conflict Management and Problem Solving: Interpersonal to International Applications.* London: Francis Pinter. New York: New York University Press.
Sandole, D. J. D., and J. A. Scimecca. Forthcoming. "Present at the Creation: Institutionalizing Postgraduate Programs in Conflict Analysis and Resolution." *Peace and Change.*

Saposnek, D. T. 1983. *Mediating Child Custody Disputes: A Systematic Guide for Family Therapists, Court Counselors, Attorneys, and Judges.* San Francisco: Jossey-Bass.

Scimecca, J. A. 1987. "Conflict Resolution: The Basis for Social Control or Social Change?" In D. J. D. Sandole and I. Sandole-Staroste (eds.), *Conflict Management and Problem Solving: Interpersonal to International Applications.* London: Francis Pinter. New York: New York University Press.

———. 1988. "Conflict Resolution: Not Just for the Children." *Peace in Action* (1): 20–23.

———. "Freedom and Reflexivity as Basic Human Needs." 1990. In J. W. Burton (ed.), *Human Needs and Conflict Resolution.* London: Macmillan.

———. "Conflict Resolution: The Emergence of a Field." In press. In K. Avruch, P. Black, and J. A. Scimecca (eds.), *Conflict Resolution: Cross Cultural Perspectives.* Westport, Conn.: Greenwood Press.

Sites, P. 1973. *Control, the Basis of Social Order.* New York: Dunellen.

Susskind, L. E. and M. Wheeler. 1983. *Resolving Environmental Regulatory Disputes.* Cambridge: Schenkman.

Susskind, L. E. and J. Cruikshank. 1987. *Breaking the Impasse: Consensual Approaches to Resolving Public Disputes.* New York: Basic Books.

Taylor, F. W. 1911. *Principles of Scientific Management.* New York: Harper and Brothers.

Tomasic, R., and N. M. Feeley (eds.). 1982. *Neighborhood Justice: Assessment of an Emerging Idea.* New York: Longman.

Wedge, B. 1969. "The Case Study of Student Political Violence: Brazil, 1964, and Dominican Republic, 1965." *World Politics* (2): 183–206.

———. 1970. "Communication Analysis and Comprehensive Diplomacy." *Social Education* (1): 19–27.

———. 1971. "A Psychiatric Model for Intercession in Intergroup Conflict." *Journal of Applied Behavioral Science* (7): 733–61.

Whiting, A. A. 1988. "The Use of Mediation as a Dispute Resolution Tool: An Historical and Scientific Examination of the Role and Process of Mediation." Unpublished dissertation, Syracuse University.

Wilson, E. O. 1975. *Sociobiology: A New Synthesis.* Cambridge: Harvard University Press.

*Lloyd Klein, Joan Luxenburg, and John Gunther*

N I N E T E E N

# Taking a Bite Out of Social Injustice

*Crime-Control Ideology and Its Peacemaking Potential*

The troops are assembled and ready to take the battlefield. Surveillance vehicles and armed infantrymen patrol the streets in a search and destroy mission. This situation is not a United States Government military action undertaken within a third world country somewhere around the world. On the contrary, these troops are actually citizens or hired private security personnel either self-delegated or entrusted with the responsibility for controlling a seemingly endless crime problem. This problem, as reflected in a growing concern over neighborhood safety, has several components.

First, community residents are agonizing over citizen victimization resulting from larger social problems (i.e., drug dependency, poverty, and systematic racial discrimination). Programs such as Crime Stoppers and Neighborhood (or Block) Watch, as well as auxiliary patrols, form the backbone of a purposefully combined criminal justice response toward the problem. Additionally, private security firms flourish in this age of dependence upon former police officers and trained security personnel (Cunningham and Taylor, 1986).

Second, systematic public-relations campaigns, guided by criminal justice personnel, seize upon this preoccupation with the crime problem. One of the more visible efforts, the McGruff campaign, promulgates an ideology supporting vigilance against the criminal element. The symbolic and ever-intense crime-dog crusades against lawbreakers in warning people about the potential for eventual victimization. This program is also noteworthy for promulgating other proactive and reactive efforts toward dealing with assaults on the general populace. Crime Stoppers, "America's Most Wanted," "Unsolved Mysteries," locally produced media campaigns (e.g., the *New York Daily News* Crime Fighter effort), and countless media-based efforts utilizing crime reenactment combine in this joint campaign. The informant approach has been utilized on network television (notably by NBC and the Fox Broadcasting Company); but it has also extended through local news programs around the country (e.g., New York, Los Angeles, Chicago, Milwaukee, and other major cities) and through newspaper publicity.

Third, mobilization against criminal violence (or potential victimization) is produced by alteration of fundamental relationships between people. Tough propaganda campaigns produce hatred and generate an aggressive reaction against particular people or groups. The citizenry implicitly accepts these messages and alters their individual outlook toward marginal social groups. Minorities or foreigners often become a priori suspects and are scapegoated in an encountered frustration toward the larger crime problem.

The criminal justice apparatus draws its strength from these altered citizen perceptions (Gross, 1985). The search for resolution of social conflict is an endless process. These divisions create an uncomfortable tension in the everyday lives of most people. Crime-control ideology emphasizes the pursuit of peace while framing its appeal in the form of belligerent social attitudes. Social injustice (and "mankind's inhumanity toward fellow citizens") is a resultant by-product stemming from this process.

How have newspaper campaigns, slick television productions, efforts of anticrime coalition groups, and the manipulation of Curtis Sliwa and other individuals produced and/or intensified these efforts? Analysis presented in this essay offers an examination of ideological messages associated with the crime-control campaign. An assessment will incorporate the nature of this process and how crime prevention efforts can potentially act as a force toward achieving peaceful resolution of social conflict rather than promoting mutual hatred.

## Crime-Prevention Efforts and Collective Behavior

Governmental authorities have historically condoned the excising of unwanted situations through either applied force or working toward purposeful isolation of a particular group. The *battles* are framed as sanctioned assaults upon socially undesirable situations (i.e., a *war* on drugs, *war* on crime, or *war* on illiteracy). A fundamental contradiction exists as we *attack* a problem in the process of formulating an acceptable solution. The formulated approach can take the form of co-opting citizens as legitimate "eyes and ears" of criminal justice authorities.

Criminal behavior has always existed as a deviant social category. Durkheim (1893) originally described the classification of criminal activity as a pathological state. This view was later reaffirmed by Lemert (1951) in an explanation of criminal behavior as a collective phenomenon. The labelling function is sustained by a collective consensus implicitly accepted by the general public. As a result, crime is interpreted as an expression of improper social reactions. The combination of the public reaction, along with purposeful criminal justice "target-hardening" efforts, sustains direct efforts against perceived antisocial behavior.

Programs encouraging the provision of citizen information are more visible in recent times. The criminal justice system, along with the cooperation of the citizenry, counterattacks against an enemy force. The rationale centers around a view that lawbreakers violate statutes specifically created for the maintenance of law and order. On one level, the state invokes all the weapons at its disposal in the targeting of criminal activity. This reactive stance consists of an attack on the crime problem through the imposition of deterrent measures. Fear of crime is an ever-present concern acting toward framing a justification of this philosophy. The threat of arrest, incarceration, and denial of social privileges encompasses a serious counterattack against the criminal element.

Criminal justice authorities manipulate crime-victimization statistics through selective reporting and interpretive statements. We consistently read about an ever growing number of robberies or violent crime committed with firearms. These trends are documented through releases by the Federal Bureau of Investigation, state criminal justice agencies, and city agencies (Flanagan and Jamieson, 1988).

On another level, comparisons between the domestic and international situation are inevitable. A larger social-control mechanism forms the basis for imposing ideological values. Harsh criminal penalties and nuclear capacity are equated in an interesting manner. These nuclear missiles form the equivalent of nuclear capability or (deterrence) and become designated as "peacekeepers." The resultant ideological approach involved with advancing this perspective emphasizes the need for programmed destruction, in order that we create a more desirable social system. Penitentiaries fulfill this role through the purposeful denigration ceremonies profiled by Goffman (1963). This contradiction ironically reflects a Marxist view that we must destroy the system before building a more perfect structure. Both sides are seeking peace from a similar perspective, but they invoke conflicting rhetoric.

Attaining peace through contradictory means is the object of this ongoing social exercise. A standard dictionary definition equates peace with security and order. The hard-line "justice-model" ideological view assumes that the fault is in the street criminal and not in society (Cullen and Gilbert, 1982). Street criminals are identified as undesirable and depersonalized names. Thus, peace is associated with the desired ends rather than with emphasizing the contradictory means through which the goal is sought.

Ideologically sustained citizen crime-patrols are predicated upon "citizen co-production of essential services." The police are the domestic link of the standing army, and citizen-patrol participants represent paramilitary reserves (i.e., the connection between the military and the National Guard). Citizens are deputized for the purpose of serving as a "posse." Collective citizens' efforts serve as the eyes and ears of the police force (Shearing and Stenning, 1987).

Law or custom has provided dual informal and formal norms of social conduct. Citizens are seeking peace through the social organization of ad hoc groups formed for the purpose of implementing a violent world-view upon the situation. An innate need for peace forms the underbelly of this mechanism. This mechanism, as utilized by the capitalist system, reinforces identification of the problem. The quest for peace is regarded as linked with diligence and aggression against the enemies of the capitalist system. The extensively imposed rhetoric, known as the war on crime, emphasizes the classic desire for peace. On the surface, peace is an ideal state of mind. Achievement of this ideal is difficult and merely serves as a vehicle for displaced motivations. Preventing violent crime is a "holy crusade" shared among members of the community and designated criminal justice authorities. Members within specific communities act out of a perceived need for preserving a state of security or order.

Certain prerequisites are necessary for acceptance of this democratized crime-fighting activity. First, the public must perceive that individual response is necessary for the potential resolution of potential or actual victimization. This condition is fulfilled through massive publicity surrounding the urban crime problem. Reiman (1984) shows that this hard-line rhetoric plays upon public concerns and creates a greater problem than might actually exist. Statistics, available in the FBI Uniform Crime Report (UCR), indicate that the average person has a 1 in 100 chance of potential victimization. The typical citizen, particularly someone watching television an average of 7 hours, 5 minutes per day, perceives his or her chances for criminal victimization as 1 in 10. Police dramas on television and the ongoing vigilante-film genre heighten the perception that victimization is a certainty. In reality, criminal victimization largely depends upon whether a person is in a given place at a given time.

Thus, the precedent is set for crime-prevention efforts as sponsored through public and private auspices. The new trend toward "tabloid television" emphatically decries the outrage of this "escalating" criminal violence. Phil Donahue, Geraldo Rivera, and other talk-show hosts thrive through exploitation of materials containing violent sexual or physical anecdotes. Additionally, "A Current Affair" offers a regular review of violent crimes against community residents. Interestingly, the most notorious program in this series consisted of videotaped material showing Robert Chambers, a convicted preppie killer in the Jennifer Levin murder case, engaged with several women in frivolous games.

"America's Most Wanted," a weekly series running on the Fox Network, has captured the attention of audience viewers from coast to coast. The program contains reenactment of several criminal incidents. The perpetrator is described in extensive detail. The public can offer information on the criminal's whereabouts via a toll free telephone number (*New York Times*, 1988). Additionally, the program offers its audience a recap of criminals captured through volunteered telephone tips from viewers.

This television program, hosted by John Walsh, whose child was a crime victim, galvanizes the attention of an indignant public. The collective behavioral dynamics center around offering a crime-wary public relief in the form of catharsis and social reinforcement. The public can identify a "bad guy" and actively seek out the profiled individuals in their own backyard. More importantly, regular viewers can find reinforcement through assurance that someone truly cares about a prevailing social problem.

One cautionary note is appropriate in this regard. The proffered offender-descriptions often result in the detainment and questioning of innocent people. One such case was documented in a prominently featured op-ed article within a major newspaper (*New York Times*, 1988b). A freelance writer was investigated by the FBI as a result of similar resemblance and profile with a wanted criminal. The man was subsequently cleared, but this case pointed out that innocent victims often become entrapped in these out-of-control public efforts.

The issue is clearly one of defining style over substance. The media campaigns play upon our predisposition toward accepting the legitimacy attributed toward the state. Analysis in the next section will concentrate upon an elaboration of the *thesis* (or original condition) that we are examining. Subsequent sections will pinpoint the alternatives *(antithesis)* and the culmination of these two conflicting processes *(synthesis)*.

## Sanctioned Surveillance and the Paramilitarization of America

Surveillance is an ongoing process of criminal justice law enforcement. Criminal justice authorities seek out and identify individuals or groups directly responsible for civil disturbance. As indicated earlier, citizens are called upon for assistance in this ever-present war on crime. The process through which citizens are directly involved in this battle has been termed "sanctioned surveillance" (Klein and King, 1982). Authorities encourage citizen participation through such devices as Crime Stoppers, Neighborhood Watch, and auxiliary patrols. Civilians function as law enforcement officers to the extent that they can spot a crime in progress and reactively contact the authorities.

The *paramilitarization* of America can take several forms. This section will focus on Crime Stoppers and the McGruff campaign (media efforts) and on the Guardian Angels (an organized citizen patrol).

Media efforts are highlighted by the development and encouragement of nationwide Crime Stoppers programs. Crime Stoppers originated in the mid-1970s through the effort of Albuquerque, New Mexico, law enforcement officials (Rosenbaum et al., 1989; Klein et al., 1983). The organization originally encouraged local community reporting of violent felony crime. Public-service announcements encouraged the reporting of violent felony crime. A further incentive was supplied through the awarding of monetary sums for information leading to apprehension and conviction of particular felons. The program has since spread to hundreds of cities throughout the United States and Canada.

The McGruff campaign was originally formulated back in the mid-1960s (Mendelsohn and O'Keefe, 1984). The intent was the creation of a public awareness program wherein both children and adults could relate to the messages. Problems addressed over the years include: teaching children that accepting candy or rides from strangers was wrong; warning adults about leaving their homes vulnerable to burglars; how citizen patrols deterred crime; and how some criminal activities were recognizable. More recently, both children and adults were warned about the dangers of using drugs. The overall campaign has also included rental of McGruff costumes. (One of the authors observed a Midwest bank promotion wherein McGruff was the feature attraction.) .

A third organization aimed at paramilitarization is the developed Guardian Angels, which was founded in 1975 by Curtis Sliwa and originally called the Magnificent 13—named for the small group formed by Sliwa, who was then a South Bronx, New York, manager of a McDonald's branch. The Guardian Angels have thrived on media exposure featuring tough talk by Curtis Sliwa and his wife Lisa (currently national president of the organization). Chapters ostensibly exist in hundreds of cities throughout the United States, Canada, and even some foreign countries. Kenney (1987) highlights citizen activism through an analysis of the New York City subway system. The Guardian Angels figured prominently in the conscientious law-enforcement efforts of the New York City Transit Authority. Sliwa challenged the system and eventually persuaded the authorities that the Guardian Angels patrol was an essential part of public mass-transit safety.

All three of the above discussed organizations—Crime Stoppers, McGruff, Guardian Angels—have certain attributes in common including (1) an expression of wish-fulfillment according to public opinion, (2) retaliation against crime while stressing obedience as underlying social behavior, and (3) an overt appeal toward the more basic human aggressive instincts. Perhaps an interesting way of characterizing the above factors is through one of Richard Quinney's remarks upon accepting the Edwin Sutherland Award (1984): "Be careful what you dream—soon your dreams will be dreaming you."

The American public is raised on violence through the media. Therefore it should come as no surprise that wish-fulfillment and public opinion become vital factors. The long-term success of the vigilante-film genre, especially popularized by the *Death Wish* series featuring Charles Bronson, subtly demonstrated how citizens can channel their active crime-fighting efforts into organized patrols. Public opinion was directed toward the plight of victims rather than the long-term Supreme Court decisions favoring the rights of the accused. Violence begat violence in an all-out effort against criminals perceived as public enemies. The famous Supreme Court decision in the case of Miranda vs. Arizona has been gradually tightened in favor of police enforcement. The recent Reagan Administration targeted the neutralization of these criminal protections as high on their agenda.

Retaliation against crime while stressing obedience is another important criterion in this analysis. These formulated programs directed at crime-control activity are intended as techniques for pacifying the public while involving them in the process. Rosenbaum (1986) indicates that many of these efforts are psychological processes aimed at containing citizen discontent as much as controlling criminality. Citizens must perceive that their needs are addressed. A failure in this regard will mean that the system loses its legitimate recognition. Reiman (1984), Sheley (1985), and Gorelick (1989) discuss similar trends within the continued public acceptance of an often inefficient criminal justice system. The populace must readily believe the rhetoric indicating that the system actually fulfills a significant function in our society.

Dubow et al. (1979) offer an important distinction between "crime control" and "crime prevention." "The former deals with a vigilance for criminal acts and efforts to apprehend, convict, and sentence violators." Crime prevention, on the other hand, involves efforts to "address the underlying social economic and environmental factors that foster crime" (Dubow et al., 1979: 71). Under crime control, Dubow and his associates list: collective surveillance of homes and streets, reporting of crimes or suspicious behaviors (including reward-reporting), education in self-defense, escort services, and the like. Under crime prevention, the same authors list programs for unemployed or idle youth and efforts to improve housing, recreational facilities, and other conditions that create incentives and opportunities for committing crime.

Our last criterion, an overt appeal toward more basic human instincts is important in this analysis. Human beings like to feel that they possess a certain degree of autonomy. Increased crime threatens their sense of well-being and promotes a lack of confidence in the overall social system. Criminal justice authorities must continually justify ever-increasing funding levels in annual budget requests. Local police departments highlight the growing incidence of violent crime. The call for more prisons—costing taxpayers billions of dollars per year ($25,000 per inmate housed in a given year and at least 53,000 inmates within the federal system)—is significant. Alternately, some small communities perceive prisons as instrumental in economic survival while others reject these facilities on the grounds of potential community problems.

The cumulative effect is that the state eventually becomes the big winner. Residents become dependent upon the state and directed efforts toward organizing citizens in achieving a safe local environment. Crime, rather than the state, is the enemy ostensibly under attack in these ongoing efforts. One must not lose sight of the fact that peacemaking is a state of mind *and* a social reality. Our quest for a comfortable place which we can call home is never-ending. The late Joseph Campbell directed us toward a succinct view of the process. The world emphasizes myths which are created by humans for ulterior purposes (i.e., social control). Campbell indicated, in a series of interviews telecast in 1988 after his death, that we must transcend these limitations in understanding our place in the world. Crime is one of the benchmarks by which people judge their safety and comfort.

Cohn et al. (1978) further clarify the important distinction between crime prevention and victimization prevention. They claim that crime prevention is reflected when neighborhood groups organize to prevent local conditions that were thought to breed crime. Efforts included providing jobs and recreational facilities for idle youth, removing abandoned houses, etc. To prevent victimization, individuals avoid dangerous areas, target-harden their homes, etc. Dubow, McCabe, and Kaplan (1979) have referred to these efforts as a "fortress mentality," where efforts are concentrated on self-protection and home-protection rather than on removing the root causes of crime. In effect, victimization prevention is "self-serving," while crime prevention is "social-science–serving."

Given these ideas as a thesis, we will turn toward possible alternatives in reevaluating this mythmaking process. We have suggested that citizen-patrol ideology perpetrates a myth that people can prove instrumental in controlling their fate. Further discussion of this trend, along with an antithesis stressing conflict-resolution processes and a synthesis suggesting resolution of these essential processes, will form the remainder of this essay.

## Nature of Conflict-Resolution Processes

The antithesis, or possible alternatives for the conditions described above, can find its roots in classical philosophical thought. Ellis (1971) pointed out the potential for Hobbesian order in an understanding of social conditions.

Hobbesian order had three basic components: normative theory, exchange theory, and coercion. Each component led toward the movement away from civil war and in the direction of civil peace.

The normative theoretical approach existed when norms and values were shared and internalized. This led to effectively mutual-rewarding and balanced relationships. The exchange approach emphasized that interdependency is vital for the sharing of scarce resources and positive relationships. Lastly, coercion was the end result when each party is equally powerful and could possibly destroy one another. Therefore, they must turn to a supra-group loyalty to impose a mutual agreement between the parties. Common-ground and pluralistic relationships must be emphasized when cooperative efforts or competing groups dominate the situation. These coercive efforts took the form of a social contract wherein a mediating force, government (acting as a supra-group), constitutes itself as an intervening force between these countervailing interests.

Governmental force is essential in controlling human basic nature toward war as a natural state. Hobbes claimed that it is a general rule of reason that every man should seek peace. But when he cannot obtain peace, he may use all advantages of war. In the absence of common power (or a social contract), man is not responsible to law. If there is no common power, then there is no law. Where there is no law, there is no injustice and, therefore, no security.

These problems breed discontent among conflicting groups. Basic human self-interest results in a virtual dissolution of the Hobbesian social contract. Government intervention is mistrusted among the collectivity. As a result, individual and collective efforts are instituted with the intent of supplementing and/or substituting formal measures of control. Such efforts include the organization of crime-control zealots represented by the Guardian Angels, urban street patrols, vigilantes burning down crack houses and other autonomous actors.

A cohesive context for placing this problem into a stronger focus exists within the social work model. The social-work model emerges as a method of understanding the impact of interventionist measures against such collectivities. The social-work perspective recognizes three models of community organization. In 1968, Jack Rothman introduced three models of community organizing for social-work practice (Rothman and Tropman, 1987). These are generally known as: locality development, social planning, and social action. The models guide macro-level social-work practice with communities.

We find several elements of all three models relevant to the current indigenous movements within communities to restore a sense of safety and well-being to residents who are particularly concerned about crack houses and crack pushers. The "invasion cycle of neighborhoods" (Horton and Hunt, 1972: 453) suggests that when a new "element" enters an existing neighborhood, it may go unnoticed initially. When residents take notice, they try to dissuade the members (a racial group, a new type of activity, etc.) from continuing to enter. If the community fails in their efforts, the new members either begin to outnumber the indigenous residents or, simply, are otherwise "taking over" (e.g., a factory, a halfway house, etc.). At this point, those who are able to begin to flee the neighborhood. A tipping point occurs, where the new element has replaced the former residents. The final stage of the invasion cycle allows the neighborhood to take shape, either to remain chaotic because of all that had taken place during the previous stages, or to remain stable. Clearly, only the beginning stages of this cycle apply to the "infiltration" of crack into comparatively crack-free neighborhoods. How the community chooses to resist the invasion is decisive for our discussion.

The community's efforts can be combative, feeding into the rhetoric of "invasion," "infiltration," etc. by the "enemy." Alternatively, communities can emerge in collaborative efforts with the authorities to problem-solve. Relevant aspects of the locality-development model that would assist communities include: the community's ability to organize to help solve its own problems, a high degree of consensus among segments of the community (allowing coalescence), and a recognition that the members of the power structure are working with them. The roles of the community organizer in the locality-development model are those of enabler and teacher of problem-solving skills. The enabler provides a sense of encouragement (and, thereby, empowerment) to replace frustration. The teacher role of the community organizer functions to provide concrete information regarding options for coping strategies, with the assumption that the capabilities are there but need to be cultivated.

The social-planning model conceptualizes the community organizer as a data gatherer and analyst working toward a rational, technical resolution of a substantive community problem. The atmosphere can either be one of consensus or conflict between the various segments of the community. In addition to fact-gathering, the community organizer may take on the task of proposing and implementing a course of action.

The social-action model views community inhabitants as "victims" of an oppressive power structure that puts the less advantaged into an even greater disadvantaged position. The goal of the community organizer is to help shift and redistribute the power. This can be done by focusing on issues and organizing demonstrations. In this model there is a conflict or contest approach that seeks confrontation and subsequent action. The primary roles of the community organizer are those of activist, advocate, and agitator. The movements of the 1960s for welfare rights and tenants' rights employed the social-action model. Very often the desperation of community residents resulted in an ideology of the "ends justify the means" (Alinsky, 1946).

With the aforementioned three models in mind, we suggest that, depending upon the resources held by a neighborhood and its history of success with responding to previous community problems, the members will employ strategies and tactics primarily associated with one of the models. Clearly, of the three models, the social-action one is the least conducive to peacemaking.

## Social Synthesis and the
## Potential for Peacemaking

Violent ends need not automatically result from a dependence upon the social-action model. The case of communities fighting crack is a perfect example of the various extremes. In Detroit two men were acquitted by a jury for torching a crack house. Angelo "Butch" Parisi and Perry Kent admitted that they burned down a Barlow Street crack house, but claimed it was done in self-defense, to rid the neighborhood of the danger posed by the house ("Geraldo," 1988; *Time Magazine*, 1989: 17).

Less drastic measures, less violent and more rational, include the actions of Molly Wetzel of Berkeley ("Oprah Winfrey," 1989; *Time*, 1989: 16). Wetzel and 17 of her neighbors (ages 3 to 65) filed suit in small-claims court (for a $6 fee) against a crack-house landlord for maintaining a "public nuisance." As a result the crack dealer was evicted by the landlord, and each plaintiff was awarded $1,000. Wetzel's precedent-setting suit inspired a similar action by a San Francisco group. Gary Brady of that group is collaborating with Wetzel to put together materials that will explain to others how to take similar action.

Going one step further (away from self-concern toward social concern) is Kimi Gray ("Oprah," 1989) who had to turn in her own crack-using son to the authorities. Gray, a veteran of the resident-management movement of public housing, is now active with the National Center for Enterprise. The organization puts out a manual to inform communities of how to start entrepreneurship programs for youth. According to Gray, the "drug problem" is only a symptom of a real problem—the economic state of the black community. Opportunities for selling crack, according to Gray, represent "the first time that black young men have a chance to be corporate leaders." In reality, the long hours, dangerous conditions, inevitability of self-destruction, etc. make the job of crack-dealing (for youth) not as lucrative as it is purported to be. Gray and her group can turn the same profit mentality that the adult drugpushers have used on the kids into a training ground for legitimate business sales. In some cases, the kids that Gray trains start with selling cookies.

Kimi Gray's approach to training would-be crack couriers for respectable enterprises has its roots in the tenant-management movement in which Gray has been active. Gray's approach to the underlying structural problems facing black communities, like her own, incorporates the principles of the locality-development model. Communities can help themselves. When Gray and her fellow tenants decided to manage their federally subsidized low-income housing project, they were able to teach the residents how to avoid property deterioration. Those who would not control their kids from criminal or vandalistic activity were evicted. New residents were screened carefully. Tenant management has "turned around" housing projects in St. Louis ("Sixty Minutes," 1986, 1987). Where activist Bertha Gilkey organized Cochran housing, Gilkey, in turn, took her message to other housing projects across the United States. Other successful tenant-management efforts include Mildred Hailey and Boston's Bromley-Heath (housing project), as well as Irene Johnson and Chicago's LeClaire Courts (*Newsweek,* 1989: 44). Such tenant groups not only have succeeded in preventing the decay of their surroundings, they have been able to institute a day-care center, job training, a private security force, free medical care (through local hospitals), and private grants to enroll in management-training classes (*Newsweek,* 1989: 44).

The tenant-management movement appears to have conformed closely to the social-action model in order to gain its initial impetus. Its reliance on data collection and rational planning, on screening tenants and formulating strict rules for residents, etc. incorporates the social-planning perspective. Its insistence that public-housing residents can manage their own projects, and only need to be given a chance to do so, illustrates aspects of the locality-development perspective.

When Gray turned her attention specifically to entrepreneurship-training for black youth, her focus was on the social-planning model. While the self-help spirit of the locality-development model is ever-present in the entrepreneurship program and in the assumption of economic power, redistribution (found in the social-action model) underlies the need to form the program, and specific strategies to accomplish its goals are clearly associated with the social-planning model. These models clearly demonstrate the potential for integrating the positive aspects of crime prevention into community organization. The last section of this paper introduces some of these salient notions and the possibility of achieving community independence from repressive crime-prevention programs.

## Empowerment, Advocacy, and Social Transformation

The notion that current crime-prevention efforts are a co-option into the capitalist order is a radical one. However, even more radical is the notion that appropriate methods of community organization can transform this co-option and confirmation of the capitalist order.

As has been previously noted, individuals in communities that have adopted the paramilitary approach to crime prevention focus on the symbolic message that they are generally being victimized by the criminal rather than by the state. This symbolic message thus becomes the standard by which community organization takes place and citizens engage in personal and political attempts to change their conditions to fight crime. This approach to crime prevention has an inherent failure built into it in that it does not bring about fundamental transformation in the societal system. Richard Flacks (1970) emphasizes this point:

> Fundamental social change in advanced industrial society is not initiated or mediated through the political system, nor is it likely to result from mass insurrections or rebellions. Instead, fundamental transformation occurs only after a prolonged period of ferment and conflict within the principal cultural, social and economic institutions.

While Flacks frames the essence of the current dilemma in crime prevention for communities, the tenets for a newer approach to community organization—which embody both the notions of community and societal transformation while acknowledging the inherent power of the state—are left unstated. To fill this void, the collective approach to community organization is suggested. Galper (1975) speaks about this approach as revolutionary in nature and as a potential building block to large-scale social change. The collective approach has strong strategy suggestions embedded in it that present an alternative to current crime-prevention strategies. The collective approach is a strong deterrent to the attributes of negative community valuations that exist in current crime-prevention strategies (i.e., expression of wish-fulfillment according to public opinion, retaliation against crime while stressing obedience as social behavior, and an overt appeal to aggressive instincts). Specific principles of the collective approach to crime prevention and community organization include:

1. A focused community collective dealing with a specific system (e.g., crime prevention) that has commitment and linkages to other small, focused collectives (e.g., economic development, housing and health coalitions). This principle recognizes that the problem is system-focused rather than problem-focused and that ultimately a broad-based coalition of interests will bring about major systems change.
2. Empowerment of individuals in the community affected by the system. The collective approach, by offering alternative explanations to communities, deflects the negative valuations given by the system which are ultimately "disempowering" for individuals.
3. By offering alternative empowered messages to communities, the structures that mediate changes in the social order (e.g., families and churches) are empowered to advocate for institutional transformation.
4. Finally, by empowering individuals, doing away with negative valuations of communities and advocating with other coalitions of interests, the stage is set for a reordering of priorities within the current social and economic order.

If we accept the tenets of the collective approach to community organizations, we recognize that true transformation and renewal of the social order can be brought about by individuals transforming in their own communities. If individuals empower themselves by not accepting the paramilitary alternatives (e.g., Crime Watch, McGruff) of the dominant society, they are thus able to present a self-determining collective alternative to the criminal justice system. In short, the community becomes the focus for dispensing community solutions, thus creating social and community control. Community-oriented conflict-resolution can become a new mechanism for social control that emphasizes not only crime prevention but transformation of the community in light of needed systemic changes, such as economic development, housing, and health. Thus, an empowered community is created that is ready to engage in proactive, primary crime prevention. Skogan (1986: 13) strongly emphasizes this point:

> Where community institutions are strong and cross-cutting, gossip, social exclusion, negotiation, and even mediation or arbitration by trusted figures can resolve disputes or contain their consequences. However, where community solidarity is so low that there are no viable mechanisms for resolving disputes informally, or where they do not embrace all major local groups, long-standing conflicts may undercut the social and economic forces underlying the neighborhood stability . . . Problem-solving mechanisms which rely upon self-initiated citizen action require community institutions which foster interaction and cooperation.

In summary, it becomes rather clear that current initiatives in the area of crime prevention are designed to sustain the dominant society's control over its citizenry. By engaging in the collective approach to community organization and emphasizing the process of empowerment, transformation, and advocacy, a newer approach to crime prevention in the community is suggested. The collective approach to crime prevention emphasizes system changes in multiple areas (e.g., economic development, housing, and health) as more effective strategies in preventing community crime. The choice is simple: McGruff and Crime-Watch programs or empowered communities!

This essay has explored the rise in crime-prevention programs drawn on the crime-control model and their eventual consequences. We have several real solutions and proposed potential methods of dealing with this ongoing social dilemma. Several points still require further emphasis and clarification as we complete this analysis.

First, we cannot underscore the need toward examining proactive alternatives before the problems engulf community settings. Specifically, community organization must take social conditions into account before accepting target-hardening as a *fait accompli*. Deficient education systems, poverty, underemployment and unemployment, insufficient healthcare systems, and unplanned pregnancies exacerbate an already strained urban setting. Community organizations must work toward dealing with these problems before casting their lot with attractive crime-control solutions. Imposed violence without accounting for the causes of the problem will merely result in a fight against an unconquerable foe (e.g., crime and its social consequences).

Secondly, many people accept violence against forces threatening the prevailing social order as the natural emotional panacea. These attitudes are hardened through constant reinforcement from criminal justice propaganda and media depictions of violent criminal activity. The domestic war against crime is promoted as actively as many foreign incursions by United States troops in overseas countries. An assault on the local crack house or against the MOVE group in Philadelphia is covered as a major tactical strike against an apparent enemy.

These trends fly in the face of conflicting messages. On one hand, President George Bush claims that we are living in a "kinder and gentler society." And yet, we accept government claims that community residents, and not funding cutbacks for ameliorative social programs, are the crux of the problem. The misplaced emphasis upon crime bears the long-term consequences of benign neglect. Social struggles are displaced in favor of endorsed government crime-control programs. Crime prevention, as applied in the classic sense, addresses the root causes rather than the eventual effects.

The Hobbesian notion of a social contract is bankrupt in this day and age. Hobbes hypothesized this ideal in an age unencumbered with the industrial revolution and the development of urban settings. The Marxian idea of class struggle and the exploitation of the working class was several centuries in the future. Government abdicated the social contract in implementing policies working against the social well-being of most citizens. Drugs and crimes are the result of social-policy failures and do not appear in a vacuum. Why should citizens blindly accept the rhetoric espoused by a political system concerned with maintaining status quo for the powerful economic and political elite? These questions are rarely asked by community residents taking up arms against other victims of political repression.

In conclusion, perhaps the late John Lennon was correct in urging that we "give peace a chance." Human beings can study and productively lessen these intractable social pressures against achieving peaceful resolution of social strain. We must understand the enemy before even offering corrective strategies. Building new prisons will not solve the drug problem or the overall crime dilemma. The resolution will require an open-minded assessment of where the social contract failed in fulfilling the implied promises. Who should bear the brunt for this failure? Ultimately, the late Walt Kelly's quote, "We have met the enemy and he is us," is still alive and well in a society characterized by self-alienation and the acceptance that "might makes right." Prospective changes rest in exploring alternative strategies. The future direction of community organization is in our hands.

## REFERENCES

Albini, Joseph. 1986. "The Guardian Angels: Vigilantes or Protectors of the Community? A Participant-Observation Study." Paper presented at the Academy of Criminal Justice Sciences, Orlando, Florida.

Alinsky, Saul D. 1946. *Reveille for Radicals*. Chicago: University of Chicago Press.

. Cohn, Ellen, Louis Keller, and Joan Harvey. 1978. "Crime Prevention vs. Victimization Prevention: The Psychology of Two Different Reactions." *Victimology*, 3 (3–4): 285–96.

Crimestoppers, International. 1980. Personal Communication.

Cullen, Francis T., and Karen E. Gilbert. 1982. *Reaffirming Rehabilitation*. Cincinnati: Anderson.

Cunningham, William C., and Todd H. Taylor. 1985. *The Hallcrest Report: Private Security and Police in America*. Portland, Ore.: Chancellor.

Dubow, Fred, E. McCabe, and G. Kaplan. 1979. *Reactions to Crime: A Critical Review of the Literature*. Washington, D.C.: Government Printing Office.

Durkheim, Emile. 1964 (1893). *The Division of Labor in Society*. Tr. George Simpson. Glencoe, Ill.: Free Press.

Ellis, Desmond. 1971. "The Hobbesian Problem of Order: A Critical Appraisal of the Normative Solution." *American Sociological Review*, 36: 692–703.

Flacks, Richard. 1970. "Strategies for Radical Social Change." *Social Policy* 1 (March–April): 10.

Flanagan, Timothy J., and Katherine M. Jamieson (eds.). 1988. *Sourcebook of Criminal Justice Statistics-1987*. Washington, D.C.: Government Printing Office.

Galper, Jeffrey H. 1975. *The Politics of Social Service*. Englewood Cliffs, N.J.: Prentice-Hall.

"Geraldo." 1988. March program on Crack House Arson in Detroit, Michigan. New York: Tribune Syndication Company.

Goffman, Erving. 1963. *Asylums: Essays on the Social Situation of Mental Patients and Other Inmates*. New York: Doubleday.

Gorelick, Steven M. 1989. "Join Our War: The Construction of Ideology in a Newspaper Crimefighting Campaign." *Crime and Delinquency* 35 (July): 401–20.

Gross, Bertram. 1985. *Friendly Fascism: The New Face of Power in America*. Montreal: Black Rose Press.

Horton, Chester L., and Paul B. Hunt. 1972. *Sociology*. 3rd ed. New York: Harper and Row.

Kenney, Dennis Jay. 1987. *Crime, Fear and the New York City Subways: The Role of Citizen Action*. New York: Praeger.

Klein, Lloyd, and Marianna King. 1982. "Sanctioned Surveillance: The Role of Citizen Crime Prevention Activity." Unpublished paper presented at the annual meeting of the American Society of Criminology, Toronto.

Klein, Lloyd, Joan Luxenburg, Marianna King, and Karen Gilbert. 1983. "Reach Out and 'Bust' Someone: The Evolution of Crime Stoppers Programs." Unpublished paper presented at the annual meeting of the American Society of Criminology, Denver.

Lemert, Edwin M. 1951. *Social Pathology*. New York: McGraw-Hill.

Mendelsohn, Harold, and G. J. O'Keefe. 1984. *Taking a Bite Out of Crime: The Impact of a Mass Media Crime Prevention Campaign.* Washington, DC: National Institute of Justice.

*Newsweek.* 1989. "When Tenants Take Charge." 27 November: 44.

*New York Times.* 1988. "Freeze! You're on TV: How America's Most Wanted has Led to the Arrest of 22 Fugitives." Frank Prial, 25 September, p. 56.

*New York Times.* 1988a. "Do I Look Like a Criminal?" Op-ed column by Dave Pauli, 3 October, p. 22.

"Oprah Winfrey." 1989. October program on Citizens Self Help Groups.

Reiman, Jeffrey H. 1984. *The Rich Get Richer and the Poor Get Prison.* 2nd ed. New York: Wiley.

Rosenbaum, Dennis (ed.). 1986. *Community Crime Prevention: Does It Work?* Beverly Hills: Sage.

Rosenbaum, Dennis, Arthur Lurigio, and Paul Lavrakas. 1989. "Enhancing Citizen Participation and Solving Serious Crime: A National Evaluation of Crime Stoppers Programs." *Crime and Delinquency* 35: 378–400.

Rothman, Jack. 1968. "Three Models of Community Organization," in *National Conference on Social Welfare and Social Work Practice, 1968.* New York: Columbia University Press.

Rothman, Jack, and John E. Tropman. 1987. "Models of Community Organization and Macro Practice Perspectives: Their Mixing and Phasing." In Fred M. Cox, John L. Erlich, Jack Rothman, and John E. Tropman (eds.), *Strategies of Community Organization.* 4th ed. Ithasca, Ill.: F. E. Peacock.

Sheley, Joseph F. 1985. *America's "Crime Problem": An Introduction to Criminology.* Belmont, CA: Wadsworth.

Shearing, Clifford, and Peter Stenning. 1987. *Private Policing.* Newbury Park: Sage.

"Sixty Minutes." 1986, 1987. Segment of Citizen Empowerment. November, 1986; rebroadcast in July, 1987. Columbia Broadcasting Company.

Skogan, Wesley G. 1986. "Disorder, Crime and Community Decline." In Sally E. Marry, *Urban Danger: Life in a Neighborhood of Strangers.* Philadelphia: Temple University Press.

*Time Magazine.* 1989. "On the Front Lines." 11 September: 14–18.

# PART FOUR

# The Peacemaking Choice

*Harold E. Pepinsky*

---

# TWENTY

# Peacemaking in Criminology and Criminal Justice

Several years ago, responding to an early draft of a study I had written on "responsiveness" in Norway (Pepinsky, 1988), Richard Quinney wrote me that he thought *peacemaking* was the direction criminology ought to move, that he sensed wide but scarcely visible interest in the subject among criminologists, and that we ought to do something about it. Kevin Anderson pitched in and did much of the work, so that over a three-year period we had a series of sessions on peacemaking at the annual meetings of the American Society of Criminology. Richard and I called for relevant essays, which now comprise this volume. Some of the talented authors herein gave us their essays at the outset, enough to show Indiana University Press that we would have a coherent work. They have since updated and revised their work; and we thank them, and indeed all our contributors, for their patience and effort.

I suspect that these essays are a representative sampling of peacemaking research among those identifying themselves as North American criminologists. They are anchored in longstanding traditions of thought and action. Three categories of tradition stand out in this collection—religious traditions, feminist or women's traditions, and critical traditions. These three categories are surely not exhaustive, particularly so for those who work in and at criminal justice but do not consider themselves "criminologists" in the North American tradition. In the process of organizing the

Fifth International Conference on Penal Abolition (ICOPA), I discovered that by far the strongest contingent among the hundreds of correspondents are workers and activists with religious affiliations, notably the peace churches and ecumenical peace groups. Religiously self-identified people cross all eight intellectual traditions which have emerged: academicians and theorists, activists and reformers, feminists, lawmakers, mediators, native traditionalists, peoples of color, and prisoners. The National People's of Color Task Force on Criminal Justice has simply merged itself into the Interreligious Task Force on Criminal Justice; and one of its former leaders, the Reverend Matthew Stephens, a prison chaplain in Ohio, is its coordinator. Each of the eight traditions has its own international networks. ICOPA participants and correspondents represent the pacifists of criminal justice.

I find to my surprise that many of the peacemaking criminologists and many ICOPA people are completely unaware of one another, although among the contributors in this volume, Kay Harris, Russ Immarigeon, and Fay Honey Knopp have also been active in ICOPA. We have paid a price for specialization and advanced data-processing capabilities in this information age. If you look in a standard college text for criminology or criminal justice, the vast literature cited there will scarcely if at all include any notice of activities of members of the ICOPA network. For that matter, most ICOPA members find little reason to read mainstream criminology or criminal justice research-journals. The result is that most ICOPA members do not see much room for their kind of knowledge and inquiry on college campuses, and even the most progressive criminologists feel nothing is being done to provide alternatives to prison, let alone punishment. Here's to the time when information and ideas are freely shared between these communities! The problem is not that peacemaking in criminology and criminal justice is new and untested; the problem is our ignorance of the vast amount that is being thought and done by peacemakers in criminology and criminal justice.

We suffer another level of collective ignorance—the connection between *crime and punishment* on the one hand and *war* on the other. There is also a vast community of scholars and activists in peace studies, as represented for instance by the International Peace Research Association. I have found it no easier either to get criminologists into peace studies or to get students of peace to show interest in criminology than to get ICOPA members and criminologists together. Specialization gets in the way again. I know of several groups which consistently transcend this breach: (1) peace churches (see the chapters by Cordella and Immarigeon); (2) radical feminists (see particularly the chapters by Harris; Caringella-MacDonald and Humphries; and Knopp, who joins Quakerism with feminism); (3) humanists (see the chapter by Anderson); and (4) anarchists (see the chapter by Tifft and Markham). Each of these groups is marginal to the mainstream both in peace studies and in criminology. Each offers a solid, well thought-out, and researched foundation for all groups working for peace to come together.

Happily, you will find that the contributors to this volume are broadly active and informed about issues of peace and war. There is a wealth of material herein about related work which belongs in criminology but as yet is not often found there. We criminologists just need to begin to look beyond the end of our collective nose.

What is the obvious connection between crime and war? Crime is violence. So is punishment, and so is war. People who go to war believe that violence works. So do criminals and people who want criminals punished. All these believe violence works because they also believe that domination is necessary. Somebody who is closer to God, natural wisdom, or scientific truth has to keep wayward subordinates in line, or social order goes to hell. The only way to tame the social beast is for everyone to agree (by "social contract": see Peter Cordella's chapter) that everyone is at times "entitled" to be subordinated and to be subordinator—ideally always to be both subordinator and subordinator in one's proper place at all times. This line of thinking appears in all religious and political traditions: as in Confucianism versus Taoism; as in bureaucratism versus anarchy; and as in old Old Testament worldly retribution versus, for example, the Prophets or the Sermon on the Mount. It is also known as the idea of the existence of a chosen people (Galtung, 1987)—in matters of conflict, some people are entitled to dictate terms to some other lesser human beings and to kill or totally incapacitate them, if necessary, to establish human virtue.

Pacifists in criminology and criminal justice can learn from one another by force of reason. So can retributionists. But to recognize that the kind of criminologist one is is fundamentally a matter of religious preference is to see that reason cannot dictate whether a criminologist chooses to learn within a paradigm of war or a paradigm of peacemaking. In 1967, I sat up late one night with a family friend whom I later heard had been head of operations in East Asia for the CIA. Back and forth we argued about the domino theory. Finally, simultaneously, it hit us that unless I could prove to him that the Communists would not eventually land in San Francisco if we did not stop them at the seventeenth parallel in Vietnam, he would find it imperative to stop the Communists now. And unless he could prove to me that the Communists would land in San Francisco, I would continue to advocate our withdrawal from Southeast Asia. We both knew that the only proof of anything is by tautology, as in pure math. We laughed and gave up on each other. That was an important experience for me to learn the limits of reason.

As radical feminists well know (see, for example, Brock-Utne, 1989), there are two kinds of "science." As esoteric as the claim to being the true scientist often is, "science" just means "learning." Learning is something we all do, but which can be done in radically different ways. When I sat in on criminology-research seminars at the University of Oslo, a number of participants echoed the criticism of a survey of introductory-psychology students' attitude formation which had appeared in a leading U.S. social-psychology journal. "How Unscientific," they kept saying. "The author didn't know any of the students. How could he have known what they meant by each of their responses? Instead he just guessed in his statistical analysis." Criminologist Les Wilkins once wrote, "Kings and queens have subjects, researchers should not!" In one approach to knowledge, we make our informants "subjects" of our own definition of the situation. We don't tell them what the study is about. We use statistical traces they have left to decide what we know about our subjects, rather than getting to know them face-to-face. In the other approach, our informants become our teachers. If we are to prevent another Ted Bundy from killing again, we need to understand what Ted Bundy did. If we badly need to understand what Ted Bundy did, we badly need to keep him alive and engage in dialogue with him. This is not just a matter of doing truly scientific research. It is an approach to learning which permeates the social existence of the believer. It is perhaps because they are free to engage in openly religious discourse that the Mennonites can see the quality of mediation we offer as the key to confronting, redressing, and preventing future violence. "Reconciliation" itself is to them a natural way of learning from conflict. More than the form itself—which just isn't the same when it is sponsored by the National Institute of Justice (see Maria Volpe's and Joe Scimecca's chapters)—it is the spirit which guides action and science and determines whether we are learning how to make bigger and better wars, or bigger and better peace.

That is why religious and humanist traditions have been chosen to lead off in this volume. There are ways to talk about paradigm choice in criminology. I was a little too smug about dropping the discussion with my CIA friend. We could not appeal to one another by what radical feminists call "male" reasoning. If we were to address honestly the issue of paradigm choice, we had to rise to another level of discourse. That is, of course, what theoretical physicists did in the early part of this century as they tried to grapple with quantum mechanics. They turned to metaphysics and theology, not because they had burned out and were dropping out of science, but because they had to rise above paradigmatic debate to address issues of paradigm choice. They were in fact turned on, although too many of them stopped asking questions and used their newfound wisdom to build nuclear destruction.

Max Weber is erroneously cited for advocating value-freedom in science. He gave a pair of lectures on the subject (Weber, 1946). In "Science as a Vocation" he did say that science could tell you whether you could do something but not whether you should. He also said that the research questions one asks and the method one uses rest on untestable presuppositions. How does the scientist choose presuppositions? In "Politics as a Vocation," he says that choosing presuppositions is the political obligation of every human being, and that the choice is primarily a matter of following one's heart. Scientists should be true to their own hearts. The object of religious discourse is to discover what truly lies within one's heart.

## Religious and Humanist Traditions

In the spirit of confronting and honestly discussing conflict, and at risk of embarrassing my much esteemed friend and coeditor, I heard many a criminologist claim that Richard Quinney had flipped out when he extended his much admired and cited Marxist work to the theology of crime. Some Marxists were angry that he had forsaken them and tarnished their respectability. Richard (who has always been Richard and not a Marxist or a Christian or a Buddhist alone) broke the ice and gave many of us criminologists courage as we have dared ourselves to become avowedly religious—as seekers rather than purveyors of religious truth.

Richard's long and extensive search for understanding across religious traditions is revealed in and informs his chapter. Is he telling us to be truly Buddhist or truly Christian? Actually, neither. He highlights Buddhist learning to show that religious traditions are essentially different ways of talking about the same truth. He echoes the famous statement by Eugene V. Debs that "while there is a soul in prison I am not free." But wait—Debs was an atheist socialist, not a Buddhist. That's the point. Richard is not talking about what a Buddhist is; he is talking about Buddhist insight into universal human experience.

In an award acceptance speech at the American Society of Criminology, criminal justice reformer Jerry Miller (1988) put Richard's main point this way: There are basically two kinds of criminologists, those who think criminals are different from themselves and those who don't. You cannot separate a criminal's self-understanding from our understanding of the criminal. More than empathy, understanding requires our sympathy— allowing ourselves to feel the offender's pain and committing ourselves to trying to alleviate the pain for us both. Buddhist teachers have put this message beautifully.

Why cite the Buddhists? There are two reasons at least. One is to show that people on the other side of the world from the contributors of this volume long ago reached the same conclusion as Jerry Miller. It should give us pause about labeling the home of this tradition "third world," "less developed," "underdeveloped" or "developing." Drawing on faraway traditions may give us a little more respect for the humanity of their bearers, and make it a little less tolerable that we live well at their expense. The other reason is that while Jerry Miller is talking about being a criminologist, the Buddhists are talking about being human, pure and simple. Criminologists who are incapable of making their own relations equitable and just—with students, informants, and colleagues at work, or women and children at home—cannot be presumed to know how to make judges, police officers, prosecutors, and correctional workers be equitable and just. This is elemental to Buddhists but not necessarily to current bearers of Greco-Judeo-Christian tradition. The Buddhists tell it like it is, not in some criminological compartment, but as a matter of how human beings get along anywhere, anytime. They make a statement that radical feminists, anarchists, socialists, humanists, and members of peace churches can readily accept as one way of stating their own position.

Those metaphysical physicists were concerned with basic issues of definition: what is mass, what is energy? Criminologists could use a good dose of the same reflection. Our most basic issue is: What is crime? And by extension: Why do we use that word? What do we feel when we use it? What do we intend to accomplish by using it? Richard offers us an idea: Crime is suffering passed on from one person to another; one kind of suffering becomes another; we have to suffer with the criminal to put an end to the suffering the criminal inflicts on others. As long as we persist in trying to make the criminal suffer for us, the problem will get worse.

East meets West again in a somewhat different way in Kevin Anderson's secular humanist analysis of the eschatological premises of an avowedly religious revolutionary, Mahatma Gandhi, and an avowedly atheist revolutionary, Karl Marx. It is ludicrous to deny that Gandhi, Marx, and Anderson are considering fundamental issues of the ultimate purpose of human existence. It is one thing to reject certain institutional forms of religious expression, another to decline to discuss issues because they are basic human concerns. Kevin like Richard aims to free us from these bounds on discourse in criminology. And when we do, seemingly opposing positions may suddenly become complementary and mutually informing like Gandhi's and Marx's.

The contrast between the "Marxists" Kevin criticizes and the radical humanism he espouses is inherent in his research method. Kevin analyzes the writings, statements, and practices of both men in their entirety, in historical perspective, to distill their personalities and hence their core beliefs. The "Marxists" take some unit of Marx's many writings and encode it as an independent variable, whose value is taken for granted. Kevin's own method of learning from Gandhi and Marx is an example of how people learn in Gandhi's utopian village and Marx's utopian commune.

In criminal courts as in Kevin's research, turning crime into peace is in essence a matter of how people learn. Those who assume they know what this "normal case" (Sudnow, 1965) means are warriors at heart and in action. Those who assume the need to understand one another in matters of crime are more likely to make peace. Kevin, like fellow humanists Gandhi and Marx, has made the latter "metaphysical" choice. His purpose in reading Gandhi and Marx is to understand what they have learned about how to make peace. In them together he finds for instance that radical peacemakers eschew political position. (I try to remember that when I find myself running for something.) I'm not quite sure where Kevin stands on this, but for myself I also find that Gandhi is right on one point of disagreement with Marx: Peacemaking must be evolutionary, built from the bottom up, rather than imposed by revolution. The method is the end. Kevin observes how prominent women were in Gandhi's marches. To the feminists whose contributions are discussed below recognize, this is the ultimate extension of *satyagraha* (Gandhi's nonviolent action). Unless we can make peace in the privacy of our own homes, men with women, adults with children and with older people, we cannot build peace outside in our other workplaces and in our nations. Research on peacemaking in criminology thus becomes the study of how and where people manage to make peace, under the assumption that the principles that create or destroy peace are the same from the Smith family kitchen to the Pentagon and the prison. By these examples we hope to be able to create more peace of our own.

This is the very theme of Peter Cordella's chapter. Peter tells us about the Anabaptists, and especially about the Mennonites, who as Russ Immarigeon also tells us have pioneered the use of mediation and reconciliation as an alternative to North American criminal justice in their Victim Offender Reconciliation Programs (VORPs).

Now that I've settled in Indiana, I am proud of the tradition of the peace churches in this state. "Peace churches" refers to Christian sects whose members—as Peter tells us—are committed to one law only, the law of agape—to love one's neighbor as oneself. Among them the Church of the Brethren established the first degree program in peace studies in the United States at Manchester College in 1948. The Quakers have established an internationally prominent peace studies program at Earlham College. The Mennonite Central Committee is in Elkhart. Even in a church that is not known as a peace church, the Catholics have established a major peace studies center just down the road from Elkhart at Notre Dame, directed by former Ohio Governor John Gilligan. And good Amish people live among us throughout the state.

Peter concludes by observing that even those peace church members who live in relative isolation, like the Hutterites or the Amish, live "mutualist" lives not to live perfect lives themselves but to show people in a troubled world that "community lived in mutuality is possible." More to the point, community lived in mutuality exists and is substantial even in as conservative a state as Indiana. We nonbelievers just don't pay much attention to it. Living a life committed to love rather than violence is therefore not just some utopian romantic idea. It is a long accomplished fact for many very successful people right in our own violent midst. Where there's a will there is a way to live peacefully rather than by crime and punishment. It is not that Mennonites and others succeed in living lives of perfect nonviolence. It is rather that when violence happens, they choose to try to restore peace rather than to respond in kind. And once again, the method is the way. Notice that Peter, too, distinguishes how those who subscribe to social-contract theory put people in categories from how mutualists try to understand and reconcile the stories of troubled people. Do you try to understand the story of someone charged with crime or put the person away? That is the basic moral choice every human being faces. Notice again, too, that what got the Anabaptists in serious trouble in Europe (as in being burned to death) was that they declined formal service to the state. No Mennonite could ever become a prosecutor. Think of a world where everyone made that choice. That is the dream of Larry Tifft, Lyn. Markham, Gandhi, Marx and every committed anarchist.

There are only two reasons for choosing to favor punishment of offenders. One is ignorance of the fact that people can and often do live like Mennonites. The other is the simple moral and religious choice to go on trying to hang onto one's own pieces of domination by violence anyway. The matter of choosing what kind of criminologist one will be—a peacemaker or a warmaker—is not a matter of advanced statistical interpretation of complex data sets, although it is a matter for profound soul searching.

Lest we lose sight of the fact that peacemaking is an established part of every religious tradition, Gregg Barak takes us to Hebrew scriptures, on which Hesed House, a shelter for homeless people in Aurora, Illinois (not far from Elkhart, Indiana), is founded. "Hesed" is sometimes translated like its Buddhist counterpart—"compassion." While Hesed is the doing of justice, Tsedeka is Hebrew for the fruits of justice, and gives the name to the Tsedeka Foundation, established by George Moore in Calgary, Alberta, Canada, to find alternatives to punishing offenders. In Hebrew as in Urdu, Hindi, Arabic (as the Sufis read the Koran), Greek, and Chinese, religious scriptures provide a rich foundation and guide to peacemaking efforts.

The homeless are the traditional primary caseload of criminal justice systems all over the world, where the homeless are variously known as vagrants, parasites, trespassers, and for being publicly intoxicated and disorderly. (As one local judge told me for a video I made, "If you're going to drink you'd better stay at home." And if you haven't got a home . . . ?) Preserving proper ownership is the primary objective of punishment of offenders, and the homeless own virtually nothing. So by definition, whatever they take they likely do not deserve, and we lock them up in reprisal. Our contempt is matched by the inability of the homeless to fight further repression. Look at national arrest figures in the United States, and you will see that offenses associated with homelessness—vagrancy, loitering, disorderly conduct, and public intoxication—invariably account for the greatest proportion. Look at Soviet jails, and you will see that "parasites" predominate even when political repression runs high. Offering Hesed to the homeless is a revolutionary alternative to a large chunk of the criminal justice caseload in any society. And again, Hesed House is not a utopia but a reality. Imagine what would happen if the thirty or forty thousand dollars we spend to imprison a person for a year were reinvested in offering Hesed. At a time when homelessness plagues so much of the world, Gregg's news about Hesed House is especially timely.

My colleague Charisse Coston has spent considerable time with one segment of the homeless population of New York—bag ladies (Coston, 1989). She tells me some bag ladies are reluctant to go to shelters because the shelters have the policy of searching one's belonging and throwing away the things they figure will attract roaches. A shelter which does not do Hesed is not an attractive alternative to the streets for many women. As Gregg describes it, doing Hesed means providing hospitality without degrading or stigmatizing the receiver, one might well add by doing agape.

Hesed and its spiritual counterparts imply a belief that what riches one has are gifts rather than entitlements, to be shared with those who need them most. It is that sense of spiritual purpose which distinguishes making peace with people in trouble from treating them as criminals.

This perspective draws its inspiration from Norwegian peace researcher Johan Galtung's (1969) famous distinction between negative and positive peace. Negative peace means meeting crime and other violence with superior might, while positive peace means giving people less to fight about. The difference is starkly illustrated by comparing the United Nations human rights documents to the U.S. Constitution. The only affirmative guarantees given U.S. citizens as a matter of constitutional right are to get census results delivered every ten years and have their mail delivered at a price. The Bill of Rights is entirely negative, enjoining courts to put state power on the side of individuals who are abused by their officials, to limit official action. What of enjoining officials to give economic and political democracy to people at the grass-roots level? The Constitution of the biggest government in the United States does not even guarantee a right to education, food, or shelter.

Like Buddhist scriptures, human rights documents provide a well-articulated alternative to warmaking in criminology. Rather than deriving their research agenda from the state (see also John Galliher's chapter for a discussion of this problem), criminologists ought to ground their research in the human rights agenda.

It does not really matter whether the foundation is a United Nations human rights document or the Bible. The point is that the alternative vision and practice is set forth in all manner of religious and secular traditions. The one element missing when the agenda is secular is the sense that peacemaking is a reality rather than merely a dream. The Mennonites, for instance, are living in a peaceful part of the world of their own making. They know it exists and that the problem is one of extending the reality of peace rather than of creating it in a vacuum.

Russ Immarigeon's chapter is an overview of efforts to supplant criminal justice with reconciliation in the United States. It is a fitting way to end a section on religious choices, by focusing on their secular consequences for criminology and criminal justice.

I have known Russ for some years and have never heard him explicitly raise religion. And yet while the Unitarian Church funded the Moratorium

on Prison Construction (NMPC, until 1987), Russ worked for them whole-
heartedly. He edited *Jericho*, the NMPC's journal about what was happening in U.S. prisons, and I consider him an encyclopedia of what is
happening in prison abolition. NMPC and VORPs worked closely together.
However he got it, Russ has a spiritual intuition for distinguishing making
wars on crime from making peace on crime. He surveys the U.S. criminal
justice scene over recent years to weigh progress against setback in the
quest to make peace instead of punishment in criminal justice.

This chapter is placed at the end of the first section on religious traditions
for two reasons. First, Russ shows that one need not declare one's re-
ligiosity to be consciously spiritual. Richard Quinney declares many religious affiliations, while Russ declares none. Second, Russ makes it a point
to stay informed as to what attempts to reconcile victims and offenders are
happening in the United States, indeed in the world, and is as capable as
anyone I know of portraying what is happening to offenders as a consequence of peacemakers' efforts. The resulting balance sheet foreshadows
the concluding chapters on critical thinking. Clearly, peacemaking criminologists and criminal justice functionaries are up against warmaking ones.
Russ distills the essence of what separates the two. Courts continually fail
to ask victims and offenders why conflict is happening and what they want.
As Christie (1977) puts it, peacemaking fails when disputes are taken out of
the possession and hands of victims and offenders, when victims and
offenders are prevented from confronting one another. Time and again in
the vignettes Russ offers, the choice is between doing Hesed and doing
violence. Sometimes the forces of violence prevail, and sometimes the
voices of peace. The challenge for peacemakers in criminology is to be able
to discern the difference, oppose the warrior alternative, and do peacemaking instead. Listening to what parties to criminal disputes know and feel
about the situation makes the crucial difference.

Les Wilkins is a gifted and recognized social statistician who like Russ
argues that information about crime and punishment helps if and only if it
presents people with more choices than advocating wars on crime or sitting
passive (Wilkins, 1984). Democracy, or peacemaking as it has been called
here, means that those who stand to be affected by a decision know options
and act on them. Knowing the issues is as important as voting, perhaps
more so, because people who stand ready to keep being informed do not
care so much for voting and getting on with business. To repeat, understanding Ted Bundy is worth more to the peacemaker than eradicating him.

Russ cites evidence that when people stop to listen to victims and
offenders, reconciliation does happen. The practicality of reconciliation
rests on whether it is tried, not whether it works. Implicitly if not explicitly,
this understanding rests not only of Russ's command of the research
literature, but on his understanding of the religious basis of the distinction
between reconciliation and punishment.

## Feminist Peacemaking Traditions
## and Women's Experience

I think we can safely presume it universal to the human condition that womanhood is associated with fertility, with nurture, and with the preservation of life. The divergence in human experience comes in choosing how to respond to this association: Do we embrace womanhood or try to subdue it?

The peacemaker opts to embrace womanhood. As Native Americans put it, the earth is our mother. This explains the close affinity of radical feminists and environmental movements like deep ecology (inspired by the Norwegian philosopher Arne Naess, 1989), Green parties in Europe and North America, and native traditionalism. Reverence and nurture apply equally to other human beings and to the universe around us, that supports us as well as the other life forms upon whose existence we depend. Hesed applies as fully to caring for the environment as to caring for the homeless, and the fertility of doing Hesed is basically womanly.

This is not an argument that women are better than men, or that biological differences ought to have much to do with how men and women are treated. Men can become nurturant, hence womanly, too. Oppressed women who, for instance, raise sons to be soldiers in a manly war can and do behave after a manly fashion. Liberated womanhood that men can live as easily as women is an ideal rather than a reality. The problem is that people who suppress womanhood inevitably suppress women as a class. Time and again, as in Native American tradition, people whose men have honored and respected rather than subdued womanhood have been relatively nonpunitive, peaceful societies (Eisler, 1987). Honoring and respecting womanhood doesn't mean letting women take charge. Rather, it means both doing Hesed without anyone having to be in charge and allowing men and women alike to be womanly. (In a world free of repression, there isn't much need for manhood at all.)

Kay Harris has pioneered in making the connection between radical feminism and criminal justice explicit. I start off my feminist justice seminar with an earlier work of hers (Harris, 1985). Victim Offender Reconciliation Programs are not only Mennonite. They are literally what the radical feminist seeks, as Kay shows us.

In response to Kay's presentation of a draft of this chapter at one of the American Society of Criminology peacemaking sessions, Kay talked freely about the moral dilemma of responding to rape victims and other women who damn well want their offenders to be punished and suffer. Kay pointed to an underlying issue: Punishing offenders is held to be a way of making women safe, and so we ought to be talking about what makes women safest. That is the premise of the response to a rape-murder in Kalamazoo, Michigan, as described by Susan Caringella-MacDonald and

Drew Humphries in the chapter that follows Kay's. Just think, for example, of how much more dramatic an impact spending a dollar on rape-awareness sessions between young women and men can have on women's safety than spending the dollar toward paying for a rapist's prison cell. And through a trusted intermediary, if not face-to-face, giving a woman a safe opportunity to confront the offender with her anger and pain, and to ask the offender to account for himself, must offer more relief than praying that one's rapist doesn't hit the streets, and will probably have a more favorable impact on the rapist. As for incapacitation, experience in Massachusetts has shown it is not much more expensive to put violent people under close community supervision—and far more effective in controlling the behavior of the bulk of violent offenders who will eventually be released—than to lock them away (Loughran, 1987). It would be very easy to keep close enough watch to ensure that a rapist was never again left alone with a woman without her informed consent, and with aid close at hand, for less than it costs to build and operate a prison cell. Generally, there are many nonviolent ways to do Hesed for women in danger.

As Kay tells us, radical feminists see no harm in trying to live happily. They want to expand the power of people to live happily together. This is the other side of the coin from the Buddhist belief in the necessity of suffering. Happiness in the radical feminist sense doesn't mean being carefree and irresponsible. Rather it rests on a recognition that human fates—rich and poor, powerful and oppressed—hang in the balance together. If we turn our attention first to those most in need, those suffering the worst oppression and poverty, we can, by eliminating human suffering at its worst, make all our lives happier. Without denying and in fact by confronting the suffering of the victim and her rapist, you aspire for them both to be able to live as happily and successfully in your midst henceforth as you are able to help them achieve. That is of course a considerable challenge, made all the greater by punitive support for criminal justice. No matter how challenging, radical feminists believe human happiness is the only thing worth living and working for; and they are prepared, like the Buddhists, to share suffering to get there.

It is remarkable to have so many U.S. radical feminists gathered in a single volume. Embedded as we are in what Peter Cordella calls the contract society, liberal feminism predominates over radical feminism in this country. As Brock-Utne (1989) puts it, liberal feminists want a bigger share of the pie, and radical feminists want to change the recipe of the pie. It goes without saying that women deserve as much of the pie as men, but neither gender deserves to eat oppressive ingredients. In her words, "Women who aspire to be equal to men lack ambition." But this is precisely the position of the bulk of oppressed feminists in the United States today, as contrasted for instance to Canada and Western Europe. Radical feminists in the United States are a pioneering lot who deserve the support of other groups of peacemakers in and out of criminology and criminal justice. The women contributors here, like radical feminists everywhere, tend to be involved in a broad array of peacemaking movements although their visibility in male-dominated peace groups tends to be overshadowed by men's. The broad participation of radical feminists across peace movements suggests that their way of knowing is like Cordella's mutualists and Anderson's humanists: They want to understand the human condition in full context rather than specializing on one element of the human body such as criminality.

The Kalamazoo experience Susan and Drew describe highlights a recurrent dynamic of successful peace movements. They respond to a problem as women experience it (rape); a broader initiative than standard bureaucratic response to the problem is initiated by women; and the women succeed in drawing the support and cooperation of powerful men (who often get the lion's share of the credit). The power of this pattern is why the most successful economic development projects for the world's poorest people time and again start by lending or giving money and ownership of property to women exclusively, in the confidence that they are more likely to share what they have with men than the reverse (Christian Science Monitor Special Report, 1989). Again, what has happened in Kalamazoo is a reality not a utopia, and a common if all too seldom noticed reality at that.

Larry Tifft and Lyn. Markham's radical feminist (and anarchist) chapter is a reminder that the issue is how men and women can be free and womanly together, rather than of whether women and men are truly, basically different. They make crystal clear that it is the spirit pervading the lives of men and women alike in the United States which lets officials and mercenaries torture, rob, beat, and murder Central Americans on the one hand, and torture, rob, beat, and murder women in their own homes on the other hand. Given opportunity in a manly society, isolated women are as likely to batter other women as isolated men are to batter women. Of course men have greater opportunity and toleration of their battering, and so they do the major share of it. But oppression breeds oppression, and builds violence in its victims. Small wonder that women who are told the criminal justice system is their only hope want to put their batterers away but good.

The trouble is that the battering only gets worse unless some peacemaker gets in the way and says, "Enough, let's confront the real issues here. What are you fighting about? Let's see if there's some better way you can get what you want." That is what Larry and Lyn. are trying to do—to confront us with the omnipresence of the will to batter in all of us, rather than compartmentalizing Central America or domestic violence and trying to treat it or stamp it out in isolation. Their anarchist roots represent another important peacemaking tradition. There have been many violent anarchists, Bakunin is perhaps the most infamous; but most avowed anarchists, Tolstoy and Kropotkin for instance, are peacemakers like Larry and Lyn. I have been labeled an anarchist myself and don't mind. Not controlling others and not submitting to others' control is the core of the anarchist's ethics. Control of and ownership of property—public or private—to prevent meeting people's needs and to obstruct their physical, psychological, and social development is the bane of the anarchist's existence. Some of my anarchist friends espouse this standard: violating property rights which stops violence to life is no vice. That is how people who live for nonviolence justify damaging missile silos and pouring blood on draft board records or on the White House fence, or how Greenpeace can try to obstruct a missile launch. This is reminiscent of the mutualist premise: All that I have is a gift to share with those in need; I own nothing; the earth is my mother.

The anarchist prefers confrontation to violence and concealment of conflict. Punishment of offenders and battering Central Americans may be a good way to bury our problems; Larry and Lyn. demand that we face them instead, try to heal the wounds in our own human spirit. And need it be said? Battering in any form is intolerable.

Walt DeKeseredy and Marty Schwartz take a hard, critical look at the potential of radical feminism to increase women's safety. They had no chance to read Susan and Drew's description of radical feminism in Kalamazoo, nor this closing chapter. I wonder what they would think now. Aren't radical feminists in Kalamazoo and elsewhere around the world providing women with genuine protection against abuse? Is it their fault that people aren't interested in learning about their experience? I understand that at least one rape case has successfully been mediated in the VORP in Batavia, New York. If radical feminism or other peacemaking has been done for women in physical danger, how can we say it is vague and untested? Admittedly, it may take considerable time and effort for people accustomed to violence to learn how to reconcile differences and offer one another safety instead. People who try will fall down as often as babies learning to walk. They can learn faster if they have access to how more experienced and accomplished peacemakers like those in VORPs succeed. it is not to minimize the magnitude of the task of peacemaking to say that a lot of people have done it and done it well, with remarkable self-awareness and willingness to share their experiences.

To their credit, Walt and Marty criticize the failure of left realists and others to acknowledge feminists more heavily than failings of the radical feminists themselves. Once one starts to look out for women's writing, its suppression becomes striking throughout the social sciences. Women's-studies programs, journals, book series, book publishers, and bookstores are one response to this problem. As long as women's experience and ideas barely make it into curricula, into research literature, or into mass media, there is an acute need for enterprises of people committed to giving women's experience and feminism a voice and a hearing.

Notice that Walt and Marty also subscribe to the peacemaking premise that we learn better by understanding the context of violence than by categorizing and statistically analyzing violence. By their method as well as by its substance, the Marxism of left realists is a marked contrast to Kevin

Anderson's humanist Marx. The issue isn't one of accepting or rejecting Marxism, but of what kind of Marxism we adopt. The writings of Karl Marx, like the scriptures of any religious tradition, are subject to the division of beliefs between those who believe in retribution and those who believe in compassion. Kevin's Marx is compassionate, while Marx to the left realists requires retribution. The crucial distinction between peacemaking and warmaking criminologists once again transcends institutional affiliation.

Lila Rucker's chapter epitomizes what radical feminists project happens when a liberated woman becomes integrally involved in shaping and interpreting how offenders are treated. We will more likely find such descriptions in women's literature than in men's these days, which is another good reason to seek out women's literature. Larry and Lyn. have shown us that we live in a spiritual prison outside the walls; Lila indicates that prisoners conversely can live in spiritual freedom with the proper support. Yes, as long as people are locked in prison, treatment or habilitation within the walls is possible. (So many prisoners aren't yet in a position to be *re*habilitated.) *Coerced* treatment is an oxymoron, as the famous study sponsored by the American Friends Service Committee (1971, the highest U.S. body of the Quakers or the Society of Friends) firmly concluded. But Hesed is already done in prison by radical feminists and penal abolitionists like Lila or the legendary Liz Barker in Massachusetts prisons.

I responded to Lila's first draft with skepticism. All of us who have known prisoners know prisoners can be very skilled at conning their treaters into feeling good about themselves while the cons are inwardly laughing at them. In this draft, Lila adopts radical-feminist method, examining context rather than isolating a behavior like "recidivism." Note for instance her telling observation that at the end of a three-day session together: "People look *at* one another rather than *through* one another or at the floor." One can well imagine the consternation of the conventional "empirical" researcher at trying to measure the difference between looking at people and looking through people. And yet anyone who has looked other people in the eye and paid attention can quite noticeably feel the difference. Nor does it matter whether there was a statistically significant change in how people looked at each other. In radical feminist terms, the crucial difference between the empiricist and Lila is that Lila pays attention to the looks and counts her progress by them. It is common knowledge among radical feminists that women are trained to attend to looks rather than to recidivism figures, that women characteristically see what men characteristically overlook. What one feels in a situation is the most crucial datum of all, for knowing the feelings is prerequisite both to evaluating one's progress in peacemaking and to explaining and thereby preventing violence. Lila may not call herself a feminist, but turning prisons into healing centers is precisely the approach advocated by Kay Harris; and citing a woman, family therapist Virginia Satir (1972), for providing a theoretical foundation for healing centers is also characteristically feminist. The labels we use for one another are not nearly so important as the transcendent approach to crime and criminality we take.

Lila recognizes that three days, no matter how positive, does not necessarily remake a prisoner's life. Research on learning and reinforcement teaches that the desired response will be extinguished when reinforcement ceases. On the other hand, participants may have learned how to find and foster reinforcing interaction in previously unseen places. Either way there is no indictment of Lila's efforts. One never knows what bit of compassion may trigger a profound change in someone's life; but even if the prisoners lapsed back into old violent patterns, the problem is not that Lila did Hesed but that the doing of Hesed stopped thereafter. And as Lila rightly points out, the fact that the prisoners participated openly and freely in a compassionate world for three days is no mean accomplishment, and is something they ought to feel proud of.

I'm still learning. Tucked away in a draft of this book manuscript I found Fay Honey Knopp's essay. I had heard her mentioned by friends like Kay Harris and Russ Immarigeon, but I had never read her work nor seen it cited in the criminological literature. I now believe she ought to be ranked as one of the giants in U.S. criminology. She wrote the case for prison abolition in 1976 long before the first ICOPA was held. Her Quakerism, her radical feminism, and her prison abolitionism have reinforced and informed one another. She scarcely separates theory from practice. She has been confronting sexual violence and offering alternatives to prison for half a century. She speaks authoritatively from firsthand experience. The fact that she is invisible in standard U.S. criminological literature helps prove the point that patriarchy reigns—that men especially don't listen to women's voices outside the home.

Ms. Knopp's chapter says all I am trying to say in this extended conclusion clearly and crisply, in far fewer words. In her rape-free society, women are respected and influential, interpersonal violence is a rarity, people revere rather than exploit the natural environment, gender roles are equal and symmetrical, decisions are usually made by consensus (the Quaker practice), and the source of energy and creativity is seen as female (the earth is our mother). Again, Ms. Knopp is not talking about utopian societies, but of an anthropological survey of 95 tribal societies, 47 of which were free of sexual assault. Not surprisingly, this study was done by a woman (Sanday, 1982).

I think the most important lesson to be learned from Ms. Knopp's strength, wisdom, and clarity of purpose is that she does not divide herself into roles. She is not a Quaker at Sunday meeting, a prison abolitionist from nine to five, and a radical feminist at home and in her "leisure" hours. She is all these things together all of the time. She has distilled the common essence from the three commitments. Elise Boulding in sociology and peace studies is a comparable figure. It's hard to be a Quaker, a radical feminist, and a prison abolitionist all at the same time without being committed to peacemaking throughout one's life.

Her approach to prison abolition is Gandhian. She is fighting with what a peacemaker friend of mine, Bill Breeden, calls "guerrilla peacefare"—a war of attrition against imprisonment. Tossing people out of prison won't work unless we have provided options people—victims and offenders especially—are comfortable with and pleased to use. It's ironic. It's appropriate to call peacemakers "socialists"; and yet as a socialist, Ms. Knopp is building private enterprise to subvert the state. Private enterprise, competing against the state, may well be the only way to reduce incarceration rates. Certainly a broad array of private, peacemaking alternatives exist should enough people want to make prison populations go down. The distinction between peacemaking and warmaking private initiatives is crucial, as Ms. Knopp is well aware, and as Lila Rucker has highlighted. If the alternative enterprises are open—participatory, democratic rather than hierarchical, compassionate rather than judgmental (of the person as opposed to the person's act), inviting rather than coercive, usually operating by consensus rather than by patriarchal management—then we can expect them to make peace, unlike for instance the private entrepreneurs who are building and operating prisons. Of course open criticism, confrontation of problems and failures, is vital to making a democratic enterprise in form be a democratic enterprise in spirit and practice (Henry, 1984). Peacemaking means being ever open to surprise and discovery of good and bad, successes and failures, what Ruddick (1989) calls "attentive love." There are, as Ms. Knopp notes, no final solutions for a peacemaker. To act on a "solution" is to stop listening and responding to one's impact on others. It is a tip-off that warmaking entrepreneurs typically promise to solve "all your problems," as has recently happened in my home county in a proposal to build a 200-bed juvenile-detention center for a five-county region of some 350,000 people. These private contractors for hire virtually promise to take all the treatment off the hands of everyone—other agencies, juvenile probation officers, and juvenile judges. The lesson is that private enterprise in alternatives to prisons is a wonderful investment, *provided that the entrepreneurs demonstrate a spiritual commitment to making peace.*

The section on feminism and women's experience closes with Maria Volpe's chapter reviewing recent U.S. experience with mediation programs as alternatives to criminal prosecution. Maria makes no claim to feminism nor to spiritual commitment to peace. I nonetheless think it is significant that this evaluation is as experienced by a woman. Her critical eye is useful to show us that all the enterprises laying claim to doing mediation are not necessarily peaceful or successful. Implicitly, what she likes and doesn't like about mediation programs is based on the feminist issues of whether confrontation is fair and open, whether mediation is intrusively judgmental, or whether it is a parody of mediation—quick, dirty, and ineffective. She closes with a set of "challenges" which are cogent, and which I think bear addressing in some detail.

I'm usually averse to quoting dictionaries as authorities, but I do think many of the problems people have with "mediation" stems from a sloppy use of the term. In law and in legal anthropology, "mediation" means that the third party can propose but in no way dictate or force terms on the conflicting parties. The measure of a mediator's success is the ability to elicit enough information and listen closely enough to understand what hurts and concerns each conflicting party, and then to brainstorm with them to find a way out of the conflict that gives them both what they truly want.

In arbitration and adjudication on the other hand, the third party listens, then dictates a finding or a sentence that declares what the issues are or the response is. The problem as Witty (1980) has found is that when you take mediation as a form out of one culture and stick it in another one, the substance changes and the form may be perverted. Inasmuch as criminal justice workers habituated to warring against offenders—notably judges who decide on referrals—play a decisive role in which "mediation" programs get funded and used, mediation programs often become arbitrative at best and, when the mediator refers cases for prosecution, adjudicative at worst.

As Peter Cordella indicates in his chapter, Mennonites who have established VORPs are well aware of this tension and struggle mightily not to be co-opted by the demands of judges, prosecutors, and probation officers. But the Mennonites are clear in their own minds that the danger is that mediation ceases being mediation and becomes an empty caricature of mediation instead.

This raises the issue just discussed of how to choose among private investors in alternatives to criminal justice. In Maria's terms, how does one know that the entrepreneurs are qualified to mediate? The plain fact is that one cannot distinguish whether mediators are qualified without examining their spirituality, a womanly datum not easily fed into regression analyses. VORP training of mediators attends closely to spiritual cues like the body language Lila Rucker describes. Most important of all, however, is for mediators literally to feel what true reconciliation achieves, to feel the importance of attentive love during the mediation process.

Nan Witcher (1986), head of the VORP in my hometown until the State Department of Correction stopped funding the program for dealing with too many children and not enough adults, had an easy answer to the issue of widening the net. If mediation really is restorative for freely consenting victims and offenders, who cares whether their cases otherwise would have gone to criminal court? The fact is that they were hurting and they got helped. You shouldn't have to be prosecutable to qualify for a dose of genuine peacemaking. All conflict that festers unresolved merits a try at genuine mediation.

This does not let criminal justice workers off the hook. Because mediation so clearly works better than prosecution—even in the few serious cases criminal justice workers let go—prosecutors, judges, and probation officers have a moral obligation to do all they can to build support for genuine mediation and to let their defendants go. Warring against defendants is not only morally reprehensible, but a huge waste of taxpayers' money.

As I reread Maria's challenges in light of a narrower definition of mediation than hers, I think they add up to one challenge: How do we make mediation rather than a warlike parody of mediation more widely available to criminal victims and defendants, and to all other people caught in intractable conflict? There are plenty of people around who know what mediation is and do it well. The problem is not that we do not know how to mediate, but that we do not let experienced mediators teach us how to transcend our own inclination to violence and punishment. Peacemakers like the Anabaptists have been waiting a long time for us to ask.

## Critical Thinking about Warlike Criminology and Criminal Justice

One thing that is often said of us "radical" criminologists is that we are free with our criticism but short on constructive alternatives. That is why the section of more nearly pure criticism has been saved for last in this volume. By now, the peacemaking alternative ought to be pretty clear in the reader's mind.

There remain many negative things to be said about the damage done by warlike criminology and criminal justice. While all authors in this volume are critical, the authors in this section concentrate more heavily on the shortcomings of criminal justice than on spelling out an alternative vision or practice.

It is especially appropriate to begin this section with the chapter by Dragan Milovanovic, because Dragan comes as close as anyone I know to being the truly "critical" criminologist. He is one of the few criminologists to have read, digested, and gone beyond the work of philosophers like Habermas, collectively known as the Critical School or the Frankfurt School. Although Dragan's ideas are literally secular, his focus on semiotics puts him in the same methodological position as feminists, Buddhists, Anabaptists, and humanists, where understanding what people mean by what they say is more important than what they say. A seriously wounded veteran of Vietnam who returned to heavy combat, Dragan knows war vividly; and it shows in his portrayal of the ideology of criminal justice. The "juridical subject" is a violent, vicious distortion and denial of humanity. Who can now doubt that peace studies and peacemaking in criminology go hand in hand?

Dragan draws on Nietzsche of all people to infer the antithesis of war-making. Just as Left Realists use Marx, so many people use Nietzsche as a proponent of fascism. As Kevin Anderson does for Marx, so has Dragan drawn on Foucault and a number of French scholars in particular to look more deeply into Nietzsche and to find the humanism there. While Hegelian analysis implies oppositional praxis like Saul Alinsky's, that is "negative peace," Nietzschean analysis implies what Dragan calls *trans-praxis*—a transcendence of violence, the practice of "positive peace."

Dragan's alternative vision looks remarkably like Hesed and Anabaptism. It is on the one hand remarkable that Hesed can be logically inferred and distinguished from the praxis of war. On the other hand, at the level of critical theory, transpraxis remains a dream rather than the reality it has become, for instance for Mennonites.

Dragan closes with a poetic statement of his vision. He reminds us that "music makers"—as celebrated for example by members of the Romantic Movement in post-Napoleonic Europe—is a vital part of peacemaking. The resonance of people singing or playing in harmony is a pure expression of compassion. Not surprisingly, arts and music have become foundations for successful peacemaking enterprises like the Craigmillar Music Festival (Craigmillar Festival Society, 1987; Crummy, 1987; described in the "societal rhythms" chapter of my book *The Geometry of Violence and Democracy*). Lyrical celebration of the spirit of compassion is important to building peace, and I am glad Dragan has brought it to our attention.

Subcultural theory has permeated U.S. criminology from the outset. There is something quite laudable in subcultural theory, for the researchers like Dragan Milovanovic are concerned to know what the world means to delinquents and to others who run afoul of the law. Like feminists, they are concerned with understanding the social and cultural context of violence and crime. Part of the attraction of subcultural theory is that many writings in the field bring life to otherwise dry and meaningless crime statistics.

Sue Caulfield is nonetheless quite justified in criticizing the violence implicit in subcultural theory. To paraphrase Jerry Miller, the problem is that subcultural theorists presume that members of subcultures have different values from the researchers'. There is a recurrent connotation in the literature that subcultures are primitive by the researchers' own standards. Perhaps members of subcultures deserve help and understanding, but still, they are implicitly lesser beings. Cultural anthropologists have of course confronted the same problem with describing cultures as "primitive" or "simple."

While it is true that "differential opportunity structures" play a crucial role in shaping behavior, it is untrue that the values or the norms vary much as between prisoners and powerbrokers. Prisoners have repeatedly pointed out the parallel to me, as between the values and practices of someone on death row and the values of Oliver North. As they see it, the difference is that Ollie North has the power to get away with it and they don't. An exercise I start one of my classes off with has proven illuminating. I ask people to compare Christopher Columbus to Charlie Manson.

From our discussions I have concluded the following: Charlie Manson thought he was God, and Christopher Columbus thought he sat on God's right hand. They were both violent and crazy. (Columbus once threatened summary execution for any soldier who suggested Cuba might not be part of the Asian mainland.) On the other hand, Columbus had a lot of power as a Spanish viceroy, and Manson was a loser. Besides, Columbus ordered Native Americans killed and Manson ordered high-class whites killed. So Columbus got to have about a hundred thousand times more people killed than Manson; and Columbus only had to go back to Spain in chains once when he flipped out, while Manson will be in prison for life.

Columbus and Manson sound an awful lot alike, except that Columbus had much greater opportunity to live out his fantasies than Manson has had. A subcultural theorist who made such inter-class comparisons and cross-societal comparisons could contribute much to our understanding of how violence happens. Unfortunately, by concentrating exclusively on idiosyncracies of the underclass, subcultural theorists have further embedded in the collective mind the belief that oppressed people are more dangerous and strange than their oppressors, much as women have been described by men. Time and again in this volume, the point is driven home that you cannot conquer violence by treating the violence of oppressed people in isolation from the continued violence of their oppressors. The same prisoners who know that their captors are fully as violent and crooked as they strive to play by "society's" rules. The criminal justice process teaches them that distinguishing between what's yours and what's mine is the paramount socially accepted objective in life. (You can after all get a number of years for taking very little property.) Inmates are taught that the most petty infringement on someone's property demands harsh protective response. Prison also teaches you're nobody unless you own something. Maybe when you're outside the only thing you can own is a woman, but by God if any man tries to mess with her he's dead meat. While there are cons and frauds everywhere—and some of the worst get created in prisons—it is a grave error to presume that many of the most violent prisoners are not people of impeccable moral dedication, struggling to master the standards of their captors. Token economies teach that one must be decisive when protecting what one owns. Learning table manners further ingrains the determination to be a cultured Oliver North. (And of course, like Ollie North, you have to take and hold what you can get and kill for it if necessary). It is obvious what is taught in another recent "innovation" in U.S. criminal justice—military boot camps known as "shock probation" for first-time offenders.

Habilitation of the violent underclass is not a matter of teaching them to be like us. We all have to learn to be peaceful if peace is to prevail over violence at any class level. As radical feminists say, domination and its corollary obedience are the problem, and peacemaking is the solution.

I resonate strongly to the importance Peter Sanzen attaches to criminal justice education. Increasingly, I find teaching to be the most rewarding and challenging part of my professional life. The rewarding part is seeing people come alive at the discovery that violence does not have to be acceptable. The challenge is, as Peter writes, "Each of us is a miniature criminal justice system—police officer, judge, jury, and correctional officer." Indeed! Many criminal justice students are or will be police officers, court or correctional workers. There they will be carefully taught to obey authority and impose discipline. In theory, the control the teacher has over a college classroom is awesome. Grades mean a lot, and hence so does pleasing and not offending the teacher. Most students have been through years of training that the teacher's word is law. Under these circumstances, a simple invitation (let alone a demand) to take control of one's own education is terrifying. I know! It took me two years, when I switched from public school to an ungraded alternative school in the eighth grade, to dare to do projects on my own initiative and, better yet, to carry them through. On the one hand, the criminal justice classroom provides, as Peter tells us, enormous opportunity to do what Lila Rucker is doing with inmates—teaching by experience that peace works. On the other hand, conversions are rare and progress slow.

Sanzen is doing what Brock-Utne (1989: 77) has called "educating *for* peace" as against "educating *about* peace." Educating about peace is a sham. Should humans live long and well enough to transcend all the other "-isms"—racism, classicism, sexism—I expect the last great barrier to peace will be ageism, the presumption that people of some ages must be or ought to be treated differently. Often the young and the old are pitted against one another by middle-aged oppression. Educating about peace means telling students what democracy means and ordering them to memorize it for the next test. Educating for peace means making the school a student-staff democracy, where students learn peacemaking by doing it—as is done in Harmony School, just off my campus, which I describe in the chapter on speaking freely with children in *The Geometry of Violence and Democracy.* Most colleges and even graduate and professional schools are but an extension of childhood and hierarchical schooling (although a large number of colleges and universities—Antioch College and the University of California at Santa Cruz are two prominent examples—try instead to educate *for* peace).

How does a teacher begin trying to make peace in the classroom? Peter's prescription sounds remarkably like Richard's, viz.: "As one broadens one's sense of freedom, one generates a new understanding of relationships with others. This is perhaps the most difficult step because it requires an inner search for freedom, equality, and dignity. . . ." How true that rings for me, and for the many criminologists I know who are trying to educate for peace. There is a vast literature on educating for peace—as by Christie (1971), Freire (1970), and Illich (1970)—which also concerns once again how people *do* educate for peace as well as how they might do more. These works, too, ought to be a standard part of the criminology and criminal justice literature. We need not invent educating for peace, and we would do well to carry on the kind of dialogue Peter Sanzen has initiated here.

John Galliher's chapter takes us out of the classroom and into the larger U.S. political arena. Much of this volume has concerned communities of peace and how they are constructed. John presents a vividly contrasting portrait of how warmakers try to build military communities by building fear of crime.

John supposes that George Bush would have denied abortion assistance to Willie Horton's rape victim. Certainly, wars on crimes have little regard for victims except to use their pain and anger to fuel national war fever. There is a deep mystery about George Bush's Willie Horton campaign commercial. Adviser's to Bush's opponent, Michael Dukakis, knew full well that CIA Director George Bush had met notorious drug trafficker Manuel Noriega and kept him on the CIA payroll. Denials that Bush knew and actively supported Iran-Contra arms sales were highly implausible to say the least. And yet Dukakis let Bush go on taking the high road on the war on crime, never once questioning Bush's sincerity. Jacqueline Sharkey (1988) reported at a plenary session of the 1988 American Society of Criminology Meeting that her old boss at the Washington Post was unwilling to print these and allegations of Reagan's own involvement, based on sworn public testimony, because "we feel we have already been hard enough on Reagan." I remember feeling at the time that Dukakis's silence was the most deafening and scariest of all. I have a hunch about it. Some of Dukakis's closest advisers were advisers to John Kennedy, and Kennedy was as up to his neck in organized crime as any recent president, as Bush well knows. I think the implications of facing the truth about crime in U.S. government are just too staggering for any knowledgeable and ambitious politician or editor to contemplate. Bill Moyers (1988), as high a political insider as anyone but a former president, apologizes for his own role in Vietnam as he charges devastatingly that every military operation of ours since World War II has been unconstitutional because Congress has not declared it. All acts which are unconstitutional are what corporation lawyers call "ultra vires." That is, these acts are done by private citizens merely posing as government officials. Which is to say that all deaths resulting therefrom are minimally first-degree felony murders under the District of Columbia Penal Code. Besides, as we have seen in Iran-Contra, federal crime statutes themselves have been repeatedly violated under every president since World War II; and deaths have resulted. (Jimmy Carter probably cut off all the drug contacts during his presidency, but almost certainly he tried to cut his own illegal arms deal with the Iranians to pull an "October Surprise" in the 1980 campaign. Reagan representatives simply outbid him. In effect, both became involved in an ongoing conspiracy to trade illegal weapons for the hostages. And the failed military mission to rescue the hostages in which U.S. soldiers were killed was unconstitutional. See Cockburn, 1987:

190–94.) The Supreme Court opted out of the issue during the Vietnam War, when it ruled that someone could not resist the draft on grounds that the war was illegal. That was a political issue between Congress and the President. Which means that the only remedy is routinely to impeach presidents until they close down covert activity. The only trouble with this is that most members of Congress have become accessories by voting appropriations for murder. Hence in an all-out purge of murderers, most members of both houses of Congress would be obliged to remove themselves from office.

See what I mean by "staggering"? As I write this conclusion, events this staggering are taking place in Eastern Europe. The difference is that Eastern European schoolchildren well knew they were being oppressed by an alien, violent government, while U.S. schoolchildren are carefully taught in home as in the classroom that the U.S. government is all that stands between them and hell on earth. It provokes a real crisis in a number of my students to confront the reality of U.S. history—as powerfully told by Zinn (1980) for instance. How do they face their parents? What about the police career they wanted? Can they live any other way?

We don't have to do a Gallup poll to know the level of fear of questioning governmental truths. Just try to talk about it where you live or work. I'm sure Mennonites and Quakers have no trouble talking about it, but in most places you are in for a shocked response. The very difficulty of finding safe and supportive places to talk honestly about the heart of the U.S. crime problem without getting fired or otherwise rejected is all the evidence we need of the grip the war on crime John Galliher describes has on us all. This is another reason why the Buddhists Richard Quinney describes ask us to change our own lives in our own daily spheres as a way of changing the world. This is precisely what the Anabaptists have tried to do for centuries. The fear, in other words, is not something George Bush has created. It is a fear he has sensed and which he has played on to obtain a mandate to rule. It is the omnipresent fear among the nation's people of acknowledging that the U.S. government has been a virtually continuous, massive criminal conspiracy. And thanks to Bill Chambliss (1988), we can be pretty sure the same goes for state and local governments. Crime permeates our lives far beyond our willingness to confront crime. Here the irony becomes the greatest of all: that peacemaking criminologists who are called soft on crime are the only ones dedicated to confronting rather than hiding from the vast bulk of our crime problem.

I must admit that the criminologists John describes, notably these days Wilson and Herrnstein (1985), make me angry. They play so heavily to public prejudice and fear. Wilson and Herrnstein have written a massive volume; and yet, of white-collar crime (which I suppose for them includes state crime), they say merely that this is not the subject of their research, for their primary concern is with violent street crime. What is street crime? It's the crime the underclass has the least alternative to committing. Would a crack dealer murder people by thousands and even millions as president of the United States? Would George Bush be a crack dealer if he had been born black and poor? Wilson and Herrnstein don't care: They just want to tell us that police, prosecutors, and government-sponsored crime-surveyors tell us that blacks commit most crime, and this could be because blacks are biologically impaired—in 800 pages with a thousand references. What a sham!

It is crucial to peacemaking that confrontation and anger not become violence and punishment. I don't want Wilson or Herrnstein, Bush or North to go to jail—although I'm not so sure I'd object to their going through a few years of mediation sessions with all the people whose fears they have increased and reinforced, or with the families of the countless victims U.S. officials and their private allies have killed. The object is neither to obtain revenge nor to minimize the true suffering caused by street crime. Once one recognizes the magnitude of crime, retribution becomes absurd. If we give a president with a life expectancy of twenty years a life sentence for first-degree murder of say 2,000,000 people (the number of Vietnamese killed in our war), how many microseconds of jail do we give a kid for stealing a $400 stereo from someone's home? Do we then do nothing about the burglary?

Robert Elias has been writing for some time on the human rights movement. He has seen the United Nations discourse on human rights go through generations of evolution until now, when peaceful collective development is seen as a condition for individual enjoyment of human rights, the basic right is to live in political and economic democracy. Without political and economic democracy, as he indicates in his essay on human rights enforcement, crime and victimization only get worse in the United States.

Joseph Scimecca addresses the development of the criminal justice program known as "alternative dispute resolution." Joe has been a leading exponent of the peacemaking possibilities of conflict resolution, writing extensively on the subject and directing the program at George Mason University. He notes in his critique that "alternative dispute resolution" as employed in the criminal justice system is not the resolution of conflict, but rather is a system of sound control and the perpetuation of conflict and violence. Conflict resolution, however, is peacemaking and promotes the establishment of social equality.

The last essay is by Lloyd Klein, Joan Luxenburg, and John Gunther. They show the broad array of ways politicians and the media mobilize people to take a bite out of crime and to play especially on racism. They go on to do what needs to be done once the problem is confronted, drawing constructively on ideas of social planning from community social work.

Community social work is another ally of peacemaking criminologists. While much of social work in the United States has individualized problems and played on stereotypes about how social disadvantage warps people (see, e.g., Platt, 1977, on the child-saving movement of early social workers), community social workers focus instead on how to help people restructure communities to meet their needs. One iconoclastic friend of mine with a traditional M.S.W. puts the difference this way: "I used to have to do case writeups for our practicum. I'd be asked to answer all kinds of questions about a guy's relationships with his parents and so forth, but I'd be thinking, 'Hell, the guy's problem is that he got laid off and can't afford to feed his family.' " The primary objective of the community social organizer is to get the community mobilized. In the Saul Alinsky tradition, this often means playing oppositional politics, such as organizing rent strikes to get places cleaned up and repaired. While there is nothing inherently wrong in oppositional politics (in Gandhi's terms, in refusing to cooperate with oppression), there is the danger that community members will turn on one another and further victimize each other unless the community organization is built on peacemaking principles. This problem is manifest in the Left Realist position as criticized in Walt DeKeseredy and Marty Schwartz's chapter. In other words, it is as important to attend to how community members relate to one another as it is to attend to how they relate to their oppressors. Either they can turn on one another as the Left Realists would have them do, or they can attend to doing Hesed with one another. Suppose tenants for instance first organized to do one another's repairs, and then went on the rent strike to pay for their time and expenses. It is like training mediators. If people are first "trained" in the spiritual experience of making peace among themselves, they stand a better chance of using oppositional politics nonviolently.

I cringe as I write the word "trained." I can understand how a peacemaker can visit another community to learn from people there, to carry new ideas and experience home. I can understand how a peacemaker like many U.S. religious workers who have gone to Central America can decide to live among a group of oppressed people and work to improve the quality of her or his life with others there. I have difficulty, however, with the notion of going in to help people, unless of course they have asked for help. There is a chance that this could turn into the patriarchal approach—doing good for people—instead of the peacebuilding approach of doing good *with* others. One test of which is happening is for helpgivers to ask how much they themselves are getting from the people they are helping, what kinds of strength and wisdom the helpgiver lacks they have to offer. It is a warning sign not to be able to envision getting as much help for one's own weakness from others as one gives in response to their weaknesses. There are, of course, peacemaking social workers who recognize this full well. It's time they and peacemaking criminologists got to know one another better.

## Closing the Peacemaking Circle

A common belief among peacemaking traditions is that understanding runs in circles rather than in straight lines. It would have followed tradition to begin this volume with the section on critical thinking and end it with the section on religious traditions. First you criticize or ground your work in conventional wisdom, then you build new ideas from there. That organization would be as logical as this. The essays in the critical-thinking section leave unaddressed the question of who is doing things right or, in the case of Lloyd, Joan, and John, with whom can we join cause besides a fringe group from a single profession? The sections on religious traditions and on feminism answer this question. Richard and I have chosen to offer the answer first, under the assumption that readers will begin the book in fear and despair enough without our adding anxiety. It is vital to strip away the mask of peace from U.S. criminal justice so that we see warmaking for what it honestly is and don't respond in kind with good intentions. It is more important still to offer people safety and security in place of war. The most important message in this work, to me at least, is that peacemaking exists, is well researched and understood, and is quite prevalent even in as violent a place as the United States.

In reality, neither issue is logically prior to the peacemaking criminologist. We find ourselves constantly oscillating between criticism and affirmation of peace. They are like chicken and egg. The criticism tells us what to avoid, and the doing of peace gives us a chance with others to go on to something better. The understanding and doing of peace, prevalent as it may be, is incredibly slow and painful. As Richard tells us, we who would make peace can expect to suffer far beyond our own lifetimes. Confronting crime makes one suffer. The only comfort is that fear and suffering become even worse when one becomes addicted to the Reagan/Bush opiate for not talking about most crime or confronting it. Noted alcohol and drug counselor and radical feminist Anne Wilson Schaef (1987) has diagnosed this approach as "process addiction," which is more lethal than physical addictions. This is the real drug problem—greater than alcohol, tobacco, valium, and crack—from which the war on drugs aims to divert our attention.

I went to Norway in the spring of 1986 to get away from all the violence, to see whether I could not begin to see peace instead. It worked for me; and to my amazement, when I returned to Indiana I suddenly began to notice peacemaking all around me. I noticed that even if the world were still pretty violent, the peacemakers I knew seemed more contented and secure in their lives than the warriors. One of the things that has helped some of my students is for me to bring in local peacemaking friends as though to say, if I can find them in Bloomington, you can find them wherever you go. Often the confidence and spiritual well-being of the visitors comes through. Then I can ask, would you get more of a personal payoff investing in friendship as these people do, or investing in Wall Street? The world does not have to change for peacemaking to have a substantial, favorable impact on one's own life. It is the kind of social security that says you know you can count on food and care in a loving home even if you're out of work or old and sick, because you have friends. For me, for example, it has been the kind of security that has enabled me to get better jobs after being fired. It is a comfort to believe that this selfish service of myself is the best contribution I can make to a more peaceful world, and that a greater inner peace and security is possible while confronting and suffering the world's violence.

It all comes down to this: You see that peacemaking in criminology is tried and true. You see that the scholarly basis for peacemaking is millennia old. You see that criminal justice is monumentally unjust, wasteful, destructive. You can well imagine that declaring oneself a peacemaker rather than a conformist risks ridicule and rejection, and peacemaking surely is not a path to wealth or to power over others. The choice may be hard to make, but the issues are simple. The choice is yours.

## REFERENCES

American Friends Service Committee. 1971. *Struggle for Justice: A Report on Crime and Punishment in America.* New York: Hill and Wang.
Brock-Utne, Birgit. 1989. *Feminist Perspectives on Peace and Peace Education.* New York: Pergamon.
Chambliss, William J. 1988. *On the Take: From Petty Crooks to Presidents.* 2nd ed. Bloomington: Indiana University Press.
Christian Science Monitor. 1989. *Grass-Roots Projects: Christian Science Monitor Special Report.* Spring Valley, N.Y.: *Christian Science Monitor.*
Christie, Nils. 1971. *Hvis Skolen Ikke Fantes (If School Weren't Found).* Oslo: Oslo University Press.
———. 1977. "Conflicts as Property." *British Journal of Criminology* 17: 1–19.
Cockburn, Leslie. 1987. *Out of Control: The Story of the Reagan Administration's Secret War in Nicaragua, the Illegal Arms Pipeline, and the Contra Drug Connection.* New York: Atlantic-Monthly Press.
Coston, Charisse Tia Maria. 1989. "The Original Designer Label: Prototypes of New York City's Shopping-bag Ladies." *Deviant Behavior* 10: 157–72.
Craigmillar Festival Society. 1987. Annual Report 1986/87. Edinburgh: Craigmillar Festival Society.
Crummy, Helen. 1987. "Craigmillar Self Treatment—The Cooperative Approach." Paper delivered at the International Conference on Solutions to the Problems of Urban Pathologies, Kazimierz Dolny, Poland.
Eisler, Riane. 1987. *The Chalice and the Blade: Our History, Our Future.* New York: Harper and Row.
Freire, Paolo. 1970. *Pedagogy of the Oppressed.* New York: Continuum Publishing Co.
Galtung, Johan. 1969. "Violence, Peace, and Peace Research." *Journal of Peace Research* 6: 167–91.
———. 1987. "United States Foreign Policy as Manifest Theology." Center for International Studies, Princeton University, Princeton, New Jersey. Unpublished.
Harris, M. Kay. 1985. "Toward a Feminist Vision of Justice." Amsterdam: Second International Conference on Prison Abolition (ICOPA II). Unpublished.
Henry, Stuart. 1984. *Private Justice: Towards Integrating Theory in the Sociology of Law.* New York: Metheun.
Illich, Ivan. 1970. *Deschooling Society.* New York: Harper and Row.

Loughran, Edward J. 1987. "Juvenile Corrections: the Massachusetts Experience." In Lee Eddison (ed.), *Reinvesting Youth Corrections Resources: A Tale of Three States*. Minneapolis: Center for the Study of Youth Policy, Hubert H. Humphrey Institute of Public Affairs, University of Minnesota.

Moyers, Bill. 1988. *The Secret Government: The Constitution in Crisis*. Cabin John, Md.: Seven Locks Press.

Naess, Arne. 1989. *Ecology, Community and Lifestyle: Outline of an Ecosophy*. Cambridge, U.K.: Cambridge University Press.

Pepinsky, Harold E. 1988. "Violence as Unresponsiveness: Toward a New Conception of Crime." *Justice Quarterly* 5: 539–63.

Platt, Anthony M. 1977. *The Child Savers: The Invention of Delinquency*. 2nd ed. Chicago: University of Chicago Press.

Ruddick, Sara. 1989. *Maternal Thinking: Toward a Politics of Peace*. Boston: Beacon Press.

Sanday, Peggy R. 1982. *Female Power and Male Dominance: On the Origins of Sexual Irregularity*. New York: Cambridge University Press.

Satir, Virginia. 1972. *Peoplemaking*. Palo Alto, Calif.: Science and Behavior Books.

Schaef, Anne Wilson. 1987. *When Society Becomes an Addict*. New York: Harper and Row.

Sharkey, Jacqueline. 1988. "The Contra-drug Tradeoff." *Common Cause* 14: 23–33.

Sudnow, David. 1965. "Normal Crimes: Sociological Features of the Penal Code in a Public Defender's Office." *Social Problems* 12: 255–76.

Weber, Max. 1946. *From Max Weber: Essays in Sociology*. Tr. Hans H. Gerth and C. Wright Mills. New York: Oxford University Press.

Wilkins, Leslie T. 1984. *Consumerist Criminology*. London: Heinemann.

Wilson, James Q., and Richard J. Herrnstein. 1985. *Crime and Human Nature*. New York: Simon and Schuster.

Witcher, Nan. 1986. "The Captain and the Cop." *ACJS Today* (September): 4–5.

Witty, Cathie. 1980. *Mediation and Society: Conflict Management in Lebanon*. New York: Academic Press.

Zinn, Howard. 1980. *A People's History of the United States*. New York: Harper and Row.

# CONTRIBUTORS

KEVIN ANDERSON has written on Marxist humanism, on critical theory, on radical criminological theory, on social change, and on the drugs-crime relationship for journals such as *Crime and Delinquency, Journal of Political and Military Sociology, Quarterly Journal of Ideology, Review of Radical Political Economics, Sociology and Social Research,* and *Studies in Soviet Thought.* Over the past decade, he has taught sociology and criminology at City University of New York, Northern Illinois University, and now at Indiana University, Northeast.

GREGG BARAK is a professor and the chair of the Department of Criminology and Criminal Justice at Alabama State University. He has written numerous articles on crime, justice, corrections, the courts, and domestic violence. He is the author of *In Defense of Whom? A Critique of Criminal Justice Reform* (1980), the editor of *Crimes by the Capitalist State: An Introduction to State Criminality* (1990), and the author of the forthcoming book *Gimme Shelter: A Social History of Homelessness in America.*

SUSAN CARINGELLA-MACDONALD is an associate professor in the Department of Sociology at Western Michigan University. Her research and publications are primarily in the areas of sexual assault and the violent victimization of women. Her interests and work focus on the relationship between enacted legal reforms, implemented outcomes, and dominant ideology.

SUSAN L. CAULFIELD is an assistant professor of sociology at Western Michigan University. Her recent work includes "Life or Death Decisions: Prosecutorial Power versus Equality of Justice," published in the *Journal of Contemporary Criminal Justice;* and "Subcultures as Crime: The Theft of the Legitimacy of Dissent in the United States," published in Gregg Barak's book *Crimes by the Capitalist State.* Susan's work centers on the role of political institutions in the creation and treatment of "criminal" behavior, and on the implications of such relationships for crime control and the perpetuation of harm.

J. PETER CORDELLA is an assistant professor in the Department of Sociology at Clark University, Worcester, Massachusetts. He has been a community mediator and mediation trainer for the past ten years. His research and writing have focused on restorative models of justice. His most recent work on John MacMurray's conception of the mutualist model of justice, entitled "Beyond Justice: Freedom, Morality, and Persons in Community," will be included in a soon to be published volume of collected essays entitled *John MacMurray's Post Modern Philosophy: The Primacy of Persons in Community.*

WALTER S. DEKESEREDY, who received his Ph.D. from York University, is an assistant professor in the Department of Sociology and Anthropology at Carleton University. He has published numerous articles on violence against women. He is also the author of *Woman Abuse in Dating Relationships: The Role of Male Peer Support*. His research interests include woman-abuse and left realist crime-control initiatives.

ROBERT ELIAS is an associate professor of politics and the chair of Peace and Justice Studies at the University of San Francisco. He has taught at the University of California, Berkeley; the University of Maryland (Europe and College Park); Penn State; and Tufts University. He has been a researcher at the Vera Institute of Justice, at the Center for the Study of Law and Society, and at the International Institute of Human Rights. He has authored *The Politics of Victimization, Victims of the System,* and *The Peace Resource Book;* and he is an associate editor of *Peace Review.* He was awarded a Fulbright to teach human rights in Sri Lanka and holds an NEH Chair at the University of San Francisco in the Literature of Repression.

JOHN F. GALLIHER is a professor of sociology at the University of Missouri, Columbia. His books include: *Morals Legislation with Morality; Violence in Northern Ireland: Understanding Protestant Perspectives; The Criminology of Edwin Sutherland;* and *Criminology: Human Rights, Criminal Law and Crime.* His current research involves the historical origins of death-penalty abolition movements in the United States.

JOHN GUNTHER is an associate professor of social work at Southern University, New Orleans. Previously, he was the executive director of Mid-Del Youth and Family Services, a juvenile delinquency prevention and remediation program, in the Oklahoma City, Oklahoma metroplex. While at Mid-Del, he developed a psycho-social restitution program for delinquents and worked actively with the local district attorney's office and police departments in coordinating delinquency programs.

M. KAY HARRIS is an associate professor in the Department of Criminal Justice at Temple University. Prior to joining the Temple faculty in 1981, she served as the director of the Washington office of the National Council on Crime and Delinquency. She previously held positions with the Unitarian Universalist Service Committee; the American Bar Association; and, within the U.S. Department of Justice, with the Office of the Attorney General, the National Institute of Law Enforcement and Criminal Justice, and the Bureau of Prisons. In 1972, she served as the assistant director of the National Advisory Commission on Criminal Justice Standards and Goals. Professor Harris frequently works with citizen groups, policymakers, and criminal justice practitioners on rethinking current punishment practices and on developing more promising approaches for the future.

DREW HUMPHRIES is an associate professor of sociology at Rutgers University, Camden. Her work on history and political economy of crime has appeared in *Social Problems, Contemporary Crises, Social Justice,* and *Crime and Delinquency.* She is currently completing work on crime and the media.

RUSS IMMARIGEON writes about criminal justice reform for various publications, including *VORP Network News, Corrections Compendium,* and *Dollars & Sense.* Formerly a state coordinator for the National Council on Crime and Delinquency and the associate editor of *Criminal Justice Abstracts,* he writes a regular column on alternatives to imprisonment for the National Prison Project *Journal.* Immarigeon is currently completing a term as a member of the board of directors for the National Community Service Sentencing Association. He has served as a consultant to different criminal justice agencies, including the Presbyterian Synod of the Northeast, the Massachusetts Council for Public Justice, and the U.S. National Institute of Justice. He is the author of *Concerned About Crime?* (cowritten with Van Zwisohn), *Probation at a Crossroads: Innovative Programs in Massachusetts, Women's Prisons: Overcrowded and Overused* (cowritten with Meda Chesney-Lind), and an *Annotated Bibliography on Jail and Prison Crowding Developed by the National Jail and Prison Overcrowding Project.*

LLOYD KLEIN is an instructor at Medgar Evers College, CUNY, and affiliated with Brooklyn College in a research capacity. Previous publications feature research on Citizens Band radio prostitution, community corrections, and private policing. Current research interests include community crime prevention, racial (or hate) crime, credit card fraud, and political surveillance.

FAY HONEY KNOPP is the founder and director of the Safer Society Program, a nonprofit research and education center on the prevention of sexual abuse. The center advocates nonrepressive alternatives for victims and offenders. Knopp is the primary author of *Instead of Prisons: A Handbook for Abolitionists.* Her current titles include *Retraining Adult Sex Offenders: Methods and Models, Remedia Intervention In Adolescent Sex Offenses,* and *The Youthful Sex Offender.* Fay has been engaged for thirty-five years in an alternative ministry (Quaker) to persons imprisoned, and she is the recipient of both the Karl Menninger Award (Fortune Society) and the DeWolf Award for Distinguished Contribution to Community Corrections in America (OAR). She serves on several task forces concerned with safety and criminal justice, including the Governors Commission on Community Control.

JOAN LUXENBURG is an associate professor of sociology and criminal justice at the University of Central Oklahoma in Edmond. She is the author of *Probation Casework: the Convergence of Theory with Practice* (1983). Her previous work has centered on the topic of CB radio prostitution. She is coauthor, with Lloyd Klein, of "CB Radio Prostitution: Technology and the Displacement of Deviance" in *Gender Issues, Sex Offenders, and Criminal Justice: Current Trends* (1984), edited by Sol Chaneles. Her current research interests include fear of crime in communities. She is coauthor, with Lloyd Klein and Maranna King, of "Perceived Neighborhood Crime and the Impact of Private Security" in the July 1989 issue of *Crime and Delinquency.*

LYN. MARKHAM is a doctoral candidate in criminal justice at the State University of New York at Albany. She is interested in the ecology of community crime-prevention strategies and is currently studying commercial-crime and economic-development policies in New York State.

DRAGAN MILOVANOVIC received his Ph.D. from the School of Criminal Justice, SUNY at Albany. His research interests include: a post-Frankfurt epistemology rooted in a materialistically grounded psychoanalytic semiotics; law; ideology; and theoretical issues on prison. He draws from his experiences, which include his position as a company point-man in Vietnam during the war as well as his work in mental institutions (dormitory setting), jails (teacher), prisons (prison inspection-team member, John Howard Association), and juvenile institutions (juvenile counselor). His current research centers on the integration and synthesis of Lacan, Marx, and Nietzsche. He is author of *The Sociology of Law* (1988), *Weberian and Marxian Analysis of Law* (1989), and *Ivory Tower* (unpublished). His current book in progress is *Law, Semiotics, and Reality Construction.*

HAROLD E. PEPINSKY is a professor of criminal justice and of East Asian languages and cultures at Indiana University. Trained in Chinese, law, and sociology, Pepinsky has written extensively on crime and punishment. His books include *The Geometry of Violence and Democracy* and, in collaboration with Paul Jesilow, *Myths That Cause Crime,* which won the 1986 Outstanding Book Award from the Academy of Criminal Justice Sciences.

RICHARD QUINNEY is a professor of sociology at Northern Illinois University. He is the author of several books in criminology, social theory, and sociology of religion, including: *The Social Reality of Crime; Critique of Legal Order; The Problem of Crime; Class, State, and Crime; Providence; Social Existence;* and a book of autobiographical reflections titled *Journey to a Far Place.* He received the Edwin H. Sutherland Award for theoretical contributions to criminology. His work continues to be an integration of the sacred and the secular.

LILA RUCKER is an assistant professor in the Department of Political Science, Criminal Justice Studies, at the University of South Dakota. Her work and research focus on the interplay between incarcerative environments and incarcerated individuals.

PETER L. SANZEN is an associate professor of criminal justice at Hudson Valley Community College, where he teaches primarily in the areas of community policing and management. He has published, with Dennis Sullivan and Kathryn Callaghan, "The Teaching and Studying of Justice: Fostering the Unspeakable Vision of Cooperation" in *Crime and Social Jus-*

*tice.* Sanzen is a member of the Editorial Advisory Board of *The Journal of Criminal Justice Education,* published by The Academy of Criminal Justice Sciences; and he is the editor of *Criminal Justice Educator,* published by The Criminal Justice Educators Association of New York State.

MARTIN D. SCHWARTZ is the vice-chair of the Department of Sociology and Anthropology at Ohio University, where he teaches criminology and social problems as well as a women's-studies course on violence against women. He has published or presented more than two dozen pieces on such various aspects of feminist theory and violence as woman battering, child sexual abuse and incest, pornography, marital rape, and forcible rape. Other publications include numerous works on sociological pedagogy, penology, and left-criminological theory. In 1990 he served as the president of the Association for Humanist Sociology.

JOSEPH A. SCIMECCA is a professor of sociology and conflict resolution at George Mason University, where he was formerly the chair of the Department of Sociology and Anthropology as well as the director of the Center for Conflict Analysis and Resolution. Among his books are *The Sociological Theory of C. Wright Mills* and *Society and Freedom: An Introduction to Humanist Sociology.* He has also contributed articles in criminology and conflict resolution to such journals as *The Journal of Criminal Law and Criminology; International Journal of Criminology and Penology; Psychology, Peace and Change;* and *Peace-In-Action.*

LARRY L. TIFFT is a professor of sociology at Central Michigan University. He has written articles on the social organization of police work, on the meanings of capital punishment in the United States and in the People's Republic of China, and on the contributions of Peter Kropotkin to criminology and social theory. He and Dennis Sullivan wrote *The Struggle To Be Human: Crime, Criminology, and Anarchism;* and Tifft is currently working on two books: *The Social Structural Roots of Crime* and *Battering and Public Policy.*

MARIA R. VOLPE, Ph.D., is an associate professor of sociology and works with the Dispute Resolution Program at John Jay College of Criminal Justice, City University of New York. Volpe teaches dispute-resolution courses at the undergraduate and graduate levels; and she conducts dispute-resolution skills-training for a wide range of groups, including police, parole officers, security personnel, lawyers, etc. She is a member of the editorial board of *Mediation Quarterly* and the *Journal of Contemporary Criminal Justice,* and she also serves as the second vice president of the Society of Professionals in Dispute Resolution. Maria has lectured and written extensively about dispute-resolution processes, particularly mediation, and about the criminal justice system.

# INDEX

Printed in the United States
144824LV00007B/24/P